DREAM
BROTHER

DREAM BROTHER

THE LIVES & MUSIC OF JEFF & TIM BUCKLEY

DAVID BROWNE

HarperEntertainment

An Imprint of HarperCollins*Publishers*

For Clifford Conklin Browne

PREFACE

"This guy is a book," one of Jeff Buckley's friends told me in the summer of 1993. "Start taking notes."

In fact, I already was. Throughout the preceding year, several associates whose music tastes I respected had been urging me to venture to a coffeehouse on the Lower East Side called Sin-é in order to see an embryonic talent named Jeff Buckley. They all cited the same reasons for their enthusiasm: He had an astonishing voice with an impressive range, he could seemingly sing anything, and he was a rising star, having signed a contract with Columbia Records. That he was the son of Tim Buckley, a '60s cult figure with whose work I was familiar, made less of a mark on me than did the startling realization that the *children* of '60s musicians were now old enough to begin their own careers.

On an August evening so stiflingly humid that pea soup would be humbled, a friend and I finally made our way to Sin-é. As we walked down St. Mark's Place, I could already see a crunch of people spilling out onto the sidewalk in front of what I first thought was an art gallery or clothing store. But no—it was Sin-é itself, and unable to wedge ourselves into the tiny club, we were forced to catch the performance outside and on our tiptoes. I could only glimpse the top of the performer's head and the pegs on the headstock of his guitar. But I heard the voice and heard the songs, and it was obvious something important was happening. Soon after, I was assigned to report on this phenomenon for the *New York Times,* and one day in the middle of September I dialed Jeff Buckley's home number to set up an interview.

At first he was hesitant, asking me what section of the *Times* the article would appear in. (When I told him it would be for the newly launched "Styles of the Times," he scoffed, "But nobody *reads* that!") Given his age (twenty-six) and his affiliation with a conglomerate, his wariness toward the media and its coverage struck me as curious. I suggested we first meet informally at a local bistro before we did a proper interview. He agreed— and then didn't show up. (As I later learned, this was far from the only time he had missed a meeting during the course of his career.) He apologized when I called him back, and we rescheduled for the following morning. This time, he appeared on schedule, wearing jeans and a long-sleeved red T-shirt and sporting a summer-short buzzcut. We ordered breakfasts and began chatting about music and the angle of the interview. "Can I ask you one question?" he inquired at the outset. "Is this going to be about my father? Because I never knew him."

Unaware of the relationship between father and son, and more interested in son than father anyway, I assured him the article was a profile of him and his seemingly blossoming career. That out of the way, he began to talk—about his background, his life, his musical tastes, our mutual knowledge of the music of Nusrat Fateh Ali Khan. Eventually I asked if I could take notes, and he nodded and gestured toward my pad for me to begin. For the next hour and a half, we talked in what amounted to his first major press interview.

It was a fascinating but somewhat bewildering conversation. As he spoke of his life, his future, and the upcoming recording sessions for his first album, his mood veered from self-assured to glum, his tone from ethereal to wisecracking. I had already learned that his contract with Columbia was an enviable one, and yet this seeming novice to the business came across as skeptical and distrustful of it all. Just when he seemed easy to understand, he slipped off into another, completely different disposition. ("Looks like he could be wounded," I scribbled in my pad.) It was apparent that this was one of the most enigmatic performers I had ever spent time with, and when we had to leave and he shuffled out with a haunted, wounded-deer look in his eyes, I knew what his friend had meant: Maybe there wasn't a book about him at this point, but there certainly was a story in there somewhere.

Nearly four years later—the late morning of May 30, 1997—I was in my office at *Entertainment Weekly* magazine when a beep announced the arrival of E-mail. It came from a coworker, and the subject header simply read "Jeff Buckley." My first thought was that there was finally a release date for that overdue second album we had been hearing about, or perhaps it was an announcement that he would be performing in the area. Instead, it was a terse, two-sentence note: A report on the Internet said he was missing somewhere in Tennessee, near the Mississippi River.

It was shocking and depressing news; his astonishing first album, *Grace,* had become a best friend and comfort to me during the last few years. That weekend, while everyone waited to see whether he would turn up in the waters of the Wolf River in Memphis, I began work on an obituary, and our meeting in 1993—and his friend's words about a book—hung in the air. From what I knew about Jeff Buckley's life based on our initial conversation and from reading the interviews he did to promote *Grace,* I now realized there *was* a book in there somewhere. It was a poignant, sprawling story about a kid who grew up the son of a semi-famous '60s rock star who had died young, a child who strove to become his own person—and then, in what seemed either a horrific twist of fate or just a horrific accident, was now gone himself at an equally young age. That summer and fall, I began my preliminary research, and a book announced itself to me.

It was clear that the life of Tim Buckley, the absentee father Jeff had barely known, would have to be explored to some degree. Jeff resented, even hated, any and all comparisons to his father, and for understandable reasons—Tim had left Jeff's mother, Mary Guibert, before Jeff was even born, and like most of us, Jeff yearned to accomplish goals in life that would surpass those of his parents. But it soon became apparent that the intense caution Jeff displayed to me had been with him since childhood and underscored his entire career. And as my research continued, it became vividly clear that Jeff did not know his biological father, and that they were two very different people in many ways, but that Jeff was painfully aware of the mistakes Tim had made in his life and career. But what were those errors? What exactly had happened to Tim Buckley that left him dead at twenty-eight and left his far-off son perpetually on his guard? The Buckley family history, along with that of the Guiberts, would have to be fleshed out as well.

All along, I was well aware that Jeff would have hated the connection. Then, one evening I was speaking with one of his closest female friends, and I told her how deep and far-ranging my research would have to be.

"That's *amazing*," she said. "Jeff wanted to know *all* that. It's such a shame he's not around, because he could have hired you to be his detective." With such words of support, my journey in search of Jeff Buckley began in earnest.

This book is the result of more than two hundred primary-source interviews conducted between June 1997 and June 2000. The conversations took place in person and by phone and E-mail, and spread from New York City, Jeff's home base, to California (both Los Angeles and Orange County), Memphis, Paris, Arkansas, Mexico, London, and Portland, Oregon. Mary Guibert, Jeff's mother and the executrix of his estate, was the first to offer her time and resources. At the conclusion of our first informal meeting, she told me she would make herself available for interviews, not ask to see the finished manuscript, and encourage others to speak with me. Later she allowed me access to journals, unreleased tapes, even answering-machine messages. For graciously enduring repeated, nagging, and sometimes difficult questions and for opening up her world to a journalistic interloper, I thank her deeply.

Of those who were particularly close to Jeff, Tim, or both, I extend the utmost gratitude to Larry Beckett, Manda Beckett, Steve Berkowitz, Judy Buckley, Dan Gordon, Mick Grondahl, Anna Guibert, Peggy and Kip Hagberg, Matt Johnson, Dave Lory, Rebecca Moore, Jane Pullman, Leah Reid, Daniella Sapriel, George Stein, Michael Tighe, and Joan Wasser. Despite the pain and sorrow that surrounds this tale, each allowed me into their homes or offices for extended interviews and the inevitable follow-up conversations, and they did so with inordinate patience and generosity. Without them, this book would not be possible, and I cannot thank them enough for their time and insights. Gene Bowen and Jack Bookbinder at Fun Palace also set aside their bittersweet memories in order to assist with fact-checking, tour schedules, and sundry facts and documentation, and I offer them my heartfelt appreciation as well.

For helping me navigate my way through the complex life and thought processes of Jeff Buckley, I also wish to thank Steve Abbott, Tamurlaine Adams, Steve Addabbo, Penny Arcade, Carla Azar, Emma Banks, Glenna Blake, Morgan Carey, Ellen Cavolina, Tom Chang, Irwin Chusid, Tom Clark, Michael J. Clouse, Mitchell Cohen, Debra Colligan, Chris Cornell, Hod David, Paul Derech, Patrick Derivaz, Michael Dorf, M. Doughty, Shane Doyle, Chris Dowd, Doug Easley, Eric Eidel, Susan Feldman, Bill

Flanagan, Keith Foti, Mark Frere, Robert Gordon, Kathryn Grimm, Jason Hamel, Daniel Harnett, Juliana Hatfield, Gary Helsinger, Robin Horry, Jerry Howell, John Humphrey, Kate Hyman, Don Ienner, John Jesurin, Sergeant Mary Grace Johnson, Holly Jones-Rougier, Brenda Kahn, Danny Kapilian, Lenny Kaye, Parker Kindred, Nathan Larson, Laure Leber, Andria Lisle, Inger Lorre, Gary Lucas, Tony Marryatt, Tim Marse, Joe McEwen, Melissa Meyer, Larry Miller, Corey Moorhead, Ron Moorhead, James Morrison, Janine Nichols, Jared Nickerson, Clif Norrell, Dave Novik, Pat O'Brien, Will Osborn, Nihar Oza, Paul Rappaport, Roy Rallo, Tom Shaner, Dave and Tammy Shouse, Brooke Smith, Patti Smith, Gayle Kelemen Snible, Randall Stoll, George Vandergrift, Tom Verlaine, Andy Wallace, Hal Willner, and Jimi Zhivago. Nicholas Hill supplied not only reminiscences and documents but gave me access to his estimable collection of concert and radio recordings. Merri Cyr shared memories and contributed some of her superb photographs.

Providing invaluable aid in unraveling the Tim Buckley saga were Stan Agol, Corby Alsbrook, David Anderle, John Balkin, Maury Baker, Taylor Buckley, Emmett Chapman, Herb Cohen, Martin Cohen, Carter C.C. Collins, Pamela Des Barres, James Epstein, Joe Falsia, Jim Fielder, Danny Fields, David Friedman, Linda Gillen, Zachary Glickman, Steve Harris, Buddy Helm, Judy Henske-Doerge, Eileen Marder Hinchey, Jac Holzman, John B. King, Al Kooper, Artie Leichter, Molly LeMay, John Miller, Denny Randell, Hope Ruff, Clive Selwood, Jennifer Stace, Joe Stevens, Victor Stoloff, Danny Thompson, Lee Underwood, Jerry and Marlene Yester, Wess Young, and Gail Zappa. The legendary Izzy Young graciously allowed me to excerpt his unpublished 1967 interview with Tim, for which I am most indebted. An extra note of appreciation is extended to Louie Dula, arguably the foremost Tim Buckley archivist, for the boxes of clips and video footage she generously shared with me.

Thanks also: Russell Duke, Laura Fletcher, John Gleisner III, Ken Hecker, Llew Llewellyn, Pam Manazer, and John and Chris Turanitza.

In addition, court documents, contracts, and government documents were consulted. Sources of interviews with either Buckley are cited; Jeff Buckley quotes that are not attributed are taken from my interview with him in September 1993. Certain sources spoke to me only on the condition of anonymity, and their recollections and perceptions were used to confirm existing information. They know who they are, and I thank them as well.

Conrad Rippy, Donna Young, and Evan Cohen were conscientious gatekeepers who nonetheless helped guide me through the sundry mazes of these men's lives. Also providing contacts and information were Larry Jenkins and Howard Wuelfing at Columbia Records, Pat Baird at BMI, Sandy Sawotka at V2 Records, Gregg Geller at Warner Brothers Records, Karie Cooper and Barrett Tagliarino at the Musicians Institute, Pattie Merklin at Bearsville Studios, Perry Serpa at Nasty Little Man, David Baker and Thane Tierney at Rhino Records, Greg Sandow, Bill Ellis at the *Memphis Commercial Appeal,* Vera Beren at Sorcerer Sound, Binky Philips, and SoundScan.

To my relief, my principal researcher, Deirdre Cossman, was able to unearth any number of obscure statistics and factoids on any number of esoteric topics. Margaret T. Cossman, Gerry Anderson Arango, and Beth Johnson also pitched in and came to several rescues. Additional research assistance came from Kathryn Danielle of the Musicians Local 47 in Los Angeles; Petty Officer H. C. Kilpatrick of the United States Coast Guard, Lower Division; Marianna Beard of the Anaheim Public Library; Dr. Andrew Vecchio of the Smithers Center; Naomi S. Engle of the Bell Gardens Public Library; Andrew Ruppenstein of the Demographic Research Unit of the California State Department of Finance; George Koskimaki and the 101st Airborne Division Association; the New York regional office of the Department of Veterans Affairs; John M. Walsh of the Irish Cultural Society of the Garden City (New York) area; the Lincoln Center Library for the Performing Arts; the Los Angeles District Attorney's Office; and the office of Clifford G. Amsler at the National Personnel Records Center.

Jim Seymore, Pete Bonventre, and John McAlley of *Entertainment Weekly* generously allowed me the time off to work on this project, and I thank them for their understanding and support. For their encouragement, recommendations, and helpful tips, I also tip my hat to Regina Joskow Dunton, Owen Gleiberman, Anne Grew, Kathy Heintzelman, Geraldine Hessler, Dulcy Israel, Betsy Lerner (and John Donatich), Barbara O'Dair, and Michele Romero. Early in this project, David Hajdu was an invaluable source of advice and inspiration, and he deserves an extra note of thanks for his selfless professional aid. I would also like to thank John Capouya, my onetime *New York Times* editor, for suggesting I investigate this mysterious figure named Jeff Buckley in the first place.

In the three years it took to conceive and complete this work, I was immensely fortunate to have associates who were never less than enthusiastic, committed, and tenacious. My agent, Sarah Chalfant, was an immediate and boundless supporter of this project, and without her and all at the Wylie Agency—especially Andrew Wylie, Georgia Garrett, Liza Walworth, Rose Billington, and Jin Auh—this book would not be a reality. Tom Dupree at HarperEntertainment and Andy Miller at Fourth Estate were not only astute, knowledgeable editors but also fans of the music, truly a dual blessing. Thanks, too, to Yung Kim, Lou Aronica for giving us the go-ahead, and to Martha P. Trachtenberg for the scrupulous copyediting. Stephanie Chernikowski lent her sharp editorial eye to the manuscript and was as always a good friend throughout. My family—my mother Raymonde Browne, my sister L. Virginia Browne, and my sister Colette Browne and the McPherson-Browne-Brotman household—have given me a lifetime of love and encouragement of my work, down to lending me the family car during my research trips to California. Last but far from least, I extend my love and gratitude to my wife, Maggie, for her compassion and support, and for the saintly patience she exhibited in a home gradually overrun with cassettes, folders, transcripts, and boxes. Her unwavering faith that I could complete this project was the greatest of gifts.

Shortly into the writing of this book, my own father, Clifford Browne, was diagnosed with non-Hodgkins lymphoma, and he left us three devastatingly fast months later. Throughout his life, he instilled in me the virtues of hard work, dedication, loyalty, and honesty, not to mention a love of big-band music and the Carpenters. He was bemused by the world of rock and roll—"weird," he would call it, with a laugh—but was never less than encouragingly positive about my decision to make a career writing about it. I'll miss his company, his phone calls, his home-repair tips and relentless perfectionism, and the moments when he would ask, "Hey, Dave! How's the book comin'?" or tease me with, "Done yet, Dave?" To use one of his favorite phrases, he was a real corker, and this book is dedicated to his memory.

DREAM
BROTHER

In the South, they call it a shotgun shack: a house so compact that one can, if so inclined, open the front and back doors and discharge a blast straight through and into the backyard. Actually, there wasn't much behind 91 North Rembert Street, mostly dirt and gravel, and that backwoods ambience was in keeping with the earthy feel of the rest of the property. The white wood siding had begun to peel, and three-foot-high brownish weeds had transformed the hilly front yard into a parcel of untamed field. No one would ever describe 91 North Rembert as the lavish accommodations of a pop star.

Inside, glancing around the bare white walls and tan plank floors of the living room, Gene Bowen realized how much work there was to do this evening. With his sandy-brown shag and boyish features, the thirty-three-year-old Bowen looked surprisingly youthful for someone who had worked as a roadie from the time he was eighteen and then graduated, three years ago, to a job as the loyal tour manager of Jeff Buckley. As anyone around Jeff would testify, Bowen's wasn't the easiest of jobs. The usual road-manager work—making sure schedules were adhered to, cars and trucks were rented at the appropriate times and places, and supplies from guitar strings to hair dye were on hand—was hard enough. Fulfilling those jobs for Jeff was another matter altogether. Jeff had a tendency to show up hours late for meetings or simply space out, although he was always a little sheepish, even self-lacerating, whenever he screwed up.

Even though Jeff's nearly two-year-long tour had ended fourteen months before, the downtime since had hardly been stress free. Although it wasn't a runaway commercial hit, his first album, *Grace,* had established him as a formidable new talent in rock, an oldfangled haunted romantic who wore his heart on both sleeves yet wasn't afraid to thrash away as if he were a bratty punk rocker. With its overspill of emotion and passion, the album set him apart from most of his Lollapalooza-era peers, as did the pensive eyes and gaunt cheekbones that had launched numerous Web sites and a reputation (one Jeff mostly loathed) as a dreamboat. Still, the making of Jeff's second album—the one his label, Columbia, was so eager to see completed and released in order to capitalize on that rising reputation—was starting to feel like an endless round of jams, fruitless recording sessions, problems with band members, and instruments being hauled from one subterranean practice room to another back in New York. For any number of reasons, the gears seemed to be stuck; the wheels of the Jeff Buckley machine weren't rolling.

Ever since Bowen had driven into Memphis yesterday morning, he had been concerned about his friend's—and employer's—mental state, as had others back in New York, where Jeff had been living for most of the past five and a half years. Jeff had always been slight of build and only about 5 feet 7 inches, still the skinny kid from Orange County, but he had lately begun to look a bit drawn and thin. His mood shifts, which had always been pronounced, had become more manic and erratic, with highs and lows even more drastic than before. Jeff's behavior during the last twenty-four hours hadn't eased Bowen's mind. Why was Jeff so insistent on buying that decrepit old car, the one that wasn't even for sale? What was he *doing* in that bathtub last night, the red ink dribbling down his chin?

As the sun began to set on this Thursday evening, though, matters overall appeared to be on track. Jeff's band, including his third drummer in eighteen months, was scheduled to arrive at the airport in about two hours, and as soon as possible—maybe even the following day—they would begin rehearsing the new songs Jeff planned to record for the second album. His producer would be flying into town on June 23. Jeff seemed pleased with his new material. After nearly two years of gestation and false starts, he had told his musicians, business executives, and friends that he was finally ready to nail the album. He had sent his band a tape of his new songs only seven days before, but that was typical; Jeff seemed to do everything, including create music, at the last possible moment.

Although dusk was in sight, the moist, breezy air still felt mosquito-muggy inside and outside the unairconditioned cottage. Jeff had grown very attached to 91 North Rembert and the block of cozy, single-story homes in the midtown district of Memphis. After a life in which commitment to anything was cause for anguish, Jeff, who had turned thirty about six months before, appeared to have turned a significant personal corner. He told Bowen he wanted to buy the house from the owners, who lived on the other side of the street, and Bowen had been instructed to visit them later in the evening to ask how much it would cost. The suggestion raised several pairs of eyebrows back in New York among Jeff's management, accountant, and record company, but they would deal with that later.

The plan called for Jeff's musicians to stay in his house, which is where Bowen's work for the evening began. It was going to be tight. The living room was empty save for a green velvet couch and a milk crate that doubled as a stand for Jeff's boom-box tape recorder, but it was nonetheless small and boxy, and the adjoining room and Jeff's own back bedroom were even more shoebox-sized. Somehow, though, they would make it work. Bowen had already scooped up toilet paper and linens for the house and, earlier today, had rented several mattresses.

Shortly before 8 P.M., Jeff emerged from his bedroom in black jeans, ankle-high black boots, and a white T-shirt with long black sleeves and "Altamont" (in honor of the Rolling Stones's anarchic, death-shrouded 1969 concert) inscribed on it. Though officially out of his twenties, he remained a rock and roll kid at heart; an Iggy Pop T-shirt also hung in his closet. After a period in which he had often dyed his hair black, his newly shorn hair was back to its natural brown. As he and Bowen stepped outside and stood on the front porch, Jeff said he was heading out for a while. Generally Bowen would accompany Jeff on expeditions while on tour, making sure his boss was where he needed to be at the appointed times. But tonight Bowen needed space. The mattresses would be delivered shortly, and the last thing the tour manager needed was Jeff bouncing around the house when they arrived.

So, when Jeff told Bowen he would be leaving with Keith Foti, Bowen was mostly relieved. Foti was even more of a character than Jeff was. A fledgling songwriter and musician and a full-time haircutter in New York City, Foti had accompanied Bowen from New York to Memphis in a rented van, the band's gear and instruments crammed in the back. Stocky and wide-faced, with spiky, blue-dyed hair that matched the wavy-blue pattern of his aqua army pants, Foti, who was twenty-three, could have been the star of a Saturday morning cartoon show about a punk rock band. The red smoking jacket he was wearing only completed the picture.

Jeff told Bowen that he and Foti had decided to drive to the rehearsal space the band would be using during the upcoming weeks. A couple of drum kits had been set up there, and Jeff felt like bashing around; Foti, always up for some form of musical expression, liked the idea, too. To Bowen, it seemed as good—and harmless—a plan as any. Once the furniture arrived, Bowen would then have to rush over to the Memphis airport to pick up the band, whose plane would be touching down at 9:08 P.M., and there wouldn't be room in the rental car for everyone anyway.

Bowen told them to be back at the house by nine to greet the band. Jeff said fine, and he and Foti ambled down the gravel driveway to the van parked in front of the house. Despite the humidity, it had been a cooler than normal spring, so Jeff grabbed his jacket on the way out.

Bowen felt the heat too, especially after a long day driving around Memphis running errands. He went back into the house, through the black-grille front door and the living room and into the white-walled kitchen, with its old stove and vintage refrigerator. He poured himself a glass of water from the tap and gulped it down.

Suddenly it dawned on him: Did Jeff and Foti know where the rehearsal space was? For nonnatives, Memphis's layout can be confusing; streets zigzag into each other, and it wouldn't be terribly hard to get lost or suddenly find one's self in a dicey part of town. And knowing Jeff, who could wander with the best of them, Bowen thought he should make sure they had directions.

Bowen bolted through the front door, but the van was gone; he must have just missed them. Oh, well, he thought to himself, they'll find the building. After all, they had just been there yesterday.

Cruising around Memphis in their bright yellow Ryder van, past weathered shacks, barbecue joints, pawnshops, and strip malls, Jeff and Foti made for an unusual sight. Foti was in the driver's seat, which was for the best; Jeff was an erratic driver, to say the least, and had had his license revoked several times due to minor accidents. In the passenger seat, Jeff gripped Foti's boom box, a black, bargain-basement $99 RCA model with dual tape decks. Foti had brought it with him from New York the day before, and when Jeff first saw it he laughed and cracked, "What are you *doing* with that?"

Tonight, though, it would have to do. They cranked one of Foti's mixed tapes, and the two of them sang along to the Beatles' "I Am the Walrus," John Lennon's "Imagine," and Jane's Addiction's "Three Days." Foti and Jeff had bonded over their love of Jane's Addiction and its shamanesque, hard-living singer, Perry Farrell. It took Jeff back to those days in the late '80s when he was living and starving in Los Angeles, trying to make a name for himself despite the name already attached to him.

It wasn't Jeff's fault that he shared some vocal and physical character-istics with his father and fellow musician Tim Buckley. Both men had the same sorrowful glances, thick eyebrows, and delicate, waifish airs that made women of all ages want to comfort and nurture them. It wasn't Jeff's fault, either, that he inherited Tim's vocal range, five-and-a-half octaves that let Tim's voice spiral from a soft caress into bouts of rapturous, orgas-mic sensuality. In the '60s, Tim had used that voice to write and sing melodies that blended folk, jazz, art song, and R&B; although he had never been more than a cult act, some of those songs had been recorded by the likes of Linda Ronstadt and Blood, Sweat & Tears.

When Jeff had begun writing his own music, he too moved in uncon-ventional ways, crafting rhapsodies that changed time signatures and leapt from folkish delicacy to full-throttle metal roar. None of this, he insisted, came from his father's influence. His biggest rock influence and favorite band was, he said, Led Zeppelin. To his friends, Jeff talked about his boot-leg of *Physical Graffiti* outtakes with more affection and fannish enthusi-asm than he ever did about the nine albums his father had recorded dur-ing the '60s and '70s.

Tonight, for once, Tim's ghost was not lurking in the rearview mirror. If anything, Jeff seemed at peace with his father's memory for perhaps the first time in his life. Whenever Jeff had mentioned Tim in the past, it was with flashes of irritation or resignation. He sounded as if he were dis-cussing a far-off celebrity, not a father or even a family member. In a way, Tim was barely either: He and his first wife, Mary Guibert, had separated before Jeff was even born, and Jeff had been raised to view Tim's life and music warily. But in the last few months, Jeff seemed to have begun to understand his father's music, and, more important, his motivations.

Jeff's years in Los Angeles hadn't been fruitful, but when he moved to New York in the fall of 1991, a buzz began building around the skinny, charismatic kid with the big-as-a-cathedral voice and the eclectic reper-toire. Many record companies came calling, and he eventually, hesitatingly, put his name on a contract with one of them, Columbia. After an initial EP, an album, *Grace,* had finally appeared in 1994. A brilliant sprawl of a work, the album traversed the musical map, daring listeners to find the common ground that linked its choral pieces, Zeppelin-dipped rock, and amorous cabaret. Certainly one of the links was Jeff's voice, an intense and seemingly freewheeling instrument that wasn't afraid to glide from operatic highs and overpowering shrieks to a conversational intimacy. The voice personified the album's mood swings; even skeptics who felt the songs were a bit meandering admired it.

Beyond being simply one of the most important and moving albums of the '90s, *Grace* branded Jeff as something even more vital: an actual, hype-be-damned talent for the ages. The record business was always eager to promote newcomers in such a manner, but here was someone with both a sense of musical history and seemingly limitless potential. Like Bob Dylan or Van Morrison before him, he appeared to be on the road to a long and commanding career in which even a creative misstep or two would be worth poring over. Comparisons with Tim were inevitable—Jeff's inches-thick press kit attested to that—and a disturbing number of fortysome-things had materialized at Jeff's concerts to ask him about his father. But much to Jeff's relief, the comparisons had begun to vaporize with each passing month.

Grace hadn't been the smash hit Columbia would have liked it to have been, but worldwide it had sold nearly three-quarters of a million copies, and it was talked up by everyone from Paul McCartney and Jimmy Page to U2 and Soundgarden; at a Rock and Roll Hall of Fame induction dinner, Jeff was introduced to Zeppelin's Robert Plant, who told him how much he loved *Grace.* Overcome with emotion, Jeff left the dinner party soon after. Fans in Britain, Australia, and France adored him even more passionately than those in America. On the downside, Jeff was in the hole financially with Columbia, and he worried about it constantly. Perhaps that was why his hair had begun looking a little thin these last few months, as if he had been pulling at it.

To his managers and record company, Jeff was a shining star, a gateway to prestige, money, and credibility. Many people in Jeff's life had treated him this way, but never so intensely as now; so much was riding on the songs he was testing out on the four-track recorder in the living room of his house in Memphis. Jeff didn't like to think about those pressures, which is partly why he was six hundred miles from New York. Here, he could think, write, create, and, with any luck, not be as distracted as he had been.

Jeff told everyone who would listen that he wanted his next album to "rock hard." He feared his music and image were considered too soft. Accordingly, his sonic interests had careened toward rock steeped in dissonance and jarring tempos. The Grifters, one of his favorite current bands, lived right here in Memphis, and he loved their howling, basement-clammy voodoo rock; it sounded as if a layer of bathtub scuzz had been recorded atop it and was then being scraped off with a rusty shovel. Jeff adored that sort of noise. And, as with his interest in buying his house and moving wholesale to Memphis, this shift in artistic direction had set off more than a few alarms back in Manhattan.

Earlier in the day, shortly before he and Foti left the house, Jeff had been blasting CDs on the boom box in his living room, mostly pogo punk from the '80s by the likes of the Dead Kennedys and Flipper. Jeff had gone outside to chat with a friend, and Gene Bowen, who wasn't in the mood for headache-inducing music, had put on a CD by Helium, a more melodic and languid alternative rock band. Jeff charged back inside, yelling, "I don't want to hear that!" Back went the Dead Kennedys.

The drive from Jeff's house on North Rembert to Young Avenue, where the rehearsal room was located, should have taken ten minutes down a few tree-lined streets. But something was wrong. Before Jeff and Foti knew it, nearly an hour had passed, and there was still no sign of the two-story red-brick building. They found themselves circling around a variety of neighborhoods, past underpasses for Interstate 240 and pawnshops. To Foti, everything began to look the same.

They knew Bowen had most likely departed for the airport to pick up the band, so there was no point in calling the house and asking for directions. Jeff had an idea: They would call the owner of Barrister's, a local club where Jeff had been woodshedding for the last two months. He loved the anonymity and low-pressure scenario of Barrister's; it reminded him of his early days in Manhattan, when he played at an East Village coffee-house, his friends and colleagues in the audience cheering him on. There was no pressure, no record contract. That was a nice time—a "pure" one, he told one of his closest friends—full of promise and potential.

When no one answered the phone at Barrister's, they decided to head over to the club. By now, they were approaching downtown Memphis, an area on which Jeff at least had a handle. The van rumbled down Jefferson Street, a four-lane avenue that runs through the heart of downtown, an area of concrete parking garages, hotels, and drab office buildings that housed state and federal offices. Barrister's was located in an alley off Jefferson, beneath a parking garage and across from a vacant lot.

They banged on the black metal door, but the club was closed. The trip wasn't entirely a loss, though. Lying on the street, waiting to be hauled off as trash, were a couple of discarded orange diner booths. "Oh, man, I need these!" Jeff exclaimed. He and Foti grabbed one and tossed it into the back of the van. Jeff needed more furniture for his house—or, in fact, *any* furniture, since all he had was that green couch and a piece of foam that doubled as his mattress.

By now, it was approaching 9 P.M.; there was still time to waste. As Foti began to pull away, Jeff turned to him and asked if he were hungry and wanted to go for ribs. Foti said he wasn't. Perhaps inspired by the time he had spent earlier in the year in this part of town, Jeff had another thought.

"Why don't we go down to the river?" he said.

The idea sounded good to Foti, who had brought along his guitar and felt like practicing a song he was writing. Having a talented, well-regarded rock star as an audience wouldn't be so bad, either.

Foti pulled onto Jefferson, and the van began rumbling up the gradually inclining street, past the Bankruptcy Loan Center, a Chinese restaurant, a bank, a nearly empty parking lot, and, at North Main, past Jack's Food market and over the trolley tracks that ran through the downtown district.

At Front Street, Jefferson took a dip. Foti and Jeff looked out the windshield, and spread out before them was the Wolf River.

The Wolf River did not look particularly wolfish, and it barely had the feel of a river. After wending its way into Memphis from western Tennessee, the Wolf intersected with the Mississippi just north of downtown Memphis. At that point lies a closure dam, resulting in a still-water harbor that the United States Coast Guard branch in Memphis referred to as the Wolf River chute. Viewed from the embankments above it, the chute, which trickled three miles along the Memphis waterfront, was hardly the rushing-rapid waterway one would expect. With its slowly rippling beige water, it more closely resembled a long, placid lake tucked away in a small valley.

On the other side of the waterfront was Mud Island, a massive sandbar peninsula that had formed naturally earlier in the century and housed a series of tourist attractions, from an outdoor concert theater to a Mississippi River museum. At the island's bottom tip, the Mississippi intersected with the Wolf River chute, at which point the swelling, powerful Mississippi waters whipped around into the chute and created occasional eddies.

The city government passed an ordinance banning swimming in the Wolf River, but no signs indicated this restriction. According to locals, there didn't have to be, since everyone in Memphis knew it was far from an ideal swimming hole. The first six inches of water could be warm and innocuous-looking, but thanks to the intersection with the Mississippi, the undercurrents were deceptive. All day long and into the early hours of the morning, two-hundred-foot-long barges carrying goods from the local granaries and a cement factory hauled their cargo up and down the Wolf. With their churning motors, the tugboats that pulled the barges were even fiercer and had been known to create strong wakes. Local Coast Guard employees had once witnessed a sixteen-foot flat-bottom boat being sucked under the water in the wake of a tug; another time, they found a boat tossed up on the bank after a tugboat had chugged by two hundred feet away.

Memphis lore had it that at least one person a year drowned in the Wolf, and events continued to bear out that horrific statistic. In 1995, an eleven-year-old boy who had jumped into the water to untangle a fishing line had been pulled under, turning up dead two hundred yards away; a year later, a man sitting on the riverbank had taken off his shoes and jumped in, presumably to crash the H.O.R.D.E. hippie-rock festival taking place in full view of him at the Mud Island amphitheater. His body washed up three days later. Everyone knew why he thought he could make it: The distance from the downtown side of the Wolf to Mud Island was less than one hundred feet and appeared to be easily swimmable.

Even if Jeff had heard these stories, he either didn't care or disregarded them as the evening wore on. Driving down Jefferson, Foti hung a turn into the parking lot of the Welcome Center, a white, country-home-style building containing statues of Elvis Presley and B. B. King as well as tourism-related pamphlets and information. The center was closed, but Foti parked in front, and he and Jeff stepped out. Foti grabbed a Dunhill

Light cigarette, and Jeff asked for a hit. Smoking was one of many habits he had picked up on the road while touring to promote *Grace,* and one of many he was trying to quash in Memphis.

Hopping over a three-foot-high brick wall, they strode across a cement promenade with picnic tables, perfect for taking in river views on a beautiful summer day. Then Jeff hiked his black combat boots onto the bottom rung on the greenish steel rail that ran alongside the promenade and jumped over. Foti, gripping his guitar, followed, and they found themselves barreling down a steep slope, swishing through knee-high brush, ivy, and weeds.

On the way down, Jeff shed his coat—just dropped it in the brush. "You're not gonna leave it here, are you?" Foti asked, stopping quickly to pick it up. Jeff didn't seem to be listening. Carrying Foti's boom box, he continued down and arrived at the riverbank.

It wasn't very much of a bank. The locals and authorities referred to it as "the cobblestones," but that name made it sound much more quaint than it was. The shore was littered with rocks, soda cans, and shattered glass bottles—if anything, it resembled a dirt road more than a beach—and it quickly sloped into the water just inches away. It didn't take a Coast Guard employee to see that the debris that littered this part of the cobblestones could easily shred one's feet, so Jeff kept his boots on.

The night felt peaceful. The marina on the opposite bank housed a small city of docked houseboats and sailboats, but there was little if any activity. Jutting monolithically into the sky above Jeff and Foti were the brown cement pillars that held up the Mud Island monorail, a train that transported people from downtown Memphis to the island. With its steel lacework, the bridge looked like a huge ladder stretching across the waterway. It was a daunting, imposing sight, especially in the near darkness of this part of the river.

As gentle waves lapped up onto the grimy shoreline, Jeff set Foti's boom box on one of the many jagged slate rocks on the bank, just an inch or so above the water. "Hey, man, don't put my radio there," Foti told him. "I don't want it going in the water. It's my only unit of sound." Jeff didn't seem to be paying particular attention to that request, either.

By now, just after 9 P.M., Foti had strapped on his guitar and started practicing his song. Looking right at Foti, Jeff took a step or two away, his back to the river. Before Foti knew it, Jeff was knee-high in the water.

"What are you doin', man?" Foti said. Within moments, Jeff's entire body eased into the water, and he began doing a backstroke.

At first, Foti wasn't too concerned: Jeff was still directly offshore, just a few feet away. He and Foti began musing about life and music as Jeff backstroked around in circles. "You know, the first one's fun, man—it's that second one . . . ," Jeff said, his voice trailing off as he continued to backstroke in the water. Foti wasn't quite sure what he meant, but he didn't give it much thought.

With each stroke, Jeff inched more and more out into the river. Foti noticed and said, "Come in, you're gettin' too far out." Instead, Jeff began singing Led Zeppelin's "Whole Lotta Love." "He was just on his own at that point," Foti says. "He didn't really observe my concerns."

Although Foti didn't realize it at the time, Jeff had an impetuous, spur-of-the-moment streak. Many of his friends considered it one of his most endearing qualities, while others worried that it bordered on recklessness. Like his father, he liked to follow his muse, to leap into projects passionately and spontaneously, even if it wasn't fashionable or appropriate. Take that night in 1975. Tim was on his way home from a grueling tour. His record sales were in freefall, but lately he had tried to cut back on his drinking and drugging and was attempting to get his music and even a potential acting career on track. On the way home from the last stop on his tour, he stopped by the home of a friend, who offered up a few drugs. What was wrong with a little pick-me-up after some exhausting road work? No one knew if Tim realized exactly what he had snorted that late afternoon, but it ultimately didn't matter; he died that night of an overdose at the age of twenty-eight. Only months before, eight-year-old Jeff had finally spent some time with his estranged father, for the only extended period of time Jeff could remember.

Although Jeff had experimented with drugs, he steered clear to avoid his father's fate, both physically and artistically; he had learned from Tim's mistakes in the matters of artistic integrity and handling the music business. Part of the reason he was here, in laid-back Memphis, was to distance himself from New York and its various temptations. He wasn't about to let the same pitfalls that debilitated his father undercut him. Onstage, Jeff would often make cracks about dead rock stars, pretending to shoot up or breaking into spot-on mimicry of anyone from Jim Morrison to Elvis Presley. Once this new album was completed, he was planning to dig deeper into his family heritage and unearth the truth behind the seemingly ongoing series of tragedies that haunted his lineage.

The genealogical research would have to wait. Tonight, as he backstroked in the water, Jeff appeared to feel freer than he had in a while. The mere fact that he was even *in* water was a sign of change. Although he had grown up near the beaches of Southern California, Jeff was never a beachcomber. Even his current lover could never get him to take a dip in the ocean; the hotel pool on tour was as far as he would venture. Jeff seemed nervous about water. It was too mysterious, too uncontrollable. But this body of water felt different; hearing his imitation of Robert Plant's lusty squeal on "Whole Lotta Love" ping-ponging between the riverbanks, Jeff felt at peace.

It was close to 9:15 P.M., and Jeff had been in the river nearly fifteen minutes. Water began seeping into his boots; his pants slowly grew heavier. He began swimming further toward the center of the river, circling around before drifting to the left of Foti and the monorail pillars. Then, he began swimming straight across to the Mud Island side, or so it appeared to Foti. Directly across from them, on the opposite bank, was a dirt road that led right up from the river. It looked so close—maybe Jeff felt he could reach it and take a quick stroll.

The tugboat came first, moments later. "Jeff, man, there's a boat coming," Foti said in his flat, dry voice. "Get out of the fucking water." The boat was heading in their direction, up from Beale Street. Jeff seemed to take notice of it and made sure to be clear of it as it passed. The next time Foti looked over, he still saw Jeff's head bobbing in the water.

Not more than a minute had passed when Foti spied another boat approaching. This one was bigger—a barge, perhaps one hundred feet long. Foti grew more concerned and started yelling louder for Jeff to come back. Once again, Jeff swam out of its path, and Foti breathed another sigh of relief. In the increasing darkness, the speck that was Jeff's head was just barely visible.

Soon the water grew choppy, the waves lapping a little more firmly against the riverbank. The waves weren't high by any means, but Foti grew worried about his boom box. The last thing he wanted was to see it waterlogged and unusable. Taking his eye off Jeff for a moment, he stepped over to where Jeff had set the stereo down on a rock and moved it back about five feet, out of reach of the waves.

Foti turned back around. There was no longer a head in the water. There was nothing—just stillness, a few rippling aftershock waves, and the marina in the distance.

Foti began to scream out Jeff's name. There was no answer. He yelled more. He continued screaming for nearly ten minutes.

On the other side of the river, Gordon Archibald, a fifty-nine-year-old employee of the marina, was walking near the moored boats with a friend when he heard a single shout of "help." Concerned, he looked out onto the water. But he saw nothing, nor heard anything more.

ONE

*My grandfather had a beautiful voice. Irish tenor. Beautiful. Too much
of a military hardass to deal with his own and his son's talents. I wish
it were otherwise. I love you, you poor bastards. . . . With a father like
this man, it is no wonder that Tim Buckley was afraid to come back to
me. So afraid to be my father. Because his only paradigm for
fatherhood was a deranged lunatic with a steel plate in his head. . . .
I know that he must have been scared shitless to think he might possibly
become like his father. Scared shitless of treating me the way his father
treated him and his family. Can you imagine the heartbreak? The
useless, shitty torture day in, day out?*

—JEFF BUCKLEY, JOURNAL ENTRY, AUGUST 9, 1995

As centuries went, the eighteenth was not a particularly desirable one in
which to be Irish in Ireland. The island was on its way to becoming
absorbed into the United Kingdom, and the British Penal Laws drawn up
between 1702 and 1719 had planted the seeds for the muzzling of native
Irish culture. One law in particular made it illegal for the Irish to study
and practice their own language, Gaelic, and their own traditions within
their own borders. For the Irish people, the Laws were demoralizing and
degrading, and they led the populace to devise increasingly covert ways to
school their children in, among others, Gaelic. Illicit instructors began
teaching in whatever ramshackle structures could be found—in old barns

and ditches, behind the ruins of walls, even behind hedges that would hide both teacher and pupils. The latter practice gave rise to the term "hedgemaster," which came to apply to any and all of these illegal practitioners of Irish tradition.

Among the hedgemasters was at least one member of the Buckley clan, said to be from county Cork in the southwestern part of the country. According to family lore, the Buckleys were already known around Cork's sloping, green-blanketed valleys for their skills as storytellers and troubadours. As hedgemasters, they now added authority defiers to their reputation. Along with their fellow educational rebels, they consciously spat on the law of the land in order to carry on the dying and suppressed culture of their own people. The hedgemasters—and the Buckleys—would do things their way.

Among their own dubious achievements, the British Penal Laws also forced thousands of Irish to flee Ireland and settle elsewhere, and some landed in the industrial towns of upstate New York. By the early twentieth century, a descendant of one of the hedgemasters—the first Timothy Charles Buckley—and his wife, Charlotte, were living and working in one of those areas: Amsterdam, a factory town twenty miles northwest of Albany. The Mohawk River sliced through the small city, but that feature was far from its most notable. Sixty-two plants clogged the streets of Amsterdam, which was populated primarily by working-class Irish, Polish, Germans, Russians, and Italians. In the proud words of its chamber of commerce, Amsterdam was "first in the manufacture of brooms" in the nation; its factories also churned out rugs, carpets, underwear, gloves, and pearl buttons, among dozens of other everyday products. (It was also the producer of actor Kirk Douglas, born there as Issur Danielovich in 1916.) Tim Buckley had an auto repair service in town with his partner, Frank Graff, but Buckley & Graff did not last long, and by 1936, Tim senior was a full-time bartender and dwelled with his family on Mechanic Street near the Chuctanunda Creek. The Mechanic Street address was merely one of many; every year, the family would relocate to a new home.

The Buckleys' initial attempt at a family failed when their first child died shortly after birth. In November 1916, eighteen-year-old Charlotte finally bore a healthy child, a son named Timothy Charles Jr. Tim Jr. graduated high school and, by age twenty, was working in the local movie theater, the Strand, on the city's bustling, fume-choked East Main Street, near the Sears Roebuck and Penney's stores. In 1939, he took a job at the Bigelow-Sanford Carpet Company ("America's style leader for over 100 years," boasted its advertisements). However, World War II altered whatever plans Tim Jr. had for his life. He had already enlisted in the National Guard in December 1937, and was placed on active duty on October 15, 1940. Then, on May 25, 1942, he was drafted and assigned to the 101st Airborne. He was twenty-five.

Even under the circumstances, it was a daunting assignment. The newly activated 101st trained and prepared soldiers for an innovative form of postindustrial warfare, parachute combat; their unofficial name, the Screaming Eagles, testified to the ferocity and intensity of their mission. Tim spent four weeks in parachute school at Fort Benning in Georgia before he and his fellow dogfaces shipped out for the European theater of operations on September 5, 1943, eventually participating in campaigns at Normandy, Ardennes, northern France, and the Rhineland. Tim's outfit was originally part of companies B and D of the 502nd Parachute Infantry Regiment—a quarter to a fifth of whom were killed in action. Tim was later transferred to ground duty as part of the 105th Infantry, Company G. In the 502nd, his official title was sergeant, but his unofficial moniker was a "demolition specialist," who, in the Army's words, "destroyed by means of explosives, such objects of military importance as bridges, roads, buildings, and railways to delay enemy action."

As with many of his fellow soldiers, Tim arrived back in America only after the war ended—on Christmas day 1945, first to Fort Dix, New Jersey, and then to Washington, DC. Judging by the slew of medals he brought back with him, including a Distinguished Unit Badge, a Bronze Star, and a Good Conduct Medal, Tim seemed a solid, honorable soldier. But he also returned with a Purple Heart (for wounds received in action), and according to family lore, the injury went beyond a scrape or the posttraumatic stress syndrome common to combat veterans. As his second wife would tell her grandchildren, a land mine somewhere in Europe had exploded close to Tim's head and, as a result, a steel plate had been inserted into his skull.

At first, Tim didn't seem drastically altered. For a short period, he stayed in Washington, where he met and married his second spouse, Elaine Doris Scalia. (An earlier marriage, to a fellow Bigelow-Sanford employee in Amsterdam, New York, had taken place and dissolved before the war under a cloud of mystery. For decades afterward, few in Tim's family, including his children, knew there had been a Mrs. Joan Buckley prior to Elaine.) To her friends, Elaine was a sweet, warm woman with a deep-seated love of music, particularly jazz and standards. On Friday, February 14, 1947—Valentine's

Day, and an unseasonably sunny and mild one at that—their first child, named Timothy Charles Buckley III in the family tradition, ventured out of his mother's womb.

A week later, the new family relocated, moving back to Tim's prewar home of Amsterdam, New York. Little had changed in his absence. The smoke plumes rising out of the now sixty-six coal, linoleum, and paint factory stacks dotted the landscape like a frenzied series of exclamation points. The Buckleys settled into a home on Garden Street, close to the Mohawk River, and Tim went to work for General Electric (and, after that, American Locomotive) in Schenectady, sixteen miles outside of Amsterdam, while Elaine became a bookkeeper for a local hardware and mill supply store. "I was living up there in the woods," their son Tim III would later comment sardonically on their time in Amsterdam and nearby Fort Johnson, where the family moved, once more, in 1955.

Young Tim started attending school in Fort Johnson, but when he was in the second grade, the Buckleys contracted the same bug that was leading so many Easterners to migrate westward. California, they heard, was less bleak than this fume-clogged portion of New York state, and there were bound to be better jobs for young Tim's father. And, just maybe, whatever problems the eldest Tim had brought back with him from the battlegrounds of Europe would be covered by a warm blanket of Southern Californian sunshine.

Anna and George Guibert began loading up their two-door Plymouth coupe just after dinnertime. On this Memorial Day 1954, many of their neighbors in Massapequa, New York, were winding down from the holiday cookouts common to other postwar, middle-class suburbs on Long Island. For the Guiberts and their three children, though, it was time to leave behind one home and depart for another, thousands of miles away.

They didn't have a choice but to move tonight, since they had already sold their two-bedroom tract home on Park Lane—was there a more appropriate name for a street in milky-white '50s suburbia?—and the new owners would be arriving tomorrow. Anna, a petite, fairskinned Panamanian with a smile large enough to bridge her ears, made sure to clean up after dinner; she was as organized and fastidious as ever. Her husband, George—a lean stalk of a man with an intense, V-shaped face and deep-socketed eyes—jammed everything from utensils to the children's strollers and dolls into a four-by-eight trailer he had built and hitched onto the Plymouth.

Leaving at night wouldn't be so bad, they thought; this way, the children—six-year-old Mary and her three-year-old brother George—could sleep in the backseat. Anna and her husband were so diminutive that they were able to share the front seats with a crib carrying seven-month-old Peggy. As George started the ignition and the car pulled away, little Mary stood up in the backseat, watching their house grow ever smaller in the distance.

For both Anna and George, the journey signified a fresh start far from the hardships each had endured on Long Island and in their native Panama. For Anna, life seemed to be little but calamity. Located on the isthmus connecting North and South America and home to the Panama Canal, Panama was tropical in its eastern half and rugged and mountainous in its west. It sounded wonderfully tranquil on paper, yet it was hardly peaceful for Anna and her family. Her grandfather, a hearty Greek named John Payablas, had moved to Panama City early in the century. One night in 1911, a fight broke out in the bar of a hotel he had opened, and Payablas went to intervene. For his trouble, he was kicked in the testicles, and the resulting infection led to gangrene, which in turn led to his death. He left behind six children and another on the way. One of those children, Antonia, would marry another local of Greek descent, Costas Smiros. Together, they had five children, all born in Panama; the fourth, Anna, came into the world in February 1924.

From the start, life was far from easy for the Smiroses. Costas had a violent, hot-blooded streak and would often hit Antonia. Thankfully, he wasn't home much, since he worked on an oil tanker that often took him to New York. He yearned to stay there, so, with Antonia still in Panama, he began sending for his children one by one. In New York, he would paint houses to make extra money, but one day he fell off a ladder and injured his leg so badly that he too wound up with gangrene. Since her husband had no money left to send for the rest of the family, Antonia was forced to stay in Panama City and raise her remaining three daughters, including Anna. They took a one-room apartment with a communal bathroom and cooked with a small coal stove. To earn a living, Antonia began making dresses, selling them to the local prostitutes for fifty cents. It took many dresses to feed the family.

When she was ten, Anna contracted pneumatic fever. Her gums became infected, and all her teeth were pulled out and replaced with dentures. Her mother then endured a bout with cancer of the uterus, at which time Anna was forced to quit school and take a job as a secretary in the Signal Corps, the military office of the nearby Canal Zone. She was all of fifteen. (Her mother and sisters thanked God for her fluency with the English language, which helped her land that position.) Antonia was treated and eventually went into remission, but only by the method of cauterizing her uterus by the insertion of scalding metal rods. To pay for the extra treatments, Anna had to borrow money from as many family friends as possible.

The George Peter Guibert whom Anna met at a friend's wedding in 1944 hardly seemed like the ideal man to rescue her from these circumstances. Born in September 1923, he had a desirable job repairing airplanes in the Canal Zone. But Guibert, pronounced *Ghee*-bert, seemed irresponsible and childlike, and he had a tendency to smoke pot, a forbidden predilection at the time. Raised in the rural city of Boquete in western Panama, he had a sixth-grade education, hadn't set foot in a city before the age of nineteen, and didn't speak or write English. He was, Anna recalls, "not marrying material."

George had had his own family problems as well. His father, George Sr., was an American from Pittsburgh who loved nothing more than to visit Panama and have as much sex as possible before returning home. In 1943, he returned to Panama in search of the two sons he had left behind. He found his son George Jr. in the Canal Zone, and thanks to his father's intervention, the younger Guibert officially became an American citizen, his income leaping from "silver roll" status (for native Panamanians) to the higher-paying "gold roll" (for Americans working in the Canal). Up until that point, George had, like his friends and family, endured the humiliating legal racism of the silver-roll status, a caste system that even extended to separate silver and gold water fountains.

Now an American making three times the salary he had the week before, George Jr. became much more desirable to Anna, and he began working hard at winning her over, even strumming a guitar and singing Spanish folk songs to her outside her window at night. "He was a good singer," Anna recalls. "He'd come and serenade me. Very romantic and all that." Years later, she would hear traces of that voice in her children and grandchildren. His newfound American citizenship also meant George was immediately drafted into the U.S. Army, but good fortune again shined on him. World War II ended shortly after he entered the service, and he received an honorable discharge and was cited for performing "general Army office work" in the post office. On January 10, 1946, he and Anna were married in a Catholic church, George in his uniform.

One of the principal reasons Anna wanted to marry—and she wasn't ashamed of admitting it—was to have children. The pneumatic fever she had contracted as a kid made pregnancies potentially life-threatening, and her doctor warned her against having a baby. But Anna wanted nothing more, and she prayed to the Virgin Mary that if she had a child and the infant was healthy, she would name the baby Mary in her honor, which is exactly what she did when her daughter, Mary Ivette, was born on February 20, 1948.

If Anna had any inkling her new husband could be volatile, those feelings were confirmed when eight-month-old Mary was in a playful state one night. In no mood for romping with her, George demanded the baby go to sleep. When she wouldn't, he spanked his infant daughter. All night, Anna walked the floor with her baby in her arms, the child sobbing continuously. She made George promise to never punish their child again; having been beaten as an infant herself, Anna was particularly sensitive to physical abuse. George promised, but he broke his word when Mary was seventeen months old. Again, Anna made him vow not to hit their child; again, George said he wouldn't.

It was 1950, and many of their friends and relatives began telling George and Anna they should head for America. George visited Dallas that July for an exploratory visit, and the warm, hospitable Texas climate reminded him of home. He sent for his family, and, after a few months in Dallas, George, Anna, and two-year-old Mary headed for New York state in September 1950.

At first, Anna liked Long Island. Their apartment, in Port Washington, was near the North Shore and close to relatives, and George found a job as a sheet metal worker. In 1951, their son, George Peter III, was born, and the following year the family bought its first house—in Massapequa—for $10,000, with $100 down. It was, Mary recalls, "a very idyllic time. My parents were in love with each other. It was Kate Smith, and Howdy Doody on television, and life was wonderful." In the woods behind the house, the family would glimpse raccoons and bunnies. In October 1953, the Guiberts' third child, Peggy, was born.

The harsh realities of living in a northern climate soon made themselves brutally clear. In Panama, Anna had never even owned a sweater, but here, she had to bundle herself and children in layers of clothes to combat the frigid winters. She would hang the children's diapers out to dry and find them frozen on the line. Anna wanted out, and fast. She had also developed spinal arthritis, and her doctor suggested a move to warmer climates—for instance, Southern California.

As soon as the Plymouth arrived in California a week later, in early June of 1954, Anna smelled the scent of oranges as they drove through the area. Just as the Buckleys would feel when they arrived, she sensed change literally in the air. Here, she and her husband hoped, they would finally leave behind the tumult of the past, and for once be a content family.

Initially, the Guiberts stayed with friends in Southgate, just south of Los Angeles, and then rented their own apartment in nearby Maywood. But they wanted a home of their own, and all signs pointed to eight hundred square miles of farmland known as Orange County. "I remember when we drove out from Southgate to look at the new house," Mary recalls, "sitting and looking out the window and seeing mile after mile after mile of orange grove after orange grove. That's all there was."

The Valencia orange groves had indeed given this stretch of Southern California its colorful name, but until the Second World War, citrus products were the only reason the rest of the country paid any attention to this vast chunk of farmland located over an hour's drive south of Los Angeles. (The fact that there wasn't even a highway connecting its towns to LA did little to attract outsiders.) Once the war ended, the area began to look much more inviting, both to the new wave of Los Angelenos in search of a suburban bedroom community, and to the servicemen who had been stationed in Orange County's dozen army bases and decided to settle there. The completion of the I-5, also known as the Santa Ana Freeway, made it easier to commute to and from Los Angeles. From within and outside the state, the rush to Orange County was on. In 1950, the county's population was 216,224. Within ten years, it would vault to 703,925, only 260,451 of whom were actually born in California.

With hills that protected its crops from the weather, Anaheim had been home to the county's first orange groves early in the century. Its name— roughly translated to "home by the river"—was derived from a combination of Ana (for the Santa Ana River, which ran through it) and *heim* (German for "home," from the fifty German immigrants who founded the city in 1857). Anaheim went about its business until the day in 1954 when the city of Burbank rejected Walt Disney's plan for a theme park. Disney hired a research firm to find a new location, and they uncovered one an hour south of Los Angeles. Disneyland broke ground in Anaheim in April 1954 and opened the following year. With hungry developers eager to cash in, row after row of tract homes began sprouting up to replace the row upon row of oranges. One hundred and sixty acres of citrus were massacred for Disneyland alone.

The Guiberts bought their first home in Anaheim the same year Disneyland opened, and even visited the theme park during its first week of business. They had heard the schools in Anaheim were above average and the homes affordable, and both reports proved correct. Anna and George had to put down only $199 for their three-bedroom, $11,000 tract home on Greenacre Avenue on the outskirts of town. As the family's sole provider, George Guibert began taking home $100 a week as a foreman on an all-female assembly line for a local electronics company. Despite his flashes of temper, he could be a personable, hardworking man, and he seemed to have a way with handling (and working with) women who were not related to him.

In January 1960, by which time Anaheim's population had tripled in a mere four years, the Guiberts had saved up enough money to afford their dream house. It was still in Anaheim but a mile away, in a community of similar-looking tract homes. Although only a one-level structure, the tan-colored house on Archer Street housed three bedrooms, dining and living rooms, carpeting, a backyard, and a laundry room—all for an affordable $19,600. "We thought we were *such* hot stuff," Anna recalls. Soon there were azaleas in the front yard, near the palm tree outside the front door. Their neighbors, all of them white, made sure their front lawns were green and abundant, and took their children to see Mickey Mouse and Donald Duck as often as possible. It was as if everyone in this development in Anaheim was living wide awake in the American dream.

Anna wanted her children to have what she never did as a child in Panama, so when little Mary began showing signs of artistic inclinations at a young age, Anna encouraged her. On Long Island, Mary had taken ballet and tap-dance lessons. At age nine, in Anaheim, her parents bought her a used upright piano from a neighbor down the street. After dinner, she would often escape chores like dishwashing by heading straight for the keyboard. In school, she played cello in the school orchestra, even taking private lessons. At age twelve, already "a show tune kid," Mary landed a small role in an Orange County summer-stock production of *South Pacific* starring actor Bert Convy. She was paid $25 a week and was instantly hooked on the idea of being onstage.

From the sidelines, the Guiberts watched Mary's creative side blossom and nodded approvingly. "She had perfect pitch, a very good ear," her mother recalls. "We had dreams for her."

*   *   *

If Anaheim was the model of postwar suburban tranquility and middle-class affluence, Bell Gardens was its hell-raising, black-sheep cousin. Tucked away between highways 710 and 5 in Los Angeles County, the town had long been admired for its rich farming soil and its origins as part of a massive, 29,000-acre land grant known as the Rancho San Antonio. When the Depression hit, a local developer, O. C. Beck, began subdividing the land into one-third-acre lots, and for $20 down and $10 a month, a family could purchase its own farm. The area began attracting households from the dust-bowl-stricken Midwest, particularly Oklahoma and Arkansas, and Texas. (One of them included a transplanted Minnesotan teenager named Eddie Cochran, who would practice guitar in his garage in Bell Gardens and record joyful-noise popabilly hits like "Summertime Blues" and "C'mon Everybody.") Thanks to its new influx of homeowners, Bell Gardens took on an even more rural feel, right down to its nickname, "Billygoat Acres," derived from the fact that local ordinances allowed families to raise livestock on their property.

The blue-collar Okies who began anew in Bell Gardens didn't simply work hard; after hours, they drank hard and partied even harder. Bell Gardens was only 2.4 square miles, yet by the '50s two dozen bars dotted one of its main strips, Eastern Avenue. The music blaring out of those bars was pure country and honky-tonk. Hank Williams had died as the decade had begun, but his chronicles of emotional turbulence and restlessness continued to strike a hard-living chord with the roughnecks of Bell Gardens. The riverbed of the Los Angeles River, which ran through town, hosted hotrod races, and local lore had it that a crazed homeless woman named Shotgun Annie lived there too, shooting salt-pellet bullets at any kids who dared bike through what she considered her private property. The town's rowdy side was offset, at least partially, by its slew of churches, many of them Pentecostal. On any given week, it wasn't uncommon to see a full-fledged revival meeting under a tent in the middle of town.

At Bell Gardens Junior High School in the fall of 1960, eighth-grader Dan Gordon noticed a familiar face on the football field. It was that wiry, crewcutted kid Tim Buckley, whom Gordon had played against when they had attended different elementary schools in town. The Buckley family, Gordon soon learned, had arrived in Bell Gardens two years earlier and bought a nondescript home in an area not far from the town's hobo camps. (Tim and Elaine's second child, a delicate-looking girl they named

Kathleen, was born in 1958.) Tim and Gordon became fast friends, drawn together by a mutual love of music, sports, and sport cars.

Gordon also learned early on that Tim had a few peculiar traits. One day when both were about twelve, they were hanging out in a Bell Gardens park and spotted two slightly older but seemingly available girls.

"Let's go try and pick 'em up," Tim said.

Gordon was game, but the girls quickly scurried off when they discovered Tim and Gordon were a year or two younger than them. However, Tim would not accept, or admit to, defeat. When he noticed a few friends arriving at the park, he turned to Gordon and said, without missing a beat, "Let's tell those guys we screwed those girls." As Gordon recalls, "We had obviously never gotten laid, but he made up this entire saga of what we had done with these girls in the park: how we got naked and balled their brains out. I just looked at him amazed. I certainly knew how to stretch the truth to the breaking point, but Tim didn't even consider that line. He went straight past it."

At the same time, Tim was the epitome of suburban normality. He inherited his mother's delicate cheekbones and warm, wide smile, and his father's thick, coarse mat of hair and dark sense of humor. For three years, he was a quarterback on the junior-high football team. ("We used to have a no-fail short-yardage play," recalls teammate Gordon. "He would pinch my butt, which meant a quarterback sneak. He was devastating with it. He didn't have a particularly good arm, but he was very sneaky.") Football (and tennis) weren't Tim's only extracurricular interests; he ran for and won the job of student body president, joined the proto-preppy Lettermen's Club, and wrote for the school newspaper. "He was smart, and he always smiled," says another classmate, Corby Alsbrook. "He was a very solid kid." Like Gordon, Alsbrook recalls young Tim wearing Oxford shirts, khaki pants, and corduroys, his hair neatly combed and parted—"a poster boy," Gordon says, "for Republican America."

Simultaneously, Tim's interest in music began to accelerate. Thanks to the influence of Bell Gardens's country music streak, he grew to love Johnny Cash's hard, syncopated Sun Records hits, like "Big River" and "I Walk the Line," as well as the wailing R&B of Little Richard. At home, Elaine Buckley would play her Frank Sinatra, Judy Garland, and Ella Fitzgerald LPs, which Tim also adored. Later, he would tell reporters he was first inspired to make music after hearing one of his mother's favorite Miles Davis albums when he was five. The sound of Davis's exploratory trumpet intrigued him so much that he learned to imitate it, or to drop his voice as low as an alto saxophone. Seemingly out of nowhere, Tim discovered he was blessed with an extraordinary voice that could span, he said, five octaves, and with it, he would bicycle through town mimicking the sounds of cars and buses. "I discovered the high voice, it all started in high school when I started singing," Tim said later in an unpublished interview. "Just happened. I could probably go higher. Or lower."

Since it was the early '6os, though, young men's fancies turned not to jazz but to folk music. In the years since the Kingston Trio had scored the most unlikely of number-one hits with 1958's "Tom Dooley," a new breed of folk—collegiate, earnest, and as freshly scrubbed as the Trio's striped, button-down shirts—had filled the hole left by the end of the first rock and roll era. Tim already knew how to play banjo; when he contracted the mumps at age eleven, his mother bought him one, and he took lessons to learn how to frail and fingerpick. With a tenor that could replicate that of folkies like the Trio's Nick Reynolds, Tim made his first steps into music-making. He began reading the folk magazine *Sing Out!* and, with Alsbrook on guitar, formed his first band, a Peter, Paul and Mary–style group, with a female classmate. They lasted only a few months, but it was a beginning.

Starting in junior high, Tim, Gordon, and another guitar-strumming classmate, Larry Boren, formed a more serious combo, heartily harmonizing on folk songs popularized by Pete Seeger, the Kingston Trio, and another nightclub folk act, the Limeliters. Calling themselves the Cobblestone Three (later the Four, when Alsbrook joined up), they dressed in black suits and ties with crisp white shirts, and earned a few dollars at local Kiwanis and Rotary Clubs, school assemblies, and at least one company picnic. The shows would often wrap up with the Weavers' "Lonesome Traveler," Tim's tenor voice and banjo building to a crowd-pleasing crescendo.

By the time Tim entered Bell Gardens High School in the fall of 1962, music had overtaken sports as his principal obsession. He still played tennis and baseball, but he was too small to throw around the football with the heftier high-school kids and joined the Latin Club instead. Whether it was true or not, Tim would claim he had broken a finger playing football and, unable to form barre chords (in which the first finger of the left hand depresses all six strings simultaneously), began writing and playing in an open-tuned style that would become one of his trademarks.

*　　*　　*

There were several parts of town into which the Cobblestone Three rarely, if ever, ventured. One was the hobo hangout near the town's railroad tracks, with its army of menacing homeless. Another was the Eastern Avenue bar strip—violent dives with lounge-swinger names like George's Playroom and the Kit-Kat Club. Tim and his friends would occasionally walk past them and listen to the country tunes blaring inside, until, inevitably, the sound of breaking bottles drowned out the music. Locals called the bars "murder-a-month places," for good reason: One night, Tim and his friends witnessed a drunk beating his wife on the sidewalk in front of them.

Later, Tim would tell friends that his musical education began in these bars, and that at fifteen he played guitar in a local country band called Princess Ramona and the Cherokee Riders, wearing a "yellow hummingbird shirt" and playing lead guitar. However, none of Tim's friends from this period have memories of any Ramona, country royalty or not. "Tim didn't take *those* kind of chances," says Alsbrook, referring to a sojourn into one of the Eastern Avenue bars. Besides, he says, teenage Tim would have been too young to enter any of them. Alsbrook, though, does recall Tim writing one of his first songs about a Bell Gardens pool hall.

One part of Tim may have *wanted* to be inside those beer-stained saloons, for as Gordon recounts, there was by now "this burgeoning dark side" within his friend. It wasn't hard for his friends to see it stemmed from another sector of Bell Gardens they rarely saw: the Buckley residence. The problem didn't appear to be his mother Elaine or baby sister Kathleen. Gordon and Alsbrook recall Elaine as friendly and nonjudgmental, a woman who pushed Tim to study and practice music even as she harbored dreams of her straight-arrow son becoming a dentist. It wasn't hard to see that her spunkiness and mischievous sense of humor spilled over into her teenage boy.

From what Tim's friends could gather, the family dilemma appeared to lie with "Buck," the family nickname for Tim's father, Tim Jr. (To his father, Tim was "Little Buck.") By now, the elder Tim was a burly, blue-eyed Irishman with a head of charcoal-gray hair. For a while, he was a stable father—Elaine would later describe him as "a wonderful man, a wonderful father" in *Musician* magazine—but that period didn't last long. As his grandson would write in his journal over twenty-five years later, "One day, years later, at his job, the workers had gone on strike and scab labor had moved in. My grandfather was the foreman. It was raining, and there was a leak in the roof. Nobody knew how to fix it, or wouldn't, and he climbed up to the roof to do it himself. A real hardass. The only thing was that his leather sole slipped on the wet roof and he slid down on his back, to the ground, landing squarely on the back of his neck. He was never the same."

Whether the fall knocked loose his steel plate or simply gave him another reason to increase his already prodigious alcohol intake, Buck grew increasingly peculiar. One minute he would be garrulous and outgoing, but he could abruptly turn "weird and scary," says Gordon, who recalls seeing the elder Buckley walking around the family's backyard wearing only a bedsheet. Tim wouldn't say much about him and discouraged his friends from spending time at the Buckley home, but it was clear that Buck's treatment of Tim did little for his son's sense of self-worth. One day, Tim and Gordon stopped by Tim's house after they had scored a football victory. "Won the game, huh?" Buck barked. "Well, you're not *faggots* after all!" If that happened in front of *friends*, Gordon wondered, what transpired when no one was around?

Instead, Tim and his gang of wisecracking pals would often kill time in their buddy Larry Boren's house. Inside the walls of the garage, Boren had stashed whiskey and bourbon bottles, and using clear plastic surgical tubing inserted into the walls, he and his friends were able to sip away and get pleasantly buzzed while flipping through dirty magazines. His father's apparent alcohol problem didn't seem to deter Tim from imbibing himself. If anything, it refined his taste in liquor. He could tell good booze from bad, which impressed his pals as much as did his budding musical chops.

By the time he hit puberty, Tim had developed recognizable traits all his peers admired: He could sing in a tenor as clear and untainted as Irish air, he could tell the most authoritative of fibs, and he knew his liquor. He appeared to master each with equal prowess.

TWO

My mom and my dad both had the shit beat out of them by their
fathers, throughout their teens. Escape, escape, escape, escape, escape
sweet Timothy and Mary.

—JEFF BUCKLEY, JOURNAL ENTRY, AUGUST 9, 1995

The flat-topped boys and bob-haired girls dutifully filed into the gym for what was billed as Loara High School's first "hootenanny." In the spring of 1964, the urban folk boom was still in full swing, thanks to the rise of a caustic urban ragamuffin named Bob Dylan and cash-ins like ABC's weekly folk TV concert series *Hootenanny*. Sales of acoustic guitars doubled.

One of the half dozen high schools built to accommodate Anaheim's population boom, Loara had a curriculum designed to encourage participation in the arts. Its sprawling complex was a series of red-brick buildings, basketball courts, and student activity centers surrounding an outdoor "quad" complete with picnic tables. The student population was almost entirely white and, despite coming from families around the country, strangely similar. "We didn't know what 'white middle class' meant, because whatever it was, *everybody* was," remembers Jim Fielder, who was a junior at Loara that year. "It was weird. Everyone came from somewhere else, so in that sense you had a lot of social diversity. But at the same time, everyone was essentially the same."

The students gathered in the gym to hear Denny Brooks and Bob and the Leveemen—"professional singers," noted the yearbook—along with a few student performers invited to complete the bill. One of the latter took the stage in a white collared shirt and a tweedish sports jacket, his curly hair cropped short on the side. To the best of everyone's memory, he sang "Geordie," a traditional British folk ballad he had probably learned from Joan Baez's 1962 *In Concert* album. Even in the realm of British ballads, the centuries-old "Geordie" was a mournful number, narrated by the wife of a man who is about to be hanged for stealing "sixteen of the king's white steeds" (and, it implied, for bedding the king's wife).

Fielder was in that audience, along with his fellow sixteen-year-old Loara junior Larry Beckett. Both kids thought of themselves as underground, intellectual types amidst Loara's straightlaced student population. Like many of his classmates, the narrow-faced Fielder was from another part of the country—Texas—and was already a fledgling musician, proficient at guitar and bass. His first love was surf music, and by the time of the Loara hoot he had already played with local instrumental surf bands. Beckett's parents wanted him to be a physicist—easy enough to imagine, given the blond crew cut and horn-rimmed glasses that lent him a bookish look—but Beckett was already aspiring to be a writer. Alone in his bedroom, he ignored his view of the Matterhorn at Disneyland and wrote poems and science-fiction stories, absorbed the works of Allen Ginsberg and Jack Kerouac, and played LPs of experimental music from jazz (Roland Kirk) to new classical (Edgard Varèse).

Despite the credentials they bestowed upon themselves, neither Beckett nor Fielder knew what to make of this unfamiliar kid crooning "Geordie." "We'd all heard stuff on the radio," recalls Beckett, "but my *God,* to hear this unbelievably strong, pure, clear, passionate man's voice, you just went, 'Whoa—*wait* a minute. This is not an amateur hour anymore.'" The 1964 Loara yearbook was a bit more reserved, if nonetheless positive: "Students were pleased with the singing of Tim and other student choral groups," it noted. As Beckett and Fielder soon learned, the kid's full name was Tim Buckley, and in the early months of 1964, he and his family had just moved to Anaheim after seven years in Bell Gardens.

At the beginning of the following school year, in the fall of 1964, Fielder met Tim—they were in the same senior gym class—and then introduced him to Beckett. Immediately, they sensed in Tim a comrade in artistic arms and began hanging out together, often at Beckett's, listening to his collection of jazz and experimental records. If they went to Disneyland, they would mock its sterility. On those rare occasions when Tim would invite his friends over to the Buckley's quaint tract home on Gilbuck Street (they would say only the quickest of hellos to his parents and then scurry off), Beckett was impressed by the range of Tim's musical interests. Typically, Frank Sinatra's *Frank Sinatra Sings for Only the Lonely* album would be playing, a Miles Davis LP would be leaning against the stereo, and a copy of *Sing Out!* would be open on his desk, to something like Bob Dylan's "Quit Your Low Down Ways." The kid's tastes were sure hard to pin down.

Compared to the wild, wild west California that was Bell Gardens, Anaheim must have struck Tim as resembling a cemetery; indeed, he would later describe Loara and Anaheim as "plastic." It wasn't long before he brought out the true rebel in his new pals, especially Beckett, who was president of the honor society. With Tim and Fielder, Beckett began cutting classes to take trips into Los Angeles—which, although only thirty-five miles north, seemed an exotic, enticing refuge of museums, art galleries, and jazz joints. Tim and Fielder joined the French Club, which was little more than an excuse to take out-of-town field trips. Beneath his outward cockiness, Tim struck his new buddies as shy and lonely. He was also the possessor of a far more adult wardrobe than they; it wasn't unusual to see Tim arrive at school in slacks, a black turtleneck, and a sports jacket. "He was a self-possessed Mr. Grown-up, whereas the rest of us were just kids," recalls Beckett. "He was already out of school in his mind. He just happened to be there."

What Tim's friends eventually learned was that his nascent maturity was not necessarily by choice or good fortune; by 1964, things in the Buckley household had begun to unravel. Beckett remembers Elaine Buckley as "a total sweetheart," but her husband . . . well, *strange* was the word that kept coming to mind. On one visit to Tim's house, Beckett saw the elder Buckley sitting in the family living room talking to his collection of kachinas, the miniature spirit dolls of the Hopi Indian tribe. "When he was sober and lucid he was a nice enough guy," says Fielder. "But it didn't take much to push him over the edge."

Old Buck was apparently in and out of various jobs, and by his senior year at Loara, Tim had to take a job of his own at a local Mexican restaurant in Anaheim to help pay the family bills. At seventeen, his future appeared all too apparent and all too grim: taking care of his family and, after graduation, enrolling in a local community college to learn how to repair his neighbors' teeth.

Sixteen-year-old Mary Guibert began noticing a conspicuous new boy in school that same fall of 1964. Preparing to enter one of her classes from the quad, she found him sitting next to the red metal door and strumming a guitar, his feet sticking out. She thought she heard him mutter something under his breath as she walked by, but she couldn't tell what he was saying. "Not a nice boy," she recalls. "Big black turtleneck shirts all the time. Wore his hair longer than nice boys should." She had never even *seen* a turtleneck before.

She next saw him in her French class, sitting in the back, then again in the quad, singing as a few students gathered around him. As she walked by, she could have sworn he was staring right at her, his eyes burning into her. She turned away and continued on her way to class; boys like that were dangerous, unlike the preppy types she would occasionally date and who would gently hold her hand.

The portrait of the ideal junior at Loara High, Mary played cello in orchestra class and glockenspiel in the marching band, and she never failed to finish her homework. "I was the teacher's pet, always sucking up," she states. She stood out in other ways as well: With her olive Latin skin and dark hair, she would never be mistaken for one of her blond, bee-hived classmates. "Mary was one of the most beautiful girls of that age I've ever seen," says Dan Gordon, Tim's old Bell Gardens pal. "For a young girl, she was very womanly. You had the impression you were dealing with a woman."

The day after seeing Tim sing, Mary was in her French class when a note was passed to her. It was, she recalls, "a love poem, about touching me and what he knew was inside me. What he could see inside my eyes, what fires he knew lurked inside. The color of my breasts. I had never been talked to like that. It was pretty arousing and pretty disturbing." The fact that the young man signed his name—Tim Buckley—didn't make it any less unnerving. Flustered, Mary asked for a bathroom pass and fled to the girls' bathroom, where she read the note again, her heart racing. Mary waited for Tim after class was dismissed, and he walked her to her locker.

Tim, as it turned out, was a senior almost exactly one year older than she, and he was taking the junior-level class as a graduation requirement. It wasn't long before they began dating, the first major such experiences of either of their lives. (Gordon recalls Tim bringing a date to a school dance in junior high, but she hadn't been a serious or long-term girlfriend.) Tim had a car, a yellow Triumph, and he would pick her up for school and drive her home. In between, he would take her to parking lots for make-out sessions. He was, Mary recalls, "like a man of the world."

She began telling Tim about her family. It seems her father was not adapting well to changing times and a changing daughter. On the surface, things were never better, what with George Guibert bringing home nearly $200 a week. (By now, they had learned they had been pronouncing the family name all wrong: It was actually the French-sounding "Ghee-*bear*," they discovered, after meeting a relative in California.) But around him, the world was transforming into a threateningly unruly place. A series of neighborhood burglaries led him to keep a baseball bat in his and Anna's bedroom. (A machete, a remnant of his life in Panama, lay in the garage, waiting to be used in a life-threatening emergency.) To his consternation, his three children were listening to rock and roll and watching male dancers like Rudolf Nureyev on *The Ed Sullivan Show*. ("*Maricón!*" he would yell at the television set, using the derogatory Spanish slang for a gay man.) To listen to the radio, Mary stuck to her portable radio and white earplug. She wasn't allowed to wear makeup and nylons or shave her legs. "In his country, they did things differently," Mary recalls. "And as far as he was concerned, that way was better."

George Guibert's way, apparently, continued to include his own style of heavy-handed parenting. If a problem arose with his children, George didn't seem to know how to talk to them about it. If they challenged his authority or forgot to complete a household chore, he would fly into a rage. He was, Mary says, "a nineteenth-century man born in the twentieth century with twenty-first-century children." Already displaying a feisty, independent streak as Latin as her complexion, Mary would frequently challenge her father, which didn't help matters. Anna, a housewife with no income of her own, had no choice but to stay put and try to break up any looming fights.

Tim listened intently and, over time, would tell Mary stories of his own: his father verbally abusing him, calling him a "faggot," or taking Tim's head and pounding it on the family car. Mary recalls old Buck working as a security guard and seeing him conduct military maneuvers in the Buckley front yard, complete with a gun. The next thing she heard, he had checked into a local Veterans Administration hospital. She knew little else about the family; Tim didn't talk much about his father or his past.

The first time Tim dropped Mary off at her family's house on Archer Street, just a few miles from his home, he didn't venture beyond the foyer in the front entrance, and he didn't say a word to Anna Guibert. He was just this kid in white jeans, a shirt with the tails untucked, and, says Anna, "the curliest, biggest hair you ever saw—and they were *just* starting to let their hair grow." There seemed to be something defiant about him, and Anna had little tolerance for rebellion. As much as her beloved Mary was attracted to this Tim Buckley, Anna was instantly on her guard. He had, she felt, "such dark thoughts."

As Tim's social and dating skills began developing, so did his music. Tim began playing a six-string acoustic guitar more than a banjo, and he was still very much an earnest young folkie, capable of imitating Odetta's version of "John Henry" or Leadbelly's of "Rock Island Line." But his own intuitive curiosity, combined with the influence of Beckett and Fielder, began to widen his artistic horizon. Beckett would introduce Tim to the sitar playing of Ravi Shankar or the *musique concrète* collages of Karlheinz Stockhausen; Tim would play them Sinatra's "One for My Baby." "Hitting high notes and singing in pitch and in time—he didn't have to think about that," Fielder recalls of those early days.

As 1964 turned to 1965, American pop music was undergoing one of its periodic revolutions. The invasion of the Beatles in early 1964 was one indicator, along with the ascendance of Dylan. Folk felt old hat, and new styles—brisk, beat-happy rock and roll, and folk played with amplified instruments—were pop's new vanguard, and most of the musicians making those sounds even wrote their own songs, expressed their own feelings. The term *rock and roll*, with its implications of '50s greasers and Chuck Berry guitar licks, was starting to become the deeper and more art-conscious *rock*. One day, Beckett made a suggestion to Tim: Why not write his own songs, with Beckett, a would-be poet, supplying the lyrics? Tim, as usual, shrugged and said "Sure."

Beckett began feeding him lyrics, and Tim would craft simple melodies for them; songs seemed to tumble effortlessly out of him. Meanwhile, Fielder continued to dream of becoming a professional musician; his bass-guitar playing was improving, and he was even teaching guitar to local kids at a downtown Anaheim musical instrument store. Beckett already had a Ludwig drum set in his bedroom—complete with pearl-gray coloring, inspired by Ringo Starr—so, with dreams of being Southern California's answer to the

Beatles, the friends formed a band. Calling themselves the Bohemians—they still considered themselves part of the underground, after all—they began gigging in and around Anaheim midway through their senior year at Loara. Most of their performances were at high-school functions, where they were forced to play Top 40 covers. If a particular current hit seemed too hokey for them, they would switch to something more amenable, like a Dylan or Beatles cover. Although initially meant to accompany Tim, they grew even more serious as a band when Fielder recruited a guitarist named Brian Hartzler, a younger friend from another area school whom Fielder had met in a surf band.

One rehearsal, Beckett brought in a potential song lyric he called "Grief in My Soul." He showed Tim the words, and Tim thought it would match a melody he had just written. "We thought, 'What in the world is going on here? How is it that you have a melody for the words I've been writing over the weekend?'" Beckett recalls. "We realized there was something going on between him and me that nobody had any words for, some kind of deep chemistry." It would be among the first of the fifty songs they would write before they had even donned their high school graduation caps.

At the same time they had formed the Bohemians, Tim, Fielder, and Beckett also began showing up at local open-mike nights at folk clubs under a different name, and with a different goal. Calling themselves the Harlequin Three, they began to explore what they saw as their truly creative, avant-garde side. Not limited to music, a Harlequin Three performance might include Beckett reciting a poem or one of them reading aloud from Kahlil Gibran's *The Prophet* or James Baldwin's *Another Country*. At a few of these gigs, Tim would grab the bow of Fielder's upright bass, tune his guitar to an open tuning, and scrape, rather than strum, the instrument. To top it off, he would sing along wordlessly, letting his elastic tenor wander. At eighteen, Tim was already refusing to typecast himself as merely a folk-rock singer; the idea of improvisatory music was beckoning.

The performances didn't end once Loara's class of 1965 graduated. Two of Tim's old Bell Gardens buddies, Corby Alsbrook and Dan Gordon, decided friends their age needed a club in town to call their own. Renting out part of an old pool hall near the bars on Eastern Avenue, they covered the billiard tables with plywood and dubbed their joint, appropriately, Two Tables; the stage was a brick-and-board coffeetable from Gordon's apartment. They charged fifty cents admission and only sold Coke and peanuts, but they discovered that, at least for the summer, there were kids their age who wanted to see and hear music of their own generation—mostly folk and country, but with a post–Kingston Trio twist. After a few weeks, they moved to another location in Bell Gardens, keeping the name but not the pool tables.

For Tim, playing Two Tables nearly every weekend that summer—sometimes solo and sometimes with Fielder or Beckett backing him—became an invaluable training ground. He didn't earn any money, since Gordon and Alsbrook couldn't afford to pay any of the performers. But it didn't matter: Tim began to come into his own as a performer. In his increasingly confident tenor, he sang the tunes he and Beckett had begun writing. They were "sort of jejune," admits Beckett, "but there was something about the melodies." Tim began toying with the range of his voice and developing stage moves, like bouncing up and down on his toes. The cleft in his chin had grown deeper and cuter.

Just as important, there were, for the first time in Tim's life, female fans in full sight. "*Every* girl fell in love with him," says Gordon, "and they came back to the club just to see Tim. No one was under any illusions that it was to see any of *us*." That summer, any dreams Elaine Buckley had of her son becoming a dentist were permanently put to rest. Tim was, in his mind and everyone else's, a musician.

If Tim was playing at Two Tables, it was always easy to find Mary—staring adoringly at him, sighing and beaming along with the other female customers. Throughout the 1964–65 school year and into the summer, Tim and Mary's romance burned on, in his car in parking lots and at Disneyland, where Mary (who worked at the Fritos-sponsored Mexican restaurant Casa de Fritos) would sneak Tim in for free.

"Until she met Tim, she probably didn't realize she had so much stuff bubbling under the surface in herself," observes Fielder, "and Tim gave her a real big outlet—*real* quick." For both Tim and Mary, the romance was their only refuge from hot-tempered fathers. How, they must have wondered to themselves, did two children who had grown up in the same eastern state, each the offspring of a turbulent father, manage to find each other on the other side of the country?

Their harbor wasn't always safe, however. If she arrived home fifteen minutes late, Mary would find her father ready to pounce, Anna attempting to get between them. As Mary and George argued in her bedroom one night,

Tim watched, standing on the shrub outside her window. On occasion, he would sneak into her window at dawn, cuddle in her bed, and then head off to the Mexican restaurant. "They were very much in love and very devoted to each other," says Gordon. "They were these *Romeo and Juliet* characters. The fact that her parents were *so* against it lent it this wonderful air of danger and romance."

As Mary recalls, "We spent one night in the parking lot of the hardware store on Lincoln, just holding each other and crying and saying, 'What are we gonna do?' I was tired of the beatings and didn't want to go home." Mary says she and Tim were already talking about marriage and that both sets of parents refused to consider it. That night, they decided to run away—or, at least, have everyone think they did. They told their families they had gone to San Diego. Instead, they headed for Gordon's apartment in nearby Bell Gardens, where they slept together for the first time and, Mary says, had "the closest thing we had that might have resembled sex." The Guiberts, especially George, were beside themselves.

Then, in August 1965, something Tim and Mary hadn't planned happened: Mary missed her period. Anna found out, and the two of them visited the family doctor, who diagnosed the unthinkable: Mary was pregnant. Suddenly, the arrangement Mary says she and Tim had made—to wed in a year, after she had turned eighteen and was out of high school—crumbled like a stilt home in a California earthquake. Anna demanded a meeting with Tim, who drove over to her house with his mother. It was the first time the two parents had met, and Elaine sat quietly by her son's side.

"The fact that she thinks she's pregnant is not a good enough reason for you to marry her," Anna told Tim. "I need to know more."

"I love her," Tim replied. "That's why I want to marry her."

Satisfied with Tim's answer, Anna talked her husband out of throwing Mary out of the house—which was his first reaction—and began planning a small wedding for the teenagers. Borrowing money from friends, the Guiberts bought Mary a used wedding dress. "I didn't want them to get married," Anna says, "but what are you going to do?" Many of the couple's acquaintances felt the same way.

Thanks to an autumn heat wave that set 100-degree-plus records in Los Angeles the day before, October 23, 1965, was an unusually warm fall day in Anaheim. But inside the dark chapel of St. Michael's Episcopal, the Guibert family church in Anaheim, the atmosphere was noticeably cool. Twenty friends and family members took their seats in the cozy chapel's twelve rows of dark wood pews and put on a brave face. As much as everybody tried to hide their anxiety, though, that collective face cracked throughout the ceremony. Just before walking to the altar, Tim, in a dark suit and carnation, turned to Beckett, his best man, and said, "I don't want to go through with it." Despite whatever he had told Anna Guibert, Tim now felt "roped in," Beckett recalls. (Adds Fielder, "He definitely felt events were carrying *him*.") Tim never glanced at his future mother-in-law, while Mary, in shoulder-length hair and bangs, put on an upbeat front. George Guibert, Mary's father, was so angry he didn't attend. Tim's father did, but on the way out he shook the priest's hand, leaned over, and said, "I give it six months." Outside, the new couple posed for a photo, and the uneasy, barely concealed frown on Tim's face spoke volumes of the unforeseen situation in which he suddenly found himself.

Adding to the less than congenial family reaction to the marriage, the reception was held in the Beckett family home, since George Guibert wouldn't allow a party to honor his deflowered daughter. Later, he told his wife that he drove by the Beckett home during the reception and briefly considered setting it afire out of anger. There was a toast, and cake was eaten—what was left of it, anyway, since the Beckett family dog had nibbled on the baked goods during the ceremony.

Afterward, Tim and Mary sped away and spent their first night as Mr. and Mrs. Buckley at a hotel in Laguna Beach. For extra romantic effect, they dropped a few coins into the vibrating bed. When it wouldn't stop vibrating, they gave up and spent their wedding night sleeping on the hotel room floor.

They wanted a home of their own, with a calm family life that would be the antithesis of their upbringings, so Tim and Mary rented a small apartment in Anaheim, less than a mile from the Guibert home. There, they attempted to play the role of bright-eyed newlyweds. Tim enrolled in Fullerton Junior College, but only stayed for a week; he later said he dropped out because he wasn't allowed to take advanced classes in music. He continued his job at the Mexican restaurant, washing dishes and mashing guacamole in the kitchen, while Mary, her stomach growing larger, returned to Loara and found herself an outcast, suddenly a bad girl who had done the deed with a member of the opposite sex, still a touchy subject in 1965. The girl whose locker was next to hers, as well as her best friend, stopped talking to her. Eventually Mary dropped out of school—

married students weren't allowed, anyway—and took typing classes at night school.

Tim's future, his only discernible exit from this scenario, was music. When his fellow Bohemians weren't in class themselves at one of the local colleges, the band slogged on around Orange County, struggling to make sock-hoppers dance to Tim and Beckett's originals at school dances and parties. "We played things no one could dance to, so we didn't get any gigs," Tim later said. In the fall, a new club called the Paradox opened in nearby Tustin, southeast of Anaheim. One of the owners was a salesman for a meat company, but that didn't stop top-drawer folk and roots acts like Sonny Terry and Brownie McGhee, Ramblin' Jack Elliott, and Josh White from gigging there on weekends. Local talent—including a shy Orange County singer-songwriter named Jackson Browne, a local rock-jug group called the Nitty Gritty Dirt Band, and another rising singer, Jennifer Warnes—signed up for the Thursday night open-mike nights. The Bohemians performed there and, when adventurous, drove up to Los Angeles to play similar open-mike nights at the Troubadour, one of the city's leading folk clubs.

That September, Tim and Beckett were further inspired when they saw one of their heroes, Bob Dylan, premiering his new electric band at the Hollywood Bowl. Dylan would sing a verse of "Desolation Row," one of the new songs he was previewing from his upcoming *Highway 61 Revisited* album, and Tim and Beckett would look at each other, laugh, and shake their heads in admiration. "This was fine rock and roll *and* powerful poetry," Beckett says, "and it set an ideal for us that we never really let go or forgot."

If they wanted to be rock stars, they would need a tape of their songs. One afternoon in November, at Fielder's urging, the Bohemians entered a stereo and appliance store near Anaheim that offered local talent the chance to put their music on tape for $6 an hour. They set up their gear in the middle of the showroom floor and, with a store employee counting off the number of songs between takes, plowed efficiently through their repertoire, twelve songs in all. They opened with a shaggy folk-blues shuffle, "Put You Down," twisted and shouted through the Beatlesque hullabaloo chorus of "Let Me Love You" and the garage-band shimmy of "Don't Look Back," jangled through the Byrdsian flair of "You Today," and displayed their courtly folk-pop sensibility in "She Is" and "Here I

Am." The differences between Tim's and Beckett's individual lyrics were more apparent: Beckett aimed for the flowery gallantry of Renaissance poetry ("She is a smile that keeps me warm . . . she is a bridge upon which I want to walk"), while Tim's more direct thoughts were steeped in accusation, melancholy, and pain. "Don't mind you trying to make me tame/But don't blow out the flame," he sings, possibly to his new wife, in "I've Played That Game Before."

The music was a little crude and ragged, the songs less than original, and, as Beckett himself admits, his drumming was less than crisp. The Bohemians sounded like exactly what they were: a scruffy little folk-rock bar band, albeit one with a secret musical weapon—a powerful, emotive singer who could slide from a falsetto to a gritty grunt, who could ooze vulnerability and tenderness one moment, petulance the next.

The Bohemians had their demo tape, but they hadn't a clue as to how to get it to the right industry people. They were all still a bunch of Orange County kids, and Los Angeles never seemed so far away.

Tim had other distractions by this time. Only a few months into his marriage, with memories of his female fans at Two Tables still dancing in his head, he already appeared to be chafing at the idea of marriage. "In the beginning, he was very taken with Mary," recalls Fielder. "He'd say how much he loved her when they first got together. And then the day-to-day realities of carrying on a relationship beyond that first passionate encounter came to roost real suddenly. It was not long before he started to think of being married as a burden." A little over a year later, Tim described Mary to writer and New York clubowner Izzy Young as "a concert pianist" and said that they "didn't communicate on musical terms. She used the classical thing to put down my thing." (Mary denies these allegations.)

One night, on a long drive home from Los Angeles, he and Mary began arguing as Beckett, now a first-year UCLA student, sat in back. "She's saying, 'What do you *want*, Tim?'" Beckett recalls. "And he said, 'Well, I need somebody to clean up, straighten up, and make food,' at which point she said, 'You don't need a wife—you need a *maid*.' Which I thought was a point well taken. He *did* need a maid and he *didn't* need a wife."

On New Year's Eve, Tim and Mary lay down on their bed for a nap. A few hours later, Mary awoke to find the bedsheets covered in blood. She was rushed to the hospital, and after a few days the bleeding stopped and she returned home. Three days after that, she felt what she thought was her water breaking: The baby was on its way. Tim and Mary returned to the hospital, but there was no baby—or, rather, no fetus.

Mary was most likely not pregnant, after all; instead, she may have been a victim of *pseudocyesis*, commonly known as hysterical or imaginary pregnancy. A condition that dated back to 300 B.C., it was, to say the least, rare (between 1959 and 1979, only forty-two cases were reported, according to the *Journal of Family Practice*), and it was generally attributed to women suffering from either depression, "wish-fulfillment theory," or a combination of both desiring and fearing pregnancy that creates, the *Journal* wrote, "an internal conflict and causes endocrine changes." Given her perceived family situation and her need to flee with the help of Tim, any of those symptoms could have applied to seventeen-year-old Mary. "She had a big stomach and the whole thing," Anna recalls. "It was the most amazing thing I've ever experienced."

The fact that there would not be a child at their young ages may have had its advantages, but it wasn't evident in the Buckley household. Tim and Mary's apartment became, in the words of Dan Gordon, "a horrible, depressing place to visit." The scent of Tim's waning lust and of the hysterical pregnancy hung somberly in the air. Just before the holidays, the newlyweds had bought a Christmas tree for their little apartment. It wasn't a particularly plush plant from the start, but it remained standing through February. By then, it was, according to Gordon, "this moldy, Godawful-looking thing." To their friends, the slowly dying tree withering away in the middle of their living room was all too emblematic of their life inexperience—and, more tellingly, of where their marriage seemed to be headed, only six months after it had begun. It was just as old Buck had predicted.

THREE

Mary Guibert and Tim Buckley got married in '66 . . . I was expected.
He went to N.Y. for some gigs some time later and decided not to be a
husband anymore. They were both eighteen or so, what the hey . . .

—JEFF BUCKLEY, UNSENT LETTER, 1990

For Tim and his fellow Bohemians, the first weekend of February 1966
was like most others of the preceding months. Every Saturday, desperate
to flee Orange County and its decidedly orthodox environs, the recent
high-school graduates would pile into a car—usually Jim Fielder's '57
Chevy—and take the hour or so drive into Los Angeles. Once there, they
did what everyone else appeared to be doing: They made an automotive
beeline for Hollywood, and then straight for the Sunset Strip.

At that moment, the future of rock and roll in Southern California—
and, it seemed, everywhere else—was sprinkled up and down a winding
stretch of West Hollywood that ran sixteen blocks and nearly two miles.
Named after the boulevard on which it was situated, the Sunset Strip had
had an illustrious history, beginning as a cow trail at the beginning of the
century and then, starting in the '30s, as a nightclub-strewn party headquarters for Hollywood swingers, celebrities, and West Coast goodfellas.
But when a rock and roll dance club called the Whisky-A-Go-Go (complete with go-go dancers shimmying in cages) opened in 1964, a new gen-

eration began elbowing its way onto the Strip. On any evening, the Strip was an endless conga line of teens and music cognoscenti in the official uniforms of the West Coast counterculture—turtlenecks, shag haircuts, black ankle boots—roaming past nightclubs, neon signs, and alluring marquees.

If they couldn't squeeze into the Tiger's Tail to see the happy-face folk-rock of the Turtles, there was always another band that was taking the melodic and harmonic trademarks of the early '60s folk boom and literally electrifying them: the Buffalo Springfield at Gazzarri's, the Grass Roots at the Whisky, or the Byrds at Ciro's. Los Angeles had never looked or sounded that way before.

The amplified-hootenanny sound of those bands wasn't limited to the Strip. Thanks to hits like the Byrds' "Mr. Tambourine Man" and Sonny and Cher's "I Got You Babe," it had broken nationally, transforming Los Angeles into a city of pop music hope, hype, and hits. "Music was just *exploding* in Los Angeles," recalls Fielder. "Anyone who could keep time and had something to say was getting a record contract. The record companies didn't understand the music, but they knew a whole new era of popular music was starting to happen, and suddenly there was an industry hungry for product." For a brief moment, Los Angeles, and the Strip especially, became nothing less than America's Liverpool.

The Bohemians knew the Strip well. Tim, Beckett, and Fielder had ditched their high-school prom in Anaheim to see pop-jazz singer Nancy Wilson at the Cocoanut Grove, and they had scored an actual audition at one Strip club, It's Boss, shortly before Christmas 1965. To their dismay, the owner asked them to play covers: the same old Orange County grind, but in a more happening locale. The band, Tim in particular, went along with the request but made no bones about their lack of interest in singing other people's material. As Tim recalled to Izzy Young a year later, "I never liked playing every night. You lose the feeling of what you're doing. Besides, they wanted us to do Top 40 stuff. We do our own thing." Needless to say, the Bohemians didn't land the gig; as Beckett recalls, "They hated us."

The rejection didn't keep Tim away from the Strip; if anything, it only accelerated his all-consuming hunger to break into the music business. It was certainly on his mind as he, Beckett, and Fielder cruised up and down the Strip on this February 5, 1966, evening, gawking at the nightlife and the mobs of sharply dressed scene makers. With their short hair and Beckett's oversized denim coat, the Orange County kids didn't look or feel especially cool—"we looked really stupid and like a bunch of rednecks," Beckett recalls—but at least Tim's hair was just starting to mushroom into a Bob Dylan–style afro. In the months since his wedding, Tim's mop had grown bushier every day, his eyebrows so thick he would ask Mary to untangle them after he stepped out of the shower.

Tonight, they found themselves walking past the Trip, planted on a hilly part of the Strip at 8572 Sunset. ("Food & dancing 'til 2 A.M.," boasted its newspaper ads.) Once a jazz club called the Crescendo, the Trip featured a huge window behind its stage, which, when a curtain was opened, afforded a spectacular view of Los Angeles Its regular lineup of bands included the Byrds, the Lovin' Spoonful, and Donovan (who wrote a song, "The Trip," about the club). The Trip also booked a slew of Motown acts, from the Four Tops to Martha and the Vandellas, attracting African-American crowds to the Strip. For an extra layer of trippiness, the "The" in the club's name was printed upside down on the marquee.

This evening, that marquee announced the evening's featured act, the Mothers. Fielder knew the name: It was the band featuring Jimmy Carl Black, a prematurely craggy Native American who gave drum lessons at the same Anaheim music store at which Fielder taught guitar to local kids. The two young men would cross paths in the store, and after a few months, Black began telling Fielder, "Jim, you gotta come hear this band I'm playing with now in LA—it's really off-the-wall stuff." He said they were led by "this weird guy named Frank Zappa." Though they had yet to release any LPs, the Mothers (their original name, before their label, MGM, requested they tag on "of Invention" so as not to offend potential record buyers) had already garnered a reputation as one of the Strip's strangest and most innovative packs of avant-rockers, with Zappa their outlandish maestro.

Tim and the band didn't want to spend what little money they had to see the Mothers, so Fielder had the doorman hunt down Black, who came out shortly thereafter and chatted up the band. They complained to Black about their dilemma—they were a working band with their own material, but they couldn't find anyone to hear them. Friendly and sympathetic, Black said he'd introduce them to the Mothers' manager. Perhaps he could help them.

One of Herb Cohen's clients would later say that Cohen—or simply "Herbie," as he was often known—should have managed wrestlers or boxers, not rock stars. In fact, Cohen resembled an aging boxer himself. Short and stout, with a sliver of facial hair framing his jaw and a hardened, perpetually frowning mug, the thirty-four-year-old could have passed for a bearded fire hydrant.

As unlikely as it seemed, given his demeanor, Cohen was also a catalyst in the Los Angeles music scene, with an enigmatic and wide-ranging personal history that surpassed even the standard rock and roll mythology. Born to a Russian father and Argentinean mother who moved to the Bronx in 1923, Cohen joined the merchant marines at seventeen and later became part of the burgeoning LA music scene as both a concert booker (for the then-blacklisted Weavers, among others) and club manager (of the Purple Onion, which he transformed from a nightclub to a folk venue around 1956). About two years later, he borrowed money from Theodore Bikel, one of the Purple Onion's main attractions, and opened his own Hollywood joint, the Unicorn. Later came Cosmo Alley, where Cohen presented everyone from Lenny Bruce to fledgling calypso singer Maya Angelou.

At that club and the Purple Onion, it wasn't uncommon for Cohen to keep a loaded .45 under the bar in case any fights broke out. If that didn't work, he would resort to whatever was available to stop a brawl. Associates and musicians recall seeing him unflinchingly smash sugar jars or coffee mugs into the faces of anyone who dared misbehave in one of his joints.

As the '60s began, restlessness and police hassles over cabaret laws led Cohen to begin another, entirely different career. Although Cohen himself won't confirm or deny it ("anything's possible," he comments), it's said he ventured into gun-running and mercenary soldiering in—depending on the source of the story—North Africa, Cuba, the Congo, or all three regions. "He was mainly seeing the world, but he was a *wild* guy," says Jerry Yester, who, as half of the Yester Brothers, worked with Cohen before the trip. In 1963, fresh from whatever adventures he had experienced outside of California, Cohen returned to Los Angeles and, with his brother and partner Martin (nicknamed "Mutt"), a lawyer, he ran and then sold the Purple Onion. Next came artist management, where his first client was Judy Henske, an imposing, big-voiced Wisconsin singer who had played at Cosmo Alley. Henske was initially skeptical about the stories of Cohen's travels. "I thought, 'This is just some more of that Hollywood stardust stuff,'" she says. Then, while reading Peter Matthiessen's '60s Africa-travelogue book *The Tree Where Man Was Born,* Henske came across a description of "a bearded American veteran of the Israeli wars with a hidden sheath knife, beret, dark glasses, and gold earring." Recalls Henske, "I thought, 'Hmmm . . . It *could* be Herbie.'"

Henske and Cohen's other clients, including the Modern Folk Quartet (featuring Jerry Yester), noticed Cohen had learned a few new lessons in self-defense during his years out of town. If approached by a potential hassler, Cohen would sometimes take a car key, grip it so the key poked out between two knuckles, and—presto—create a makeshift knife. He would then hold it right up to the combatant's face, at which point the offending party would generally back off. "A lot of people made the big mistake of thinking Herbie was this soft, pudgy guy, and they'd get the shit beat out of them," recalls Yester. "Herbie had the killer instinct." Cohen's brusque, gruff voice only accentuated his image.

The Bohemians were in the dark about Cohen and his background when Black introduced Tim and Fielder to him at the Trip. "I want to hear you guys," said Cohen, staring at Tim. "Herb was immediately intrigued with Tim," Fielder recalls. "Didn't know the first thing about him, hadn't heard him sing or heard any of the songs. But that's the way things were—potential attracted interest." An afternoon audition was set up for the following weekend at another local club, the Action, and the band played a short set of originals, Tim in typically strong voice. After the audition, Fielder and Tim went over to Cohen's house in Hollywood and played him their appliance-store demo tape. As they were listening, Cohen picked up the phone and called his brother Mutt. "There's something here," he told him. Before he knew it, Tim had signed a publishing contract with Cohen's company, Third Story Music. "I said, 'Who writes the songs?'" Cohen recalls. "I liked the songs. So I said, 'Fine, come to my office tomorrow,' and I signed them up." No one thought much about implications or contracts; if this LA wheeler-dealer liked them, that was good enough for Tim. "Herbie always had this icy calm about him, this sort of 'make my day, sucker' attitude," Fielder remembers. "He was young but *hard*. He was a made guy, as far as we were concerned."

Many of Tim's friends wondered if had chosen the right guardian for his career, but to fellow clients like Henske, Cohen's appeal was obvious. "Nobody wanted to work at business," she says. "It was, 'We're bohemian artists and we don't care.' The artist wasn't *supposed* to be good at business. You were supposed to be a piece of jelly, and that's what most of us were. Herbie was so strong, and he had this reputation—which he *told* everybody—of being a mercenary. We thought, 'Wow, no one can hurt us!' We were all very fearful people, and Herbie was not afraid of anything. Also, we weren't ready to be out in the world alone, so Herbie stepped in and said, 'I'll protect you. You be the kids, and I'll be the father.' We were like birds that needed a strong tree to light on, and that tree was Herbie."

"Tim was very unsophisticated," recalls Dan Gordon. "This was not someone who'd been out on the road paying his dues for three or four years. He hadn't a clue about anything. So pretty much whatever Herb said was it." What Cohen said, almost immediately, was that the Bohemians were history. "Tim had the greatest voice in the world," Cohen says, "but Larry wasn't really a drummer." In Cohen's eyes, the clear star, the ticket to the big time, was Tim. No one needed another rock band. What *was* needed, especially on the LA scene, was a new Dylan, and this kid with the mop of curly hair, the cleft in his chin, and the silken, potent voice could be it.

Sheepishly, Tim told Beckett, Hartzler, and Fielder the news. They took it fairly well—Beckett was by now dreaming of being a writer, not a percussionist—and the sting was eased somewhat when Tim promised to continue writing songs with Beckett and use Fielder and Hartzler on his albums. The band accepted Cohen's, and Tim's, dictum. They sensed, as Cohen did, that Tim was on the road to his particular destiny.

His foot jammed firmly in the door of the LA music community (and with Cohen setting up club showcases for his new client), Tim began commuting into Los Angeles more regularly, eventually quitting his job at the Mexican restaurant. At first, Mary stayed behind in Anaheim, but then Cohen suggested a plan: Why not have Tim live with Fielder in Fielder's apartment on Hobart, while Mary would reside with the Cohen family and help look after their daughter? "Herb said, 'You can't drag your wife around like that—she needs a place to live,'" Mary recalls. Again, Tim did what Cohen instructed him to do, and he and Mary spent days together and, at night, returned to their separate residences.

Tim appeared more than willing to accept what was by all accounts a curious arrangement, even by the loose-knit standards of the growing counterculture. "It was pretty tacitly understood," says Fielder, "that the reason Timmy and I were rooming together was so he could get out of that whole living situation with Mary, if not the marriage itself." Others, Mary included, felt the setup was Cohen's way of breaking up the marriage for the good of Tim's career, which Cohen denies. "Did I talk to them about it?" he asks. "Yes. But we're not talking about normal people. If they were normal, they couldn't be able to do what they do, which is get on a stage and say, 'Look at me.' Is that normal?"

Conventional or not, Tim continued to ply his craft at clubs in Los Angeles. Almost every Monday, he'd wander over to the Troubadour, the well-regarded folk club on Santa Monica Boulevard, at the end of the Strip. Unlike its chief rival, the Ash Grove, the Troubadour attracted folk and blues acts who were a bit more unorthodox and cutting-edge, from Muddy Waters to the Blues Project. Owner Doug Weston would later describe Tim's early style in the *East Village Eye* as "a little mealy-mouthed," adding, "His diction wasn't what it should have been initially." But Tim persisted. Every Monday night was "hoot night"—anyone could take a number and, when called, take the stage for a few songs.

One evening at the wood-paneled club, Tim walked offstage and past a small, intense girl with straight, dark hair sitting at a table in the second row. She had seen him there a few other times and had been increasingly impressed with his talent. "You're really good," she told him, frankly and directly. Tim stopped and thanked her. He seemed to lap up the attention, drinking up every word she said. He was too skinny for her taste, but she was nonetheless intrigued; instantly, she wanted to comfort him.

Jane Goldstein had been a regular at LA clubs since she was a high-schooler in Santa Monica. Five months younger than Tim, she had been raised in Yorktown Heights, sixty miles north of Manhattan, and with her family had already had moved back and forth between New York and California several times. She had big eyes, a strong gaze, and a lithe, dancer's figure, and she loved a good party. When she wasn't attending Santa Monica City College, Jane frequented the clubs, seeing the Byrds and befriending the Doors; Jim Morrison once crashed at her pad on Ocean Park. Perhaps because her mother was a part-time poet, Jane loved music and hanging out with musicians, and Tim became her latest discovery. "I don't know why he picked up on me so fast," she recalls. "I think he was just looking for someone. He pretty much approached me, and I pretty much responded."

The two began spending more and more time together, going for walks on the beach or to Tim's club performances around town. Jane visited Tim's apartment and was appalled at how cruddy and empty it was; furniture was nonexistent. One day she brought over doughnuts, and Tim cracked, "Doughnuts? Bring me something *real* to eat." Only then did Jane realize that both the apartment *and* the refrigerator were empty. ("Everyone told me how great I was, but it didn't mean anything because I wasn't eating," Tim told Izzy Young later.) For the time being, Tim didn't mention his wife or marriage. "When I met him, he was just very sad inside," she recalls. "Partially he was born like that. But he was sad because of his father. That had a huge impact. He really missed having a father."

Across town, in Herb Cohen's apartment, Mary began to sense Tim pulling away and growing distant. Sometimes, when Cohen and his family would take one of their frequent trips to Europe, Tim would stay with Mary in the house, and they would act like a family. "We'd play house for two weeks," Mary recalls. "He wasn't screwing around on me. He was having sex with me as *well* as other people." Other times, he would vanish for days on end, and no one would tell Mary where he was.

While his personal life began to grow increasingly complicated, Tim's professional life took another leap forward. In early spring, he told Jane he needed to go to New York and asked if she would accompany him. It seemed there was a record company interested in his music.

The electric rock revolution that had taken hold of Los Angeles was being felt around the country, and no one felt it more than Jac Holzman. Tall, thin, and suavely handsome—Joe DiMaggio after a few months on the road with a rock band—Holzman had been obsessed with folk and classical musics since his college days in the late '40s. During the same period, he decided to start a record company, and, using all $300 of his bar mitzvah money, Holzman launched Elektra Records in the fall of 1950 with a recording of a lieder recital featuring soprano Georgianna Bannister. Elektra's second release, in 1952, was a collection of mountain folk laments by Kentucky-born balladeer and dulcimer player Jean Ritchie, whose doleful version of "O Love Is Teasin'" defined the unvarnished purity of Elektra's folk artists.

From then on, Elektra became a haven for everything from sound-effects collections to albums of traditional British, American, and Mexican folk songs. By 1962, when Holzman signed a troubadour of pure voice and even purer looks named Judy Collins, the New York–based Elektra had become an outpost for the new breed of literate, urban folk balladeers. In quick succession, Tom Paxton, Phil Ochs, and David Blue (né Cohen)—the vanguard of the new urban folk and protest-song scene—had joined Collins in the independent label's stable.

The amplification of pop music hit many in folk circles hard. In New York, Mike Porco, owner of Gerde's Folk City, the club that helped launch Dylan, Simon and Garfunkel, and many others, wouldn't allow electric instruments in his venue. The times they were in the midst of a-changing, but Holzman, for one, was not about to let them change without his participation. Although committed to vernacular and classical artists, Holzman was a businessman (he was one of the first executives to argue for the elimination of the mono LP in favor of stereo, which cost record buyers a dollar more), and he knew the future lay in rock. It didn't take an industry prognosticator to see that million-selling albums and singles by Dylan, the Rolling Stones, and, of course, the Beatles had pushed record sales to an all-time high of $789 million in 1965, up 14 percent from the year before. Besides, folk was beginning to run its course. "The existing folk repertoire was just worn out," Holzman recalls. "There wasn't anything *left*. You had to turn to people who wrote their own material."

Elektra got its feet wet in this arena in 1965, when Holzman signed the Paul Butterfield Blues Band. But in March 1966, the thirty-four-year-old label head made his crossover move official with the creation of a new line of pop-oriented Elektra releases, the Series 4000, which would sell for $1 less than the label's non-rock releases. The first Series 4000 releases would be an album and single by the underground LA band Love, an album by singer-songwriter David Blue, and a compilation—featuring, among others, new but revered British guitarist Eric Clapton—called *What's Shakin'*. If the lower list price of the Series 4000 releases wasn't enough to attract hip teenyboppers, then the series' more sophisticated album covers would do the trick instead.

It was while Holzman was in the midst of his company's expansion that a black lacquer demonstration disc—a ten-inch disc smaller than a standard LP—arrived on the desk of his office at 51 West 51st Street in midtown Manhattan. The sender was Herb Cohen, a friend of Holzman's who had brought Henske and Theodore Bikel to Elektra. Holzman had never heard the name of the person listed on the acetate, Tim Buckley, but he tended to trust Cohen's taste. ("Herbie didn't sign fifteen acts and throw them against the wall," says Steve Harris, Elektra's marketing and promotion man. "He was very discriminating, which was good to know.") At the time, Elektra's entire staff numbered less than a dozen people, so rather than hand it off to a lower-level executive, Holzman played the disc himself.

The lacquer contained six songs from a nearly two-hour session Tim had done in Los Angeles just after signing with his new manager, with only Fielder's bass accompanying Tim's guitar. "I can generally tell in five minutes of listening whether it was something I'd be interested in or not, and I was just grabbed immediately," Holzman recalls of that first listen to Tim's demo. "I don't want to say I was knocked out, but I was taken by the direct-ness and the purity of what I thought he was doing. It seemed effortless." Twice a day for a week, Holzman played Tim's acetate. "When things got troubled," he says, "I found listening to Tim very clarifying. It was like a smog chaser." The fact that Tim resembled a cuter version of Dylan didn't hurt, either; Elektra could use one of those as much as Cohen could.

Although Tim would later tell interviewers he was pursued by other record companies, including Columbia and Capitol, these boasts appear to be more of Tim's omnipresent tall tales, his own developing mythology. Cohen says he went to Elektra alone, since "Tim wasn't folk per se, but it wasn't rock and roll. I knew Jac would be understanding of that." Holz-man was more than understanding. Within a week, he had made a deci-sion to sign Tim to a standard six-album contract—a guarantee to release one album, with options to put out five more. The contract, typical of business dealings at the time in the record industry, ran only a few pages, with Tim receiving a 5 or 6 percent royalty per album. (The deal wouldn't be announced in print for several more months. In the October 8, 1966, issue of *Billboard*, a small "Signings" box on page twelve read, "The Doors and Tim Buckley, both to Elektra.")

Several days after the deal was done, the label's Steve Harris flew to Los Angeles and found himself, as he often did, conducting "market research" with a group of girls between ages eighteen and twenty-two. At that point, Tim's signing was known only to those within the company. "These girls said, 'We don't care about Jim Morrison anymore,'" Harris recalls. "I said, 'Somebody's taken his *place?*' And they said, 'Tim Buckley. He's beautiful, he's wonderful, he's fabulous.' And I said, 'Oh my God, he's on Elektra.'" Apparently it wasn't just the company and Herb Cohen who felt a star was about to be born.

As winter turned to spring in 1966, Jane Goldstein didn't have any qualms about traveling across the country with a nineteen-year-old boy she'd only just met. By coincidence, her father wanted her to drive the family's Volks-wagen bug to New York, since they were in the process of one of their numerous cross-country moves. Besides, Jane felt insecure, and Tim's attention flattered her. She felt Tim was lonely and vulnerable himself, and being "the little rescuer I was," she agreed. She temporarily dropped out of college and threw what few belongings they had in her car and began their drive to New York City. Tim told Mary he had to go east to meet with his new record company and perform; he made no mention of a traveling companion.

By the time they left town, Tim and Jane hadn't yet slept together, and Jane was nervous; she knew the topic was bound to crop up. Soon it did, just as they arrived in Amarillo, Texas. At a motel, the clerk asked, "One bed or two?" "We were just stupid teenagers, and said, 'Eh, it doesn't matter,' " she recalls. Although their room had two mattresses, they ended up in the same one. Tim asked Jane to be careful with his feet; he claimed they had been trampled in high school football and were sensitive as a result.

Driving into Greenwich Village, Tim and Jane temporarily settled into an apartment on Thompson Street in the café-strewn heart of Greenwich Village. All around them was music, a more compact Sunset Strip. At clubs like Folk City, the Village Gate, the Village Vanguard, and the Gaslight that summer, Tim could have caught jazz wildcats John Coltrane and Thelonious Monk, rising singer-songwriters Eric Andersen and Tom Rush, spunky rock bands like the Blues Project and the Youngbloods, bluesmen Mississippi John Hurt and Muddy Waters, even Latin folkie José Feliciano and R&B crooner Lou Rawls. Through a connection with the owner, Cohen landed Tim a gig at the Night Owl, a one-hundred-seat joint on West Third and MacDougal that was next to a pizza parlor. Once in a while, lucky customers would catch a glimpse of Dylan huddling with his songwriter pal David Blue in a corner, their identical bushy heads silhouetted against the wall. In New York, says Cohen, "It was *the* place to play."

As an out-of-towner with no records in the stores and little in the way of a reputation, Tim didn't attract large crowds, but the few who attended knew there was something special about the sensitive-looking kid with the sports jackets who belted out tender, mournful originals. "His singing was different, with that Irish tenor," recalls waitress Marlene Yester (née Waters). "You knew he was real good and interesting. I thought, 'He belongs in here, like a lot of the other great people.' " Tim himself took in performances by local legends like Tim Hardin and Fred Neil (another client of Herb Cohen's), who blended folk, jazz, blues, and rock into dark, compelling hybrids that felt both deeply personal and universal. As Tim quickly noticed, they made music (and took drugs) on their own terms.

After settling into a new apartment, a basement-level pad on the Lower East Side, Tim and Jane set up a temporary home. Jane found a job at a supermarket—ever independent-minded, she wanted her own cash—

while Tim began performing weekly at the Night Owl, Jane seated in the front row each night. Holzman traveled downtown to see his new signing, whose shows only confirmed Holzman's feeling he had made a good decision, and plans were laid to record Tim's first album toward summer's end in Los Angeles. Strolling from the Bowery to the narrow, boisterous streets of the Village in the heat of a New York summer, Tim absorbed the city mania exploding around him. Here at last was the bohemia he had read and heard about, flowering before his eyes. "The music—*our* music, the music of the kids—was pouring out of the windows of restaurants and apartments," recalls Beckett, who joined his friend in New York. "It was heard in the street while you were walking down the street. You didn't even have to *go* to a concert. You were *in* the concert."

On one of their jaunts, Tim and Beckett also provoked Jane's ire when all three drove upstate to see her family. Upon arriving, Tim and Beckett immediately retreated to a bedroom, where they stayed the entire time repeatedly playing Bob Dylan's new double album *Blonde on Blonde*. "They were both assholes in that respect," Jane recalls. "They had no regard for somebody's parents."

New York also brought a new mentor into Tim's life. One day at the Night Owl, he was introduced to a handsome and unremittingly serious-minded singer and guitarist with short sandy-blond hair named Edward Lee Underwood—Lee, to his friends. A former high school English teacher who taught in a private school in Hightstown, New Jersey, Underwood was eight years Tim's senior but still struggling to find his musical way. The previous year, Underwood had left his wife and began traveling the club circuit playing folk-blues fingerpicking guitar with his girlfriend and musical partner Jennifer Stace. The two wound up in San Francisco, by which time Underwood was a solo act but still romantically linked with Stace, but since he had entertained fantasies of recording with Elektra himself, Underwood eventually headed back to New York, where he found himself at the Night Owl and was introduced to Tim by a mutual friend. It wasn't long before Underwood was sitting in with Tim at the club. According to Stace, Underwood "wrote me and said he met this kid who had a voice like an angel and couldn't play guitar very well and that he needed a lead guitarist and had a recording contract with Elektra, and his name was Tim Buckley."

Underwood was initially hesitant ("Lee wasn't at all pleased to be a backup player, but it was a recording contract with Elektra," says Stace), but he and Tim struck up an immediate friendship. Tim, young and eager to absorb any input, was impressed with Underwood's grasp of literature and jazz; to Underwood, Tim was a clean slate. "I liked him," Underwood says, "thought his voice was fantastic, saw enormous talent and creative potential, quickly realized how smart, funny, charming, and insightful he was, and decided to give it a go."

When Stace arrived in New York, she met the object of Underwood's attention at the Tin Angel, a Bleecker Street bistro that became one of Tim's regular haunts. Like many women before her, Stace was instantly taken with the terribly thin teenager slumped over at the table. "He was a beautiful, poetic presence," Stace remembers. "He was like a little bird. He had an absolutely gorgeous smile. His teeth were perfect. He had that big dimple on his chin. Gorgeous eyes and hair. He really did exude star quality." In early August, after two months in New York, everyone piled into Stace's blue Rambler—Beckett sitting on his Dylan albums, since there was no more room for them in the trunk—and drove west to officially start Tim's career as a recording artist. Stopping in Las Vegas along the way, Beckett won a slew of coins from a slot machine. Since they were all broke, it felt like a good sign.

Tim, Jane, Underwood, Stace, and old pal Jim Fielder (who had by then joined the Mothers of Invention) set up home in a rented house in the Hollywood Hills. Fielder introduced them to pot, their collective first drug, while Jane's stabilizing role in Tim's life began to take shape. Efficient and practical, in search of equilibrium after a childhood spent on the move, Jane set up house, even buying dishes. There was little, if any, talk of Tim's wife or an impending child.

If Tim was focusing at all on a birth, it was that of his first album, on which work began immediately upon his return to Los Angeles. Holzman recruited staff producer Paul Rothchild to oversee Tim's debut, which was recorded at Sunset Sound Studio in two days, August 15 and 16. Tim's voice and rhythm guitar were supported by a small, tight three-piece band comprised of Underwood on lead guitar, Fielder on bass, and Mothers drummer Billy Mundi, with session ace Van Dyke Parks overdubbing keyboards at a later session. They cut fourteen songs, some written by Tim alone, some collaborations with Beckett. Jane accompanied Tim to the studio, and, she recalls, "We had a blast. It was so exciting. He went from being sort of a bum to all of a sudden making a record." To prime his voice, Tim would drink Harvey's Bristol Cream sherry between takes.

Tim Buckley, as the album was simply called, often feels as earnest and formal as the checker-jacketed, doe-eyed teenager on its cover. The arrangements alternate between charging folk-rock, in galloping remakes of "It Happens Every Time" and "She Is" from the Bohemians' demo tape, and sullen, after-hours art songs, as in Beckett's ode to his girlfriend, "Song Slowly Song," with its celestial percussion and spacey Underwood guitar. As a first single, Elektra chose "Wings," a bittersweet, set-her-free farewell with the windswept orchestration of a Glen Campbell single from the same period.

Emotionally, the songs appear to be in as much transition as the music. At least half of them—"Aren't You the Girl" ("Oh, do you ache inside, do your eyes wanta cry/Do you want me back again?") and "It Happens Every Time"—are ambivalent declarations about Tim's feelings for Mary. "Valentine Melody" finds Beckett placing words in Tim's mouth to describe the precarious state of his and Mary's relationship ("You came to me with fire inside/Your movements and your pride," ending with, "Today the coin is in the air/And we are here and there"). The song's backdrop of guitar and strings is, coincidentally, the album's most intimate. Even the Beckett lyrics about *his* girlfriend—"Wings" (from which Beckett's name was dropped in the credits) and the ode to the "autumn temptress" in "I Can't See You"— may as well be about Mary.

Conversely, it isn't hard to realize the inspiration behind one of the last-minute additions to Tim's repertoire. Set to a bright, piano-laced cadence, "Song for Jainie" praises the "free-giving ways of a woman" of Tim's new flame, the one "who took me in and showed me love again." (For reasons even Jane does not understand, Tim misspelled her name in the title.) It's as if the songs are torn between two lovers.

In his phrasing, Tim comes across a little stilted, his wholesome folk sing-along roots still poking through. Yet in the way it winds from a sensuous falsetto to an operatic foghorn to a low growl, his voice reveals unmistakable individuality. The five-octave range he had discovered as a child in Bell Gardens springs forward and announces itself even in these relatively restrained settings. There is also a hint of an impassioned wail during "Understand Your Man," a piece of period chauvinism conceived in the studio at the last minute. ("Grief in My Soul," an early Beckett-Buckley collaboration also resurrected for the record, is a similarly callow blues vamp.)

Flaws aside, *Tim Buckley* is at least far from conventional. Few troubadours of the time attempted such challenging departures as the dirgy, rippling electric guitars and tempo of "Song Slowly Song" and "Song of the Magician" or a piece like "Strange Street Affair Under Blue," whose tempo accelerates with each verse before winding up as a Sunset Strip polka. The album was very much a first step—"the popping of the creative zit," as Holzman calls it—but it made the steps to follow impossible to predict.

Thirty miles south, in Anaheim, Anna Guibert thought all was going well between Tim and Mary. She assumed her daughter and son-in-law were living together in a cute Hollywood apartment, dining at hamburger stands and taking strolls on the beach. She was therefore surprised when, one early summer evening, Mary called shortly before midnight. Her daughter sounded upset, and, it turned out, with good reason: She was three months pregnant, this time very much for real. Even more confusingly, Tim seemed to be out of town and didn't appear to want the baby. "Come pick me up," Mary told her. Anna jumped into the family car, drove into LA to the Cohen house, and brought Mary home that night.

The pregnancy had been only the most recent surprise for eighteen-year-old Mary, who had earlier heard about Tim's record contract while at the Cohen house. The unplanned baby had probably been conceived during one of Tim's trips in February or March, just a few months after Mary's hysterical pregnancy. Even before Tim left for New York, his wife suspected he was spending time with other women, but blames her denial on self-worth problems associated with battered children. "By no stretch of the imagination was this a marriage made in heaven," she says. "He hadn't been faithful to me for very long. And I thought that was perfectly acceptable because, after all, he was so wonderful, and I was so nobody."

Mary says she told Tim about the pregnancy before he left for New York, but that he told her he had to leave town and that she should move back in with her family in Orange County, get a job, save money, and "maybe get an abortion or whatever you want to do," she recalls him saying. Even then, Tim made no mention of another woman or his fading interest in his wife. "I just had no idea," Mary says. "A lot of denial going on. Tons of denial on both sides, because he wouldn't bring himself, to the very end, to say, 'You know, I really don't love you very much.'" She sent Tim letters to various addresses in New York; his replies came fitfully and were pointedly vague. Finally, a mutual friend gave her the news: Tim was in New York with a new girlfriend, and would be back in Los Angeles shortly.

Underwood recalls the situation being a topic of discussion while he and Tim were in New York that summer. Given the choice of returning to Mary and Orange County or following what Underwood calls "his destined natural way," Tim, says Underwood, "decided to be true to himself and his music, fully aware that he would be accepting a lifetime burden of guilt. Tim left, not because he didn't care about his soon-to-be-born child but because his musical life was just beginning, and, in addition, he couldn't stand Mary. He did not abandon Jeff; he abandoned Mary."

Perhaps, yet for whatever remained between Tim and Mary, the fall became a sad and confusing time. In high school, they had sought refuge in each other, but Tim, it seemed, increasingly felt that refuge had grown too constricting. With a debut album in the can and tours to promote it in the works, Tim grew even more conflicted—and, at times, spiteful. He began telling both Jane and his friends that Mary had "tricked" him into marrying him because of her nonexistent initial pregnancy. Mary, desperate to hold onto Tim, tracked him down in his house in the Hollywood Hills. "She put on a real nice, smiling bubbly front," recalls Fielder. "Whatever her true feelings about Tim and Janie, she kept them to herself." Despite the visit, Tim didn't return to Mary. They both realized they had married too young, and to Tim at least, the whole mess, baby and all, had been a mistake born of naïveté, youth, and hormones.

Finally, action needed to be taken. Tim drove down to Anaheim and met Mary at a coffee shop within walking distance of the Guibert home. It was awkward from the start. Eventually, Mary asked, "How's Jane?"

"Fine," Tim mumbled, a little embarrassed.

The events that transpired in that coffee shop remain somewhat unclear. Tim never talked to his friends about it, while Anna Guibert recalls Tim giving Mary an ultimatum: divorce or abortion. According to Mary, she asked Tim what they should do about the marriage and pregnancy, and he replied, "You do whatever you have to do, baby," and hung his head. "He never said, 'No, I don't want you to get a divorce,' or 'Yeah, I want you to,' " Mary says. "He was so guilt ridden he couldn't say either way. He couldn't say, 'I want you,' either. He was sad and remorseful."

Afterward, many months pregnant, Mary walked home, told her mother the news, and cried. As Anna remembers, "I said, 'That's the best thing, honey. If he doesn't want you, be free.' She was crazy about Tim. But he wanted his career. There was no place for a baby in his life." Anna asked her daughter about an abortion, in 1966 a life-threatening and illegal proposition. Mary said no; she wanted the baby.

Some of Tim's friends from this period, like Fielder, maintain it was Mary who gave Tim a "career or baby" ultimatum, which she denies. "If he had said, 'I want you to come back with me now,' I would have left that coffee shop and gone home and packed a bag and gone with him," she says. "I did not want to end that marriage. But I did not want to stay in a loveless marriage, either." Reluctantly, Mary filed paperwork for a divorce, which would be finalized nearly a year later, on August 29, 1967.

The contractions began in the very early hours of Thursday, November 17, 1966. When the pains started coming five minutes apart, everyone in the Guibert household sensed this was no false alarm. Anna drove Mary to Martin Luther Hospital in Anaheim, where her daughter began an agonizing twenty-one hours of labor. It was, Mary says, as if the baby just didn't want to come out. Anna stayed with her daughter as much as possible, and to everyone's surprise, Mary's father George visited the hospital, thrilled at the prospect of a grandchild. Finally, at 10:49 P.M., out plopped a blond, pudgy baby boy, a literal golden child.

The issue of identity loomed even before the child left the hospital. Mary named her son Jeffrey Scott—"Jeffrey" after her last high-school boyfriend before Tim ("my last pure boy-girl relationship, my last pure moment") and "Scott" in honor of John Scott Jr., a neighbor and close friend of the Guiberts who died in an accident at the age of seventeen. Yet because Mary preferred Scott, and because "Scott Jeffrey" didn't flow as smoothly off the tongue as "Jeffrey Scott," the child was instantly called Scotty by his family. Tim was not available for consultation, since no one knew his whereabouts.

FOUR

I remember awful brown carpeting
I remember desert all around
I remember roaches all night
I remember washing dishes
I remember the garden
I remember my records thrown in the street
I remember grandpa holding me over the water
I remember Ted Nugent blasting from Chuck's car in Nowhere CA

—JEFF BUCKLEY, JOURNAL ENTRY, 1996

From the beginning, everyone was in awe of him. He was a child born of pain and turmoil, yet he was so bubbly with laughter that the cloud under which he was conceived appeared to drift away. He would sit in his high chair and bang on the tray with a spoon as if he were keeping a beat with any music he heard. Even when he was baptized at St. Michael's, the same church where his parents had been wed a little over a year before, he made his mother smile by looking up and loudly passing gas during the ceremony.

Intent on being a single working mother, Mary found an apartment in Anaheim. It was there that Tim had his first glimpse of his child, but baby Scotty took one look at his father's unruly tousle of hair and began crying. Soon after, Mary took ill with an infection of the fallopian tubes and, as a result, lost her clerical job at a local bank. With Scotty in tow, she returned to the Guibert household. Although her father adored the baby, cooing to him and coddling him as much as everyone else did, family matters had not dramatically improved in the Archer Street house since Mary had moved out. Her two younger siblings, George III and Peggy, were now teenagers, and the same disciplinary measures that applied during Mary's adolescence became a part of her siblings' lives. "He wanted the children to do what he said, no matter what," Anna says. "He didn't allow for the kids to make mistakes."

It wasn't long before George Guibert's pressure pot began to boil over, and lamentably, the moment arrived on Christmas Eve 1967. The family was preparing to attend an afternoon church service, followed by dinner at home with friends. As they were about to leave, George senior discovered fourteen-year-old Peggy hadn't unloaded the dishwasher and exploded just as Mary walked into the room with Scotty in her arms. It was only a matter of minutes before Mary was yelling "Daddy! Daddy!" and the elder Guibert was pulling her hair and even starting to lunge at the baby. They never made it to church, and the dinner was called off. "It was," Anna recalls, "the most horrible Christmas."

With that, Mary took to the road. Still hopeful of a career in the arts, she moved to North Hollywood and, to earn a living, took jobs at the phone company and a pharmaceutical office. For the next year and a half, Scotty spent weekdays with his grandparents while Mary lived and worked in Los Angeles, spending time with her baby on weekends. For a brief time in Los Angeles, she dated Tim's old Bell Gardens friend Dan Gordon, who recalls little blond Scotty exuberantly chasing seagulls on the Santa Monica boardwalk. In his apartment one day, Gordon came across one of Mary's drawings—a face half in darkness, half in light. It was, he says, "Tim's face, no question about it," but Mary denied it, saying the illustration was merely something she had doodled.

Mary's ambivalence was understandable. During Scotty's first three years, Tim made what amounted to only guest appearances in his son's life. Once he visited Mary in her Hollywood apartment, bringing the child a gift, a picture book about the circus. Another time, he and Gordon drove down to Anaheim to see the infant, and Gordon watched as Tim stared wistfully at the sleeping child "like he was a holy creature. He was looking with wistfulness and awe and almost a kind of reverence." On the drive back, Tim cracked cynical jokes; Gordon always noticed that the more caustic Tim's sense of humor turned, the sadder he was.

In the fall of 1968, Mary and Scotty showed up at Tim's home in Malibu. All of them sat on the beach, wrapped in blankets and staring out at the ocean. Tim brought Scotty into the house, cradling the golden-haired two-year-old asleep in his arms. "It's my *son*," Tim said to a visiting friend, flashing one of his warmest smiles. Jane Goldstein, Tim's central love at the time, remembers Mary dropping off the baby another time at the same home. Tim, Jane recalls, "was so completely in love with this baby. We were just sitting there looking at him." Since Jane would often grow jealous of the baby (and Mary), Tim was forced to reunite with them once at the nearby Santa Monica apartment of his friend Daniella Sapriel on Memorial Day weekend, 1969. Tim was again carrying the conked-out Scotty in his arms, and he told Sapriel he simply wanted to spend time alone with the baby and his mother. For a short moment, they felt like a family. But the moments were as rare and fleeting as rain in Los Angeles; there were other families, and other worlds, beckoning. In his absence, Tim sent Mary and Scotty some money: child-support payments of a little over $80 a month, totaling $330 for the last months of 1967, $1,055 for 1968, and $1,065 for 1969, according to court documents.

Being so young, Scotty was unaware of these visits, although years later, he would half-recall sitting with his parents at the beach in Malibu. ("We all three had a big blanket around us. Just sitting there saying nothing," he wrote in a letter.) At two, he began attending a progressive Montessori school in Anaheim. Everyone was still marveling at him: the way he sang children's songs (especially "I'm a little teapot/Short and stout"), mimicked a Sri Lankan instructor, or named any state pointed out to him on a map. While attending public school, he grew enamored of Harry Nilsson's album *The Point* and sang along with the Muppets on television, and he would sing and dance in front of the Guibert family fireplace, which became his stage. "Scotty was the center of attention," recalls his aunt, Peggy Hagberg. "And he ate it up."

One day, Anna bought an acoustic guitar as a gift for a neighbor, but when pint-sized Scotty found it in a closet, he immediately asked if he could have it. It seemed like an odd request, given he was just a few years old and knew little about musical instruments. But Anna relented; this baby, she thought, just seemed determined to get someplace.

The commute to Los Angeles was too much for mother and especially child, so Mary returned to Orange County in 1969 with the idea of working part-time while attending a local college. After she had found an apartment in Anaheim, the landlady informed her that the garage was being utilized by a man who repaired cars. Mary pulled open the garage door and saw two large feet sticking out from under a Porsche. Out rolled a strapping, six-foot-two ex–football player with, Mary remembers, "the most beautiful blue eyes you ever saw."

Ron Moorhead was, in every way, the anti–Tim Buckley. Born and raised in Pennsylvania by a conservative family, Moorhead had moved with them to California in 1960. His first love was cars, and he had taken a job as a mechanic at a Porsche shop in Huntington Beach while repairing autos on the side. Strapping and straightlaced, with a head of curls and muttonchop sideburns framing his face, the twenty-one-year-old Moorhead was the strong-silent archetype sprung to life. It was only a matter of months before he and Mary began dating and two-and-a-half-year-old Scotty started handing Moorhead tools in the garage. To everyone's surprise, they were married soon—in December 1969 at Anaheim Unity Wedding Chapel, little Scotty carrying the rings. Although Mary's parents thought the couple wed too soon, and Moorhead's folks were less than thrilled about their son marrying a divorcée with a child, both sets of parents attended.

The following year, the new Moorhead family moved to Fullerton, a blue-collar town north of Anaheim, and purchased a cozy, gray-stucco house on Pritchard Street. The $18,500 dwelling was affordable for a transparent reason: Behind it was an aluminum siding company, and two houses down was the Fullerton Municipal Airport. Between the incoming Cessnas and the siding plant's twenty-four-hour shifts, the Moorheads were surrounded by noise, especially Scotty, whose back bedroom faced the plant. Still, it was a home, and while Ron Moorhead never officially adopted the child, he immediately took to the polite, well-behaved Scotty. Moorhead became, in turn, Scotty's first real father, the man who took him to parks and to his office. Moorhead had opened his own business, a Volkswagen repair shop called the Bug Inn that was only a few blocks away and allowed him to be home for lunch with Scotty.

Despite the clatter, music was everywhere. A devout rock fan, Moorhead would always buy the must-own LPs of the day, and Scotty was never far from the sounds of the Moody Blues, Grand Funk, Cat Stevens, Crosby, Stills & Nash, and Chicago. Moorhead's VW camper panel van was equipped with a stereo, and Scotty would often fall asleep next to the speakers as Led Zeppelin and the Doors blared, the music becoming implanted into his subconscious. Mary, meanwhile, introduced her son to the music of Barbra Streisand, Carole King, and Joni Mitchell—"your basic drag-queen music diet," he would later crack to a reporter—and played Bach, Chopin, and Mendelssohn on the living-room piano. "Lots of music," the child wrote later, "lots of singing."

"Man, I even *performed* a piece I'd made up when I was in the second grade!" he also wrote once to a friend. "All the piece was was me plucking the first four strings in an arpeggio in 3/4 time very slowly and the change was, I think, substituting the D string with the A. All open strings. It was *so* nothing, technically. But when I played it, I was completely mesmerized."

Financially, the Moorhead household was struggling: The Bug Inn wasn't flush with cash, and Mary's first venture (a clothing-design business) hadn't moved beyond their garage. The family made ends meet whichever way they could. One Halloween, Scotty wore an American Indian costume made from a paper bag.

Slowly and painfully, though, a schism between Mary and her second husband began to crack open. Both were volatile, and when Mary began taking courses to resume her stillborn music and acting career, her husband objected. "He wanted me at home cooking and cleaning and taking care of Scotty," Mary says. "He didn't want me out at night rehearsing until eleven." Moorhead confirms this scenario—"I was a little immature in that respect"— but feels the problems were a two-way street. Tim's manager would send his client's latest LPs to Mary, and she would play them for Scotty, who seemed not at all interested, being barely of kindergarten age. "At that time, I'm going, 'Look, don't push it on the kid,'" Moorhead recalls. "'If he wants to listen to it, fine.' But that was an issue with Mary and I." Moorhead never met Tim, but he resented the recorded intrusion of Scotty's wayward father into their lives. It wasn't long before arguments, exacerbated by their financial woes, joined the clatter of airplanes and the crunching of aluminum.

When marriage counseling failed to help, Mary resorted to a time-honored way of saving a marriage: pregnancy. Their first son, Corey James, was born in March 1972. ("My mom has a baby, and I'm jealous because I'm not getting as much attention," Scotty matter-of-factly informed his relatives.) But the newborn arrived too late. Moorhead had already begun an affair with another woman, and after what he calls "a number of heated discussions," they separated shortly after Corey's first birthday, in early 1973. Mary kept the house, a car, and both children; Moorhead took the car-repair business and the LPs. The first real father figure of Scotty's life drove away with his Volkswagen bus.

On a spring day in 1975, eight-year-old Willie Osborn was skateboarding up his street in Riverside when he spied a new family moving in. He observed "this little hippie kid" with flaxen locks, so he skated over to introduce himself.

Starting the day Ron Moorhead had moved out, the last two years had been rough ones for Mary, Scotty, and Corey. Mary's clothing business hadn't taken off, and she had taken various day jobs to support the kids. Corey was also growing into a miniature demon; one day, at three, he was discovered scampering around the landing strip of the airport near their Fullerton house. Filling in for her mother at a faucet-importing company in Buena Park, Mary met a salesman six years her senior. Although married and the father of two children, stocky, mustached George Vandergrift soon became romantically linked with Mary. In 1975, they bought a home in Riverside, forty-two miles east of Anaheim, by which time Vandergrift had divorced and opened his own plumbing-supplies business.

Lined with imposing maple trees, oversized homes, and old-fashioned lampposts, 12th Street was quieter and more stately than any other place Scotty had lived. The same went for the house Mary and Vandergrift purchased: a turn-of-the-century, Mission-style clapboard with refurbished hardwood floors and a beige, four-car barn in the sloping backyard. Small, round cement balls that had been horse tie-ups were still sitting in front of the house. Scotty could look up the street and see the picturesque, massive rock formation known as Mount Rubidoux jutting into the sky.

Mary had reverted to her maiden name, Guibert, after her separation from Ron Moorhead. Scotty had other ideas. That spring of 1975, Mary had taken him to see his natural father in concert, and when he was filling out his registration form for his new school in Riverside, the nine-year-old informed his mother that he wanted to be called Scotty Buckley in his father's honor. It was not the only indication that music was increasingly becoming a major part of Scotty's vocabulary. He and his new friend Osborn would walk together every day to their nearby elementary school while singing Yes and Styx songs, and Scotty turned his friend on to the first major band of Scotty's life: Kiss. Scotty owned *Kiss Alive!*; months later, when the makeup mavens released *Destroyer,* the two kids would run around in their underwear playing air guitar and lip-synching "Detroit Rock City." "He exuded happiness," Osborn says. "He always smiled. I thought he'd grow up to be a politician."

At school, Scotty was the eternal clown, making jokes, craving attention, and being more interested in music (including cello lessons provided by the school) than grades. His second-floor bedroom became a rock enclave, his most valuable possessions being a *Hemispheres* picture disc by the prog-rock band Rush and all four of Kiss's solo albums. He still had the guitar given to him by his grandmother, and although he hadn't learned to master it, he would sit and cradle it, "like Linus's blanket," Osborn says. Although he had taken his father's name, his music tastes reflected none of Tim's influence. Neither did his lifestyle; Scotty and Osborn would talk about how bad drugs were. (Strangely, one thing Jeff and his father shared at this age was an ingrown-toenail problem. "Look, Mom, I finally found comfortable shoes," Jeff said to Mary one day. Looking down, she saw the same style of gray, lace-up Hush Puppies Tim always wore. According to Mary's sister Peggy, Mary was "horrified.")

With his wide-ranging expertise in everything from business to gourmet cooking, the California-born Vandergrift proved to be Mary's intellectual equal. He was, she says, "my mentor, my Svengali, the guy who saved my head in so many ways." Mary once again shelved her show-business dreams and, with Vandergrift's financial backing, opened a small greenhouse near the house to cash in on the potted-plant craze. Unfortunately, it wasn't the only part of the period lifestyle felt in the household. Very much in keeping with the times and locale, both adults loved to party. ("It *was* the seventies," Vandergrift admits.) Two decades later, in the *Pop Culture Press,* Scotty would recount one of their weekend getaways: "When I was little, the two of them took [Vandergrift's] sister and her boyfriend and me to Mexico for some sort of lost weekend."

Once again, the idea that this home would be a stable environment for Scotty and his half-brother Corey began to crumble. According to Vandergrift, he and Mary argued over "the profitability of her ventures. Most of the arguments I remember always seemed to be over issues of where we were going in our lives. Neither of us would give. That doesn't always make for the most harmonious time." Mary was once again battling with a forceful male in her household, what she deems "classic Freudian, marry-your-father stuff."

Scotty was polite to Vandergrift but never particularly close to his mother's boyfriend (Mary and Vandergrift never married). As the years progressed, Scotty grew quieter and spent more time in his room, and visitors recall relations between him and Vandergrift growing so chilly that Scotty would be found upstairs during dinner. ("He didn't come to you a lot and say, 'I can't do this or that,'" Vandergrift recalls. "He always seemed to figure things out himself, even with his homework.") When the arguments between the two adults grew too heated, Scotty would escape to his friend Osborn's home three houses down, where they would sing rock tunes or, if they felt mischievous, throw tiles off the roof at passing cars. "You drove us mad, both of you," Scotty scolded Mary in an answering-machine message nearly twenty years later. "Me and Corey were *insane.*"

Whether it was the lifestyle or simply the clash of personalities, the situation reached the direst of straits late one night in 1979. A quarrel climaxed with Mary running down a flight of stairs as Vandergrift picked up and hurled a television set at her, shards of glass and TV tubes smashing at her feet. "Just another one of our arguments," Vandergrift recalls. Mary shook Scotty and Corey awake in the middle of the night and told them to get dressed.

Down the block, Willie Osborn heard the shouting and then the sound of something smashing. He went outside in time to see Mary's white pickup truck pulling out of the driveway, Scotty in the front seat. It was the only frown Osborn recalled ever seeing on his friend. The sight was a far cry from Osborn's most vivid memory of Scotty—a luminously smiling kid running down the hilly 12th Street, his blond mane flowing in the wind.

The pickup came to a stop in Sunnymead, but it must have felt like the last outpost of civilization. Ten miles west of Riverside, Sunnymead was nestled deep in the most arid, airless part of Riverside County: all dry brush, trailer homes, and stark, rocky hillsides. A pizza parlor and a video-game room were the principal local entertainment. In 1978, Mary and Vandergrift had bought a parcel of land at the end of one long, sidewalk-less street and built a 5,000-square-foot, wood-framed greenhouse for Mary's plant business, Emerald Enterprises. The small pink cottage in the front of the property would serve as both office and plant store.

It wasn't intended as a home, but it became one as soon as Mary's pickup pulled into the driveway. On and off during the next two years,

Mary would reunite with Vandergrift and return to Riverside. When the situation would collapse, as it inevitably would, she and her two sons would head back to Sunnymead. "All I could say to them," Mary says, "was, 'Wherever the three of us are, guys, this is home.'"

For both boys, though, Sunnymead became a modest hell. Young, mop-topped Corey grew increasingly angry over the separation of Mary and his father Ron Moorhead and became even more troubled and destructive. Scrawny, concave-chested, and artistically inclined (he starred as Snoopy in his elementary-school production of *You're a Good Man, Charlie Brown*), Scotty was bullied almost daily for his lunch money by the tough local kids and jocks. ("On the bus they used to call him 'the dirty kid,'" his friend Inger Lorre remembers him telling her two decades later. "I said, 'Why?' He said, 'I don't know—I washed and everything. But maybe it was because my hair was long.'") A rare reprieve would come when Mary would drop off the two boys with Ron Moorhead and his new wife Glenna Blake in nearby Carbon Canyon. Low on cash, Mary would pack the kids' laundry and belongings in paper bags. "I would have bought them suitcases," she explains, "but we didn't have money to live on, so brown paper bags were suitable." Along with his unpleasant school bus trips, the image would haunt Scotty for years.

Two days a week, Scotty would help his mother with her business, placing plants in sleeves and then hoisting them into her pickup truck. Unfortunately, the plant trade was in the process of growing bigger and more corporate, and Emerald Enterprises ran aground; at best, it only earned the family $9,000 a year. All along, Tim's $80-a-month child-support checks continued to trickle in. For extra food and income, Mary bred livestock, including chickens and geese, in the backyard. One year she raised a turkey called, ominously, Dinner. When it was big enough to eat, Mary went to kill it with a butcher knife. Terrified, both Scotty and Corey ran away—Corey behind Mary's truck, Scotty into his room, sobbing.

Music continued to fascinate him and provide an escape from the ever-present household upheaval. For Christmas 1979, the Guibert family chipped in and bought Scotty a copy of a black Les Paul guitar, which thrilled him to no end. The first song he learned to play was the Knack's "My Sharona," a huge power-pop hit that summer. In his room in Sunnymead, he would tape *The Dr. Demento Show,* a syndicated radio show specializing in the most twisted of novelty tunes. One of them, Ogden Edsl's 1977 "Dead Puppies," particularly delighted him. ("My puppy died last fall/He's still rotting in the hall," warbled Edsl over a faux-sentimental acoustic backdrop.)

During the summer of 1980 and into the following school year, Scotty and Corey had yet another new home, this time, with the Moorhead family in Willits, a small, rural community north of San Francisco where they had just moved. Scotty was a diligent student, always doing his homework and playing guitar in the school band. At football games, Ron Moorhead would hear a strange, discordant riff on a guitar and would instantly know it was his stepson.

One night, the family—including Moorhead, Blake, and their own two children, Keith and Annie—went to see *The Rose*, the Bette Midler *film à clef* inspired by the tragic life of Janis Joplin. Afterward, Scotty cried. The movie's depiction of a hard-living '60s rock star on a downward, drug-fueled spiral reminded him of his father. Had the Moorheads known more about the film, they would not have taken him to it.

During this period of constant transition, Willie Osborn saw his old friend Scotty registering one day at North High School in Riverside. Osborn didn't even know his pal was back in town. Scotty was now going by his real first name, Jeff, occasioned by finding his birth certificate. He joked to Osborn about wanting to be a musician and naming himself "Jeff Buck" after his latest guitar-god hero, Jeff Beck. His hair had grown darker and his face leaner, and he seemed somber, a far cry from the happy-faced kid Osborn had known a few years before. Jeff only noticeably brightened when he and Osborn went to see a metal concert featuring Blackfoot and Def Leppard in 1981. The concert—Jeff's first arena-rock experience—was gaudy and cheesy, full of the period coliseum-rock clichés like pounding lights and self-indulgent guitar solos. Yet when Osborn looked over at his friend at one point, Jeff had a glazed look about him as he stared at the stage. He appeared to be overwhelmed.

In the fall of 1981, with Mary's relationship with George Vandergrift crumbling to a final halt, she and Jeff returned to Orange County. The greenhouse having run aground, Mary took a sales job with a company that sold plants to retail chain stores, and Jeff, who had grown bored with the placid Willits, moved in with her again. He and Mary (and, occasionally, Corey) began renting the first in a series of homes in the area, initially in Garden Grove. At each, there was inevitably a clash with the landlord, followed by an eviction, over incomplete repairs and broken landlord promises. By now, Mary was working long hours and driving to and from Los Angeles on sales trips, and it fell upon Jeff to become the premature man of the house. The first to rise each morning, he made coffee for his mother and breakfast for himself and Corey. If Mary worked late, Jeff also had some sort of meal prepared for the three of them. Mary referred to Jeff as "my rock," while his grandmother Anna began calling him "El Viejito," Spanish for "little old man," because Jeff appeared to be wise beyond his years. The job, Mary admits, "paid a great deal more, but it took me away from the boys more. That was the time they felt most abandoned. They had to be better equipped to take care of themselves."

Using his grandmother's address in Anaheim, Jeff began attending Loara High School, his mother and father's alma mater and still considered one of the best schools in the area. Loara hadn't changed much since Tim and Mary had attended it seventeen years earlier, although the quad, where Tim and his gang had played guitar and hung out, was now the domain of the stoners. The school still emphasized the arts and encouraged students to play music and indulge their creative sides. (There were 180 students in the school band, compared to a mere thirty-five in the mid-'60s.) As in so many schools around the country in the early '80s, the preppies ruled: the girls were blond and mall-haired, the athletes Izod-shirted and buff. Porsches and Ferraris dotted the student parking lot. Jeff felt estranged from it all; if he associated with anyone, it was generally with the Asian kids or other outsiders or, more importantly, his fellow student musicians.

That fall 1981, during his sophomore year, Jeff joined the jazz-band spinoff of the school orchestra. The curriculum involved two guitar classes a day, so each morning he dragged his new, cream-colored Ovation Viper electric guitar in its brown plastic case onto the bus to school. In class one day, Jason Hamel—a junior who played bass in the jazz ensemble and sported a frizzy mushroom of blond hair—checked out the small, scrawny kid with the long brown hair, tennis sneakers, and California Angels cap. Rather than sit during practice like most of the other fledgling musicians, this kid *stood*, aping the moves of AC/DC headbanger Angus Young. "We said, 'What is *with* this guy? Easy on the chocolate bars,'" recalls Hamel. With Jeff comping jazz chords, the band entered competitions with ensembles from local high schools, playing big-band and jazz tunes by the likes of drummer and composer Louie Bellson.

Although just barely fifteen, Jeff was exhibiting impressive musical skills, as another school band member, drummer Paul Derech, discovered when he visited Jeff in the Guibert home in early 1982. Sitting on his bed, Jeff played songs from Al DiMeola's *Electric Rendezvous* and the first album by Asia. Even though Derech had to listen closely to Jeff's guitar—Mary couldn't yet afford an amplifier for her son—his dexterity was so apparent that Derech literally took a step back.

Once Jeff pulled out a picture of Tim from his closet and softly said, "I've spent a lot of time looking at that picture," before moving on to another topic. Derech, like other kids, sensed immediately that the absent father was a sore point. Instead, they talked music, particularly their mutual love of Rush and Genesis. Although punk and new wave were the predominant rock styles of the moment, Jeff had little interest in them. "We despised that stuff," says Hamel. "Jeff would ridicule those people." Instead, Jeff preferred music that challenged him and transported him to imaginary worlds. In the late '70s and early '80s, that music was prog (short for progressive) and art rock—bands like Yes, Genesis, and Rush that reveled in complex structures, science-fiction-themed lyrics, and virtuosic, fleet-fingered guitar parts only a few teenagers could hope to master. In a friend's garage, Jeff and Derech soon began jamming on versions of Rush songs. Jeff declined to sing, though; he told friends and family he wanted to be a guitarist plain and simple.

The reason, some felt, was because he didn't want to be compared to the musician father he barely knew. "He had exactly the same speaking voice as Tim," recalls Herb Cohen's daughter Tamurlaine, who befriended Jeff when he and Mary would visit the Cohen family for dinner. (Cohen and Mary had kept in touch after Tim and Mary's breakup.) During those meals, Jeff's vocal and physical resemblance to his father led Herb Cohen, Tim's one-time manager, to often mistakenly call Jeff "Tim."

Cohen began keeping an eye on the teenager's embryonic musical talent, and in that regard he had the right instinct. In his garage in Garden Grove, Jeff constructed a drum kit out of coffee cans and taught himself to play. In another Garden Grove apartment, on Walnut Street, egg crates were tacked onto his bedroom wall for soundproofing. There wasn't enough money in the household for a stereo of his own, or for many albums, so Jeff learned to play songs by taping them off the radio with his little boom box. Friends began noticing something peculiar about him: He could hear a song once, instantly memorize it, and then play it straight through. It was uncanny, a gift of the gods that seemed like a blessing and, if the song was bad, a strange sort of curse.

*   *   *

Robin Horry, a junior at another Anaheim high school, was in his family's garage one afternoon in April 1982, waiting for his friend Jason Hamel. Together with another Anaheim high-schooler, a drummer named Tim Marse, the three boys had formed Powerage, a local metal band specializing in AC/DC, Jimi Hendrix, Def Leppard, and Judas Priest covers. But they were always looking for extra guitar players, and Hamel kept telling Horry about a new kid in school who shared their rock tastes and smart-ass sensibilities.

Hamel came strutting into Horry's family garage; behind him was a chipmunk of a kid in jeans, sneakers, and baseball cap. His Ovation Viper guitar impressed the kids immediately—it wasn't cheap—but he made an even larger impression when he plugged into one of their amplifiers. At fifteen, the little guy could *play*. Before long, they were jamming on intricate prog-rock songs like Yes's "Long Distance Runaround" and a few Rush songs. After school and into the summer of 1982, they became closer friends and band mates. Jeff would break into a dead-on impression of Michael Jackson, complete with dance steps, and they would all watch *Monty Python* and *Goodies* reruns on TV and repeat the skits back to each other the following day. They also became an official band: Mahre Bukham, named during a brainstorming session in Horry's bedroom, and comprised of portions of each of their last names.

As with Jeff's other school musician pal Paul Derech, none of Jeff's new friends knew much of his past. Even when they discovered his father was a musician, they had never heard of anyone named Tim Buckley. "And if *we* didn't hear of the guy, then he probably wasn't too big," Horry says. "Jeff showed me a couple of his albums at his house, and I went, 'Nope, never heard of him.'" Jeff seemed indifferent anyway; he only showed Horry the albums as he was flipping through his collection in search of something else and, in the process, passed by the battered old Tim LPs in the stack.

None of this mystery concerned his friends much; single-parent homes were becoming increasingly commonplace. What amazed the members of Mahre Bukham was Jeff's seemingly effortless chops. During "Long Distance Runaround," he mimicked singer Jon Anderson's elf-from-planet-Zondar voice while simultaneously playing the snaky guitar lines; he even *held* his guitar just like Yes's Steve Howe. Although Jeff wasn't keen on singing, someone had to imitate the high-voiced lead singers of Yes and

Rush, and Jeff, with his naturally tenor-style timbre, was recruited for the task.

His tastes in music weren't limited to prog-rock. One night, he and Hamel drove to a Count Basie concert in Pasadena. Before the show, they ran into Ella Fitzgerald outside, of whom the wisecracking Jeff was, shockingly, in utter awe. Hamel had never seen his friend like that before. After the show, though, they saw Johnny Carson sidekick Ed McMahon walking up the aisle. Jeff looked up at the comedian and cracked, "Aren't you Martin Mull?" McMahon snorted his usual chortle, totally unconcerned he was being mocked.

The band's ambitions went beyond mastering prog epics like Genesis's "Squonk" in a garage. Opening for four other local bands, Mahre Bukham made their debut on Tuesday, September 21, 1982, at the Woodstock Concert Theater. A theater in name only, the Woodstock was actually a four-hundred-seat, all-ages metal club in a strip mall on South Knott Avenue in Anaheim. Although the club owner mispronounced their name as "Mary Bukham" in the club's phone listings, the boys were primed. Hamel insisted they have a flashy look like so many of the rock bands of the time, so Jeff went to a local Victoria's Secret mall outlet and, much to his initial embarrassment, bought a pair of silver spandex pants.

A couple of dozen friends and family showed up to hear Mahre Bukham play an opening set for the other acts. Although onstage just shy of an hour, they made the most of their time. The set included a few of their own songs, including one sung by Hamel called "Murder in Ojai," but it was on the covers where they—and Jeff—shone. With the spotlight making his shag haircut seem blonder than usual, Jeff offered up note-perfect renditions of the Police's "Roxanne" and Rush's "Spirit of Radio" and jumped around making goofy faces and playing air guitar during a version of Hendrix's "Fire." "His stage presence at that first show was amazing," recalls Horry. "All the photos our relatives took from that concert, we looked like a bunch of dopes, and Jeff looked like he was straight out of a stinking rock and roll teen magazine. He was so photogenic we wanted to *kill* him." They didn't make a dime from the gig, but no one cared much; they had their first taste of rock stardom. For Jeff's sixteenth birthday, in November 1982, Mary, eager to encourage Jeff's talent, bought him his first amp, a Roland Jazz Chorus, inspired by Jeff's love of Andy Summers of the Police.

Mahre Bukham only lasted four gigs, including one at a bar near a Marine Corps base in Tustin that nearly ended in a fight when Jeff directed sarcastic cracks at the Marines in attendance. But Jeff clearly relished every moment of teen rock life. One night at the Woodstock, he and Hamel flirted with two local girls. One of them rubbed up against Jeff, who was sporting his spandex pants. "Hey, *look!*" Jeff said to Hamel, pointing to a very evident erection.

Mahre Bukham also resulted in Jeff's first-ever interview, in the November 5, 1982, edition of the *Saxon Shield*, Loara High School's student newspaper. "Mahre Bukham 'plays around' with style," read the headline; two onstage photos of Jeff were included. "The members of Mahre Bukham, of course, want to succeed in the world of rock and roll," wrote one of Jeff's classmates, "but unlike many other musicians, they do not want instant success. Says Jeff Buckley, 'We'd like to get more of our repertoire and not get a recording [contract] right away. We want a good slow climb to the top. . . . when you start at the top, you can't go anywhere but down.' " As with his virulent antidrug stance, it was further evidence that the arc of his father's career had left more than a small imprint on him.

Jeff left a larger impression on his classmates six months later, at the annual "Senior Follies" show at the end of the 1982–3 school year, when he and Hamel performed Rush's "Tom Sawyer" and the Police's "Roxanne." "Senior Follies is so amateurish, and he really surprised everyone," recalls Holly Jones, a friend and Loara classmate. "It was astounding—like watching a real rock band." Yet another Buckley was knocking the collective socks off his classmates at a high-school talent show. By that point, Mahre Bukham was history, but Jeff still played with drummer Marse, this time concentrating on his own compositions: knotty fusion instrumentals with titles like "Stupid Shoes" that were extremely advanced for someone his age. Says Marse, "We wanted to create a new style of music, totally different."

It was poignantly clear to Marse, Jones, or anyone who knew Jeff that he never seemed to have any money. Frequently, his friends would buy him after-school burgers or take him on what felt like his first-ever trips out of town. One afternoon at Huntington Beach with Horry, Jeff rented a raft and drifted out into the water, eventually out of sight of Horry. The next thing Horry knew, Jeff and the raft were back ashore. Much to Jeff's annoyance, lifeguards had to swim out and rescue him. He thought he was doing just fine.

Once more, it was time for the Guibert household to relocate. Before the start of the 1983 school year, Mary had landed a high-paying job as a saleswoman for yet another large agricultural firm and was preparing to move.

Although he told friends he hated Anaheim and its environs—he referred to the area as "the Orange Curtain"—Jeff decided that this time he was not leaving. "Scotty said, 'I can't take this anymore—I don't want to change schools,'" Mary remembers. "He was sick and tired of moving around. He was fed up with my instability. He'd say, 'Come on, Mom, can't you just keep it *together*?'"

With Mary gone, Jeff moved in with his grandmother Anna Guibert, who was still residing in the same house on Archer Street in which Mary had grown up. Anna's husband, George, was long gone; he had left his wife in 1970 and moved back to Panama with a younger woman. The house on Archer was now empty except for Anna, who welcomed her young grandson. Anna still kept a tidy, orderly home, and Jeff gave her no reason to be anxious; he was, as ever, well-mannered and levelheaded. Anna gave him the copies of Tim's old LPs Mary had left behind, along with the notes Tim had tossed to Mary through her bedroom window. Jeff, she recalls, "got a kick out of those."

At seventeen, Jeff had adopted what was known regionally as a "hesher" haircut: spiky short on top, sloping down to the shoulders on the side. As contemporary as his hair style was, it couldn't hide the facial characteristics he had inherited from both parents. His wavy brown hair and slender face were pure Guibert, as were the deep-socketed eyes. Hovering over those eyes was what he called his "uni-brow," the thick eyebrows he shared with Tim; he also had a developing cleft in his chin that was very much his father's. Although some of his female classmates thought his looks cute, Jeff referred to himself as "monkey boy," the geeky twerp who couldn't attract the interest of any girls his age—and perhaps didn't deserve love anyway.

In school, Jeff was often assigned to advanced-placement classes. He joined the debate team and the Kiwanis, which competed in the Orange County Academic Decathlon competition; one of Jeff's essays helped place the team in the county's top ten. In one class, he wrote a near-perfect Ernest Hemingway parody for an essay. Shy around strangers, he would let down his guard only around his small circle of friends, joking relentlessly or breaking into "Gee, Officer Krupke" from *West Side Story* at lunchtime. The wisecracks and mocking comments made it easy for him not to talk about his past, his father, or his mother, toward whom he seemed exceedingly protective. "It wasn't this group of touchy-feely people," says another classmate, Melissa Hawley, of the times she would hang out with Jeff and Holly Jones.

"It was these people who were together because they didn't have anybody else to be with."

Although a goofball on the outside, Jeff struck many of his friends as inordinately complex and hard to read; his cutup side could easily give way to a dark-cloud moodiness or a blistering putdown. For his aunt Peggy Hagberg, he would execute devastatingly accurate caricatures of each Loara clique. But when asked which group he belonged to, he told her, "None of them. I don't belong to anyone." During cheerleader programs, recalls Jones, "he'd scream out comments and cut them down. The cheerleaders would be doing their dances, and he'd yell, 'You're fat!' He hated hierarchy."

"They hated me," he later wrote about his high-school classmates. "I hated them and their pet teachers and their mamas, too. . . . My yearbook is in the ocean, now. . . . They bellowed 'fag!' to my long hair from their speeding cars—so puerile, too hilarious, the irony was a billion miles wide and they never caught on."

Jones, like Jeff a senior in the school, became one of his first major crushes. With her blond hair dyed black, she thought of herself as a practicing witch, yet she considered him nothing more than a friend. She introduced Jeff to her longtime childhood friend Roy Rallo, who attended a local Catholic school and was already steeped in opera and classical music. He and Jeff traded tapes and played music together in Rallo's bedroom. One of the tapes Rallo made for Jeff included a recording by British mezzo-soprano Janet Baker of Benjamin Britten's choral piece "Corpus Christi Carol," which Jeff took to immediately. On the few occasions when Jeff sang, he would almost always use a silly voice, as if he were uncomfortable with the sound of his real one.

After school, Jeff would sit alone in his grandmother's living room, his guitar cradled in his lap, watching television and playing along to every commercial and sitcom theme song that came on. One of his favorite shows was *Late Night with David Letterman*—Letterman's mocking asides and gags cracked him up—but Jeff also took a musical interest in the show. He would make tapes of the different ways bandleader Paul Shaffer would arrange the show's opening theme and then play along with the tapes. To everyone who knew him, Jeff appeared to be headed for a life as a musician; no other vocations, options, or even colleges were discussed. "His name is Jeff Buckley, and he is well on his way to becoming a professional musician," read a profile of the graduating senior in the Loara 1984 yearbook. ". . . Jeff's major goal is to become 'an expert with enough recognition to fill my own potential and ability; that's what it's all about!' " The blurb added: "After Jeff has reached his higher peak, he intends to stay single yet have many affairs and acquaintances. Jeff explains that marriage would take up most of his energy; therefore, staying single, he will be better off."

No one was surprised by the latter comment, but the same couldn't be said of the yearbook section in which students printed slogans and club memberships next to their names. Jeff's simply listed "Jazz Band," followed by an unusual send-off: "Years from now we'll look back at these high school days and beat our wives."

"You can't imagine how radical that was," recalls Jones. "The whole school talked about it the next day."

On graduation night, Jeff and his friends Jones, Hawley, and Hawley's boyfriend ditched the elaborate senior-class parties and instead bought a bottle of wine and rented a room at a local fleabag motel. There they stayed until the early morning hours, talking about their futures and sipping wine. Jeff lay down next to Jones. He couldn't wait to leave it all behind: the bullies and jocks, the girls who saw him as a lower-class nobody, the memories of a disjointed childhood he kept wishing was happier than it had been. He already knew where his future lay: thirty miles north, in Los Angeles.

FIVE

Two days after the birth of Jeffrey Scott Buckley, Elektra Records heralded the arrival of a child of its own. The November 19, 1966, issue of *Billboard* sported a front-page advertisement announcing the release of Tim's first LP. "Tim Buckley is certain success," read the accompanying copy. "His debut album on Elektra Records, *Tim Buckley*, is a powerful yet sensitive statement in the new idiom, superbly performed by this young songwriter." Since "Wings" had failed to chart as a single, the ad also declared that a new 45, "Song for Jainie," would be Tim's next. (Elektra logs, however, indicate that "Aren't You the Girl" was, in fact, the follow-up single.)

Success may have been certain for Tim, but it didn't arrive with his first work. *Tim Buckley* made only the smallest of dents, selling twenty thousand copies during the fall and winter of 1966 and failing to make *Billboard*'s Top 200 album chart. Even those close to Tim viewed it as merely the first of many steps. Underwood would dismiss the album as "high-school folk music," while Beckett came to regret the inclusion of songs like "Grief in My Soul" at the expense of what he felt was stronger material from their early collaborations. In a later press release, even Elektra referred to it, in amusingly blunt language, as "a lovely album—albeit not a great album."

Still, no one was distressed by the album's lack of impact or its artistic shortcomings. Everyone, Elektra's Holzman included, knew some musicians would take two, three, perhaps even four, albums before they matured and connected with a larger audience. If a first effort did the job, wonderful; if it didn't, there would always be another. No one was making, or losing, fortunes; time and opportunity appeared to be plentiful.

Shortly after the album's release, Tim and Jane rented a home of their own, a flat-topped adobe-style house in the rustic hills of Topanga Canyon, the rising hippie community west of Hollywood and just north of Malibu. Unfortunately, Tim wasn't in the house very much. With Underwood and Fielder, he returned to New York before Christmas 1966 to open for the Mothers of Invention at a nine-night stint at the Balloon Farm, a club on St. Mark's Place in the East Village. New York was cruelly cold that winter, and Tim bundled himself into a new black peacoat, baggy sweaters, and billowy brown corduroy pants and girded himself against the frigid blasts. Neither Fielder, Underwood, nor Beckett recall any mention of a newly born child, nor have any recollection of where Tim was the morning of November 17.

Tim also returned to the Night Owl, the club at which he had made his New York debut that summer. He befriended waitress Marlene Waters, who one chilly December evening found herself seated next to Tim at the bar of Googie's, a restaurant down the street from the club. Waters, who was already taken with Tim's singing, found him "incredibly sweet and warm, and very cuddly. He certainly appeared to be someone who was very single and available." Tim began rubbing up against her like a cat until there was little air space between them. Given the sexual mores of the day—bed first, mental bonding later—it was inevitable they would spend a few nights together, in the apartment of one of Waters's friends. Only when she was informed that Tim had a girlfriend named Jane who had just flown into town did Waters have any idea Tim was attached, much less had an estranged wife and child.

It would not be Tim's last such encounter in the months ahead. He turned twenty on Valentine's Day 1967, and the frizzy-haired, conservatively dressed adolescent of barely a year before had given way to a new persona. From his sloping nose to his crinkly, fuzzy smile to the cleft in his chin, Tim now resembled nothing so much as a flower child from ancient Rome. In conversation, his head would bob left and right, as if the weight of his wiry (but surprisingly soft, like fleece) head of hair was too heavy for his slender face. The combination, both sexual and nonthreatening, proved hard to resist. "A lot of his power over women was his vulnerability, projecting a sense of weakness," says Beckett. "They felt they could mother him, help him, elevate him, set him on the right path, help him fulfill his promise. He was a great-looking, curly-haired singer-songwriter. Gimme a *break*."

Downtown New York became Tim's home base into the early months of 1967. He and the band took up the first of many residences at the Hotel Albert on University Place and East 10th Street in the Village, a favorite of rock and rollers for its affordable rent and unstuffy ambience (although not for its peeling walls or dripping faucets). The Lovin' Spoonful rehearsed in its basement, and members of the Mothers, the Byrds, or the Mamas and the Papas could be seen drifting in and out of its minuscule lobby. Money was tight—for one series of gigs, opening for the Youngbloods at the Cafe Au Go Go, Tim made only $10 a night—and Jane would often fix meals for the entire band on a one-burner hot plate in her and Tim's room, washing the dishes in the bathtub. "No money—we starve and then we work after long periods of starving," Tim wrote to Beckett on Hotel Albert stationery. "It's meaningless, it kills my spirit . . . no one to see my beauty—no one to love my thoughts . . . my black jokes poison my eyes . . ."

Still, New York fed Tim's musical imagination and social life. He met and was photographed by Linda Eastman, a young, up-and-coming rock photographer who quickly developed a crush on him. (Whether Tim and the future Linda McCartney had an affair remains a source of debate among Tim's friends, especially given his tendency toward fabrications.) In February 1967, Tim was offered a slot at another East Village nightspot, the Dom, as an opening act for Nico, the imposing German model and singer who had made a name for herself as a onetime member of the Velvet Underground. Tim (who was tipped to the gig by friend Jackson Browne) needed the cash and Nico had a certain degree of credibility, so he signed on. "All of a sudden a blonde European chick called Nico offered him a gig," Tim, referring to himself in the third person, wrote to Beckett. "He was scared at first. But within the next two weeks he accepted—he made $200 a week and nobody listened to what he sang. When he sang loud the talking got loud—when he sang soft he couldn't hear himself. So he would become very irritated and wished himself in some other situation. But after the first weeks more people came and he grew more used to the utter confusion while he sang."

In the same letter, Tim scribbled that he was about to buy a new acoustic guitar with twelve, rather than the usual six, strings, which lent the instrument a rich, full-bodied chime. "I can't wait," he wrote. "The sound is so mystical I almost seem to hover when I hear it." He also wrote of a visit to the Dom by Canadian poet and soon-to-be-singer Leonard Cohen, for whom Tim had enormous respect ("he writes all the time, he's not like us"). "In Canada he is called God by his fans," Tim wrote, before adding a final thought almost to himself: "A horrible responsibility, I would think."

In the mid-'60s, the college market was a lucrative one for musicians lumped into the folk or folk-rock categories—which Tim, to his increasing disgruntlement, was—so Herb Cohen booked Tim into a slew of schools in the Northeast, including Swarthmore and the State University of New York at Stony Brook on Long Island. At Bard College in upstate New York in February, someone had the idea that Tim should be backed by an ad-hoc group of students from the arts-oriented college. So, before his scheduled concert at the gymnasium, Tim ambled into the church on Bard's ambling, green-grassed campus for a rehearsal. Among the student musicians waiting for him were two Bard undergraduates, future actor Chevy Chase and future Steely Dan mastermind Donald Fagen, on drums and piano, respectively. With Jane a firm, silent presence at his side, Tim sat down, nodded when he was introduced, and, without a word to the gathered players, launched into a new, unrecorded song, "Hallucinations," a baroque-sounding ballad with a tricky, stones-skipping-on-water rhythm.

Another of the accompanists was Carter Crawford Christopher Collins, a twenty-two-year-old African-American conga player from Boston who wasn't a Bard student but was crashing with friends who were. With his muscular, 160-pound build and green beret (it was, he recalls, his "Black Panther days"), the nearly six-foot-tall percussionist was an imposing physical presence, albeit one with a gentle soul. The student musicians, he recalls, "were trying to play along with Tim, but nobody was communicating," Collins recalls. "Nobody said what *key*. Chevy Chase was shuffling cymbals and moving this and that, and Fagen didn't know where to be. Tim was just playing."

After two songs, by which time Collins was the only musician keeping tempo with Tim, Tim took off his guitar capo, pulled out a towel from his case to wipe the neck of his guitar, looked up without actually looking at anyone, and, in a meek voice indicating Collins, said, "I just want *him* to play with me." Although Collins had never heard of Tim nor any of his songs, he accompanied him for that evening's concert in the gym. Onstage, the shy LA kid became a wailing, impassioned gypsy, and afterward, Collins forthrightly asked Tim if he could join his band. Tim agreed, and to a fifty-fifty split.

The addition of a conga player was unusual; even Dylan didn't use such relatively esoteric instrumentation. It was merely one indication that Tim's artistic visions were beginning to expand in unconventional ways. A few weeks later, on Monday, March 6, he returned to the Village for a show at the New York Folklore Center, a musical instrument and record store that would host concerts for $1.50 admission. Ten days later, Tim showed up at Folklore Center owner Izzy Young's apartment for an interview. Tim came across as alternately cocky and self-pitying: complaining that "no one came to see me" at the Night Owl the previous summer while dismissing the current crop of topical singer-songwriters like Phil Ochs and Tom Paxton as ones who "stayed in the same thing. They showed me they didn't grow." He opined that Dylan, his longtime inspiration, had "a lot to learn—everything comes out as a sneer or a putdown, even in love songs. But his voice is better." He talked of wanting to hire a flute player and travel to India to study meditation, and of how different his next album would be. "Elektra told me they'll put a billboard of me on Sunset Boulevard," he mentioned, adding that his still unrecorded second album would this time sport "a smiling cover."

He and Young talked folk music and, briefly, Tim's personal life. "My father's doing a mental thing in some hospital," Tim told him. "That's another story." (He failed to mention that his parents had separated the previous year as a result of old Buck's increasing psychosis.) At one point, Tim also mentioned "the kid."

"What kid?" Young asked.

"The one that we had, Jeffrey," Tim said, rattling off his four-month-old son Jeffrey Scott's birth date. Speaking of the Guiberts, he added, "They won't let me see it. Won't let me in the house. . . . I'm not allowed to see my wife—they hold guardianship over the child, who's living there. She's getting welfare, although she's living with her parents." (Again, Mary Guibert claims Tim was more than welcome to visit.) He told Young he hadn't met Mary's parents until the day of the wedding—which wasn't true—and that "they hate me, for I ruined their name."

"As far as my career, I don't know what I'm going to accomplish, but something else may happen," Tim told Young. "Everything usually falls into place. . . . I'm always trying to stretch myself, explore. I love to see change."

*　　*　　*

Jerry Yester was at his house on Oak Court in Laurel Canyon, with its majestic view of the canyon, when he heard the rumble. It was a '38 Chevy with no taillights and dotted with body rust. The clunker came to a halt in front of Yester's house, and out hopped Tim and Larry Beckett.

After the breakup of the Modern Folk Quartet, the tall, lanky Yester decided to take a stab at producing. Early in 1966, he had been invited to Herb Cohen's house to see one of Cohen's new signings, a kid named Tim Buckley. In Cohen's living room, Tim shyly sang a few numbers. With his suit, tie, and short hair, Tim looked, Yester thought, as if he were at a high-school dance. When someone—most likely Cohen, who liked to keep business dealings in his company family whenever possible—suggested Yester as a possible producer for Tim's second album, the two men had a get-acquainted meeting in New York in early 1967. Yester mentioned his main client, the pop band the Association, which included Yester's brother Jim.

"Well . . ." Tim said quietly, "I'm not really a big fan of theirs." Yester laughed and told him it was fine to admit it. The Association had sold many records, thanks to Top 10 hits like "Cherish" and "Along Comes Mary," but no one in the pop underground considered them in any way hip or cutting edge.

On this spring Laurel Canyon afternoon, though, the Tim who sauntered up Yester's driveway was a changed man from the Orange County youth Yester had met a year before. Gone was the suit, replaced by Tim's standard outfit: laced chicken-boot moccasins, brown cords, and blue denim shirt. Gone also was any postadolescent naïveté lingering from Anaheim. With Holzman and Cohen also at the house, everyone sat down to discuss the creation of Tim's second album.

The plan Tim and Beckett presented to their superiors was for a grandly produced work. "We had written songs that were more substantive," says Beckett. "We felt the quality of the music and lyrics was way above, and we wanted really good production for it. Like the Beatles' *Revolver* we wanted each piece to be free to be itself completely, not limited by any particular instrumentation or musical style." Tim and Beckett went so far as to present Yester and Holzman not only with the songs but the order in which they were to be sequenced on the record. "They weren't going to take any shit from Holzman," Yester remembers. "They really wanted to record, but not if it meant bastardizing what they believed in. The attitude was real spunky." Given that Tim had by then recorded only one album—and one that was far from a bestseller—Yester was caught off guard by what he calls the duo's "crusty and arrogant" attitude, yet he found them, Tim especially, lovable. Although only a few years older than him, he and his wife, singer Judy Henske, instantly wanted to adopt Tim.

Tim and Beckett drew part of their inspiration from the new atmosphere of rock creativity, albums like *Revolver* and Dylan's *Blonde on Blonde* that pushed boundaries in production and songwriting. They were also encouraged by one of Tim's heroes, the gruff-voiced, gruff-living Fred Neil. Prior to the meeting at Yester's house, Tim and Beckett had been invited to attend a Neil recording session at Capitol Studios in Hollywood. For over an hour, Neil and his musicians worked on a wistful shrug of a ballad called "Dolphins," constantly altering the tempo and feel and exploring every available musical option. "Seeing Fred Neil experiment haunted Tim forever," Beckett recalls. "It inspired him to perfect something in different ways with the same material, to take chances." Standing and staring awestruck in the control booth, Tim glimpsed the possibilities of his own future.

Before his own album was to be made, though, Tim first had to create a single—to break in Yester, try to make Tim a pop star, or both. "I remember Herbie saying, over and over and over, 'Listen, man, you gotta have something that's gonna go on the *radio*, man, 'cause you can't have this fuckin' art *shit*,'" recalls Henske of one meeting at her and Yester's home. "Herbie said they were too poetic, too literary; you had to think too much." Tim and Beckett went along with it. They were, Beckett says, "just playing ball" with Elektra.

For two days straight, Tim and Beckett listened to Top 40 radio non-stop at Beckett's apartment in Venice. "We were coldly analytical," says Beckett. "And after two days, we decided that pop music was either about fairy tales or about drugs and sex in a strange, mixed-up way. So we decided that would be our single." The results were "Once Upon a Time," which satisfied the former criteria, while the latter requirements were filled by "Lady, Give Me Your Key," a double-entendre ballad built around the slang for pot. "They worked and worked and worked and worked, and then came back up to the house to play this song," Henske recalls. "And it was *so* terrible. It was so funny because here are these artists trying to do something they can sell."

Despite Henske's reservations, the recording date proceeded on May 2, 1967, at United Recorders on Sunset Boulevard, with Yester at the control board. "Once Upon a Time," which Beckett calls "a piece of fluff," was in fact a vibrant slice of folk rock, with electric guitars and a harder rhythm than anything on Tim's first album and, courtesy of Yester, a cathedral-like organ in the chorus. "Lady, Give Me Your Key" had a folkier feel with what Beckett deems "an entrancing melody and chord progression" courtesy of Tim.

For reasons that remain vague, the single was assigned an Elektra catalog number but never issued. ("*Aah,* we don't need it," Yester recalls Holzman saying.) Since it was what Beckett calls "our cynical attempt to comply with the record company's request" and was never considered part of the second album, it was relegated to the vaults with few reservations. Still, Tim learned two lessons from the experience: first, that Yester would suffice in the producer's chair and, second, that Tim would never again make such a market-driven compromise.

The timing couldn't have been more perfect for the making of Tim's projected masterwork. In rock, it was the beginning of not only the summer of love but the summer of musical experimentation. Increasingly, rock was seen not as merely youth expression but as an art form unto itself, and the LP was the double-sided canvas on which the new generation of musicians was painting. From peace-and-flowers song topics and conservatory-pop production to the cardboard sleeves in which they were encased, LPs reflected the new, mind-expanding, and often more sophisticated underground sensibility and flower-child persona of the day. (Even the Sunset Strip was beginning to transform into more of a hippie, headshop-heavy enclave.) The music business was more than happy to indulge these new musician-prophets. In the first eight weeks of 1967, $43.2 million worth of LPs were sold, up 22.9 percent from the same period the year before.

The sessions began Monday, May 8, 1967, at Western Recorders, the Hollywood studio that served as a home base for the Mamas and the Papas and the Beach Boys; the latter band, with Los Angeles pop kingpin Brian Wilson at the helm, had recently recorded their *Pet Sounds* album and "Good Vibrations" single there. Yester assembled a large backup band that included Tim's regular players—Underwood, Collins, Fielder, and former Bohemians member Brian Hartzler—along with Yester and session man Don Randi on keyboards, Phil Spector regulars Jimmy Bond on bass and Ray Pohlman on guitar, and Eddie Hoh and an uncredited Jim Gordon (later of Derek and the Dominos) on drums. No expense would be spared for the creation of what many around Tim thought would be his grand statement and commercial breakthrough. According to Danny Fields, a teen-fanzine editor who became Elektra's publicist in the spring of 1967, Elektra albums also had what was jokingly called within the company a "landscaping budget"—money (usually around $250) to buy grass for musicians while they were recording.

The songs Yester had been handed varied in mood and tempo, and the producer, whose taste tended toward the baroque and polished, heard innumerable possibilities in them; besides, he says, "Tim didn't want any formulas." Over the course of a month at Western and Whitney, a former Mormon church in Glendale that had been converted into a recording studio, Yester, Tim, and Beckett took to the job like children making increasingly larger and more elaborate sand castles. "Carnival Song" was lent not only a horse-ride calliope beat but was framed with circus sounds and background noise from an Elektra sound-effects LP. Tim's complex, Near Eastern–inspired melody for "Hallucinations," featuring a Beckett lyric about his breakup with his girlfriend Tracy, was given a muted cacophony of glistening percussion and exotic effects for its bridge. "Knight-Errant" sported a coy Beckett lyric about oral sex ("'My lady's chamber' is supposed to be her cunt, not to mince words," he says), but Yester devised an arrangement that was pure psychedelic Renaissance fair, driven by Randi's madrigal piano. Throughout the sessions, Tim rarely made explicit comments, generally articulating his feelings with a shrug or a facial gesture.

At Herb Cohen's home one day, Tim asked Beckett to write a song about a hobo, perhaps recalling his childhood in Bell Gardens. Beckett chose the image of a morning glory to symbolize blossoms "that open quickly with the coming of the light." (In later years, Tim would introduce the song in concert as being about "a hobo beating up on a collegiate kid outside of Dallas, Texas," which Beckett says was not the inspiration.) In hindsight, Beckett feels his lyrics for "Morning Glory" are "clunky," but Yester worked up a quietly spine-tingling arrangement built around tender piano and an ethereal choir that, in actuality, consisted of Tim's and Yester's combined multitracked voices. "Pleasant Street"—a blistering, near operatic song about, as Tim told Izzy Young, "an acid-head in Brooklyn"—was framed with a harder, organ-driven arrangement that lent it the feel of a soul-scorching church service for drug addicts.

Tim and Beckett wanted each album side to open with social commentary, so side one begins with "No Man Can Find the War," whose lyrics ("Bayonet and jungle grin/Nightmares dreamed by bleeding men") constitute Tim's (and Beckett's) most explicit antiwar comment. (Beckett says the actual topic is less combat than "the plump American sitting in front of the TV letting all this happen with his tax dollars.") The music is stern and rigorous, a death march of congas and guitars. For dramatic emphasis, the song starts and finishes with atomic bomb explosions also taken from a sound-effects LP.

The other, less obvious war song is "Once I Was," an homage to Fred Neil's "Dolphins" ("Sometimes I wonder just for awhile/Will you ever remember me?" is a blatant nod to the refrain of Neil's song: "Sometimes I wonder, do you ever think of me?"). The war reference is limited to its opening line, but the song's mood of loss and longing could easily apply to an American soldier in Vietnam. With its clip-clop beat and old-West harmonica (the latter courtesy MFQ member and photographer Henry Diltz), the track, like everything around it, sounds like nothing else on the album.

Half of the album's lyrics were written by Tim alone, and one of them, "I Never Asked to Be Your Mountain," is particularly personal. Although it mentions no names and refers to his ex-wife by her zodiac sign, it is Tim's song to Mary and his barely year-old son:

> *The flying Pisces sails for time and tells me of my child*
> *Wrapped in bitter tales and heartache, he begs for just a*
>   *smile*
> *Oh, he never asked to be her mountain*
> *He never asked to fly*
> *And through his eye he comes his love*
> *And tells her not to cry*

Elsewhere in the song, Tim addresses what he sees as Mary's dependence on him ("I never asked to be your mountain/I never asked to fly") and what he imagines Mary was telling their son about his father ("She says, 'Your scoundrel father flies with a dancer called a queen,' " an apparent reference to Jane) before bidding a last goodbye to Mary ("I can't swim your waters/And you can't walk my lands/And I'm sailing all my sins and climbing all my fears/And soon now I'll fly"). The song is striking not merely for its personal, if oblique, lyric but for its music. Built on a dense thicket of guitars and congas, it throbs with pain and confusion, and

Tim's voice grows more impassioned, more desperate, with each line. Charged with emotional electricity—as well as a certain lack of responsibility—"I Never Asked to Be Your Mountain" was the most unrestrained and fiery performance Tim had written and recorded to that point.

Tim, Yester, and Beckett spent the most time mapping out "Goodbye and Hello," an elaborate and inordinately intricate piece—"a ballet, an opera," raves Cohen—that splices together two different songs. The first is sung in the voice of their parents' generation, and the other in the voice of the free-living counterculture that was supposedly taking its place. In standard antiestablishment '60s style, Beckett's lyric castigates television ("the electronic shrine"), war, and deadening marriages as symbols of a decaying culture. Tim wove the two melodies together into one piece, and Yester arranged the sections as separate entities as well. Hiring a string section, he made the verses relating to the older generation bustle and clatter (at one point, the strings imitate car traffic), while the "children" sections were prettier and freer. Holzman was initially less than enthused about the orchestration and its cost; according to Yester, the Elektra president called the studio one afternoon and threatened to cancel the session because Yester hadn't cleared the hiring of string players. When he heard the finished track, though, Holzman recalls being "really wiped out. I couldn't wait to get a copy." Even its length—eight and a half minutes—wasn't perceived as a problem, particularly in the nascent world of FM underground radio. "DJs loved those records," Holzman says. "It meant they had eight minutes to go to the bathroom."

According to Holzman, the tab for the album's production came to just under $5,000 (Cohen and Yester feel the cost was double that amount). "It was a massive production for its day," Fielder recalls, although he recalls the recording as proceeding "pretty smoothly. It wasn't a pulling-of-teeth session." Tim sang live with the band but, an increasing perfectionist, did twenty-three vocal takes of "I Never Asked to Be Your Mountain." After the sessions, Tim, Yester, and Beckett would head out for a beer and talk ebulliently about the progress of the album.

During the sessions, Beckett joked about calling the record *Timbuktwo,* since it would be Tim's second album; Tim himself preferred *Topless Lunch,* after a sign he saw in Los Angeles. Eventually, they settled on a title taken from the album's most ambitious track: *Goodbye and Hello.* And as Tim had predicted to Izzy Young a few months before, the cover photograph did indeed picture Tim flashing one of his most angelic smiles, the cap from a soda bottle playfully inserted in his right eye like a makeshift monocle.

For years, fans would ask about the significance of that bottle cap, yet, as Jane says, "There *is* no mystery. Tim told me it didn't mean shit. They were on the beach for the photo shoot, and Tim picked up a bottle cap and stuck it in his eye. A pop bottle top—that's all it was." Tim shouldn't have been surprised by such interpretations. In the unfolding rock counterculture, nearly everything was becoming invested with deeper significance than may have been intended. What did these people think he was? Tim wondered. An oracle?

At Elektra, Holzman's excitement over the completed album extended beyond his sneak preview of the album's rock-operatic title piece. He personally played it for every employee at the label's new Manhattan offices at Broadway and 61st Street, near Columbus Circle. "It took my breath away," publicist Fields recalls. "I said, 'It's a number-one album!' I loved the passion behind the singing, the diversity of the songs, the scope of it. I thought, 'Everybody's going to want this.'" David Anderle, Elektra's West Coast head, remembers spending "many, many hours in Jac's apartment and with Jac at my house in LA, lying on the floor listening, both of us stoned out of our brains and wondering how somebody could be so good. We thought it was going to be huge." The Beatles's own ornate wall of sound, *Sgt. Pepper's Lonely Hearts Club Band,* had been released about midway through the *Goodbye and Hello* sessions, which made the timing of Tim's album seem even better.

Like *Sgt. Pepper, Goodbye and Hello* is sometimes overbaked or too ornate, very much a piece of its period. ("There is some weird sixties kind of junk on it," admits Beckett.) While the lyrics aim for a level of high art, some are a bit too pretentious or cloying. Yet for all its pretensions, *Goodbye and Hello* includes an inordinate amount of beautiful soundscapes, from the shimmering beauty of "Morning Glory" and "Hallucinations" to the overpowering "Pleasant Street" to simpler, understated folk-rock pieces like "Phantasmagoria in Two" (whose title refers to the song being in 2/4 time and to its subject of two lovers). The vocal elasticity Tim had exhibited on his first album begins to take root as well. Throughout the record, his singing is more assured and diverse than on *Tim Buckley:* lilting on "Carnival Song," feverish on "I Never Asked to Be Your Mountain," wisely bittersweet on "Phantasmagoria in Two." And for all its acid-era presentation, *Goodbye and Hello* isn't naively blissed-out. It carries a wistful undercurrent of failed romance, as well as hints of horror in "Carnival Song," with its distant, dissonant organ, and the gothic apocalypse "Pleasant Street." The record may allude to hallucinogenic worlds, but it also hints at the darker comedown to those same trips.

When *Goodbye and Hello* was released the last week of September, Elektra prepared a fanfare that would crown Tim as the next minstrel prophet. "One will never forget the clossal exhileration [double *sic*] at the Elektra offices when the tapes came in," read a press release. ". . . A massive promotion was launched, the only goal being what the album and artist merited, which is to say, Elektra is aiming very, very high, and with confidence." Record buyers who swung open the album's elaborate (for its time) gatefold sleeve were confronted with reprints of the lyrics, intended to emphasize how important Tim and Beckett's thoughts were. A *Billboard* article headlined "Elektra Push for Buckley's 2nd LP" mentioned radio and magazine advertisements and a promotional tour. Earlier that year, Holzman had rented a billboard on Sunset Strip for $1,100 a month; shortly before the release of *Goodbye and Hello,* up went a huge reproduction of its cover, Tim literally hovering above Los Angeles.

Reviewing the album in its September 30, 1967, issue, *Billboard* praised it, saying: "The 10 songs, all written by Buckley, deal with the writer's introspective view of himself and society. Much of it is moving. It's not in the traditional folk bag, and it has suggestions of Dylan. Cover art is arresting, and the gatefold packaging attractive." Holzman's attention to fanciful cover art had paid off, and there was no reason to assume the rest of his gamble on Tim wouldn't fly as well.

In Venice, the business felt even farther away than the few miles between its boardwalk and Hollywood. Located next to Santa Monica, Venice was Los Angeles's artist-friendly, occasionally seedy beach community, with a boardwalk gauntlet of street musicians, painters, and drug dealers stretching out over a mile. For musicians, artists, and anyone else with limited income, it was the cheapest and most comfortable place to live in Los Angeles. A nondescript shack could be rented for as little as $100 a month, sometimes right on the water or at least with a view of ocean and sand. Tim and Jane (whom Tim nicknamed "Peaches") eventually relocated from Topanga Canyon to 613 ½ Ocean Park Boulevard, a main block in Santa Monica, while Beckett and Underwood shared a small pink house at 59 Navy Street. Carter Collins, new to California, would take his congas down to the beach and play in the sand with other percussionists. It was, he recalls, "a whole seafront panorama of humanity I'd never experienced before."

The days were as free and easy as sex and hallucinogens. It wasn't unusual for Tim and his friends to roll a few joints or down a tab of acid, and then while away the time discussing art and music or taking long strolls on the beach. "You might take a walk in the morning and not come back until the next day," recalls Jane's high-school friend Manda Bradlyn (later Beckett). With his sweet smile, pigeon-toed shuffle, and poetic slouch, Tim was the center of this universe. When they weren't rehearsing songs, Tim and Underwood would hurtle into intense discussions about literature and jazz, with former English teacher Underwood introducing Tim to the likes of Joyce and Dostoevsky. Tim's thirst for new input—ethnic and classical music, literature, art, film—seemed insatiable.

Money was rarely an issue. Everything Tim earned, from concert appearances to record and publishing royalties, would be sent to Cohen and dispersed to Tim during visits to Cohen's office on Wilshire Boulevard. Financially, Tim became completely dependent upon Cohen; Tim had no bank account nor any sense of how much money he had. Even if he and Jane rented a car, the office would do it for them. "I didn't like it," Jane says. "I'd ask, 'How much money do we *have?*' Tim would say, 'Oh, don't worry about it.' " To earn extra cash of her own, Jane sewed clothing with Manda Bradlyn.

Another neighbor (and Cohen client) was a sensuous young singer from Tucson, Arizona, named Linda Ronstadt. Jane knew Ronstadt as the somewhat chubby girl who hid candy bars under her bed and seemed to be exceedingly insecure. With her band the Stone Poneys, Ronstadt recorded versions of several of Tim's songs, including "Morning Glory" (retitled "Hobo"), "Wings," and "Aren't You the Girl" (once again, probably a case of Cohen keeping the publishing money in the family). According to friends, Tim wasn't fond of Ronstadt's belting style and was upset when Cohen called one day to say she would be covering his songs. Still, they were friendly. One day, Tim and Jane were asked to come down the street to Ronstadt's house, where a photo was being taken for Ronstadt's next album. When the album, *Stone Poneys & Friends, Vol. 3,* was released the following year, its back cover sported a group shot on the steps of

Ronstadt's clapboard Venice home, Tim and Jane huddled together amidst the friends.

David Anderle, Tim's point man at Elektra in Los Angeles, recalls visiting Tim's apartment, where they would listen to Miles Davis and smoke abundant amounts of marijuana. In those days, Anderle says, "You wanted enough money to buy pot, a nice bottle of wine once in a while, and a bit of gas to get around, and once in a while some clothes." Tim became a regular at the Troubadour, his old open-mike-night haunt, but by now he was a paid headliner. Attending many of those shows, Anderle would put his feet up on a seat in the second-floor balcony and watch as Tim—usually accompanied by Underwood and Collins—lost himself in long, improvised jams, the songs stretching to three or four times their recorded lengths. After the show, everyone would stay up until 4 or 5 A.M., and then, says Anderle, "try to race home before it got yellow outside."

"He was so inspiring and so *cute*," recalls Pamela Des Barres, who, as a music fan and groupie on the LA scene, attended several of Tim's Troubadour shows. "He had a real tenderness and vulnerability. You just wanted to hold him and comfort him."

Tim had by now acquired two '30s Chevys, one for transportation, one for parts. The one he drove, with its rusted exterior and oversized fenders, "*looked* like a 1938 car," according to Henske. As Collins sat beside him, Tim would cruise around Los Angeles, and the sight of the brawny conga player flexing his muscles and intimidating other drivers never failed to make Tim burst into laughter. One night, cruising around the Strip, Tim, Henske, and Larry Beckett pulled over for gas; in the next gas line was a new, shiny red Corvette. "The guy in the Corvette is filling up his car with gas and Buckley is standing there looking at him with a real nasty look on his face," recalls Henske. "The guy looks up and says, 'You got a problem, man?' And Buckley says, 'No, man. Just . . . see ya at the *drag*.' And he gets back in this terrible car. He was so arrogant—he just *had* to say something!" The three of them laughed loudly on the way out of the gas station; they showed *that* square doofus.

In the confines of the apartment he and Jane were now renting in Santa Monica, Tim adopted seemingly freeform but subtly productive work habits. Manda Bradlyn moved in with them, and the two women would throw together meals of bean stew or whatever was available while Tim wandered around the house with a massive-looking twelve-string guitar that seemed to dwarf him. He would generally play or sing only snippets of songs, inspiration seemingly darting in and out along with the ocean breeze, but there would always come the day when it would all coalesce and out would flow a finished number.

One fall morning over breakfast, Beckett came over with his latest well-honed, slaved-over lyric, yet another inspired by his breakup with his girlfriend. (The inside sleeve of *Goodbye and Hello* featured a poem by Beckett that was an actually an acrostic, a form in which the first letters of each line spelled out a phrase: in this case, "I Love Tracy.") Guitar in hand at the dining table, Tim looked at Beckett's lyrics and pushed them away "like unwanted mail," Beckett remembers. After eating, Tim took his guitar, pulled Beckett's poem back over, and out of nowhere began playing a melody that complemented the words. "He just started playing this song, maybe half an hour after Larry got there, and in maybe an hour and a half it was polished," recalls Manda. "It was impressive to see it happen. He and Larry just had this *fit* back then."

The song, which owed a debt to Homer's *The Odyssey* as well, was "Song to the Siren," a forlorn ode to unattainable love that used the call of a mythic siren as a chilling metaphor. Both its music and lyric captured the fatalistic Irish part of Tim's soul.

> *Long afloat on shipless oceans,*
> *I did all my best to smile*
> *'Til your singing eyes and fingers,*
> *Drew me loving to your isle*
> *And you sang, "Sail to me, sail to me*
> *Let me enfold you*
> *Here am, here I am,*
> *Waiting to hold you"*

In late November, not long after it was written, Tim premiered the song at the taping of the final episode of the Monkees's television series, starring the wonderfully prefabricated sitcom rock band notorious for being saddled with outside material and musicians. Tim had befriended wool-hatted Monkee Michael Nesmith at the Troubadour's hoot nights. "This is Tim Buckley," announced Monkee Micky Dolenz. With Beckett standing offstage, holding the lyrics in case his friend forgot them, Tim walked onto the set—an old car with a smashed windshield—and slumped atop the hood. Accompanied only by his crystalline twelve-string, he caressed the melody, his large brown Afro slowly bobbing back and forth as he sang.

Before the taping, Nesmith saw Tim's garb, the de rigueur tan corduroy pants and blue denim shirt, and said, "Hey, you're still wearing the same old clothes."

"Yeah," Tim shot back, "and I'm still singing my own songs."

SIX

My music has never sounded more closer [sic] *to what I am than right now. The last few years have been very insane, no one knows but me. I'm not very good at communicating such things to friends or family.*

—JEFF BUCKLEY, UNSENT LETTER, SPRING 1990

In the fall of 1984, the intersection of Hollywood Boulevard and Highland Avenue didn't look or feel like anyone's future, much less Jeff's. Its flower-power heyday as faded as old denim, this stretch of Hollywood—and the old Sunset Strip one block south—was but a shadow of its former self. Winos hobbled over markers for Milton Berle, B. B. King, and Ray Charles on the Hollywood Walk of Fame, and the long blocks were littered with hookers, gang members, and seedy souvenir shops. The once beguiling Strip had become the geographical equivalent of a decrepit hippie burnout.

Yet for six hundred guitar players and drummers from around the globe, the second-floor space above the Hollywood Wax Museum at Hollywood and Highland was an oasis. Once home to a speakeasy and a bra factory, the 30,000-square-foot quarters were now the home of Musicians Institute, a vocational school for anyone who considered himself or herself a serious musician. With its wooden desks and chipped-tile hallways, MI resembled any other urban school, but at those desks, student guitarists and drummers studied scales and power chords in hopes of becoming the next Eddie Van Halen or Neil Peart, the flashy drummer with Rush. On their way to class every morning, flaxen-haired guitar gods in training could be spotted holding their guitars and practicing licks as they walked down Hollywood Boulevard.

Jeff had heard about Musicians Institute (and its subdivision, the Guitar Institute of Technology) while in high school and told everyone it was his one and only destination. However, potential superstardom did not run cheap. The school charged $4,000 for its one-year course, and by the time Jeff graduated from Loara High School, Mary Guibert was beginning to fall on hard financial times as she went in and out of sundry jobs. In need of money for herself and her two sons, she prematurely broke into a $20,000 fund that had been set up after Tim's death. The money was earmarked for Jeff, but only after he turned nineteen. Once Mary proved to the courts that Jeff needed the cash for his education, he and Mary received it a year early. In a deep irony, the father Jeff had barely met and increasingly resented would be paying his son's way through music school.

With little more than his Ovation guitar and amplifier, Jeff arrived in Hollywood shortly before the start of the fall 1984 school year. His old pal Jason Hamel, who had attended the institute the year before, suggested Jeff rent an apartment at 1810 Cherokee, a housing complex two blocks and a brisk five-minute walk from the school. The drab, brown-brick building looked less like a residence hall than a motel; beyond its black wrought-iron front gate was a swimming pool, around which the apartments were arranged roadside-style. As Hamel recalls, the dorm-like structure was "half MI students and half derelicts," and several buildings nearby were home to Mexican gangs, forcing the students to walk to and from school in packs to ensure they weren't mugged for their instruments.

For Jeff, who was two months shy of eighteen but looked even younger, accommodations and material possessions were not of tantamount concern. At Musicians Institute, he could spend up to seventeen hours a day in classes and rehearsal rooms practicing his guitar chops and taking courses on rhythm guitar, sight reading, and improvisation. Students were also required to form bands, which, by the end of the first week of classes, the exceedingly shy Jeff did, with two transplanted Canadians, drummer Randall Stoll and bass player Tony Marryatt. Bonding over their love of fusion heroes like Allan Holdsworth and Pat Metheny, they rehearsed each morning before class; Stoll also became Jeff's roommate at 1810

Cherokee, splitting the $700 rent. Since neither had much money, it wasn't uncommon for the two to dine on Kool Aid and macaroni and cheese, into which Stoll would toss a tomato for extra flavor.

To his classmates, Jeff was bashful and unflinchingly dedicated to playing guitar. At a building-wide party at the Cherokee complex one night, everyone was having a blast—except for Jeff, who sat alone on a couch in his apartment, wearing headphones and transcribing a Steve Morse guitar piece. For him, there was little time for dating, socializing, or partaking in Hollywood nightlife; life was a routine of trudging with his luggage-style guitar case back and forth between apartment and school. He struck everyone as so earnest and green—literally the Orange County kid in the big city—that friends worried when he ventured out alone in the tawdry neighborhood.

As his guitar skills improved, Jeff continued writing fusion instrumentals, and it wasn't long before he, Stoll, and Marryatt began rehearsing one of them, "Black Tattoo," a Frank Zappa–influenced piece in challenging 7/4 time. Such displays of dexterity, perfect pitch, and prowess—part Tim, part Mary—continually caused the jaws of many of his fellow students to drop. "He came up with this technique where he'd strum chords and stab them with his finger and bring out the harmonics, so it sounded like a keyboard stab," recalls Marryatt, who says Jeff focused more on rhythm parts than on tangled, Van Halen–style guitar showcases, or, for that matter, on singing. During his entire time at Musicians Institute, he never sang a note. Recalls another classmate, guitarist Barrett Tagliarino, "You never had the sense he'd turn out to be a singer or frontman."

For Jeff, that tack was far from accidental. The world of souped-up, amplified jazz known as fusion appealed to him in numerous ways. It was dexterous music that played into his musical strengths, and it was almost entirely instrumental. The combination made for a genre that was worlds removed from his father's; with fusion, Jeff could forge his own path and avoid any comparisons. ("Every time a friend of my mom's who was a failed musician would see me with my guitar, he'd pull me aside and give me 'the talk,'" Jeff said once with a chuckle. "'Nobody cares, the business is awful, you shall be destroyed.'") Not that he had to worry much about comparisons, since hardly any of Jeff's classmates recognized Tim's name. By the mid-'80s, he was all but forgotten, a cult figure from the '60s whose LPs were mostly out of print. "Jeff downplayed it," says Marryatt. "He was like, 'Yeah, my dad was a musician.' But a lot of people told you that." Jeff, in fact, rarely discussed anything about his past, whether it was Tim, Mary, or his nomadic upbringing. "He was so quiet," recalls his friend Tamurlaine Adams, Herb Cohen's daughter. "It drove me crazy because I wanted him to speak and tell me what was inside his head. But it was real hard for him. I'd say. 'Hey, what are you thinking?' But he was so incredibly pensive. I got so frustrated: '*Say* something!' "

On graduation night, September 15, 1985, at the Odyssey in Granada Hills in the San Fernando Valley, Jeff, Stoll, and Marryatt closed the ceremony by playing Weather Report's "Pearl on the Half Shell." Renowned jazz guitarist Joe Pass, who was attending the ceremony, watched Jeff intently and was so impressed that he congratulated the young guitar hotshot and shook his hand. Even then, Jeff couldn't say much; he meekly accepted his praise.

Armed with a vocational certificate from Musicians Institute, the nearly nineteen-year-old Jeff confronted the world on his own for the first time in the fall of 1985. With Marryatt, he relocated to a one-bedroom apartment at 7000 Hawthorn, a three-story building with a red stucco roof in the middle of Hollywood. From the outside, the building looked more amenable than his old haunt. Outside the window of their ground-floor apartment stretched the football field and bleachers of Hollywood High. But early each morning, Jeff and Marryatt would be awakened by school marching bands; late at night, the gunfire of gang warfare rang out from the field. Whenever a bright light shone into their window at night, they knew it was another helicopter scouring the field in search of Crips or Bloods. In the summer, the apartment grew so stuffy Jeff would often take three showers a day to counter the suffocating heat.

As Jeff quickly learned, a certificate from Musicians Institute opened few doors he wanted to walk through. To pay his rent, he took a job as an electrician's assistant at the school while scouring "guitar player wanted" ads in the local press. There was little to do but practice and wait for the occasional gig—which arrived sporadically, including with what he called an "electric jazz outfit" called B# ("for profit mostly," he wrote later). Friends who stopped by his apartment more often than not found him perched with his guitar in his fake-brown-leather practice chair, surrounded by sheet music and tapes and wearing one of a slew of interchangeable pairs of brown corduroy pants, V-neck T-shirts, and sneakers. Whenever Adams would visit to drag him out for a meal, it was always clear from Jeff's "ghostly white" complexion that he hadn't been out much. "All he did was sleep and play guitar," says Adams. "I'd be like, 'You have to *eat* something.' Three days later I'd come back and it looked like he hadn't moved."

Roommates came and went, and so did, for periodic visits, his mother and half-brother Corey. Homeless, Mary had moved back in with her mother in Anaheim for a short while, yet the plan crumbled when they had a clash, and Mary wound up renting rooms with friends. Corey was having his own rough journey. The devilish if lovable tot had turned into a rebellious teenager, wounded by his parents' divorce; he was arrested for hitchhiking and spent three weeks in a juvenile jail. Jeff took in his mother and brother for periodic stays, allowing them to sleep on the floor of his Hawthorn living room.

"He was happy in that he was absorbed with his music," says Adams of that period. "But there was something behind his eyes that was so far away and dark, like a deep pool. The sadness and melancholy were always there."

In June 1987, Jeff made one of his rare returns to Orange County, attending a backyard party at the home of Robin Horry, his friend and former Mahre Bukham bandmate. Everyone was glad to see Jeff, but they were also surprised. The wiry cutup with the spiky hairdo they had known five years earlier had been replaced by a thin, somber, close-cropped twenty-year-old in an oversized T-shirt who sat alone in a corner. During a jam session on the patio, Jeff joined Horry and Hamel for the Rolling Stones's "(I Can't Get No) Satisfaction," but remained stock-still, hardly the animated stage presence he was in Mahre Bukham. No one knew who this Jeff was.

Like so many others in Hollywood, Michael Clouse wanted to break into the music business with a vengeance. Big and hulking, with a dark mane of hair and a boxer's nose, the transplanted thirty-three-year-old New Yorker had set up a studio in Glendale, just north of Hollywood, to record demo tapes for local talents. One summer afternoon in 1988, Clouse was working with R&B singer James Morrison and his band, and, he recalls, "these guys were talking about this young gunslinger they could get to play. I'm thinking I'm going to see some R&B cat come in the door." Instead, into Clouse's studio walked a bony, pasty-faced kid in denim jacket and jeans carrying a guitar. "Disheveled is the word that comes to mind," recalls Clouse. To his surprise—given what he had been expecting—the kid was also white.

Jeff plugged in his electric guitar as Clouse cued up a tape of the track in progress, a smooth R&B number called "Lift Them Up." The song called for "a funky, chicken-grease" guitar part, Clouse says, which is precisely what Jeff played in a few quick passes. Afterward, as the band took a break, Jeff sat down. "Anything else you want?" he asked Clouse. Soon enough, they began talking, and Clouse asked his last name.

"Tim Buckley's kid?" Clouse asked when he heard.

"Yeah," Jeff said, flatly. "You know him?"

Clouse thought it odd that the kid asked him if he hadn't only heard of Tim but actually *knew* him (which Clouse didn't). Although Jeff normally shut down when anyone brought up his father's name, he and the gregarious Clouse began talking. With their shared hunger to break into the business, they realized they could help each other out. For his demo-tape business, Clouse needed a partner who could arrange songs and play instruments while Clouse engineered and mixed the tapes. They formed an informal business—dubbed "the X-Factor," since they aimed to add that something extra—and agreed to split whatever money came in, usually $25 or $50 each for a day or two's work per song.

The fledgling singers who wandered into the Hollywood recording studio that became their home base were a mangy lot desperate for record contracts. For one singer who imagined herself the new Janet Jackson, they concocted "Black Cat Dance," a hard-rock number similar to Jackson's "Black Cat"; for a Tom Waits clone, they devised a delicate, boho-songwriter track with Jeff adding his own white-gospel harmonies. Power ballads, upscale R&B—whatever was called for, Jeff imitated on guitars. In a rare moment of vocal confidence, he even sang one of the demos himself. Called "Snowblind," it was a hard rocker in the then-prevalent hair-metal style, intended for a movie that was never produced. Sounding uncannily like Whitesnake singer David Coverdale, Jeff moaned Clouse's lyric about "sitting here with my head in my hands/It's four o'clock in the morning, girl." Sitting in the studio, his guitar pick often sticking out between his teeth as he worked out an arrangement, Jeff knew it was all hack work, but it was experience and money. Just as important, Clouse had become a combination coworker and father figure, the first in Jeff's life in a decade.

The previous September, Jeff had relocated yet again, this time to a two-bedroom apartment at 3270 Oakshire in a residential Hollywood Hills area, a view of the 101 Freeway up the street. Jeff had by now acquired his first set of wheels, a green 1973 station wagon that made him look even more diminutive when he was behind the wheel. By day, he worked at the Magic Hotel on Franklin Avenue in Hollywood, a low-slung hotel populated by actors, authors, rock bands passing through, and sundry showbiz hopefuls and washouts. Earning $7 an hour, Jeff answered phones, ran the front desk, made reservations, sorted mail, and most of all watched with pensive eyes as the parade of freaks wandered in and out.

At the time, Los Angeles had a jazz scene that was fragmented at best, and most of Jeff's Musicians Institute friends had left town for work elsewhere. Still, Jeff always appeared to be transcribing and composing music, although no one knew what *for*. In the Oakshire apartment, his friend and roommate John Humphrey, a former MI bass teacher ten years Jeff's senior, recalls Jeff "hitting the books every day, and this was after school was *over*." Visiting the apartment one day, another of Jeff's new friends—Carla Azar, a twenty-year-old, red-haired drummer from the South—saw a note in Jeff's familiar over-sized lettering on the refrigerator. "It was literally, 'Eight to eight-thirty A.M., work on string arrangement; eight-thirty to nine, practice guitar exercises,'" she recalls. "His day was literally mapped out like that, that regimented."

Starting in 1987 at his friend James Morrison's home studio, Jeff began putting those ideas onto tape. The result was his first demo, called "White-boy Music" after the name of his song publishing company. Its three tracks—"Aigeedhe," "Promise Ring," and "Gravestone Man"—were fluid if derivative instrumentals, easy-listening homages to the likes of jazz guitarist John Scofield and the fusion side of rock guitar hero Jeff Beck.

Beyond being musically disciplined, Jeff also struck his friends as honest, quiet, sincere, nonjudgmental, and perhaps a little too innocent for his own good. At his Oakshire apartment, he would often lug his guitar amplifier down three flights to the street and then run back up for his guitar, never considering that someone could steal his unprotected amp. No one ever saw him imbibe any alcohol nor take a single drug or smoke a cigarette; if a joint made its way to him at a party, he simply said no. "He was *so* pure and required so little in the sense of what humans need," says Adams. "He was hardly interested in women or sex as a younger person." He had to stay focused on music; it was the only tomorrow he saw for himself.

Concurrent with his work with Clouse, Jeff's musical horizons began to expand. His love affair with fusion was waning, and he had yet to discover a style he could call his own. What *was* clear was his ability to expertly copy any genre he desired, and that eerie proficiency became his meal ticket. With the help of former roommate and bass player Tony Marryatt,

Jeff joined the AKB Band, a reggae combo led by saxophonist Al Kirk. At rehearsals, Jeff amazed the band by breaking into a Jamaican dancehall rap. Before long, he had acquired a nickname—"Scalp Cutta," for his slashing reggae riffs—and was making $50 weekly playing with the band (and their frequent singer, dreadlocked keyboardist Pablove Black) at a ganja-smoke-filled Jamaican club in town. The band landed its most prestigious gig when they backed a wide range of reggae acts, including former Bob Marley singer Judy Mowatt, at the annual Bob Marley Day Celebration concert at the Long Beach Arena.

He also played with his friend John Humphrey's roots-rock band, the Wild Blue Yonder; contributed guitar to funk and R&B demos with another producer; and volunteered for the guitar slot in Group Therapy, another band fronted by a friend from the MI days, singer and guitarist Kathryn Grimm. With Group Therapy, Jeff was thrust into the world of heavy-metal dives strewn up and down West LA, clubs with names like Madame Wong's and FM Station. As the band's long-haired, vest-sporting, metal-dude lead guitarist, he ably cranked out the riffs and solos in hard-rock numbers with titles like "War Between Man and Woman" and "Don't Make Me Beg." Still wary of comparisons to his father, Jeff refused to sing anything but the occasional background vocal.

Not that anyone minded; Group Therapy's main attraction was Grimm, a sharp blond who self-consciously took the stage in skin-tight spandex and teased-to-the-hilt hair. (Jeff's aunt, Peggy Hagberg, attended one gig and was "a little shocked" by Grimm's outfit.) It wasn't uncommon for headbangers in the crowd to grope Grimm when she walked to the lip of the stage, or salute Jeff with devil's-horn hand gestures—the metalhead's tribute—whenever he took a solo. The generally acknowledged highlight of a Group Therapy set was "Hot Date with Buzz," an ode to masturbation that ended with Grimm singing to a vibrator (and Jeff using the same pleasure device for his slide-guitar solo). "He's one of those guys who seems like the guitar belongs in his hands," wrote a local music magazine, *Music Connection*, also praising Jeff's "unnaturally energetic" musicianship.

Although Jeff never saw Group Therapy as his future—throughout 1989, he rarely told friends about their gigs—the music was in keeping with yet another shift in his evolution: Out went fusion, in came rock. He began reimmersing himself in childhood favorites like Led Zeppelin as well as Jane's Addiction, Los Angeles's leading alternative band, and Keith Richards's *Talk Is Cheap* album. In a recording studio one day, Jeff announced he "was going to make an album that would make people forget about *Led Zeppelin II*," Clouse recalls with a chuckle. "And I thought, 'How fucking arrogant is *that?*'" Reflecting his discovery of punk, Jeff showed up for one Group Therapy show with a semi-Mohawk, half the side of his head shaved to the scalp. Through Azar, he began to discover the funky likes of James Brown, to whom Jeff had never been exposed to as a suburban kid in Orange County. That same insatiable hunger for music also applied to literature. Once, Azar suggested Jeff read Arthur Rimbaud's *A Season in Hell;* later, he told her he had not only read it but everything else by, and about, the nineteenth-century French poet.

To Azar, Jeff was an outrageous, perpetual cutup and unnervingly talented musician who could pick up a new instrument—a trombone, a harmonica—and begin playing it as if he had been practicing for years. She saw little of the melancholy side others glimpsed, and she also glimpsed another part of Jeff rarely revealed. In her apartment one day, she overheard Jeff singing and playing guitar in her living room. It was the first time she had heard his voice, and both it and the melody were, she thought, beautiful. She asked him what song it was, and he simply replied, "It's a cover." Later she discovered it was called "I Never Asked to Be Your Mountain." When she learned it was written by his father and that that parent was Tim Buckley, a fact Jeff had never shared with her, Azar began to realize how complex and enigmatic her friend was.

Between his day job at the Magic Hotel, his alternating band gigs, and his studio work with Clouse, Jeff's schedule was full yet barely fulfilling. As musically confident as he could be, he struck his friends as amorphous, fuzzy around the edges—a photographic negative still developing. That lack of self-identity manifested itself in his music. Was he a jazz-fusion guitarist? A reggae sideman? A producer? A skinhead punk? A studly metal rocker? The son of a semi-famous rock star? A *singer?*

Before Jeff could answer those questions himself, his career in Los Angeles began to dry up. He and Marryatt bailed out of the AKB Band after gunfire broke out in the middle of one of their shows at a reggae club. Group Therapy was working steadily, but for little money and, says bassist and main songwriter Mark Frere, at "every toilet in West Hollywood." The Sunset Strip experience itself was not proving to be as beneficial as Jeff hoped. In the wake of the success of Strip metal bad boys like Guns N' Roses and Mötley Crüe, the area had reinvented itself as leather-

and-studs nirvana, a gathering place for drooling-for-success hard-rock bands in leather pants and scarves. (Their lusty female fans were dressed in even more provocative outfits.) It added up to a nonstop party—so much so that the LA County Sheriff's Department patrolled the Strip on weekends—but there were so many bands (estimates began at five hundred) that in 1989, owners and bookers at many of the Strip's metal and hard rock clubs instituted an audacious policy known as pay-to-play. To ensure enough customers attended their shows and made it worthwhile for the venues, bands had to literally buy a set amount of tickets for each of their own shows (usually between 50 and 120, adding up to an out-of-pocket expense of as much as $1,000 per show per band) and then convince friends and family to buy the tickets. The musicians would only make money once the door sales surpassed the deposit.

In such an atmosphere, Los Angeles began to feel stultifying to Jeff, a creative and inspirational dead end. After six years in Hollywood, he had little to show beyond his fusion demo and a range of stage and studio experience that didn't point in any particular direction. He always appeared to be broke, even with his job at the Magic Hotel, and his green station wagon was always in need of repairs. He began to talk about leaving town to get, as Grimm says, "some life experiences" outside of California.

Before he went anywhere, there was one important matter that demanded his attention. Enigma Records, an independent record label, had unearthed a previously unreleased Tim Buckley concert tape, recorded in London twenty-two years earlier. Before the album was scheduled to arrive in stores that summer—titled *Dream Letter: Live in London 1968*—Jeff (by way of Judy) asked to hear it, and one late afternoon in February 1990, he visited the company's offices in Culver City. David Baker and Thane Tierney, two Enigma executives, greeted the low-key, reserved twenty-three-year-old, and the three men chatted in Baker's office, which overlooked Holy Cross Cemetery.

The tape—a dazzling, pristinely recorded performance Baker and Tierney had excavated in a storage closet of Tim's manager, Herb Cohen—ran two hours, so Tierney suggested they chat as it rolled. Fiddling with the buttons on his flannel shirt, Jeff made small talk with the men as the music filled the office. Every so often, he raised a finger, a signal for the conversation to stop while he listened more closely. "There was a glissando Tim did in one song," Tierney recalls, "and Jeff's eyes got like saucers and he said, '*I* do that!'" It was, Baker recalls, like watching a family member flip through a photo album for the first time. When the tape arrived at a song called

"Dream Letter," Jeff asked them, "Do you know that's a song he wrote about me?" The men sensed an immense curiosity; any flashes of anger or resentment on Jeff's part toward his father were withheld.

They also sensed a sadness. "This was the only way he was going to learn about his dad, through these visual or oral images left behind," says Baker. When the tape ended, they talked for a short while longer before Jeff hugged the men and thanked them, "as if we had done him this great honor by permitting him to hear this," Baker says. There was a noticeable tremor in his voice as he said good-bye.

The precise reason for Jeff's first trek to New York in the brisk early months of 1990 remains shrouded in mystery. Some of his Los Angeles acquaintances say the trip resulted from a brief tour with reggae rapper Shinehead, with whom Jeff most likely connected through his ties with the AKB Band. Others say he was spurred to leave California by his frustration with the music scene, an unrequited love affair, or the simple lure of Manhattan, whose musical diversity and energy he had long heard about through friends like Group Therapy bass player Mark Frere. "Can you really take the subway to Harlem?" Jeff began asking Clouse one day. And could one then proceed from there to the legendary R&B and soul venue the Apollo Theater? And where was that club called the Bottom Line? Where do you eat? How do you get around? Do you even *need* a car?

In a sense, Jeff couldn't have picked a worse time to visit New York. The city was in the grip of a period of high crime and low morale; six murders were being committed per day, adding up to the highest homicide rate of any American city. Coming down after the Wall Street boom of the previous decade, Manhattan felt grimmer and grimier than ever; somewhere, the city had taken a wrong turn, and no one seemed to be able to grab the wheel.

Nonetheless, Jeff rid himself of his apartment and station wagon and flew to New York in February. "It was," he later told the Philadelphia *City Paper*, "the most extreme and successful self-rescue operation I'd ever implemented. Otherwise I was going to rot from the inside." After briefly living in Harlem with a drummer he had met years earlier at Musicians Institute, he moved in with a platonic friend, actress Brooke Smith, whom he had met during his Magic Hotel days when she was in California filming a role in *The Silence of the Lambs*. Smith remembered Jeff vividly—the nice kid who worked behind the front desk and drove her around Hollywood, blasting Beethoven's Ninth Symphony and shouting to her over the din that the piece was at heart a hardcore punk song. Smith had a small two-bedroom place on West 89th Street on Manhattan's Upper West Side and invited Jeff to take the other room and split her $1,000-a-month rent. He immediately took her up on the offer, sleeping on a bare mattress on the floor and dragging along his collection of Led Zeppelin, Jimi Hendrix, Neil Young, Jethro Tull, and Queen albums.

Often sporting his black Hendrix T-shirt, Jeff immediately took to New York, hauling his guitar into the subway to play for change and roaming the streets. "I talked to him right after he got to New York and he was loving it," recalls his MI friend Tony Marryatt. "He said it was just like a Woody Allen movie." To support himself, he took a series of day jobs, from working at an answering service (for actors like F. Murray Abraham and Denzel Washington) to landing a job at a Banana Republic around the corner from Smith's apartment. ("Drag," he wrote to Grimm. "But I do it well. They always think that 'Maybe Jeff should . . . well, lose the earring, don't you think? You don't wear a belt? Oh my!'") At night, he and Smith would smoke pot—somewhere along the line he had been introduced to it—and talk about the problem of finding true love. Other nights Jeff would roam the streets by himself. At 1 A.M. one night in April, he found himself at a deli on West 57th Street, down the street from Carnegie Hall, eating a slice of Black Forest cake and watching as the wealthy and weary walked past him outside. "So, here is New York . . . the filth and the filthy rich rubbin' elbows while the in-betweens gradually take sides," he wrote in a letter to a friend. Meanwhile, Cat Stevens's "Wild World" played in the background, "All the fucking lyrics hitting home like I don't want them to," he wrote.

Given his father's history in New York, it was inevitable a few ghosts would haunt him. Once he stopped into "some bodega-type record shop" and saw *Dream Letter,* the Tim concert album he had previewed two months before. Whether out of sorrow or pain, he immediately walked out. Killing time at bookstores, he would look up his father in rock history books. "I'm always testing him," he wrote in a letter to Tim's friend Larry Beckett. "Born, wrote, sang, changed, changed, grew, grew, grew, ignored, rejected, revolution over evolution, gotta move, don't have much time, critics, rejected, dead . . . revered. You fucks."

"I've tried to really believe it, that he really loved me," he wrote to an inquisitive fan of Tim's that summer. "I question that. He longed to see me, I believe that. He regretted not seeing me, yes. But he was too afraid for a very long time, 'just a young kid going down his own road,' right, I understand, but I don't get it. It seems so overromanticized, all of the accounts of his actions . . . How does a baby keep you from making records? . . . I don't know—he just didn't want to be stuck with Mary, so typical, no frills, no big deal, I totally understand. But, love me? I don't know what that means."

As for New York's music scene, Jeff wrote to Beckett that it was "just in a flux . . . But you can see it's in transition, and that's *good*, 'cause I'm feeling something inside me kicking into place. The timing could be excellent. That's why I moved to N.Y. in the first place, so I'd at least be in the right town when I finally 'hatched.' "

Indeed, Jeff threw himself into hardcore punk and reggae bands, and through his Harlem roommate, he discovered *qawwali*, the devotional music of India and Pakistan. In particular, he became obsessed with its greatest proponent, a serene fortysomething Buddah named Nusrat Fateh Ali Khan. Built around group chants with interweaving, trancelike voices, the accompanying rhythms tapped out by tablas and harmoniums, *qawwali* was unlike anything Jeff had experienced. Both secular and overtly religious, it was music as mystical, elevating experience, designed to lift both *qawwal* and listener into what one critic called "mystical love, even divine ecstasy—the central experience of Sufism," a mystical movement within Islam. As Jeff wrote in his liner notes to a later Nusrat compilation, "My roommate and I stood there, blasting it in his room. . . . [Nusrat's] every enunciation went straight into me. . . . I remember my senses fully froze in order to feel melody after melody crash upon each other in waves of improvisation. . . . I felt a rush of adrenaline in my chest, like I was on the edge of a cliff, wondering when I would jump and how well the ocean would catch me." The concept of total immersion in melody, wordless chant, and improvisation resonated profoundly within Jeff. It validated the concept of music as everything, a pure, ululating form of expression unconnected to anything crass or trendy.

Despite such inspiring input, Jeff's New York "hatching period" didn't yield the results he had hoped. Potential auditions for guitar slots in hardcore bands like Murphy's Law and Agnostic Front didn't pan out. "Imagine me with a band of hulkin' skinhead 30 year old stage-divin doodz who could probably chew me up for a breakfast with beer," he wrote to Grimm during a lunch break at Banana Republic. In a fit of despair, he added: "I got to work in about five minutes. I never talk to anyone because if I try to make a joke about anything, they just go, 'O-KAY, ummm . . . whatever you say!' Like I'm a bloody maniac . . . When will I stop folding shirts? When will I leave my loser job and stop being a loser jobwad?" Equally depressing was news that a planned audition as guitarist for former Prince band members Wendy and Lisa—with whom his LA friend Carla Azar served as drummer—fell through.

Then one day, he returned to his apartment in tears. At Banana Republic, a woman's blouse was reported missing, and Jeff had been blamed. According to what he told Smith and other friends, he was interrogated and then told he either had to sign a release admitting to the crime or the store would call the police. Reluctantly he put his signature on the admission. (Banana Republic no longer retains records of employees from that period.) He told Smith he hadn't done it—*why would he want a woman's blouse?*, he told her—and, still upset, called friends and family in California and repeated the story, tearfully telling them he would never do such a thing.

The incident only reinforced Jeff's feeling that day jobs had to become a thing of the past. From now on, it would be music or nothing.

Rescue came from the least likely of sources: Herb Cohen, Tim's former manager. Despite his friendship with Cohen's daughter Tamurlaine and his childhood get-togethers with Cohen, Jeff maintained a healthy distance from the man who, depending on the source, had been either Tim's greatest benefactor or obstacle. "Herb has kept tabs on me ever since I could pick up a guitar—5 or 6," Jeff wrote to Beckett from New York. "'Is he writing anything, Mary?' 'So, you got a band together yet? Why don't you just get some guys, teach them to play, be the leader, get a tape to me and uuuuh . . . see what happens?' I don't want to hear that shit. Other artists would *die* to hear those words from Herb Cohen, but *he's* basically asking *me* to carry the bloody torch a few more miles for him. $$$. There *is no torch*." Jeff later referred to Cohen's occasional contact with him as "the quarterly, gravy-train-watch-tower phone call."

One of those calls, though, amounted to something tantalizing. Cohen had seen Jeff perform with Group Therapy in Los Angeles and offered to help Jeff record a demo tape of his own material. For all his apprehension—and even the concerns of Cohen's daughter Tamurlaine, who had a rocky relationship with her father ("I was concerned for Scott, because of the past between Tim and my dad," she recalls)—Jeff felt the powerful tug of a world from which he had been shut out for five years. Whether he found an association with Cohen appetizing or not, Jeff knew the offer was the only way he could afford to have his music recorded. "I'm going to use him," he told Azar. "At least I'm recording this stuff. At least I'll get a tape out of it."

In September, he returned to the city he had grown to loathe. Having given up his apartment, he crashed at the Hollywood apartment of his friends (and former band mates) Kathryn Grimm and Mark Frere. When he wasn't sleeping on the tattered beige couch in their living room, he was using it as a workstation to prepare for his recording debut. He put the finishing touches on "Eternal Life," a scorched-earth raver he had begun writing in New York. He would later say the song was inspired by thoughts "about having a kid"; Michael Clouse, though, recalls Jeff saying it was about Tim:

> *Eternal life is now on my trail*
> *Got my red glitter coffin man, just need one last nail . . .*
> *And as your fantasies are broken in two*
> *Did you really think this bloody road would pave the way for*
>   *you?*
> *You better turn around and blow your kiss hello to life eternal*

On the couch, Jeff also wrote a new song, "Unforgiven," a forlorn farewell to a lover that, according to sources, was at least partly inspired by a relationship he had had in Los Angeles with an older German woman, possibly a nurse.

In early September, at the San Fernando Valley studio Eurosound, Jeff put *his* voice, singing *his* songs, onto tape for the first time in his twenty-three years. Using a drum machine and playing all the guitar and bass parts himself, he recorded four songs. "Eternal Life" became a brawny wall of sound, with a sleek guitar solo that hinted at his Musicians Institute period. (Adhering to his now-standard work method, he finished the lyrics in a cab on the way to the studio.) "Radio," a grinding, puerile rant against the music business, reflected his love of hardcore, while "Strawberry Street," infused with Dylanesque surrealism, was propelled by metallic, rafter-shaking riffs that recalled his Group Therapy days. "Unforgiven," a midtempo ballad with a sweet, wistful edge and slide guitar, was altogether different. Throughout the tape, his voice was tentative, but its range, from wistful lilt to full-on rage, was clear. The four songs were a summation of everywhere he'd been and everywhere he could conceivably go.

He called it *The Babylon Dungeon Sessions,* in honor of the dank studio in which it was recorded, and slapped a photo of Jodie Foster on the cover of the tape box. Once he and Clouse finished mixing it, they jumped into Clouse's 1971 Buick Skylark convertible and, top down and two female friends along for the ride, sped through the Hollywood Hills, the tape at full volume. One of the women was intended to be Jeff's date, but he didn't seem to notice anyone else in the car. "He got this look on his face and was squinting his eyes and you knew he was listening real hard to certain things," recalls Clouse. "And occasionally something would happen and he'd make a comment about it or make a gesture with his hands, like he didn't like something." Jeff then began playing the tape for his friends, who were dumbstruck by its quality and by the singing voice they had never heard. "I was totally freaked," says Humphrey. "All of a sudden here's these fully realized songs with vocals, and he played all the parts. I knew right then that whatever he wants is going to happen."

Precisely when it would happen was still very much a question mark. While Jeff waited for the record industry's verdict on the *Babylon Dungeon* tape, he lapsed into a vagabondish existence. For three months, he continued to stay with Frere and Grimm, who returned home one night to find their poverty-stricken friend frying baloney in a pan for dinner; the several hundred dollars his grandmother had given him had been spent on CDs. He was, by then, deep into British pop—not surprisingly, the sulkiest and most sensitive of it, bands like the Cocteau Twins, the Smiths, and the Cure.

During this period, Azar introduced him to her boyfriend, Chris Dowd, the dreadlocked, gregarious, bearlike keyboardist with the insanely energetic LA punk-ska-reggae band Fishbone. To Dowd, Jeff was "a big lump of clay"; the kid clearly loved music, but he rarely *said* anything, so much so that it was months before Dowd discovered Jeff was a musician. Still, the two men—who were born the same year but two months apart—shared a manic sense of humor and a demonic love of funny voices, and they became close allies. As self-effacing as Jeff could be, Dowd also saw his new friend as "more like Robin Williams playing the guitar." At restaurants, they would purposefully annoy customers with loud banter and jokes, or hang out in Dowd's loft apartment on South Lake Street doing demented imitations:

Michael McDonald singing Jimi Hendrix, Elvis singing the Doors. One night, Jeff, Dowd, and Azar took Ecstasy, and Jeff, Dowd recalls, turned "super mushy," repeatedly telling them he loved them.

Having spent time as a child in Arkansas, Dowd would tell Jeff about the TV commercials he had seen in the South that warned residents about "not getting in lakes because they have these pockets of air at the bottom that'll just suck you under," says Dowd. "I used to tell him about shit like that all the time." Jeff would listen to those and other of Dowd's stories, but they would invariably revert to cracking each other up with sick jokes and oddball imitations.

Like almost everyone else from Jeff's life in Los Angeles, neither Azar nor Dowd had any idea their friend's father was a musician from the distant rock and roll past. Jeff never mentioned it; the specter of his parent was too hurtful, and for similar reasons, Jeff exhibited little interest in connecting with Tim's side of the family. "None of the Buckleys ever kept in touch, including Tim with the one exception," he wrote to a Tim devotee during his initial foray to New York. "Now, I can't say that I sincerely care where they are. They never did for me, apparently. I don't see how they would benefit from a meeting with me now, nor I with them. Could you imagine? What in the world would we say?"

In fact, Jeff wasn't being entirely truthful. By 1990, he had already been in touch with and spent time with Tim's widow, Judy, and her twenty-seven-year-old son, Taylor, whom Tim had adopted. In 1987, Judy and her third husband, former rock road manager Llew Llewellyn, had tracked Jeff down in order to send him royalty checks from Tim's music. With that connection, Jeff reconnected with Judy Buckley for the first time since 1975. Recounting the meeting later, he wrote to a friend: "Judy freaked on my eyes: 'Aren't you lucky?' (I could've wretched [sic] when I heard stuff like that.) She thought they looked like his, but I think it was the Buckley big-uni-brow hunched over them that fooled her into that statement. Judy said Tim shaved his down the center. I don't."

Nonetheless, Jeff was intrigued by these mysterious Buckleys he had never known, and it made him realize how little he knew about his biological father's life and history. Given Mary's ambivalence toward Tim, those topics were rarely brought up during Jeff's childhood. Hungry for more information, Jeff began his search for Tim. He obtained addresses and phone numbers of his father's associates in and around Los Angeles, from friends to Tim's sister Kathleen, a teacher in the area. The oddest fluke came when he tracked down Tim's mother; in the waiting room of his chiropractor, he overheard her name and "begged the doctor," he later said, for her number. Elaine Buckley was warm and welcoming to the grandson she hadn't seen in over a decade, and took him to a jazz festival and laid out the story of her husband and his sad postwar life.

Around Halloween 1989, Jeff visited with Tim's longtime guitarist, Lee Underwood. "Basically I did the talking," says Underwood. "Jeff let me know virtually nothing about himself or his feelings toward Tim." Underwood felt Jeff's "physical resemblance and gestures were uncannily like Tim's," although Jeff, writing in his journal years later, felt otherwise: "I must've seemed pretty bizarre: black-death rock-loser, very mohawked, stick legged wierdo [sic] at his door . . . asking another stranger about his dead father. He mentioned 'Tim's good looks,' 'Tim's charm with the ladies,' 'Tim's vocal technique—epiphany,' 'Tim said, always said, he'd never live to see thirty,' 'Tim liked booze and reds,' 'Tim pushed the boundaries.'" Jeff referred to Underwood's talk as "the mantra," and added, "I just can't be a disciple to my own father."

He said more when he reunited with Dan Gordon, Tim's pal from junior high. Seeing Jeff show up at his West LA office was, Gordon recalls, "like seeing Tim walking through the door." Gordon, by then a successful screenwriter, found his own head reeling. "His posture was the same," he recalls of Jeff. "He would sit in the same positions Tim would sit in—a slouch with elegance, like a yoga move. The hand gestures when he spoke were the same. He carried himself like Tim did. I told him that, and he didn't like hearing it."

For the better part of a day, Jeff grilled Gordon about his father's life. He asked basic biographical questions and why Tim had never called nor visited. Gordon didn't know what to say other than to agree that Tim had been self-centered and that his actions were unforgivable. They talked about Jeff's bitterness, and to placate it, Gordon suggested Jeff delve into Tim's recordings as a way of communing with his father. "Yeah," Jeff shot back, "maybe we'll be together in the [record store] bins." Jeff was also annoyed when he heard he and his father shared a love of French chanteuse Edith Piaf, whom Jeff had discovered while watching public television at age thirteen.

Through Kathleen Buckley, Jeff also met Daniella Sapriel, a close friend of Tim's from his Venice days. Jeff interrogated Sapriel as well, and they bonded immediately. In need of a new place to stay—he couldn't continue crashing on Grimm's couch—Jeff accepted Sapriel's invitation to use an extra room in the house in West LA, where the divorced lawyer was living with her young daughter Nicole. Jeff took to the white cottage with the blue shutters, the tree in the backyard, and Sapriel's lovable lug of a dog, Bear. At night, he read Nicole bedtime stories and played board games with her. He appeared to have found both a home and a sense of stability.

Still, the basic facts about his father didn't appear to entirely satisfy him. The same appetite Jeff brought to the arts—absorbing a musician's or writer's body of work—was applied to his search for Tim. When Judy Buckley gave him tickets to a concert by the Cocteau Twins, Jeff told a friend he kissed Judy on the mouth—partly, he said, out of appreciation, and partly to feel *exactly* what Tim had seen in this woman. Sapriel, meanwhile, remembered she had Tim's old peacoat in her garage and decided his son should inherit it. She had the decaying garment cleaned, relined, and rebuttoned, and, still in its plastic cover, gave it to Jeff. When he put it on, she felt a chill. If anything, it seemed to fit Jeff better than it had his father, since Jeff was a little taller and more broad-shouldered than Tim. Even in warm Los Angeles, Jeff shuffled around Sapriel's house wrapped in a quilt, so the thick, heavy peacoat became a favorite piece of apparel.

That fall, Sapriel had one more gift for Jeff. In November, she threw him a twenty-fourth birthday party at her house, and unaware of the frictions that still existed between the Buckley and Guibert households, invited a wide, contentious cast of characters. The event became a gathering of all the factions of Jeff's world: members of the Guibert family (Anna, Mary, and Mary's sister Peggy); Tim's mother Elaine and his sister Kathleen; Mary's second husband, Ron Moorhead; Tim's widow Judy and her son Taylor; and a smattering of Jeff's LA friends. Although Mary recalls the event as "a total party, nothing but positive vibes," complete with cake, champagne, and gifts, another participant calls it a "David Lynch, Warhol, and Fellini movie all in one." Elaine Buckley and Anna Guibert exchanged cordial hellos but didn't speak to each other for the rest of the day; feeling ostracized, Judy Buckley sat alone in the backyard. When she did speak with Jeff, one topic of discussion was Tim's royalties; she and Llewellyn felt they had not received their fair share and were considering a lawsuit against Herb Cohen. Taylor Buckley showed up with a tape of another newly unearthed live recording by Tim, this time from the John Peel radio show in London in 1968, and played it.

To his friend Kathryn Grimm, who also attended the bash, Jeff "seemed comfortable," and the underlying tensions between the family members appeared to have been put aside. Jeff himself never talked much about the party, and one can only imagine what went through his mind as he navigated his way through this jungle of players and emotions. Some were simply happy to reconnect with Tim's son, while others looked to him as the answer to their prayers—a new Tim to whom they could transfer any lingering, unresolved feelings. The entire group would never again assemble under the same roof.

Even as he attempted to sort out the good, bad, and ugly in his family's story, there remained the matter of his own music and career. Nothing was happening with the *Babylon Dungeon Sessions* tape (Cohen claims he never sent it around to any labels, and that it was merely a first step for Jeff), and Jeff's lack of a band meant he couldn't perform. Reluctantly, he resumed working with Clouse on those dreary demo tapes submitted by would-be stars. Through his former roommate John Humphrey, Jeff was introduced to Carole King, in whose band Humphrey played bass. In January 1991, Jeff and King spent a few days writing together, emerging with one finished (but never recorded) song. Yet as with so many of his creative pursuits, little life-changing emerged from it, and once again, Los Angeles began to feel like a dead end. The name of his song-publishing company changed from the bemused Whiteboy Music to Death Machine Music.

Then, early in 1991, the phone rang at Sapriel's house. A woman was calling long-distance, from New York, to tell Jeff about an upcoming concert she was coordinating. It was a tribute to his father, and she asked if he would like to attend.

SEVEN

About his songs: "My new songs aren't dazzling; it's not 2 minutes and
50 seconds of rock 'em, sock 'em . . . I guess it's pretty demanding." . . .
About his music: "Mess up my body, man, but don't mess up my music."
About his direction: "There's going to be a change."

—ELEKTRA ADVERTISEMENT FOR HAPPY SAD, APRIL 1969

Slouching on a fire escape overlooking Bleecker Street, Tim glanced
around and caustically observed the panhandlers and tourists strolling by
four flights below. During his frequent trips to New York that began in the
summer of 1967, he continued to rent rooms at funky Greenwich Village
hotels like the Albert or the equally downscale Earle. But according to one
of Tim's new friends, a local political-science major named John King,
Tim didn't enjoy the crowds or the scenes, so he and Jane would crash at
King's apartment at 88 Bleecker, near Broadway. Bright, witty, and caustic,
Tim reminded King of nothing less than Eddie Haskell, the wisenheimer-
next-door on the sitcom *Leave It to Beaver.*

King's fire-escape view only afforded Tim a limited panorama of
downtown-Manhattan tenement buildings and bakeries, but the city must
have nonetheless seemed ready for the taking. During that summer and
into the winter months, one celebrity or another was in the audience of his
club gigs: George Harrison and Beatles manager Brian Epstein at the Cafe

Au Go Go in August, Andy Warhol at another Bleecker Street club, the Garrick Theater, in November. Of the latter performance, *Billboard* praised Tim's "dazzling display of folk-rock-blues," while the *New York Times* noted that he "appears to have inherited Bob Dylan's old tailor, barber, and ability to stun his listeners." The show also included a rare rendition of his epic "Goodbye and Hello," whose complexity and original orchestral arrangement normally prevented its live performance.

On the other side of the country, Mick Jagger popped in to see Tim at the Troubadour in Los Angeles—and, according to Jane, chatted so loudly during his set that Jane had to shush him. At the same club, another rising star, a husky-voiced Texas blues mama named Janis Joplin, tried to pick Tim up at the bar. Tim also made acquaintances with the Doors's Jim Morrison after they ran into each other at the Whisky-A-Go-Go. "One day Tim was drunk, and Morrison drove by on acid," recalls Larry Beckett, "and they looked at each other and laughed because they each recognized that the other was on the drug of the *other* guy's choice."

In New York that fall, Al Kooper, the former Dylan sideman and Blues Project singer-keyboardist, was selecting material for his new horn-rock band, Blood, Sweat & Tears, which also included Tim's buddy Jim Fielder on bass. Fielder had taken Kooper to see Tim at the Troubadour (where Tim was "amazing," Kooper recalls), and Kooper, an industry tastemaker at the time, became a fan of Tim's two albums. When Blood, Sweat & Tears guitarist Steve Katz needed a number to sing, Kooper suggested "Morning Glory," since Katz's silken folk voice seemed a good match with the melody. The song was arranged in what Kooper calls a "Curtis Mayfield-meets-Bob Dylan style—I wanted the horns to sound like Curtis Mayfield and the rhythm section to be very Dylany."

When the remake was released the following year on the band's first album, *Child Is Father to the Man,* it became the best-known cover of one of Tim's songs, although Tim's opinion of it remains a mystery, to both Tim's acquaintances and Blood, Sweat & Tears. Neither Beckett nor Fielder remembers their friend commenting on it at all; says Beckett, "We didn't think it was good enough to bother reacting *to.*" Still, it isn't hard to imagine Tim's reaction to the remake's brassy opening fanfare and conventional folk-rock groove, both of which obliterated the delicacy of the original recording. Nonetheless, the song's inclusion on the album, which became an underground FM-rock favorite soon after its release, bestowed further credibility upon Tim and his music.

The teenybopper fan magazines began to take notice of Tim as well. "Tim Buckley is a happening thing," went an item in the gossip column of *Flip*. "His hair is frizzier than Micky [Dolenz]'s, his songs better than Dylan's, his future fabulously exciting. And Tim's only 20!" In a celebrity gift guide, *16* printed the sizes of his shirt, hat, sweater, shoes, and socks, along with his birthday and favorite colors and gifts ("baubles, bangles, beads and bells"). The *Los Angeles Free Press,* in reviewing a show at the Troubadour, referred to Tim's fans as "a great mass of underage girls." Backstage at these shows, Jane, who accompanied Tim on his road trips, took on the job of warding off that seemingly endless mass, the wide-eyed girls bearing flowers and beads for their idol. "He'd say, 'Peaches, get them out of here,'" she recalls. "And I was such a bitch. I'd go to the door and say, 'Sorry, fuck *off,*' and slam the door. It was awful. Sometimes he'd say, 'All *right,* let 'em in.' And one or two would come in and go gaga and talk in soft voices, and he'd play right into it."

One matter the willowy readers of *Flip* and *16* didn't read about was Tim's first drug bust. On the blustery late afternoon of December 22, Tim and his entourage—Jane, Lee Underwood, Carter Collins, and their new, hulking roadie Barry Schultz, nicknamed "Bear"—had barely checked into the Robert Morris Hotel in Philadelphia when there was a pounding on Tim and Jane's door. When Jane asked who was there, she heard someone say something about management. But upon opening the door, she realized their guests were actually the police, who had received a tip from an informant that marijuana was to be found in the room. Finding two plastic baggies with a total of twenty grams of pot ("prepared for smoking," said the police report), the cops arrested both Tim and Jane. Guns drawn, they then went next door to Underwood and Collins's room, where they found two miniature whiskey bottles (in a shaving kit on a nightstand) filled with "ground green weed." After Tim signed a confession that none of the pot belonged to his "wife" Jane, he, Collins, and Underwood were arrested on possession of narcotics.

Behind bars, Tim was belittled for his long hair (it probably didn't help that, according to one news report, he was wearing "gold tight pants with flower designs at the cuffs"), but a phone call to Herb Cohen's office resulted in the $300 bail and a release. The band arrived two hours late to Tim's show that night at the Trauma (referred to in the media as "a downtown hippie club"), but the audience, apparently aware of the arrest, gave him a standing ovation before he sang a note. At two trials the following April and August, at which Tim wore one of Cohen's suits to look more presentable, Tim was found not guilty, while the charges against Underwood and Collins were dropped on a technicality: The police hadn't bothered to ask if the two pot-filled whiskey bottles had belonged to them.

Despite such press, and his blossoming reputation in the music business, *Goodbye and Hello* did not significantly alter Tim's life or career. Commercially, the album fared better than its predecessor and even made the *Billboard* charts, entering at number 192 the week of November 4, 1967, and slinking up three weeks later to 171. (An accompanying star designated it as one of the week's LPs that had the "greatest proportionate upward progress.") But there the album stalled, selling a total of approximately fifty thousand copies, and "Morning Glory," released as a 45 at year's end, garnered minimal airplay and didn't make *Billboard*'s singles chart. Despite its quality, Tim's slowly enlarging following, and Elektra's promotional push, *Goodbye and Hello* was not the career-making smash everyone had expected.

Part of the problem lay with media exposure. "I knew it was never going to go to AM radio," says Elektra promo man Steve Harris, referring to the songs' lengths and intricacies. "And without AM radio at the time, you weren't going to sell a lot of records. It was wishful thinking." Two potential outlets for Tim—freeform FM radio and the rock press—were only beginning to become forces; the latter amounted to one underground pamphlet, *Crawdaddy!*, and an upstart Bay Area magazine called *Rolling Stone*.

Then again, media coverage and airplay would not have necessarily made a difference. Much to Harris's puzzlement, Tim wasn't like other Elektra acts who pestered Harris about which radio stations were or weren't playing his records and which interviews he was set up to do. Harris wasn't alone in his nagging feeling that Elektra's rising young star was not particularly interested in rising. "*Goodbye and Hello* was intended to be a breakthrough album," says publicist Danny Fields. "But it also takes the energy and will of the artist. And I just had a feeling the will of the artist was not there. He didn't want to be glamorous or famous. It always seemed *I* was more demoralized about it than he was." In New York, Tim was more inclined to spend time with Fields and his friends at Fields's apartment, watching television and listening to jazz, than he was in schmoozing or plotting career strategies. "We didn't pay attention to that junk," says Beckett. "We just wanted to make records."

These and other concerns were topics of discussion during Tim's chilling-out periods at John King's Bleecker Street apartment. "He wanted to play his *own* music," King recalls, "and they wanted him to do more commercial stuff. I would say, 'Do the commercial stuff, make enough money, get famous enough, and then do what you want. If you have enough money, you have the power.' "

Tim didn't answer. Huddled on the fire escape, he would shrug in that indecisive way of his. He was still figuring it all out.

John Miller, a compact, bearded University of Michigan music student, had a weekly routine: Every Friday night, he crammed his standup bass into his car and drove over to the Canterbury House, one of many coffee-houses in the Ann Arbor area. The club was a magnet for big-name folk and blues acts who passed through town, and for both enjoyment and experience, Miller would pop in with his bass and sit in with whomever was playing. One Friday in the spring of 1968, he noticed a frizzy-haired kid with a massive guitar accompanied by a guitarist and a black conga player, all of them weaving a complex pattern during a soundcheck on the cramped platform stage. The scenario was crying out for a bass player, so Miller joined in.

"With Janis Ian or Odetta, you knew what it was, but Tim's stuff was really something special," Miller recalls of that jam. "It was refreshing and startling in its new sound." He had never heard of this Tim Buckley person, but he was struck by the kid's "big, open spirit" and accepted an invitation to join them for the gig and then to become a full-time band member.

With his love of jazz and improvisational music, Miller was the right bass player at the right time for Tim. Tim's musical passions had already begun to encompass everything from the Brazilian jazz guitar of Laurindo Almeida to the minimalist avant-classical compositions of Erik Satie, thanks largely to the encouragement of Underwood, who had an active disdain for rock and pop. Clearly, though, jazz had blossomed into Tim's primary musical love: not just longtime favorite Miles Davis but also pianists Bill Evans and Cecil Taylor and woodwind player Roland Kirk. While many of his peers were digesting albums like Jimi Hendrix's *Axis: Bold as Love* or Dylan's abrupt return to austere folk and country on *John Wesley Harding,* Tim more often engaged in extended conversations with his band members about sleepy-voiced jazz-blues singer-pianist Mose Allison.

Miller soon introduced Tim to one of Miller's New York music compadres, a twenty-four-year-old vibraphone player named David Friedman. The day after he met Tim, the Juilliard-trained Friedman joined the band for a show at the Fillmore East on May 17. (This was Tim's second gig at pro-moter Bill Graham's new downtown theater; he played the hall's opening night on March 8, opening for Janis Joplin and Big Brother and the Holding Company.) The influence of Miller and Friedman on Tim's music was felt immediately. During rehearsals and soundchecks, it wasn't uncommon for the two musicians to warm up with a bass-and-vibes rendition of Miles Davis's "All Blues." During one such jam, Tim, who was already familiar with the composition and its wafting chord pattern, overheard them and announced he wanted to use it as the basis for a song of his own. Swiping the song's first eight bars and writing a lyric to complement it, Tim called it "Strange Feelin'."

"I saw a guy responding to jazz harmonies, jazz rhythms, and impro-visatory interpretations of his songs that he couldn't get enough of," Miller says. "With a lot of people from deep folk backgrounds, you throw in a sev-enth or a ninth chord and you're out of there. With Tim, it was just the oppo-site. He would say, 'Oh, baby, *yeah*—gimme more of that.' "

With sales of his two albums middling at best, the road became Tim's steadiest source of income during the summer and fall of 1968. He and his new, expanded lineup traveled to Europe for the first time in the spring, playing the Royal Festival Hall in London as the opening act for the Incredible String Band, and then returned to the States for a series of festi-vals, club shows, and opening-act stints for, among others, the Velvet Underground (at San Francisco's Avalon Ballroom) and the Paul Butter-field Blues Band (in New York City's Central Park). The music they con-jured along the way grew increasingly distinctive, as the band effortlessly eased into an unheard-of blend of folk, blues, and jazz. Tim began dotting his vocal delivery with exhortative wails and shrieks, while, standing stu-diously behind him, Miller played elegantly buttery bass lines and Fried-man sprinkled the songs with the melodic dust of his vibes. Underwood's electric guitar playing began to lose its folk fingerpicking style in favor of sweet phrasing more like that of jazz guitarist Jim Hall.

As Tim began encouraging his players to take extended improvised solos, the songs, even structured ones from *Goodbye and Hello,* often dou-bled in length. "He was like Miles Davis," Friedman recalls, "in that he'd make comments when you were soloing: 'Yeah!' 'C'mon, do something else—you *played* that!' He would motivate and encourage you during a solo. At heart, he was an improviser." Visually, the band was equally strik-ing. Sweat-drenched and bouncing on his toes, Tim often took the stage in moccasin boots and fringe jacket, while Miller adopted an Edwardian-suit look. Surrounded by twin conga drums and a battery of cowbells, tambourines, and percussive devices, the bespectacled, earringed Collins was the most flamboyant; with his brightly colored African robes, sandals, and knit caps, he resembled an African-American beatnik professor.

Those congas, as well as Friedman's forty-four-bar vibes and Miller's standup bass, made for often grueling road trips. With assistance from only roadie Schultz, the band would often haul their own equipment from airplane to rented station wagon to hotel. But for Tim, the grind was worth it. With this music and this lineup, he had found not only a forum for his multi-octave voice but an overall musical voice as well. "He was a jazz singer, he really was," Friedman says. "He didn't want to do a tune the same way twice. That's why he liked working with jazz musicians—we were on his wavelength."

To Friedman, Tim was also a "very poetic" presence, but the vibraphone player also sensed within his boss a developing antihero, "a James Dean guy." On the road, in restaurants or city streets, it wasn't uncommon for Tim to be heckled for his mushroom of hair, with the beefier Schultz or Collins often rushing to his aid. For his part, Tim could provoke back: Friends recall him egging on redneck patrons in bars or, in one case, yelling "faggot!" to a group of men who looked gay (and then hiding behind Underwood to hide his identity).

Tim's confrontational side equally began to rear its stubborn, Irish-rooted head in his dealings with the decidedly unhip world of mainstream show business. Increasingly, something within Tim—perhaps an antiauthority complex that sprang from his father's army background—couldn't resist biting any hand that wanted to feed him. On June 3, he and the band appeared on comedian Steve Allen's syndicated variety show, but it became "a disaster" (as Tim told *Changes* magazine) after Allen dropped food on the floor and Tim began eating it. (The previous December, Tim, along with Woody Allen, had also landed a coveted spot on one of his few favorite TV shows, *The Tonight Show*. But after guest host Alan King made several cracks about the size of Tim's hair, Tim retorted that King was "a piece of cardboard.") On July 28, Tim performed at the Newport Jazz and Folk Festival as part of a lineup that included Judy Collins, Taj Mahal, Pete Seeger, and Arlo Guthrie. According to John King, who drove his friend to the show, Tim told the audience during his set that the reason they were hearing so many Woody Guthrie songs throughout the festival was because Guthrie's management wanted to make more money on royalties. The peace-and-love crowd was instantly deflated.

Tim's trips to Europe during the spring and fall were dotted with equally defiant exploits. Clive Selwood, the head of Elektra's London office, was given the task of escorting Tim to sundry media-related appointments. Selwood managed to land Tim a spot on a popular variety show hosted by British personality Julie Felix, and the two men arrived at the television studio to rehearse what was intended to be a three-minute number. Instead, Tim launched into an extended folk-blues jam that lasted nearly an hour, Tim sweating and wailing all the while. When it was done, he turned to the show's producer and said, "Okay?" and strolled out into the afternoon sun. "It was a nice way of saying, 'Screw you, I don't need you, this is what I do,'" Selwood recalls. "And he did it supremely well." Tim never returned that day; there would be no well-placed promotional TV appearance.

During the fall trip, there wasn't enough money for airplane or hotels for John Miller and Carter Collins, so Tim recruited bassist Danny Thompson, whose supple playing in the British folk band Pentangle had earned him a well-deserved reputation as a premiere musician. Thompson accompanied Tim on several jaunts, including a performance on a live British TV broadcast. The entire band assembled at the studio, Tim in his moccasin boots ("with very little sole left in them," Thompson recalls), and rehearsed the designated song. Afterward, the director turned to Tim and said, "That was lovely, Tim. Now, if we can just do it again . . ."

"Why?" Tim responded, blankly.

The director explained that the crew needed to know exactly how long the song would be and which camera angles would be used; it would, after all, be performed live on the air, and the lineup needed to be airtight. Dutifully, Tim and his musicians rehearsed the song again, after which yet *another* take was requested. "By this time, Tim was really fed up with it," Thompson recalls. Nonetheless, the song was performed once more and clocked in at just over four minutes.

After a lunch break, the band reassembled in the studio for their on-air performance. When their time came, the director pointed to Tim, who simply said, "Huh?" To get Tim to start playing, the director furiously began playing air guitar—*anything* to communicate to Tim that it was time to start singing. Instead, Tim turned to the band and directed them to play an entirely different song, which ran two minutes longer—a major problem for a carefully planned live broadcast that had been mapped out to within a second of its life. Thompson glanced around and, he recalls, "saw everyone, all these technical people, running around."

Herb Cohen, Tim's manager, was also beginning to take notice of the noncommercial drift of his client's music. Cohen loved *Goodbye and Hello* and couldn't understand why Tim was suddenly trying to be a scat singer. In London on April 2, Cohen accompanied Tim to a radio performance on disc jockey John Peel's show. After dutifully performing favorites like "Morning Glory," Tim, Underwood, and Collins launched into a medley of "Hallucinations" and a new, unrecorded song called "Troubadour" that itself shifted time signatures and mood, from despondent to jubilant. The performance logged in at close to eleven minutes, after which Cohen turned to Selwood in the control booth and remarked, "You know, I don't normally care much for this kind of shit. But as shit goes, that's pretty good shit." What Cohen didn't realize was that the control-booth microphone was turned on, and Tim overheard his remark. "Just tell Herbie to shut up and turn the thing on," he jabbed back. (Tim's part of the exchange was heard on the 1991 EP *The Peel Sessions*, later reissued as *Once I Was*.)

Yet once he took the stage, most of Tim's bratty streak fell by the wayside, and what emerged was music with the delicate grace of a ballerina. Headlining at the Queen Elizabeth Hall in London on October 7, with Thompson replacing the stranded-in-America John Miller, the band gave an especially magnificent performance. Underwood's darting guitar and Friedman's chiming vibes danced around each other and the melodies, and Tim sounded emotionally committed to every note he sang. The set list was in itself more eclectic than that of any of Tim's peers: He tipped his hat to his Bell Gardens folk days with the traditional "Wayfarin' Stranger," warbled an utterly unironic "Hi Lili, Hi Lo" from the movie *Lili*, and sang like a man possessed on an unaccompanied rendition of "Pleasant Street," which then led into a snippet of the Supremes' "You Keep Me Hangin' On." (According to Dan Gordon, the latter was actually inspired by Vanilla Fudge's slow-motion cover, a U.S. hit that summer.) A recording of this magnificent performance was eventually released over two decades later, as *Dream Letter: Live in London 1968*. (Due to a misreading of the British method of writing out dates—day first, then month—the day of the concert was listed incorrectly in the credits as July 10.)

Although Tim was technically touring to promote *Goodbye and Hello*—

which, according to Selwood, sold a respectable ten thousand copies in the United Kingdom—he played only five of its songs that evening; his first album was completely ignored. In Tim's mind, *Goodbye and Hello* was already a distant memory, and it was time to move on.

Although Tim's music was entering a new, fertile period on the road, the demands of touring and traveling were beginning to eat away at his world. Just before Friedman joined the band, Lee Underwood was gone. A drinking problem had caught up with him, and Tim dismissed his guitarist of two years.

At home, Tim and Jane were still complementing each other. In conversation and body language, Tim always seemed to be floating somewhere in the clouds (especially when he was driving, which concerned his friends), and Jane's no-nonsense qualities helped ground him. She cooked dinner, wrote out the lyrics to his songs for his publishers, and trimmed his ever-uncontrollable locks. Although they weren't married, she used the name "Jane Buckley" on her driver's license. In the middle of 1968, they moved into a new home, this time in the remote community of Malibu. Built into the beachside cliffs, the single-floor house at 19550 Pacific Coast Highway jutted out over the ocean with the help of wooden stilts. Rickety wooden stairs led from the street to its main floor, but once Tim and Jane navigated their way down, the blue Pacific and a private beach spread out before them. Tim loved to listen to the waves crash against the window; it was, a friend says, "a healing place."

When she was on tour with him, Jane continued to act as Tim's part-time bodyguard. "I was a bitch," she says, "but he liked that about me. Maybe it gave him a feeling of security." But when she wasn't around, Tim easily strayed. After each show in a different city, Collins would glance around and see ornately wrapped gift boxes littering the stage floor. Tim could be seen taking the gifts back to his hotel room, and Collins says Tim would "pick up the phone and call someone if it sounded right." With his waifish, nurture-me looks, Tim continued to be an irresistible magnet for women and had, in Collins's words, "*jillions* of ladies on the road. It was just allowed back then."

Jane wasn't blind to Tim's wanderings. He often joked about having "a Rosie in every port," she recalls. "He didn't have to remember their names— he called them all 'Rosie.'" But the joke became reality when she learned Tim had given her gonorrhea. In the doctor's office, Tim cried and said he was sorry, and Jane thought his indiscretions were over, that this sort of incident would never happen again.

It was optimistic at best. As the '60s progressed, sexual mores were evolving even faster than rock and roll, and the postwar generation of which Tim was a part saw itself as harbingers of a new era of free-living sexual and social liberation. "We had rejected the old roles of men and women and we were trying out new territory," says Manda Bradlyn. "It was *so* easy—and so safe—to get sexually involved with people." Between Tim's dalliances and Jane's desire to forge a life of her own (which included a return to college), tensions between the couple began to mount. Although she ingested acid and smoked pot as did most of Tim's tightly knit group of friends, the more traditional Jane had little tolerance for, or interest in, partner swapping. "It was uncool to express jealousy or to even put a stake in the ground for monogamy," she says. "There was free love and nobody owns anybody and don't be jealous. You couldn't even talk about it." At dinner with Tim and his friends at the Tin Angel in New York, she recalls a woman entering the restaurant, and that Tim "slid his arm around her like a man does when he knows the woman intimately. I knew he'd slept with her." Jane stormed out, Tim following behind her apologetically.

To exacerbate matters, Tim's flirtations weren't limited to the road. During their stay in Santa Monica, Manda quickly fell in love with her roommate Tim. "He wasn't explicitly propositional," she remembers, "but he'd sidle up to you and lay his head on your shoulder or rub up against you and say sympathetic things. He was so tender you'd melt. He'd make you feel like you were really special to him." While driving with the two women, it wasn't uncommon for Tim to stroke Manda while he was talking to Jane, who, needless to say, would be less than amused by Tim's actions.

When confronted, though, Tim would always feign innocence. "He could excite people musically, sexually, and romantically," says Manda, "and then he wouldn't know what to do with this power he had over people. It would scare him. He'd say, '*I* didn't do that. *I* don't know what you're talking about.'" Starting with Mary, this element of Tim's personality was becoming a pattern: He was nothing but the innocent victim of another woman's wiles. Although he never seemed to articulate his feelings for her, Tim would sing to Manda late at night, which didn't help the situation. Eventually Jane asked her old friend to move out.

Pressures to be faithful—or, in a sense, to *not* be—were not the only ones Tim felt encroaching on him in the late months of 1968. The music industry demanded at least two LPs of new material a year, and Cohen and Elektra were getting itchy for a new album now that *Goodbye and Hello* was a year old. Not that Tim hadn't tried: In March, an early attempt at recording had taken place at Mayfair Studio in Manhattan, what Underwood calls "a cold, sleazy room built of concrete." They recorded a batch of new songs, but, Underwood says, "Nothing felt quite right, and none of us knew why. We decided the New York scene wasn't for us." Only one song, a gentle caress called "Sing a Song for You," was even remotely finished. Further sessions took place in the summer, this time at TTG Studios in Hollywood. But even with the expanded lineup of Underwood, Friedman, Miller, and Collins, the tapings yielded mostly early drafts of songs.

Throughout this period, Jane maintains Tim was under pressure from Elektra and Cohen: "They were both pretty much saying, 'Your stuff's not going to sell, you're not going to get on the radio, you're not going to make it if you don't do these certain things.' And he would be like, '*I'm* not doing that. That's not what I am. That's not my music.' They weren't threatening him, but the feeling was, 'You better do this because if you don't sell records, we'll drop you.' He would have liked to have sold more records and been more widely known, but he wouldn't have taken one *step* in that direction." At Elektra's New York offices, the idea of writing an explicitly commercial song would be broached at meetings, but Tim would mostly stare into space, as if he couldn't even begin to grasp what was being asked of him.

Another seismic shift occurred that fall: Tim was beginning to write by himself. According to Jane, tension between Tim and Larry Beckett began to increase over authorship of the lyrics. Tim's reasons for wanting to pen his own words were multiple. Never the most verbal when it came to his feelings, he needed an outlet for his tangled emotions, and his experience writing the lyrics to "I Never Asked to Be Your Mountain" and "Pleasant Street" encouraged that process. Underwood, meanwhile, grew to increasingly criticize Beckett's contributions and encouraged Tim to write lyrics himself. "Tim finally realized and recognized that he didn't need or want the limitations of Beckett's intellectually academic and emotionally superficial perspective," maintains Underwood. To others, it was clear that the intellectually curious, non-college-educated Tim was moving from one well-read intellectual (Beckett) to another (Underwood). Whatever the reasons, Tim informed Beckett that he planned to write alone from now on. The point became moot when Beckett was drafted that fall.

As Tim grappled with music business politics and changes in his personal life, Elektra's David Anderle continued to act as a laid-back mediator between Tim and the label. Yet the carefree troubadour Anderle had met a year before appeared to be vanishing behind a haze of tension and distrust. "I saw Tim cracking, big-time," Anderle says. "The last conversation I had with him, at his house, he said, 'I'm going to make my own music, I don't give a shit what anybody says, I'm not gonna fuckin' do *this*, I'm not gonna fuckin' do *that*, there's nothing Herbie can do, I'm gonna go do my jazz thing, fuck *them*.' Somebody was laying some shit on him." In late 1968, Anderle was fired because, as Elektra's Jac Holzman wrote in his memoir *Follow the Music*, Anderle "so identified now with the artists that his company perspective was lost."

Before Beckett was thrown into army life, Tim wrote to his close friend and collaborator during one of his trips to New York, updating him on the next album. "The music is happier or at least more positive and coherent a bit more—ha ha," Tim wrote. "I've got too many ideas for it. . . . It'll be different, somehow more musical." He signed it, "Love, Timmy the fading superstar."

As 1968 drew to a close, Tim's new musical direction was finally zooming into focus. Having temporarily conquered his drinking problem, Lee Underwood rejoined the band, and with the gestation period over, everyone settled down to nail the third album. Given the positive results of *Goodbye and Hello*, Jerry Yester was again recruited for the producer's chair, and brought with him Zal Yanovsky, the former Lovin' Spoonful guitarist who had become a production partner with Yester. (Yester had briefly replaced Yanovsky in the Spoonful the year before.) In late fall, band and producers assembled at Elektra Sound Recorders, the company's new Hollywood complex, and went to work.

There was trouble from the start. According to Collins, Tim had no interest in making a blatant sequel to *Goodbye and Hello*. "He was not able to be in command or in artistic control of that album," Collins says. "I never heard him say he was disappointed by it, and the tunes were beautiful, but he wanted to go somewhere else." Using the new songs Tim and the band had been road-testing for the better part of the year, the plan was emphasize an uninhibited spontaneity over studio polish. "It was," says Miller, "more of a jazz album concept: 'Let's do it again, but with a different solo.' "

For Yester, the Tim who entered the Elektra studio was even more confident than the kid who had driven up his Laurel Canyon driveway the year before. On *Goodbye and Hello*, the producer had felt like a collaborative partner; this time, though, he instantly felt relegated to a secondary role. "He had very little to say to me," Yester says. "It was obvious to me that he wasn't interested in me producing. We turned the mikes on and they played. There was no conversation."

"Tim was a renegade," admits Friedman. "No one was really happy with what he was doing, but he was doing what he wanted to do, so of course it was Tim against everybody. And if we were in his band, we were with *him*." Adds Underwood: "Yester was great producing Pat Boone [Yester was also working on a rock-oriented album for the former bobby-sox idol], but he had no business producing *Happy Sad*. Tim was into taking risks, improvising, doing everything he could to capture the beauty of spontaneously created music. Yester was a conventional producer, well-equipped to work with well-rehearsed artists who didn't try things and make mistakes."

As Tim and the band worked out the material, complete with extended guitar and vibe solos that reflected Tim's newfound jazz orientation, Yester grew increasingly irritated. "The attitude was so different from *Goodbye and Hello*," he says. "It was so cliquey. 'You guys behind the glass, you don't understand what an *artist* is going through.' Zal and I were 'the suits.' I thought, 'Who are you snot-nosed fucks out there?' It was arrogant and undeservedly so. If they were backing Miles or Mingus, I could take the arrogance—but they weren't. . . . Tim had a lot to offer besides being a great jazz artist, which he wanted to be. He had a great compositional gift and a great singing voice. He was *more* than scat singer."

In this environment, it was a wonder anything was accomplished, yet the album was wrapped in less than a week of nightly sessions. "The music flowed better, the atmosphere in the studio felt better, and everything more or less clicked into place," recalls Underwood. One of the few major problems occurred after the musicians played what Tim considered the best take of "Love from Room 109 at the Islander (On Pacific Coast Highway)," a three-part folk-classical suite. (Although the Islander was a local hotel, Jane maintains the reference was to Tim's nickname for their house.) A melding of two different songs ("Danang" and "Ashbury Park") from the summer sessions, the song ran over ten minutes. According to Yester, engineer Bruce Botnick had made only one mistake: He had forgotten to turn on the Dolby noise-reduction switch, resulting in a layer of hiss throughout the track. When Tim learned what had happened, his voice, according to Yester, "went up *three octaves* to the point where only bats could hear him. There could be no other performance of that song—that was it. He was shrieking at Botnick."

To salvage the take, Yester devised a plan: Given the title of the song, why not blend in actual oceanic effects to drown out the noise? Thus, microphones were set up under each side of Tim's Pacific Coast Highway home, and the incoming tide was recorded in full stereo and then dubbed onto the flawed take to hide the hiss. "That," says Yester, "was about as creative as I got on the album."

Yester may have felt frustrated and squandered, but *Happy Sad,* as the album was called, is an exquisite, unified work that unfurls gently and subtly, like a carpet slowly rolling out. Most pop albums of the time opened with a grabby, punchy number. Indicative of where it was headed, *Happy Sad* begins instead with "Strange Feelin'," the Miles Davis–inspired vamp that glides over seven languid minutes; during Underwood's darting guitar solo, Tim yells out "yeah!" and "oh yeah!" The lyrics, particularly moments like "When you're home all alone/Don't you need somebody to talk your troubles to?" seem to refer to his increasingly strained relationship with Jane. The remaining songs average seven minutes each and range from the joyous twelve-string clarion call of "Buzzin' Fly" to the somber, baroque "Dream Letter," Tim's ode to the son he rarely saw, sung with an aching fragility:

> *Oh, is he a soldier, or is he a dreamer?*
> *Is he mama's little man?*
> *Does he help you when he can?*
> *Oh, does he ask about me?*

On that and other songs, Tim sings in a lower, deeper register; the Irish tenor was purposefully relegated to history.

The casual mood the band aimed for—and Yester deplored—is in full glory on "Gypsy Woman," a twelve-minute vamp that, while featuring a sharp bass marimba solo by Friedman, overstays its welcome by several minutes. (Miraculously, Friedman was able to record the song despite suffering a 102-degree fever that day.) The beachfront sound effects lend "Love from Room 109 at the Islander (On Pacific Coast Highway)" an even dreamier quality, the equivalent of lying on a beach at sunset and watching the day fade away. The song's lyrics read like Tim's intimate musings to his female friends, which, in fact, they partly were. A portion of the second section—"how can my loving find the rhythm and the time of you/unless you sing your songs to me?"—was lifted from a love letter written to Tim by Manda Bradlyn after she had moved out of his house. (Bradlyn, however, feels the song overall is a composite of several relationships.)

With its wistful undertow, its feeling of floating on air as hope hangs gingerly nearby, the song—and *Happy Sad* in general—remains a perfect distillation of Tim. As he had earlier promised Larry Beckett, the record was indeed distinct. Manda Bradlyn recalls being particularly startled hearing "Dream Letter," Tim's lament to Jeff: "I hadn't realized he had feelings—that he'd ever given it that much thought."

If Tim's friends or family read the interviews he did before the album was released, they would have been equally taken aback. Not wanting to reveal much about his traumatic past—or, perhaps, simply indulging in the fool-the-media hijinks Bob Dylan had instigated years before—Tim gave straight-faced interviews filled with the type of fanciful stories he had been telling since childhood. In the most notable case, he told the *East Village Eye*'s Jerry Hopkins he had hung out as a teen with roughnecks who "were always getting busted for rumbles and maybe stealing things." He claimed that during high school he traveled "the beer-bar circuit" from Arizona to Georgia, and "it was during these early ramblings," wrote Hopkins, "that he found and shed a wife." Even Hopkins was dubious about parts of Tim's saga. Writing of the Bell Gardens days, the journalist noted, "He'd been gigging occasionally with country and western bands when they came to town, groups like Princess Ramona and the Cherokee Riders (he says)." In much later interviews, Tim would often deny even having grown up at all in the shadow of Disneyland, saying he only discovered Orange County when he ventured south of Los Angeles to resell pawnshop guitars to wealthy suburban kids.

Tim was less enigmatic talking to the *New York Times,* admitting to the existence of his son ("Yeah, Jeffrey. Great kid"), his troubled father ("a brilliant guy, but he never should have gotten married, never should have been in the war—he was in the paratroops, heavy stuff . . . I just learned he's in prison in Chattanooga"), and the music business ("They want to control you—they don't want you to be yourself"). Most tellingly, he talked about what he had gleaned from a course in college philosophy Jane was taking. "The cat, Socrates, starts spewing truth like anybody would, because you gotta be honest," he said. "And the people kill him. Ha. I don't know if I'm being pretentious, but I can see what happens . . . I don't know what to do about that."

Comments like those betrayed Tim's developing sense of embattlement, even martyrdom. Yet when it came to altering that mindset, few around him knew what to do about that, either.

EIGHT

I got my first electric guitar at 13. Left home for L.A. at 17, spent some time in a so-called music school, went on the road with some reggae acts. Escaped to NYC in '90 for about 7 months; got into hardcore and Robert Johnson. Right now my band is almost complete. I'm showing up at club jams around town trying out new songs. My life is now complete and utter chaos.

—JEFF BUCKLEY, "GREETINGS FROM TIM BUCKLEY" PROGRAM

No one working on the "Greetings from Tim Buckley" tribute concert at St. Ann's knew there was a son, and that included Janine Nichols, the church's salt-and-pepper-haired program director. All Nichols knew was that the arts center at St. Ann's, a combination sanctuary and progressive private school tucked next to the brownstones of Brooklyn Heights, was preparing its annual "Arts at St. Ann's" concerts. It was hard to find a more varied live-music series in New York; past concerts (all of which took place in the church itself) ranged from the premiere of Lou Reed and John Cale's song-cycle tribute to Andy Warhol, *Songs for Drella,* to shows by Marianne Faithfull and bluesman Robert "Jr." Lockwood. One of the planned shows for the 1990–91 season was a salute to '60s cult figure Tim Buckley, to be helmed by New York producer and hipster-around-town

Hal Willner and to feature renditions of Tim's songs by local musicians and singers.

Early on, one of Nichols's tasks was to find a publicity photo of Tim for use in advertisements and a concert program, and she tracked down the name and number of Tim's old manager, Herb Cohen. In his cut-to-the-chase manner, Cohen said he not only had photographs but news: "You know he has a kid?" And, he continued, the child was *more* talented than his father. Only in need of an eight-by-ten glossy, Nichols didn't think much of the information; offspring of '60s rock stars had begun sprouting up on the fringes of the music business, and most of them inherited their parents' looks but rarely their talent. Nonetheless, she jotted down the kid's name and number; the least they could do was invite him to the concert as a courtesy. As for allowing him to perform, they would have to wait and see.

Nichols dialed the Los Angeles number, and the first thing she noticed about the voice on the other end of the line was how tiny it sounded. After introducing herself, Nichols told Jeff why she was calling. He immediately sounded hesitant. Yes, he said, he had heard of Willner, but he'd never sung his father's music in public and had spent only a very limited amount of time with Tim. Nichols could tell he was very conflicted, and the faint voice asked for time to think it over.

Given Jeff's all-consuming passion for music and late-night television, it was natural he would be familiar with Willner's work. The son of an Auschwitz survivor, the Philadelphia-born Willner was raised on jazz and '60s underground FM rock. After moving to New York in 1974 and attending New York University, he entered the music business, paying his dues as an assistant to producer Joel Dorn (known for his work with a wide cast of characters from Mose Allison to Roberta Flack). Although he came to New York "a jazz snob," in his words, Willner's outlook changed when he saw Talking Heads perform at CBGB. In 1980, he became the music coordinator for *Saturday Night Live,* selecting offbeat background music for sketches, and in the mid-'80s, he began producing a series of all-star tribute albums on everyone from Kurt Weill to the tunesmiths of the Walt Disney movies. The albums were creative, idiosyncratic, and playful—much like Willner himself, whose bemused-stoner persona always made him seem both mischievous and half-awake.

For *Night Music,* his late-night television music series, Willner had been mulling over a tribute to Tim Buckley. As a teenager, he had seen Tim perform several times, including an early '70s appearance at a Philadelphia club that Willner calls "one of the greatest shows I've seen in my life." In the last few years, Tim's status as overlooked, underappreciated avant-folk-jazz pioneer had vaulted upward thanks to a slew of CD reissues of his work, as well as the unearthed *Dream Letter* concert album Jeff had previewed in Los Angeles and which had garnered overwhelmingly positive reviews upon its release the previous summer. Willner mentioned the tribute idea to his friend Nichols, a former *SNL* coworker. To her and St. Ann's artistic director Susan Feldman, it sounded like an ideal addition to the "Arts at St. Ann's" series. Still, Willner, known equally for his multitude of ideas and his fondness for pot, needed motivation, so Nichols and Feldman went so far as to list the concert in their season calendars as an incentive. With that, Willner had no choice but to put on the show. A date—April 26, 1991—was firmed up, and Willner went to work contacting musicians and making tape copies of old Tim LPs for anyone unfamiliar with the music.

Three thousand miles away, encamped in Daniella Sapriel's house, Jeff mulled over the unexpected invitation. He still had ambivalent feelings about the paternal figure he barely recalled, and he had long studiously avoided any public connection to him. Yet something about the idea intrigued him. He called Mary in Orange County and informed her about the call. In turn, she asked him about the people organizing the event, and he told her it seemed legitimate and was to take place in a church. "I said, 'Well, what's your purpose? What do you want to get out of it?' " Mary recalls. "And he said, 'I always missed not going to the funeral.' I said, 'There you go—there's your reason, you'll pay tribute to your father.' " At the same time, she warned him to stay away from anyone who approached him about becoming "the next Tim Buckley." "You don't want to do that," she told her son.

By the time Nichols called back, about a month before the concert, Jeff had warmed to the idea; it helped that St. Ann's would cover his $338 roundtrip airfare. She told him they wouldn't be able to pay him if he performed; even the name musicians who were participating would only receive between $200 and $500. But neither Feldman nor Nichols were sold on the kid's talent. They had listened to the demo tape he had sent and found it noisy. Still, Jeff agreed to come.

Willner was in his apartment at 10th Street and Avenue B in the East Village when the phone rang. "It's Jeff," said the voice. The producer had no idea who "Jeff" was, but soon made the connection. They talked about the concert ("he knew he had to be there—there was no question about it," Willner recalls) and the proposed set list. As Willner rattled off each song title, Jeff confidently said he knew how to play each one; in particular he seemed proud of his ability to sing "Sefronia—The King's Chain." Willner didn't know what to make of this puzzling and self-assured person on the other end of the line, but warily agreed to let him perform out of obligation.

At Chris Dowd's loft in downtown Los Angeles, Jeff announced his return to New York. "I'm going to go do this tribute for my dad," he softly declared. Dowd was thrown for a loop: What did he mean, a tribute to his *dad*? Who was his dad? A famous doctor or something? What was Jeff *talking* about?

"Well," Jeff said, "my dad was, like, this folksinger guy Tim Buckley." Dowd was stunned. By this point, he had known Jeff for nearly a year, and his friend had never before mentioned this important piece of information. "It's something I don't really like to talk about at all," Jeff replied when asked. Later, Azar told Dowd not to mention it again; it was a touchy subject.

By the time United Airlines flight 8 arrived at John F. Kennedy International Airport at 8:28 P.M. on Saturday, April 20, the night had turned unseasonably cool, and a light drizzle pelted the city. Although the concert was six days away, Jeff was so eager to participate that he went directly to Brooklyn. Clutching a small bag and a guitar and wearing Tim's peacoat, he arrived at the church on Montague Street, pulled open a side-entrance door, and stepped inside.

If Jeff was nervous before he arrived, he must have been doubly so when he entered. The Church of St. Ann and the Holy Trinity was a subtly imposing presence alongside the diners and small businesses on Brooklyn Heights's main thoroughfare. Inside, the Episcopal church dwarfed the Anaheim chapel Jeff had seen as a child. Built in 1855, the church was conceived in the gothic-revival style. Stained glass windows— the first made in America—surrounded the wood pews, while six chandeliers dangled from its sixty-foot ceiling.

Standing near the elevated stage that had been erected in front of the altar, Willner had no idea what Tim Buckley's son looked like, but he stopped wondering when in walked a kid with long, lanky hair and an earring in his left ear. It was, Willner recalls, "the kind of thing you see in your life only a few times." The sight was so spiritual that he expected to hear the sound of a heavenly choir—"*aahhhhh!*"—accompanying the sight. "You must be Jeff," he said by way of introduction.

Onstage, veteran punk Richard Hell was growling a woozy-jaunty version of Tim's ordinarily delicate "Moulin Rouge"; Jeff seemed perplexed but intrigued. Willner introduced him to the other musicians, and Jeff took a seat in one of the back pews, resting his head on his hands and soaking in the hectic rehearsals. Feldman was working in her narrow, file-cabinet-crammed office on the second floor when Nichols came upstairs and remarked of the new arrival, "Well, this younger Buckley is quite a looker." One of their concerns was finding him a place to stay, since he seemed to have very little money. Those concerns instantly faded. Recalls Feldman, "We had a feeling that this was someone women would want to take care of."

Eventually Jeff mingled with the musicians, who began looking to him for approval when arrangements were discussed. Still, Willner—who, like the St. Ann's overseers, was praying the kid could carry at least a portion of a tune—wanted a safety valve, and for that he called upon his friend Gary Lucas.

At thirty-eight, Lucas had developed an imposing reputation as a guitarist's guitarist on the New York scene. A Yale graduate, Lucas cut his musical teeth with Captain Beefheart's Magic Band in the early '80s. After Beefheart retired from music to devote himself to painting, Lucas took to supporting himself as a copywriter with Columbia Records. But he continued refining his guitar playing and, both as a solo act and with his loose-knit band Gods and Monsters, had become known as an agile musician whose fusion of lickety-riff fingerpicking and effects pedals felt like twenty-first-century folk music. His curly Afro parted in the middle by a receding hairline, Lucas looked like the stoner brother of comedian Steven Wright.

Willner asked Lucas to accompany Tim's son, and Lucas agreed to check out the situation. When they were introduced, Jeff immediately recognized Lucas's name from the credits of the Beefheart albums Jeff had discovered and grown to love in California; Lucas, in turn, sensed a creative live wire. "He totally got my attention," Lucas recalls. "He looked like he was about to jump out of his skin."

The following day, Jeff visited Lucas's West Village apartment after spending the previous night in his old Harlem place. With a view of the Hudson River outside the window, Jeff sat on a couch as Lucas began playing a drony, raga-style loop for Tim's "Sefronia—The King's Chain." Jeff began singing, and Lucas gasped to himself. Not only was the kid able to reproduce Tim's voice note for note, but he seemed to have his own formidable range. Afterward, Lucas picked out a back-porch blues lick, and Jeff improvised a lyric; the result was their first collaboration, "Bluebird Blues."

Everyone was charmed and instantly protective of the pale, sweet kid from California. Willner took him out for meals; Feldman and Nichols, who had both lost younger brothers, saw in Jeff memories of their siblings. But for Lucas, Jeff's arrival felt particularly heaven-sent. For the last few years, the guitarist had been plagued with personnel problems in Gods and Monsters (named after a line in *The Bride of Frankenstein:* "To a new world of gods and monsters!"). Lucas had a reputation for zigzagging virtuosity, but he wasn't a frontman or much of a singer, and he had developed an unfortunate habit of recruiting singers who eventually deserted him. In Jeff, he saw the answer to his dreams of mainstream success. After rehearsing, he took Jeff for food at the White Horse Tavern and told him about the band, and Jeff seemed interested.

Jeff encountered an even more intriguing personality during rehearsals at St. Ann's on April 24. Trolling around backstage, he caught sight of a delicate-looking woman with pearly skin, an impish smile, and straight, shoulder-length black hair cut in Caesar-like bangs, who was setting up a buffet for the musicians. "I want to meet her," he said to Feldman, making a beeline for her.

Rebecca Moore looked over and saw an exceedingly thin kid, his face hidden by a waterfall of hair, making a miniature mountain of a sandwich and singing "If I Had a Hammer" with dirty lyrics. She had no idea what to make of him, but he certainly seemed, well, unusual.

With Jeff's assistance, "Greetings from Tim Buckley" began on a whimsical note. Jeff had presented Willner with a tape of Tim reciting, of all things, a public-service radio ad for the U.S. Army Reserve. "This is Tim Buckley," boomed the familiar voice throughout the church. "You know, the Army reserve pays in a lot of ways . . . You get the chance to further your present skills and learn new ones, a chance that can really pay off in your civilian career." (As startling as the ad seems, given Tim's antiauthority impulses, Herb Cohen says it was a standard promotional chore musicians did at the time to help them land on the radio—"that kind of bullshit.")

The concert began in earnest with a curveball: an interpretation of "Strange Feelin'," from *Happy Sad,* performed even more quirkily by a group of downtown jazz musicians, including guitarist Elliott Sharp and pianist Anthony Coleman. Singer Shelley Hirsch then joined them for renditions of "Cafe" and "Come Here Woman," both of which featured sawing cellos, assorted noises and scrapes, and Hirsch's swooping, theatrical delivery. Hell sang his jagged version of "Moulin Rouge" ("Gosh, it's reverent in here, ain't it?" he cracked upon taking the stage), followed by a genuine shock: a punk boogie version of the Ramones' heroin anthem "Chinese Rocks," in honor of New York Dolls guitarist Johnny Thunders, who had died in New Orleans three days before.

So it went for most of the first half of the concert. Despite moments that adhered to Tim's versions—veteran folkie and Tim acquaintance Eric Andersen's low-voiced reading of "Song for Jainie" and a sweet, unplugged take on "Tijuana Moon" by the pop-folk trio the Shams—the show was not the evening of pleasant-street folk-rock many had expected. In their tendency toward experimental reworkings of the songs, the performers (intentionally or not) tipped their hat to Tim's envelope-pushing side. But as one attendee, local disc jockey and music aficionado Nicholas Hill, recalls, the concert focused on "avant-garde versions of stuff that was avant-garde to begin with. At times it was pretty painful. It was not an easygoing concert." Inevitably, the audience began shifting in the cushioned pews.

After an instrumental interlude, a new group of musicians took the stage. One of them was a long-haired kid wearing a black T-shirt. Danny Fields, Tim's onetime publicist, was in the audience, keeping an eye out for the supposed son. Though Jeff had his back to the audience as he tuned his guitar, the spotlight caught his profile and one cheekbone. "And I said, 'Whoa—there he is,'" Fields recalls. "I didn't have to wonder too hard. It could take your breath away."

Jeff, who had billed himself as Jeff Scott Buckley, began strumming rigorously as Lucas surrounded him with waves of soaring-seagull guitar swoops. It was "I Never Asked to Be Your Mountain," Tim's song to Mary and her son. The audience suddenly stopped glancing at their watches. After an hour of esoteric music, here was one of Tim's most recognizable songs, emanating from a very recognizable face and sung in a familiar (if slightly deeper) voice. Halfway through the performance, a light behind the stage suddenly flashed on, throwing Jeff's silhouette against the back wall; it was, as Willner says, "like Christ had arrived." ("My God," Jeff said to a friend on the phone after the show, "I stepped onstage and they backlit it and it was like the fucking Second Coming.")

Just before he went onstage, Jeff had finished writing his own verse for the song: "My love is the flower that lies among the graves," it began, ending with a plea to "spread my ash along the way." Anyone familiar with the subject matter of the song knew this performance was more than a faithful rendition of a '60s oldie. It was a tribute, retort, and catharsis all in one, and as soon as Jeff left the stage, the audience was literally abuzz with chatter: So *that* was the son.

Although the second half of the concert had its highlights—Syd Straw's fervent "Pleasant Street" and an elegiac, chamber-music instrumental rendition of "Morning Glory" that featured cellist Hank Roberts—the concert now belonged to Jeff. With Lucas in tow, he returned to sing "Sefronia—The King's Chain," his voice soaring and cracking when he hit the line, "I am king here/Tied to this hut by the king's chain." With singers Julia Heyward and Shelley Hirsch providing tweeting-bird harmonies, Jeff also sang "Phantasmagoria in Two," another *Goodbye and Hello* song.

When it was time for a finale, Jeff appeared onstage alone. "Uhh," he started, with a nervous giggle, "a *long* time ago, when I was a little kid, my mom sat in a bed and she put this record on. And, uhh, it was like the first song where I ever heard my father's voice. I must have been ... umm ... six. I was bored." He chuckled winsomely. "I was bored. I'm sorry. But you know, what can you expect from a cat who's into *Sesame Street* at the time?"

Then he exhaled and began singing "Once I Was." At rehearsals, Nichols of St. Ann's had asked Willner if Jeff could sing the song—it was one of her favorites—to which Willner replied, "He has this thing about his father." Nichols then asked Jeff herself, and he seemed noncommittal: "I've only sung that in the shower," he told her. The next day, though, he agreed to do it, and now, here he was, onstage, singing his father's wistful remembrance of an old affair.

Suddenly, before the last chorus, a string broke on his acoustic guitar, and Jeff sang the lines "Sometimes, I wonder for a while/Do you ever remember me?" unaccompanied. If that weren't dramatic enough, his voice spiraled up on the last word—"me"—like a thin plume of smoke, holding on for a moment before drifting up to the ceiling. He took a quick bow, said "thanks," and trotted offstage, and the concert ended. It would not have been a more perfect finale if he had planned it.

Backstage, he cried and accepted sundry congratulations and compliments, as well as a few business cards passed to him. He couldn't believe he'd been allowed to sing so many songs, and he was overwhelmed.

Danny Fields brought him a note from Linda McCartney, and Jeff told him that her photo of Tim in Central Park was his favorite of his father.

Across the country, in the living room of her Orange County apartment, Mary Guibert watched the clock, knowing when the concert would start and finish. She says she knew Tim was in the church listening, and in her mind was a mental picture of "this huge vortex of light forming above the cathedral. I knew this was a moment in time that was going to change our lives forever—*his* life forever."

"In a way, I sacrificed my anonymity for my father, whereas he sacrificed me for his fame," Jeff said years later, discussing the concert with the *Philadelphia Inquirer*. "So I guess I made a mistake."

The weeks after the show, however, hardly made his participation in "Greetings from Tim Buckley" seem an ill-conceived move. The days were filled with opportunities that had never presented themselves to him, almost as if New York was atoning for treating him so poorly the previous summer. Willner and assorted music scenesters treated him to meals and concerts; Debbie Schwartz, a manager and old friend of Willner's, introduced Jeff to sundry record executives and looked into shopping around the *Babylon Dungeon Sessions* tape. On Monday, April 29, Lucas—already convinced Jeff was destined to front Gods and Monsters—brought his new ally to the offices of Columbia Records (although, according to Lucas, Jeff refused to shake the hand of an A&R executive who worked with his friend Chris Dowd's band Fishbone). Reviewing the concert in the May 2 edition of the *New York Times,* critic Stephen Holden noted diplomatically that the show "devoted more energy to exploring interesting instrumental juxtapositions than to lyrical expression" but singled out Jeff as one of its noteworthy acts, noting he sang "in a high droning voice that echoed his father's keening timbre." Adding to the moment, a photograph of Jeff from the concert ran over two columns above the review.

Jeff had been scheduled to leave town almost immediately, on Tuesday, April 30, but instead decided to stay longer, and St. Ann's gladly paid the fee to extend his plane ticket. Another important reason to stay was Rebecca Moore. On the cusp of turning twenty-three, Moore was literally the daughter of the art world. Her father Peter was a photographer and a contributor to Fluxus, the underground, anti-gallery art community that sprang up in the early '60s. Encompassing visual artists, sculptors, painters, and musicians (including Yoko Ono in her pre–John Lennon years), Fluxus embraced "a certain irreverence toward the idea of rarefied art and commercialized control of the art movement," says visual artist Larry Miller, one of its early members. Peter Moore not only photographed artists at work but created animated works of his own, like a table whose top was a laminated photograph of . . . the top of a table.

In their brownstone on West 30th Street in Manhattan's Chelsea district, Peter and Barbara Moore raised their daughter Rebecca on a steady diet of Fluxus art and events. Her own interests drifted toward acting and theater, yet despite what would appear to be an intimidatingly arty background, Moore had an open, innocent quality, a demure naïveté very much like Jeff's. Not surprisingly, they were instantly smitten with each other. A few days after "Greetings from Tim Buckley," Moore called her friend Penny Arcade, a proudly confrontational downtown performance artist. Moore was, Arcade recalls, "very, very excited because she told me she met this special boy."

In the middle of May, Jeff finally returned to Los Angeles, and when Azar and Dowd asked him about the tribute concert, all he could tell them was that he was in love. "He didn't feel particularly deserving of someone's love, and here was this person that had this unconditional love for him," says Dowd. To Dowd, though, Jeff's adventure remained a momentary diversion. He, Jeff, and Azar had begun jamming together—Dowd handling the singing and keyboards, Azar on drums, and Jeff on guitar— and Dowd, who was pondering leaving Fishbone, was juiced.

Whether the trio (which Dowd informally dubbed the Insouciant Inbreds) would have ever become a serious band is still cause for debate, but along the way, Dowd and Azar began putting Jeff through intensive musical combat training. To them, he was a raw talent whose Musicians Institute-schooled abilities were little more than a detriment. Jeff could play, but mostly by the book; he needed to loosen up. "He had all the gifts to be a great artist, but he didn't know *why* a song worked a certain way," Dowd recalls. "A lot of times we did cross the line with him in terms of being overbearing, like, 'That fucking guitar part doesn't work! Don't you know how to write a *hook?!*' It may not have been exactly the most conducive and constructive way to teach somebody. We were *hard* on him. But there's a time for Chick Corea shit and there's a time for something to be really simple and groove and be melodic." Jeff, who was still searching for a sound and a voice to call his own, took every criticism to heart, but he followed their lead nonetheless.

Like a siren, though, New York kept calling. He began leaving long, ardent messages on Moore's phone machine. In one, he sang the Johnny

Mathis oldie "The Twelfth of Never" (which Jeff may have heard via Nina Simone's cover) in its entirety; in another, referring to himself as "Nusrat Buckley Ali Khan," he launched into a nine-minute imitation of Nusrat, turning Moore's name into a Sufi chant ("Rebecca *Moooooooore*") and transforming the Kinks's "You Really Got Me" and Stevie Wonder's "Isn't She Lovely" into *qawwali* chants. In late June, Lucas, anxious to jump-start a collaboration, mailed Jeff a tape of two new instrumentals, "Rise Up to Be" and "And You Will," and suggested Jeff write lyrics.

Eager to return to New York, Jeff found an opportunity under the most unusual of circumstances. *The Commitments,* a film about a fictional Irish R&B bar band, was about to open, and the producers needed musicians to play behind the movie's star, actor Andrew Strong, at premiere parties in New York, Los Angeles, and Chicago. Hired to assemble a band, Azar recruited Jeff to play guitar. It wasn't the most prestigious gig, but it paid well—$2,000 for a week's work for each musician as well as first-class air-fare—and it was easy work; at the parties, Jeff only had to play five or six songs, mostly covers like "In the Midnight Hour." Jeff also auditioned as a guitarist for Mick Jagger's touring band, but the musical director deemed Jeff inappropriate.

Back in New York City during his Commitments trip, Jeff regrouped with Lucas in his apartment on a steamy Manhattan night. As the guitarist sat near him and played his melodies over and over, Jeff began singing poetry from one of his spiral-bound notebooks, contouring the words to Lucas's melodies (and vice versa). Gradually, fully realized songs bloomed. "Rise Up to Be" opened with a cascade of notes like rain on a fretboard, then dove into a rugged melody with enough rocky crevices for a mountainside. Singing along, Jeff retitled it "Grace," inspired by the time he and Moore said their goodbyes at the airport on a rainy day. "The rain is falling and I believe my time has come/It reminds me of the pain I might leave behind," Jeff sang. With its images of a woman crying on his arm and of his contemplating mor-tality, the song equated love with pain, rebirth with death.

The same process transformed the rippling guitar chords and more languid structure of "And You Will" into "Mojo Pin," a song that could have easily been about a drug addiction or, most likely, the addictive, feverish pull of love. The song tossed together strings of images—"pearls in oyster's flesh," "whips of opinion down my back," a mane of hair that resembles "black ribbons of coal"—that were jumbled but visceral. Jeff told Moore the song was inspired by a dream in which he saw a young

black woman shooting up heroin between her toes. (Later, he told *Art &
Performance* magazine that the phrase "mojo pin" was "a pin with black
magic in it"; pressed for more detail, he said, "Plainly speaking . . . it's a
euphemism for a dropper full of smack that you shoot in your arm.")
Whatever the connotation of the phrase "mojo pin," both that song and
"Grace" tapped into two subjects Jeff, thanks largely to his father, had
grown to accept as part of life: drugs and death.

The combination of Jeff's oblique metaphors and Lucas's hypnotic
melodies made for music unlike anything either man had conjured, and
Lucas, more excited than ever, wanted to get them on tape in order to
secure a record deal. On one of Jeff's return trips to New York, on Saturday, August 17, Lucas booked time in a downtown studio and rehearsed
and recorded the backing tracks with bassist Jared Nickerson and drummer Tony Lewis. The songs sprang even more to life. Jeff showed up later
and delivered his parts, singing with his back to Lucas and facing an
amplifier. Lucas added a galloping midsection and a guitar freakout to the
end of "Mojo Pin"; during "Grace," Jeff played harmonica and overdubbed a wailing "wait in the fire" section onto the closing part.

"Is that good?" Jeff asked after the session. "Did you like that?"

After he left, Lucas excitedly mixed the tapes and told his wife, "This
is the shit—this is what I want to devote myself to." After years of false
starts, here was what he sought: music that "would really blow up the
world." Jeff himself seemed to agree. When he returned to town during
September and October, he joined Gods and Monsters onstage for a few
songs at downtown clubs, Lucas introducing the mysterious kid with the
flowing hair to audiences like a proud father. Another of Jeff's early champions was Nicholas Hill, a Tim Buckley fan and one-time concert pro-
moter who began presenting Jeff and Lucas on his radio show on the New
Jersey station WFMU. Jeff's first live-on-air performance, on November 10,
was typically auspicious. Sitting on the studio floor, he took off his shirt,
lit candles, and surrounded himself with finger cymbals and bongos. The
two ripped through "Grace," "Mojo Pin," and "Bluebird Blues," finishing
with Bob Dylan's "Farewell, Angelina." With Lucas's symphonic array of
guitar loops and effects swirling around Jeff's delivery, which grew more
confident and heavyhearted with each verse, the latter bloomed into a
magnificent space-rock raga.

By now, Lucas's lawyer had sent the tape to several record business
types, including Kate Hyman, an A&R executive at Imago, whose roster

included Aimee Mann, Paula Cole, and the Rollins Band. (A&R—"artists and repertoire"—people are the company conduits between musicians and label heads and help the acts with material, choice of producers, and overall baby-sitting.) Hyman considered the tapes "too busy" but thought Jeff's voice was "spectacular." Hyman, who was such a fan of Tim's that she had a photo of the elder Buckley on her office wall, heard the two men perform in Lucas's living room and later invited them to her midtown office. In his army fatigues and hole-ridden T-shirt, Jeff noticed the photo of Tim on Hyman's wall but said nothing. Hyman found him "deep" and "sardonic." Hyman offered the men a development deal, wherein the label would front them $10,000 for preliminary recording, after which the label would either pursue or drop the project. It was, at best, a cautious commitment, but it was something. The money would go toward relocating Jeff to New York, paying for musicians and rehearsal space, and subsidizing a showcase concert for the band the following year. Gods and Monsters were officially green-lighted.

Jeff returned to Los Angeles before Christmas to pack, but there wasn't much left to box up. Dowd's apartment, where Jeff had been staying, had been robbed, and everything Jeff had of value—his customized Ovation guitar, his amplifier, even his answering machine—was gone. Dowd and Azar weren't supportive of the demo tapes Jeff had recorded with Lucas (Dowd called them "masturbatory") and both resented losing a friend and fellow musician. Between the robbery and the tense emotions, there seemed little reason for Jeff to remain in his home state any longer. After giving his leather hat and jacket to his niece and nephew in Orange County, he left California once and for all.

Beginning in the late '80s, Manhattan's Lower East Side had begun fighting gentrification as much as it could, ceding certain buildings only like a jealous pit bull. The co-op buildings, coffee bars, art galleries, and $25-entrée restaurants that had begun to pop up hadn't yet filtered down to Stanton Street, a sliver of a block deep in the heart of the area. Brick tenement buildings with fire escapes sat atop bodegas that only seemed to sell food layered with dust, as drug dealers scoped the surrounding blocks.

Moore's apartment, at the intersection of Stanton and Allen Streets, had all the trademarks of a typical downtown home: the steam radiators, the wood floors painted red, the bathtub with the corroding rim, the white cement walls streaked with vein-like cracks. But it was also a homey place with a brick-walled kitchen and separate bedroom and work rooms, all for an inordinately affordable $400 a month. Jeff moved in. From the living room, he would see the blue sky and the tip of the Brooklyn Bridge.

Very much the young artistic couple in love, Jeff and Moore scraped by, dining on omelets and scouring thrift shops for used vintage clothing. Discovering he could buy used clothes right on the street, Jeff returned home one day with a one-dollar pair of wool pants so smelly that a horrified Moore instantly threw them into a plastic bag for cleaning. "I'm buying old-man clothes," he would tell her, "so I'll have them when I'm old." Every morning, they watched the television game show *The Price Is Right,* cheering on the underdogs who competed for prizes and often crying out of delight when, say, an elderly woman from the Midwest took home the cash. In the small workspace room, they painted a poem on the window pane in blue stained-glass paint. Alluding to the nicknames they had for each other—Jeff was "Scratchy," Moore "Butterfly"—it read: "The tip of her wing grazed the water lightly where only moments before she had seen the shadow move. She heard the rumors about a lone scratchy fishy. Possibly the only one of its kind. Roaming the dark water with his eyes to the sky. With each careful swoop she moved close to the swirling, beautiful blue."

In these new surroundings, Jeff began to reinvent himself. Nothing—not his family, not Tim, not his stage or studio experiences in California—was brought up. "It was like he arrived with a clean slate and a very dark history," says Hyman. "He was 'mystery man.' " If anything, Jeff presented himself as an orphan, and everyone pitched in to help him: One of Moore's friends lent Jeff a pink paisley Fender guitar and amp, while Janine Nichols gave him her white Telecaster.

All the while, Gods and Monsters—Jeff, Lucas, bassist Jared Nickerson, and drummer Tony Lewis—began rehearsing for their coming-out concert, scheduled for March at St. Ann's. Jeff and Lucas had written a slew of songs together, Imago Records was eagerly awaiting the show, and the band was jelling. "Gary was the engine," says Nickerson. "All Jeff had to do was sit in the passenger side. The music sounded fabulous." But Jeff was already showing signs of bridling at the situation being handed to him. Lucas didn't want to see Jeff depart the way previous Gods and Monsters singers had. Accordingly, he asked Jeff to sign a "partnership agreement," a two-paragraph document binding Jeff to the band and designating a fifty-fifty split between them. "I thought it was a wise idea to protect myself," Lucas says. "I wanted to take it to a grand level. I wanted to be the next Led Zeppelin." Jeff balked—possibly because, as he told Moore, a clause in the agreement stated only Lucas could play guitar (which Lucas denies). Adding to the increasing tensions between the two men, in February, Jeff decided to have his own lawyer—not Lucas's—look over the Imago contract.

Through Feldman and Nichols of St. Ann's, Jeff was directed to Zissu, Stein & Mosher, a Madison Avenue law firm that represented both musicians (Lou Reed) and supermodels (Liv Tyler). George Stein, an affable, elastic-mugged attorney who was the son of firm founder Alan Stein, remembers the quiet, well-spoken kid who dropped by his beige-walled office and slouched in the wicker chair across from Stein. The lawyer read the Imago contract and realized it gave the label first right of refusal on anything Jeff did after Gods and Monsters; if another label offered Jeff a solo contract, Imago could match it and sign him regardless. Finding the clause "unacceptable," Stein advised Jeff not to sign it. "I saw that Jeff would be attached at the hip to these people, and from talking to him, I surmised that that was the *last* thing he wanted," Stein recalls. He told Jeff it was "fraught with danger."

Three weeks before the concert, Jeff dropped another bombshell: He wanted to fire the rhythm section of Lewis and Nickerson. "It's not working for me," he told Lucas. Afraid Jeff would bolt if he didn't give in ("I went back and forth to make it as democratic as possible, but he was bristling," Lucas says), Lucas reluctantly agreed, and both Lewis and Nickerson were axed. At Jeff's suggestion, Lucas hired two accomplished professionals: Pere Ubu bassist Tony Maimone and Golden Palominos drummer Anton Fier, who had both recently concluded a stint backing up former Hüsker Dü singer-guitarist Bob Mould. In less than two weeks, the duo had to learn over a dozen songs, all of which featured knotty melodic lines and roller-coaster dynamics.

Fier and Maimone managed to accomplish that, but the bandage was only temporary. As soon as Gods and Monsters took the stage at St. Ann's on March 13, and a Friday at that, the rift between Jeff and Lucas was noticeable in more than a few ways. Wearing a long-sleeve shirt unbuttoned to the navel, his newly shorn hair (topped by a spiky tuft) accentuating his lean cheekbones and haunted stare, Jeff exuded charisma as soon as he walked on. Across from him stood Lucas, who, thanks to Jeff's youthful new look, suddenly looked older than even the fourteen years between them would indicate. As towering folk-art skeletons flanked them, the band launched into its first song, "Cruel," and it was instantly apparent to the audience that some-thing *else* was off too. Being a church, St. Ann's was not designed to handle amplified rock concerts, so what the crowd experienced was a bass-heavy muddle.

As he had eleven months earlier, at the Tim tribute, Jeff again seized the show. While Lucas tuned up, Jeff sang snippets of other songs or indulged in comedic voices ("Gods and Monsters *stylee,* y'know what I'm sayin'?" he rapped, complete with hip-hop hand gestures). Lucas would often look to Jeff across the stage during the songs, but Jeff rarely returned the glance. "It wasn't really pretty," says attendee Nicholas Hill. "It made the vibe between Jeff and Gary uncomfortable." Musical clashes were evident as well: Jeff's voice and harmonica often collided with, or were drowned out by, Lucas's splay of riffs, manic slide-guitar solos, and air-raid effects. "The guitarist was over here going, 'Watch what I can do!' and Jeff was over on the other side," says Nichols. "It was like a train wreck."

Unfortunately, the combination of onstage friction and the thumpy sound system often overshadowed the music, which at best felt like a refreshing variation on classic rock. The combination of Lucas's corkscrew guitar lines and the purity of Jeff's falsetto-to-a-scream voice made for silken battering rams like "Distortion" and "Cruel." Jeff played guitar as well, but as he sang—often with his eyes closed, his hands cupping the microphone—the developing, supple power of his throat announced itself. His renditions of Edith Piaf's "Hymn to Love" and Van Morrison's "Sweet Thing" had a lulling tenderness, although he also showed a skill for chant in "Story With-out Words" and snarled the lyrics to "Cruel."

Jeff's white-boy blues moments were often callow. Starting with his verbal introduction ("All about da *blues,* now!"), the borderline-embarrassing "Harem Man" felt like an imitation of Led Zeppelin imitat-ing the blues. (No one knows whether Jeff intended its opening line—"I wanna be your harem man"—to suggest Tim's "Honey Man," which starts, "I wish I was your honey man.") But those moments were thank-fully few. In his lyrics, Jeff painted himself as a tormented loner, lamenting over a departed lover in "She Is Free" or castigating himself in "Malign Fiesta" ("Twenty-four years, you still don't know which way the wind blows!"). "One day I was cleaning up my room and I was thinking that, um . . . a usual obsession with death and dying," he said by way of intro-ducing "Grace." "And there comes a point where you really don't care 'cause there's someone . . ." His voice trailed off, and Lucas broke into the song's rippling riff. At the end of the song, Jeff let loose with an octave-shattering howl that matched Lucas's firepower.

At one point, Lucas left the stage, and Jeff, cradling his borrowed white guitar, stood alone. For his solo spot, he chose "Satisfied Mind," which had been covered by everyone from country singer Porter Wagoner to the Byrds but which Jeff had learned from a Mahalia Jackson boxed set. A song of deep regret, sung by a narrator who has lost it all, the song was ideal for a church. Without Lucas or the other musicians, Jeff revealed an entirely new self: the sullen male chanteuse who sang as if he were older, wiser, and more heartbroken than he appeared.

"By the time of the St. Ann's gig, it was 'Jeff's a star, or he's going to be, with or without Gary,' " Hill recalls. "It was absurd that Gary was going to such great lengths to try to control Jeff's career when obviously Jeff was about to fly right out of the box, and there was nothing Gary could do about it." Although the band encored with a shattering version of "Mojo Pin," Imago's Kate Hyman says she was by then nearly in tears. In her eyes, Jeff "was overpowered at every moment." The concert confirmed what Hyman had suspected all along: that the band was "just a stepping stone," and that Jeff should be on his own. After the show, she stormed out of St. Ann's, Lucas trailing after her.

The situation grew uglier in the weeks ahead. The day after the show, Lucas listened to the concert tape in his apartment and heard magic. Just then, Jeff called to say he didn't want to continue with the band. Lucas was devastated. An even heavier dose of salt in his wound arrived in the form of a *New York Times* review of the concert, which deemed Jeff "the focus" of the concert, called the band "B-team musical celebrities," and slammed the material as "plain rock, as gray as yesterday's potatoes." About two weeks later, Hyman called both Jeff and Lucas into her midtown office and bluntly announced she wanted to work with Jeff only; Lucas could be a sideman or songwriting partner, but nothing more. The Gods and Monsters deal was officially terminated, and Lucas left in disgust. Jeff followed Lucas outside and shared his concerns, but the next day, Jeff returned, alone, to Hyman's office to talk further about his future.

Later, Lucas and his attorney and musicians began to wonder if their young frontman had purposefully sabotaged the show—by recruiting a new rhythm section at the last minute, for example—as a way to make Gods and Monsters look weak, and hence pave the way for his own career. "If he *didn't* plan it, it worked out perfectly," says Nickerson, who was nonetheless impressed with Jeff's talent. "I never saw him as innocent or as being manipulated. He knew his skills and how to work them." To Jeff's friends and champions, though, no such machinations existed. "Gary wanted Jeff to be his Jim Morrison," says St. Ann's Feldman, "but Jeff didn't want to be the pretty-boy singer. Gary had something to offer Jeff as a backup, but Gary could be so overpowering."

The truth most likely lies somewhere in between. Though he had been initially flattered, humbled, and moved that Lucas asked him to form a band, especially coming on the heels of his dreary experiences in Los Angeles, Jeff grew to resent Lucas's attempts to shape and control the band. After he expressed those fears to friends, they in turn began suggesting a solo career. As someone still coping with abandonment and father-figure issues, Jeff had never thought of himself as special or deserving of attention or love, so a group of supportive friends egging him on must have been a tremendous, intoxicating shot to his sense of self-worth.

Gods and Monsters had one more commitment: a performance nine days after St. Ann's at a club called the Knitting Factory, part of a live radio broadcast on WFMU. Although Lucas feels the St. Ann's show was better, others recall the Knitting Factory show as more powerful, perhaps because everyone involved knew it would be their last. (In fact, Jeff and Lucas did a few more shows together, as a duo, over the next two months.) For one of the encores, Jeff took the stage by himself and sang a song on his own.

"It was very clear that Jeff Buckley was a *staaaar,* with three syllables," recalls M. (Michael) Doughty, a musician and Knitting Factory employee who attended the show. "The first thing that caught me was when he was stomping the mic stand with quarter notes during one of the songs, a very intense, John Lee Hookeresque percussion thing. You look at some people and it's like, 'That's it—he's got the thing.'" Fewer than one hundred people witnessed it, and some (including Lucas) don't recall it so grandly, but it was nonetheless a watershed moment: Jeff stepping out for his first solo perform- ance on a Manhattan stage. Afterward, he walked directly offstage and into Moore's arms, and as they were hugging, Steven Abbott—the young British head of Big Cat, an esteemed British indie label—tapped Jeff on the shoul- der, complimented his performance, and gave him his business card.

Arriving on newsstands just weeks later was the April 16 issue of *Rolling Stone,* which featured an upbeat article on Jeff and Lucas's band. By then, though, Gods and Monsters was a dead issue for Jeff. "From my perspective,

I acted like a father figure," Lucas says. "Someone said to me, 'That was the problem. He had to get rid of you to kill his father.' Slay the father in order to become a man.'"

To prepare himself, Lucas could have looked no further than St. Ann's. Before the Gods and Monsters showcase, both he and Jeff were asked to write statements to be included in a program that ultimately wasn't printed up. Whereas Lucas described Jeff as "my main support/figure-head," Jeff, in his hand-scrawled note, described himself as "singer, guitarist, songmaker, post-modern, 25 years old. Style: Ultra violent romantic." After listing the bands in which he had played, he ended his résumé with a statement: "I'm in the process of radical development musically which will culminate in a new project of mine sometime in '92." Lucas never saw the document.

The preceding twelve months had been dizzying ones for Jeff. Although he had agonized over the Gods and Monsters debacle, he had leapt from nowhere to become the talk of the New York music community, complete with a supportive circle of friends in the business and his first serious love affair. All he lacked was a venue at which he could fully develop into whatever it was he would be.

Daniel Harnett, an actor so gaunt he had played Charles Manson in the avant-opera *The Manson Family,* was in the dressing room at La Mama, a theater space on East 4th Street. Next to him was his costar and friend Rebecca Moore; both were preparing to go onstage in a theatrical production. As she applied her makeup in the mirror, Moore began telling Harnett about her boyfriend and his musical talent. Moore sounded so in love and the boyfriend seemed so wonderful that Harnett—who had his own band, Glim—was almost jealous. Moore said her boyfriend had nowhere to gig and was rehearsing in their apartment, and could Harnett recommend some clubs?

Harnett told her about one of his regular performance spots, a way-off-the-beaten-path space in the East Village called Sin-é. He thought it could be just the right fit.

NINE

Check out the electric piano on "Lorca." Hah!! The vocal—haa! So
funky. That song is nasty funk. Nightmare sex funky. In the context of
Tim Buckley land . . . That work Tim did was it. That was it. In my
memory of my father, when I die, you can all remember my admiration
of that period. They hit it. They certainly hit something that no one
can touch. . . . "Gypsy Woman" and "Buzzin' Fly" irk me. Although I
appreciate them. I just don't get to them, chemically. Give me "The
River," give me fucking "Monterey," give me "Mountain," don't give me
hobo's and blah blah blah. . . . It's just my personal opinion of my
father's work.

—JEFF BUCKLEY, JOURNAL ENTRY, AUGUST 9, 1995

"Look outside, man."

Tim was standing in the middle of the sweeping stage of New York's
Philharmonic Hall when he heard the voice of Steve Harris. It was the
early evening of Friday, March 14, 1969, and the Elektra promo man,
standing offstage in his usual suit and tie, was visibly excited. Part of the
new Lincoln Center complex on Manhattan's Upper West Side, Philharmonic Hall was already one of the city's most prestigious venues, an
acoustically immaculate, wood-seated home to classical music and opera,
and Tim wasn't merely performing there but headlining. "Tim Buckley is
not a teacher, prophet or spokesman like Dylan," read the concert pro-

gram. "More than that, he is a mirror of the times, chronicling a generation of kids and their hangups."

Tim himself appeared less than overwhelmed to be playing Philharmonic Hall. Earlier in the day, he went about his business, lugging a duffel bag of clothes to a laundromat and then crashing on the floor of Barry Schultz's midtown studio, using a burlap bag filled with pot as a pillow.

For his part, Harris had been a little nervous. Tim wasn't what anyone would call a star, and tickets, which were priced between $2.50 and $4.50, were still on sale that day. Harris arrived early and had been backstage much of the afternoon, and had little idea how many of the remaining tickets had been snapped up. Just before the show began, he peered out between the curtains and saw, to his pleasant surprise, not empty rows of seats but a nearly packed hall.

Now, standing onstage with the curtains drawn, preparing for the show to begin, Tim heard Harris's call to peer outside. As Harris watched, Tim pulled the curtain apart ever so slightly and glimpsed the estimable crowd. As success literally stared back at him, his face dropped. "At first, it was a look of a little bit of disbelief," Harris recalls. "And then it was a look of annoyance—a look of, 'I'm not happy with *this.*' "

The show itself was exemplary, mixing songs from his first album ("Wings," "Grief in My Soul") with *Goodbye and Hello* favorites ("Once I Was," "Pleasant Street"). Tim also previewed songs from *Happy Sad,* which was a month away from arriving in record shops. "Hanging out with him prior to it, you wouldn't think he cared at all," recalls Joe Stevens, a photographer and friend who helped with the lighting that night. "But you could tell in the way he delivered the show that he was turned on." In its review of the concert, *Billboard* praised Tim for being in "his best form, singing and communicating to perfection," while the *New York Times* noted that "he left poetic sensitivity behind and just sang his head off." As he wailed, streams of teenage girls made their way to the stage, depositing notes and envelopes in front of him or breaking the hall's rules by taking photos.

At one point, what the *Times* described as a "tall blonde" approached the stage with a red carnation. Worshipfully, she held it out to Tim—who shocked her by taking a bite out of it, chewing up the pedals, and spitting them out. "That really tastes terrible," he cracked.

Backstage, Harris spent time with Tim and his musicians, and Tim expounded on his latest musical passion: combining Latin jazz and Afro-Cuban music. "It was really interesting," Harris says, "but while I was talking to him, I could see he didn't want to do what he was doing anymore. The feeling I got was: 'I did this—now I want to do something else. Then nobody will ever hear of me again and I can play little clubs and maybe thirty people will be there.'" Harris found the conversation deeply disturbing.

When *Happy Sad* was finally released the week of April 19, 1969—over eighteen months after *Goodbye and Hello,* an unusually long time between LP releases for the time—the music didn't cause any initial alarms to be set off. Elektra head Jac Holzman seemed pleased with the record ("He was working stuff through, and I thought the record succeeded"), as did *Billboard,* which called it "probably his best LP to date . . . his mood and delivery seemingly weightless." The album debuted on the *Billboard* charts at number 178 the week it was released, eventually peaking at number 81—Tim's strongest showing yet. It would linger on the chart for a respectable three months.

But the carnation-munching incident was symbolic of Tim's evolving attitude toward his art and his audience. The insecurities that had been instilled in him as a child began bubbling over into his more-or-less adult life. Why would anyone *like* me, he thought? The reason, he concluded, was that his fans didn't respond to his music at all; they were just, as Jane says Tim put it, "a sucker for a pretty face." More and more, he began putting the fans down, calling them "lo-bos"—from the word "lobotomy," as if his admirers were literally brainless.

"He was in love with the myth of the failed, misunderstood artist," says Manda Bradlyn. "We'd all talk about Van Gogh. He started thinking, If you do something really interesting and intelligent, then your audience will hate you, and if they love you, you must be a failure, doing something lowbrow." To Jane he would say, "If they fall asleep, that means it's really good." The attitude extended to his view of himself: Tim would only begrudgingly accept compliments. Before he was drafted, Larry Beckett would be backstage at one of his friend's Troubadour shows and watch painfully as Tim shrugged off any praise while willingly accepting criticism. "If someone said, 'Well, you know, that blues went on a little long, it was kinda tedious,' he'd say, '*God,* I know. What possessed me to go into that?'" Beckett recalls. "He would always listen to the negative and ignore the positive, as if he had it in for himself."

Similarly, the businessmen around Tim struggled to understand the changes he was going through. "It would have been nice to have had an album that built on the previous record and which exploded for him," says Holzman of *Happy Sad.* "We wanted the world to love Tim, and he wasn't helping us. And I think he wasn't helping us on *purpose.* He thought of himself increasingly as a jazz musician. He saw a different light for himself."

Despite its promising start on the charts, *Happy Sad* ultimately sold less than *Goodbye and Hello,* moving roughly twenty thousand copies. In August 1969, Holzman announced Elektra had had its best-selling month in history, thanks to the Doors, folkie Tom Paxton, soft-rock crooners Bread, and a new signing, a group of punk-rock wildmen from Detroit called the Stooges. There was no mention of Tim in the label's rundown of its roster.

By this time the album was released, Tim and Jane had moved yet again. With Tim on the road, Jane had grown lonely in the house on Pacific Coast Highway; it was far from her friends, and the highway noise right outside her door only made her despise Malibu even more. When Tim was out of town performing, Jane moved their possessions to a two-floor clapboard house on Park Place in Venice.

A block from the beach, Park Place was something of an enclave. The houses on either side of the street were separated by a small alley not wide enough for cars, so the street felt secluded even amidst the carnivalesque beach scene within sight. Tim and Jane could still smell and feel the ocean breeze as it blew up the street into their sparsely furnished living room, yet Tim would still have enough privacy to create. Lee Underwood lived just a few houses down Park Place with Jennifer Stace and her young son Michael, from a previous marriage.

The days and nights were still carefree, filled with trips to the beach, long talks over dinner and drink, or visits to their favorite pool hall on Wilshire Boulevard. In various combinations, Tim, Jane, Underwood, and Stace would drop by the Troubadour to see shows by jazz drummer Elvin Jones or the soul-gospel diva Nina Simone. Tim rarely failed to catch the must-see films of the day, from *Butch Cassidy and the Sundance Kid* to the porn classic *I Am Curious (Yellow).* His interest in literature had extended to Latin writers and poets, and for his twenty-second birthday that February, Daniella Sapriel, an Egyptian-born Sephardic woman who had met Jane through a mutual friend, had given Tim a collection of poems by Spanish author and dramatist Federico Garcia Lorca. (Interestingly, one of those poems, "Gacela of Desperate Love," contained a reference to a "chewed carnation.")

In the range of his musical interests, Tim continued to leave many of his contemporaries in the dust. It was the summer of Woodstock, of Crosby, Stills & Nash and Led Zeppelin. Tim had none of it. More and more, he felt indifferent to rock; on July 1, he and Sapriel attended a Doors concert in Los Angeles and walked out halfway through, Tim disgusted by Morrison's inebriated manner. Instead, Tim was swept away by mezzo-soprano Cathy Berberian, a fortysomething classical singer with an octave-leaping voice and an ability to sing contemporary vocal pieces by Stravinsky and John Cage, among others. Linda Ronstadt may have been Tim's neighbor and an occasional interpreter of his songs, but it was Berberian Tim aspired to imitate.

It was therefore par for his course when Tim became fascinated with Richard Keeling, a twenty-three-year-old UCLA student who lived behind Underwood and Stace. A graduate student in the university's ethnomusicology department, Keeling had black hair, a muscular build, and an air of shadowy mystery. "Richard was involved with music from all different lands, and he would bring home horns made of steel and bones," recalls Stace. "Tim was fascinated with that, and with Richard. He glommed onto him." With Keeling, Tim and Jane attended a show of Balinese dancers at UCLA on May 1, and the music's interlocking rhythms (played on gongs with mallets) resonated with Tim. To support himself, Keeling sold drugs on the side; as he later told *Musician* magazine, he couldn't afford to be a graduate student "without having some kind of business." Tim nicknamed his new friend "CR," for "cool Richard."

To Dan Gordon, who also lived nearby and was beginning a career as a screenwriter, Keeling's appeal to Tim went beyond music appreciation. Keeling reminded Gordon of a Bell Gardens classmate named Rodney, an early '60s greaser who wore a leather jacket and appealed to all the girls. "The ability to be cool in any situation, to rise above it, was something Tim wanted and never had," Gordon says. "Tim didn't have that coolness—he had passion."

To Tim's friends, a pattern began to emerge, one of discovery and eventual departure. "First he lets them fire the band [the Bohemians] and goes on his own," observes Larry Beckett. "He makes a couple of albums and then he fires the lyricist and goes on his own. Then he gets rid of the tenor voice. Everything that had gotten him to where he is, he then closes the door on, and goes into an unknown place."

In a way, that philosophy appeared to be applying to Tim's personal life, as his love affair with Jane was wilting on the vine by the spring of

1969. The initial thrill of rock touring gone, Jane had stopped joining Tim on the road. But when she would pick him up from the airport upon his return, the void between them felt more apparent and awkward than ever. "I'd have been living my life, and he'd have been living *his* life," she says. Jane's interest in making and selling clothing continued; on the back of *Happy Sad*, a forlorn-looking Tim, his eyes begging for nurturing, wore a sweater she had hand-knit. "I recognized I was living in the shadow of somebody else's glory," Jane says. "My own life was standing still." According to friends, Tim still loved Jane, but he needed someone who would devote herself to him full-time, and he seemed threatened by her side interests. Even when she took kung fu classes, he complained that her shoulders were now broader than his. "He was not about marriage in those days," says Collins. "He liked his open life."

That open life involved other women, including a new love three thousand miles away. Through Elektra publicist Danny Fields, Tim had befriended Hope Ruff, a small, forceful brunette five years his senior. A musician in her own right, Ruff was a pianist with a degree in music and made a living as both a social worker and as a transcriber of lead sheets (writing out sheet music for singer-songwriters who couldn't do it themselves). She, Tim, and Fields would often spend time together in New York, and even after Fields was fired from Elektra in January 1969—he, too, clashed with Holzman—Tim maintained a friendship with Ruff. Before long, the platonic feelings turned romantic, and Tim began dropping by her apartment on Jones Street in Greenwich Village. Tim told Ruff he and Jane were in the midst of a breakup, and Ruff didn't question him.

Ruff was awed by Tim's instinctual gifts and the range and control he had over his voice. She was less than enamored of her lover's disparaging side and what she calls his "tongue of a killer." Over dinner in the Village, she would often watch as Tim and Underwood openly belittled waitresses. "He could cut people down to size, and he would think it was funny if they couldn't take it," she says. "From feeling so weak and so defenseless, he had to strike first." Yet beneath the machismo, Ruff felt there was "an incredibly delicate human being inside, very fragile. He could chew up a million carnations, but the real guy in there was a vulnerable little kid, and it scared him." At her birthday party that year, a book with blank pages was passed around, and guests were asked to write inscriptions. Tim contributed a romantic poem: "My hands were crippled/And the city breezes filled my lungs with death/And just when I was all ready to sleep forever/Hope woke me/She held me/Even when I was too weak to give/She held me/I hold Hope in my heart." When Ruff heard "Love from Room 109 at the Islander (On Pacific Coast Highway)," she, like Manda Bradlyn, felt part of it was about her.

During one of Tim's sojourns to New York, Jane, in a moment of weakness and loneliness, had a fling with a neighbor in Venice. Tim continually called her that weekend, to no response. When he came home, she confessed to the affair.

"So what are you gonna do now?" he asked her. Jane said she didn't know.

"Well," Tim replied, "I think we're breaking up."

Distraught, Jane moved out of the Park Place apartment in the early summer.

Even with his beard and his long white hair pulled back into a ponytail, John Balkin was a far cry from the typical rock and roll bass player. Born and raised in New York City—even in his forties, he still had the gruff accent of a borough kid—he had earned a degree in string bass at the Manhattan School of Music, after which he had played with the St. Louis Symphony before moving to Los Angeles in the mid-'60s. Balkin supported himself playing in Top 40 cover bands and at weddings, but his heart lay with classical and experimental music; whenever he could, he participated in symphony tours on the West Coast. Concurrently, he had been introduced to Frank Zappa and played a few bass parts on Zappa's 1967 album *Lumpy Gravy*.

The following year, Balkin had met Lee Underwood when both men toured briefly with the Mariachi Brass, a Tijuana Brass knockoff. Then, in 1969, Underwood told Balkin his friend Tim was looking for a new bass player, and Underwood invited Balkin, who was unfamiliar with Tim's work, to Tim's house on Park Place. During an informal jam in the living room, Balkin impressed both men with his jazz roots and his background in avant-garde composition. Before long Balkin was part of Tim's band; together, they played a few live gigs, including the Troubadour on September 4.

The reason Tim needed a new bass player that summer was not made immediately clear to Balkin. Tim's previous lineup—Miller, Friedman, and Collins—was never better as a performing unit, but tensions both artistic and financial had formed a wedge between bandleader and musicians. Although Tim wasn't touring on a steady basis, he earned between $2,500 and $5,000 a week when he was. Yet Miller, Collins, and Friedman felt they weren't being paid "what we were worth," says Collins (Jerry Yester claims they asked to be paid double scale during the making of *Happy Sad*). Tim's lack of interest in business affairs—he left it to Herb Cohen, who himself showed little interest in Tim's jazz accompanists or their music—only aggravated the situation. "We loved the music," says Collins, "but we didn't like what was going on." Within the band, there was also dissatisfaction with Underwood's guitar playing; some felt he wasn't as accomplished as his bandmates.

Gradually, Miller eased back into his life in New York as a freelance musician, and Friedman—who recalls a series of noteworthy gigs featuring only him and Tim, the vibes and twelve-string guitar playing off each other during extended improvisations—says he was cut out without warning. When he heard that Tim was performing in Boston with other musicians, Friedman flew there to confront his boss, and after a screaming match, Tim told the vibraphonist that he "wanted to do something else." Says Friedman, "The band was becoming too strong musically, and maybe it was too difficult for him to handle." With little fanfare, Tim's most able backing unit to date crumbled away.

John Balkin knew little of this back story when he arrived at Whitney Studios in Glendale on Thursday, September 18, 1969. He didn't know what he was supposed to do, either. The plan, he had been told, was to begin recording Tim's next album, but even though he had played a few new songs with Tim at the Troubadour two weeks earlier, Balkin hadn't been given any sheet music or any tapes of the material they would be laying down. "There was no music, no arrangements, no charts," Balkin says. "I thought it was kind of weird."

It only grew stranger once he entered the studio. For the first song to be tackled, Tim wanted to take a crack at an experimental piece named after Lorca and inspired by Miles Davis's spacious, spectral *In a Silent Way*, which had been released the previous month and had become one of his favorite albums. Anyone stopping by his home heard the album blasting on his tape deck.

In the studio was a massive pipe organ, and as soon as he spotted it, Tim said, "Wow, that would be a trip." At first, none of the studio employees knew how to turn on the keyboard. Once Balkin figured it out, Tim began playing a descending bass line on his twelve-string—in 5/4 time—and Balkin imitated it on organ, which itself sounded as if it belonged on a horror-film soundtrack. Before they knew it, the number had stretched out to almost ten minutes, with Underwood adding improvised, dots-and-dashes lines on an electric piano. In its use of electric piano and organ and its motionless feel, "Lorca" wore its *In a Silent Way* influences (particularly the song "Shhh/Peaceful") on its sleeve.

Such emphasis on the freeform was the rule of thumb throughout the sessions, which extended to two more days, September 19 and 26. Holding his twelve-string guitar, Tim would say, "We're going to do this tune," hum a few bars, and begin playing, and Balkin, Underwood—and, on a few occasions, Collins—would fall in behind him, finding notes and grooves as they went along. "I didn't know what was coming at me," says Balkin. "I did the best I could. I didn't particularly like doing that—give me some sort of lead or directions on paper so I know where I'm heading. But it was fun to do. Precocious, but fun."

With only a recording engineer in the studio (Cohen, listed as executive producer in the credits, has no recollection of attending the sessions), Tim and the band were free to wander, and they took full advantage of the opportunity. The four songs they recorded after "Lorca"—many of them done in one take, according to Balkin—continue the loose ambience of that track. Any consideration of radio airplay or sales is nowhere in sight or sound. "Anonymous Proposition"—a nearly eight-minute number that, like "Lorca," has essentially no rhythm—is a spacey, motionless ballad; Balkin's standup bass slides around the melody as Tim dips his voice down low on lines like "Love me/As if someday/You'd hate me." Only "Nobody Walkin'" has a standard verse-chorus structure, but it too ambles over the course of seven minutes. "I left my baby standing in the back door crying," goes the first line, seemingly about Tim's confrontation with Jane, but the sentiments quickly turn to rationalization: "Sometimes you gotta turn your back," Tim intones, "just to show that little girl that there's something she's gonna lack."

Lorca is very much a tentative step. The lyrics and the arrangements meander and are at times too skeletal. With its strummed twelve-string and conga beat, "I Had a Talk with My Woman" has the most traditional feel of all the songs, but its lyrics ramble from declarations of love ("She's this memory that I hold around/She's this dream that I always hope to believe") to nonsequitur references to Moses and Jesus. In terms of songwriting, the album is a step back from *Happy Sad,* but what everyone else considered "songs" no longer appealed to Tim.

The album is primarily a vocal showcase. Revealing his expanding range, Tim dots the songs with grunts and groans and toys with single-syllable words, holding a note or stretching it out until a word like "ease" becomes multiple syllables. On "Driftin'," he dips his voice to a foghorn and tosses off a high wheeze-moan, while Underwood's curlicue guitar takes its mellow time finding notes during his solo. Though a problematic album, *Lorca* stands as a testament to the power and versatility of Tim's vocal cords. Inspired by Dylan, many male rockers of the period were happy to flaunt unsophisticated vocal chops and channel their virtuosity into guitar solos, but the Tim heard on *Lorca* uses his voice as an instrument, sending it soaring, circling, and plunging down seemingly at will.

As soon as it was finished, and before he himself had heard it in its entirety, Tim invited his friend Daniella Sapriel over to Park Place to hear the completed album, which he decided to call *Lorca* (Sapriel, after all, had given him the book that most likely inspired the title song). After rolling a few joints, they played a reel-to-reel tape of the album. "He was excited about it," recalls Sapriel. "He knew it wasn't popular or accessible, but he was really intrigued by the musical possibilities of what he was doing."

Tim and his friends and fellow musicians were thrilled, but just as many around them didn't share the excitement. "I was very unhappy," says Collins. "There was nothing for me to do. I couldn't get behind it." Soon, he too drifted off to play with other musicians. Elektra's Jac Holzman was already irked after hearing reports that Tim and his band had left Elektra's new LA studio a mess during the *Happy Sad* sessions. ("If I put a tuna fish sandwich on the sound console, it *stayed* on the sound console," admits bass player John Miller.) Holzman didn't know what Tim's new project would sound like until a tape arrived in his New York office. "I recognized this was something he wanted to do and something he had to get out, but I just wasn't happy with the record," Holzman recollects. "It made no effort to connect to people. It was, 'This is what I've got, take it or leave it.' It wasn't that we weren't willing to support the vision. It's just that it wasn't Tim anymore."

Clearly, Tim's association with Elektra was grinding to an unexpectedly sudden halt. Fields says the label actually began to lose interest when *Goodbye and Hello* wasn't a hit. "His stature at the company just plummeted," the publicist recalls. "There was such disappointment that he was set back. The Doors and rock and roll started to be much more viable for them." In later interviews, Tim would claim he left Elektra when Holzman sold the label to Warner Communications in 1970, but it's more likely that he left voluntarily or, according to Herb Cohen and Holzman, that Holzman simply decided not to renew Tim's option for another album. Tim himself may have known all this was coming: He told Balkin during the *Lorca* sessions that the album would most likely be his last for Elektra, so he was going to do whatever he wanted in the studio.

Before he knew it, Tim was already signed to another label. As early as July 1967, Frank Zappa had announced plans for a "producing firm" to be called Bizarre Productions, which would also include a record label of the same name. What had developed instead were two independent labels, both co-owned by Zappa and Cohen, his ongoing manager. (The company's motto was: "Just what the world needs—another record company.") Bizarre Records was Zappa's playground, home to his own work both solo and with the Mothers and to oddball acts like deranged Hollywood street singer Wild Man Fischer. Straight Records, its sister label, was run primarily by Cohen, who signed up his personal favorites: the GTO's (Girls Together Outrageously, a barely competent ensemble of singing groupies that included Pamela Miller, later Des Barres), a fledgling Arizona-based hard-rock band called Alice Cooper, and an eccentric blues-based growler named Captain Beefheart (whose *Trout Mask Replica* was his first Straight release). At the two labels' offices on Wilshire Boulevard, "there was always a Mother or two hanging around, waiting for a check, or a member of Alice Cooper's band," says Des Barres. "It was always a scene."

By 1969, Warner Brothers had stepped in to handle distribution for Bizarre/Straight, adding to its market viability. So, when Tim split with Elektra, it seemed only natural—to Cohen, at least—for his client to sign with Straight, thereby keeping both the record *and* publishing money in the family. Besides, Cohen said, "Nobody else wanted to sign him." Whether Tim liked it or not, or even cared, he was in an even deeper bed with his manager. Cohen also hired Tim to occasionally open concerts by Zappa and the Mothers, which, according to Gail Zappa, never sat well with her late husband. Regarding Tim's music, she says, "Frank always talked about the 'sensitivity factor'—people talking about emotional things and sitting in a corner as opposed to really opening up your mind to different types of reality." As a result, she says Zappa "resented" having Tim forced on him as an opening act, even though he grew to respect Tim's music.

According to Holzman, there was another reason for his reticence to re-sign Tim. By 1969, it had become no small secret within Tim's inner circle that his experimentation with pot and acid had expanded to include the occasional snort of heroin. By now, Tim was referring to himself less as a pop star and more as a jazz musician. The *New York Times* agreed; in a review of Tim's Carnegie Hall concert on November 2, which featured an extended, half-hour version of "Gypsy Woman," the critic remarked it was more appropriate to call Tim "a jazz singer with a guitar than a folk singer."

For Tim, heroin's allure was obvious. It had long been associated with jazz musicians, from Charlie Parker to Chet Baker, not to mention Fred Neil and Tim Hardin, two of Tim's musical idols. Heroin was also revered for the way it comforted and depressurized its user, creating a womb-like state of repose and calm. In that regard, its appeal to Tim was apparent. By 1969, he had a divorced wife and a child to support, he and Jane were splintering, and both Elektra and Tim's management were less than enthused about the decidedly abstruse bent of his music. For his part, Cohen denies applying pressure to his client. "That's bullshit," he says. "He asked, 'Why aren't the records selling?' I said, 'Because they're not commercial.' I put them out *knowing* they weren't commercial." Yet others recall Tim returning from business meetings upset and teary.

Another theory regarding Tim's dabblings in heroin involved his rarely seen son. Driving into Orange County earlier in the year, Tim's ex-wife Mary heard "Dream Letter" on the radio and was deeply offended by the song's tender evocation of their two-year-old boy. "This was a lie," she says, "a myth he was telling people. Here was this delightful child who wanted nothing more than to be approved of and loved, almost pathologically so. And this father was writing this *phony* song so the rest of the world could feel sorry for *him?* It cut me to the quick."

In late 1969, Tim heard Mary was remarrying, and friends say he was under the impression that Mary, her new husband, and young Jeffrey Scott would be moving to Australia. (Ron Moorhead had relatives in the country and often fantasized about relocating there, which could explain Tim's perception.) Mary claims that two weeks before her wedding to Moorhead, Tim called and asked if they could reconcile. Friends believe that the depressing thought of never seeing his son again—even though he barely saw him at all during the first three years of the child's life—added to Tim's mental strain and, thereby, his interest in heroin.

"All we are saying is give smack a chance," Tim cracked during his Troubadour show that September, a reference to John Lennon's new, hippie-chant single. Tim cackled at his own joke, but others didn't find it so amusing. Earlier in the decade, Holzman had had painful dealings with an Elektra artist addicted to dope, folksinger Bob Gibson, and the thought of revisiting that ordeal displeased him immensely. Holzman says he had a friend, a recovering addict, talk with Tim and that Tim was less than receptive. "I remember my friend saying to me, 'You didn't create the situation. There's nothing you can do about it. People have to do it on their own,' " says Holzman. "And I believed that." With few regrets, he let Tim go.

Was it over between them, a relationship that had lasted over three years? Jane Goldstein wasn't sure. Her last conversation with Tim, in which she confessed to her tryst, left her devastated but nonetheless hopeful. Like many of Tim's friends, Jane was frequently confused by his indecisiveness; even the straightest question was rarely met with a direct answer.

About a month after their supposed breakup, Jane, who was sleeping on a friend's couch a block away, walked over to the apartment on Park Place. Sitting on the front porch was a mysterious woman with long, dark hair who appeared a little older. Something about her felt familiar; Jane seemed to recall the woman, her husband, and her son visiting the house not long before. But as she ascended the steps, Jane had no idea what this stranger was doing there now.

"Tim's asleep," said the woman. Nonetheless, Jane went into the bedroom and found Tim half awake in bed. She asked him what was going on.

"I have feelings for her," he replied, sleepily.

"And I said, 'Well, we need to work it out or talk about it or something,' " Jane recalls. "And he said, 'No, I'm gonna hang out with her now.' I was devastated. I just couldn't believe it. I thought, Where did she *come* from?"

TEN

Ever read the Mahabharata*? There's a story about a boy who wants to be a warrior. He goes and finds a teacher but the teacher keeps putting him off. So the boy builds a copy of the teacher made of mud and he washes it every day, and he learns to do his thing. And the whole symbolism is that the teacher is inside. I made teachers out of Ray Charles, Billie Holiday, Dylan, Judy Garland. I learned about phrasing, pitch, everything.*

—JEFF BUCKLEY, INTERVIEW WITH THE AUTHOR, SEPTEMBER 1993

Everywhere Shane Doyle turned on the streets of the Lower East Side of Manhattan, he seemed to encounter one of his fellow Irishmen. A native Dubliner, Doyle was a tall, taciturn man with a lean, crevassed face and a graying, shoulder-length mane. In another century, he could have passed for an especially intense scarecrow, but in fact Doyle had spent years in his native country attempting any number of upstart businesses, from selling used tires to dealing in soybean futures to hauling around rock band equipment. Finally, in 1983, he boarded a plane for America.

He was by no means alone. During the '80s, Ireland was suffering through a lengthy depression; unemployment climbed to a staggering 18 percent, as high as any nation in Europe. Desperate for work and to escape their own country, thousands of Irish began streaming out; at Shannon Airport, it wasn't unusual to see immigration officials stopping kids with backpacks and asking, "You're coming back, right?" and the kids would just laugh and offer a half-hearted nod before boarding their planes. The Irish Immigrant Act of 1990 made even more resident-alien permits available. In 1992 alone, the *Irish Echo,* a prominent U.S. newspaper of that community, reported seventeen thousand new Irish in New York, where the booms in real estate and babies had created a market for construction workers and nannies, respectively. Those were merely the legal figures; they didn't take into account the untold numbers of Irish who hadn't bothered to obtain green cards.

Legal residents or not, they all needed settings in which to unwind and imbibe cheap beer and coffee, and with his entrepreneur's eye—and no other job prospects on the horizon—the fortysomething Doyle smelled a potential market. Deciding his fellow expatriates needed a relaxing, low-maintenance coffeehouse, he prowled the blocks around his apartment on 10th Street and Avenue B for two weeks in 1990, pen and paper in hand, jotting down the names of small spaces for rent. His goal was to find someplace less "business-oriented," he says, than the local bistros that would push customers out the door as soon as they'd finished eating.

As soon as he came across 122 St. Mark's Place, Doyle knew he'd found his locale. In terms of size, it wasn't much; at under one thousand square feet, the street-level space was so small he could walk from one end to the other in a few large strides. Its entrance—a black metal door flanked by two large, floor-to-ceiling windows—made it look more like a small grocery store than the art gallery it had been in a previous incarnation. But its scuffed hardwood floors and faded-brick walls lent the spot a comfortable, unpretentious atmosphere. With the help of wealthier friends, Doyle borrowed $15,000 and forked over two months' deposit and one month's rent, and the place was his. He christened it "Sin-é" (pronounced "shin-*ay*")—Gaelic for "that's it," a common way of ending a conversation in Ireland.

Three decades after its beatnik-era heyday, St. Mark's Place—and the East Village in general—was still defiantly squalid. Even with incoming gentrification, the area retained its anything-goes bravado, its tense claustrophobia. In the early morning, it wasn't unusual to walk down one of its tenement-lined streets and tally how many cars had been broken into the night before; all one had to do was count the trail of piles of broken glass on the sidewalk. St. Mark's Place, which ran from Fourth Avenue to

Avenue A, was the area's commerce hub, yet it was hardly a trendy one, home to everything from used-record stores and a movie revival house to tattoo parlors and cafés with scarred wooden tables.

When Sin-é opened in 1990, the walls were still wet with paint. Friends and local businesses lent cutlery; the waitresses brought in homemade food to serve to customers. "Shane was always mellow, but he had his own sneaky way of getting people to do things for him for nothing," recalls Tom Clark, a transplanted Illinoisan and Sin-é regular. "And for some reason, you didn't mind doing it." From the start, Sin-é was intended to be loose and casual; it had no outside sign, nor did Doyle advertise in newspapers. In the beginning, no liquor was served, either, since Doyle didn't have a green card yet himself. "The idea was to get people here and have them make it whatever it was going to be," Doyle recalls; if that meant having the same customer ask for tea refills all day, so be it. With $1,800 due every month in rent, Sin-é needed to make $100 a day to make rent and payroll, so some nights Doyle and his partner Karl Geary kept the place open until 4 or 5 A.M., "waiting," Doyle says, "for that last hot chocolate."

Eventually, the very casualness of the tiny storefront attracted not only recently arrived Irish, but writers working on screenplays and poets daydreaming and scribbling. After one musician talked Doyle into letting him play, others followed—Irish troubadours, jazz bass players. Since there was no stage, they would huddle to the left of the entrance, in front of the brick wall, playing a mere foot or two away from customers sitting at round, nightstand-size wood tables. Anyone walking down St. Mark's Place could look right through the front window and watch performances from the curb.

Once word spread to Ireland and the music community, suddenly Sinéad O'Connor or the highly touted (if plodding) band Hothouse Flowers would be spotted there, wedged between the tiny tables. Just as important, Sin-é also became a home for a slew of local rockers and singer-songwriters. There was Clark, "the human jukebox" who could sing any song anyone requested and whose tiny street-musician PA became Sin-é's sound system. His friend Tom Shaner would jam with a small Western swing band. For all of them, it was a perfect place to try out new songs, play covers with no pressure, and pass around the plastic pitcher that could bring them up to $100 on a good night. Since Doyle didn't charge admission, it was the musicians' only way of making money.

Some nights the place would be packed—meaning about fifty people—

while other nights only a few stragglers would be there. It didn't matter to Doyle or the musicians. Where else in Manhattan, they felt, could one play whatever music one desired, make a little cash, and have such an easygoing time doing it?

The name "Sin-é" rang an immediate bell for Rebecca Moore. By coincidence, Jeff had been there once before. At Moore's suggestion, he had wandered into various downtown clubs in the fall of 1991, clutching a copy of his *Babylon Dungeon Sessions* demo and a tattered copy of the *New York Times* review of the Tim tribute concert. At Sin-é, he was politely informed that the owners had still not listened to the eighty or so tapes that had already been submitted, and perhaps he should come back at a later date. Jeff shrugged and put the place out of his mind. "It was something I've never, ever stooped to doing before," Jeff later told a Sin-é documentarian, "but I was desperate."

The Jeff who shuffled into Sin-é six months later, accompanying his friend Daniel Harnett, was noticeably changed. With his tattered pants and T-shirt, he looked about the same, but there was, Doyle recalls, "a blend of arrogance and humility" to him. Doyle didn't remember the kid from his first visit, nor had he listened to Jeff's or most of the other tapes that were dropped off. Harnett, a Sin-é regular, put in a good word for his new friend, and Doyle, who had nothing to lose, agreed. "I was like, 'Yeah, whatever,'" he recalls. "'All right, whatever, do a thing.'" Jeff was thrilled, telling Harnett, "I love you, man—thank you so much. I love you."

On one of the first Fridays in April (the coffeehouse never kept records), Jeff ambled back into Sin-é, clutching the white Fender Telecaster he had borrowed from Janine Nichols of St. Ann's. He still hadn't replaced the guitar stolen from his LA apartment, and he didn't have anywhere near enough money to purchase a new one.

With a small group of friends in attendance, the Jeff who began performing that night was almost entirely unlike any previous incarnation. Gone were the Rush covers, the jazz guitar instrumentals, and the hard rock of Group Therapy. His hair was still short, buzzed close on the sides. But when he opened his mouth, out came the delicate vocal caress of a sorrowful altar boy—an achingly pure, almost virginal, tenor that could just as easily give way to a punky snarl or dirt-beneath-the-nails blues grit. It was the voice he had debuted in his solo spots at the Gods and Monsters St. Ann's show, now magnified. The fact that he accompanied himself on electric guitar, as opposed to the typical acoustic format of most singer-songwriters, added another sonic dimension. Rebounding off Sin-é's brick walls, the clean, fluid strums of the Telecaster enveloped the coffeehouse and lent it the hushed, reverent feel of a church folk mass.

Along with his new presentation came a revamped group of musical heroes assembled with input from his New York friends. The teenager who had been introduced to Edith Piaf on television and was taken with the naked emotion she conveyed, even in French, reemerged, and soon Jeff was in love with the music (and very idea) of doomed, tragic souls like Piaf, Judy Garland, and Billie Holiday (whose version of "Strange Fruit" he first discovered through a cover by the Creatures, featuring goth queen Siouxsie Sioux). Songs from all of them popped up during his first show at Sin-é, along with "Satisfied Mind" and "I Know It's Over" by the Smiths, another one of his beloved British bands from the '80s. Morrissey being something of a modern-day cabaret singer, it was easy to see how his songs would fit into Jeff's overhauled repertoire.

During the fall of 1991, he had purchased a copy of Van Morrison's *Astral Weeks,* and Jeff soon adopted not only "Sweet Thing" but also "The Way Young Lovers Do." He also became so taken with the husky, emotive ballads of '60s R&B-gospel priestess Nina Simone that he began covering several songs associated with her in his sets: "Lilac Wine," "Be My Husband," "I Loves You, Porgy," and "Wild Is the Wind." Songs like those—and Leonard Cohen's hymnlike "Hallelujah," learned from John Cale's version on a Cohen tribute album—formed the core of Jeff's new set list, along with the few originals he dared to sing: "Eternal Life" and "Unforgiven" from the *Babylon Dungeon* tape, and "Grace" and "Mojo Pin" from his collaboration with Gary Lucas. It wasn't rock, per se, or folk, or gospel, or blues, but an incorporeal mixture of them all.

What was startling wasn't simply the range of the material, which was as eclectic as that of any musician performing in New York. It was the way it was tackled. Although nearly all the songs were covers, few of them sounded like bland carbon copies. Whether it was "Strange Fruit" (an impressionistic song about a lynching), Morrison's almost feverish "The Way Young Lovers Do," the old-timey blues "Dink's Song," or "The Twelfth of Never," Jeff sang each as if he wasn't merely doing a remake but inhabiting the song like a favorite old coat. His emotional bond to each was so strong that it was easy to imagine he was singing his own words. (His interpretations were so personalized that many assumed Jeff wrote these songs himself.) One remarkable early favorite was "Calling You," the recurring theme song to the 1988 indie film *Bagdad Cafe*. The song was haunting in the film, but Jeff's version was a genuine goosebump-raiser. When his voice rose up in the chorus and stretched the notes—"*I-I-I-I-I am caaaaalling you*"—women scattered around Sin-é would invariably begin sniffling. (Part of one of its verses—"A coffee machine that needs some fixing/In a little café just around the bend"— may have reminded him of Sin-é itself.)

Very quickly, Jeff was given a regular slot on Monday nights. In his usual outfit of crumpled V-neck T-shirt and one pair or another of baggy pants, he would relax first at one of the tables where he'd sit with Moore or a friend, eventually stand up, take a few steps to the performance area around 10 P.M., and plug in his guitar while customers were merrily drinking or chatting away. Sometimes he would tune up for fifteen minutes; sometimes he would start strumming and humming, which would eventually lead into a song. At Sin-é, there was no strict schedule, and performers could play as little, or as long, as they wanted. "I just wanted to coast on these songs and learn to be a singer," Jeff said a year later. "I figured if I played in the no-man's-land of intimacy, I'll learn how to be a performer." Adds Doyle, "My needs and his needs were in unison at the time."

As much as he tried to hide it, Jeff's past came along for the ride. Watching him perform was akin to observing a rabid music fan rifle through a record collection and play treasured songs. From the days with his mother and Ron Moorhead in Fullerton came renditions of Joni Mitchell's "People's Parties" and songs by Bob Dylan (particularly "If You See Her, Say Hello") or Elton John. From his first trip to New York two years previous, he might wail out a note-perfect version of Nusrat Fateh Ali Khan's "Mustt Mustt" or the Bad Brains's hardcore raver "Pay to Cum." "He was playing for himself," says WFMU disc jockey Nicholas Hill, who was a regular at many early Sin-é performances. "He wanted to connect with himself more than anything."

At first, the other regular performers at Sin-é were skeptical or jealous of this broodingly handsome newcomer, especially Clark, whose Monday slot Jeff had taken over when Clark briefly left town. "You'd be half a block away and hear the sound drifting down the street and go, 'Oh, Jeff's playing tonight,'" says Clark. "And probably five hundred girls standing outside waiting to get in—that *also* told you Jeff was playing that night." But like so many others, Clark was eventually won over. One night, Tom Shaner, another Sin-é performer, stopped in, and Jeff began singing Leon Payne's "Lost Highway," popularized by Hank Williams. Sliding a bottleneck up and down the guitar strings, Jeff made his instrument buzz like a mosquito, lending the performance an even eerier feel.

"He wasn't just playing a song someone might know and love," Shaner recalls. "He was doing his best to create a total sonic environment with one guitar. And it was the way he phrased it that made it completely alive. It wasn't just a folk song about a guy in jail singing about how he did wrong. It sounded like an emotional crisis coming from someone filled with incredible regret. Most of us would play it like a two-step, like the original. But to make it a slow elegy was a remarkable choice."

The young goofball from Anaheim was never far from sight, either. His sets were peppered with standup-comic quips: He could mock heavy-metal stage patter ("Vee are zee Scorpions—vee rock with *hair!*"), riff on his California past (what he called the "Disneyland Nazis"), or imitate the voices of clueless tourists who had wandered in the week before. Or, expounding on the highs and lows of the current music scene, he might toss in a quick bar or two of current hits like Nirvana's "Smells Like Teen Spirit" or the Red Hot Chili Peppers's "Give It Away." Then there was the Tree Man—a mysterious, disheveled World War II veteran named Lloyd who would tie tree-size branches to his head and wander into the space. Most of the performers tolerated him or saw him as a beloved character; Jeff did both, incorporating Tree Man into his act and even dueting with him one evening on "Ol' Man River."

Often, Doyle and his coworkers would turn off the tea and cappuccino machines so as not to disturb him; if they were kept on, though, Jeff would just as easily imitate the foaming and grinding of the coffee machine. (He could also pull off an uncanny imitation of a nearby car alarm that would go off during a set.) At Sin-é, he learned that singing softer and with more subtlety would catch the attention of especially noisy patrons, like the jocks and frat boys who would drop by and serve as distasteful reminders of his childhood. Most important, there would be no Tim Buckley covers. One day, Doyle was playing a Hothouse Flowers CD. Thinking it was his father's voice, Jeff shot Doyle a sharp look until he realized who it actually was.

That spring, Jeff began playing other downtown venues, including Skep and the Cornelia Street Café. In April, he partook in avant-jazz eccentric John Zorn's *Cobra,* a performance piece in which a group of vocalists were given instructions onstage (on pitch, sound, or lyric) and had to improvise on the spot. When his turn came, Jeff sang as if his voice were emanating from a Thomas Edison phonograph. Still, it was Sin-é that became his regular haunt. Some nights, he would drift in and, if no one was performing, sing a few songs; other times, he would help the small staff wash dishes at the end of the night. To everyone, it seemed he treated the coffeehouse not as a workplace but as a home, as if he hadn't had one in a very long time.

On a relatively cool spring evening, Hal Willner was walking down St. Mark's Place on his way home to his nearby apartment. He often took this route, but this time, he had a friend in tow: Steve Berkowitz, an A&R and product-management executive at Columbia Records. With his chunky build, mop of frizzy dark hair, and sliver of a goatee extending vertically from lip to chin, Berkowitz resembled a next-generation beatnik. The son of a Boston truckdriver, Berkowitz, who had just turned forty, had plowed his way through various aspects of the music business since the '60s: working in record stores, playing guitar in blues bands, and acting as a comanager for the Cars in the early '80s. In 1987, he was hired as a product manager for Columbia, initially working with everyone from Shawn Colvin to Loverboy; by 1991, he had worked his way into the A&R department. Berkowitz was blunt and singularly opinionated, yet he also managed to exude a laid-back jazzbo-fan cool.

Despite his involvement with various pop and rock acts, Berkowitz was primarily a devotee of blues, jazz, and R&B, reflected in his earliest signings for Columbia: jazz saxophonist Henry Threadgill and the reunited Memphis soul unit Booker T. and the MG's. "I leaned toward the artier artists," he says. "It was just my natural tendency. If a rock band was to come by my desk, I would share it with another A&R person and say, 'This is more your bag.'" His current project was *Weird Nightmare*, a Charles Mingus tribute album produced by Willner, and he and Willner were on their way to hear some of it in Willner's apartment. The night was filled with planning, dreams, and music.

Willner suddenly paused in front of a window at 122 St. Mark's Place. *Remember Tim Buckley's kid, the one I told you about?* he asked Berkowitz; *he's playing here tonight.* Berkowitz had met Jeff at some earlier point, but had never heard the kid sing. He *had* seen Tim perform, during three consecutive nights at a Boston coffeehouse in the '60s, and recalls the elder Buckley as "one of the most intense performers I ever saw." Intrigued—and trusting Willner's taste—Berkowitz agreed to stop in and warm up with some coffee at the same time.

Berkowitz watched as a kid in rags, whom he presumed to be the club soundman, set up a microphone stand and guitar. Berkowitz looked around, waiting for the main act to start. Then the kid himself began singing, and Berkowitz suddenly realized this *was* the show. Like many in those days, Berkowitz was instantly transported. "I was just amazed by this voice," he recalls. "Hal was talking to a waitress, and I'm tapping him on the shoulder going, 'Hal! Listen to this guy!'" Afterward, Willner introduced them; Jeff told them he was playing that night in part because it was too cold in his apartment.

Berkowitz was immediately fascinated. His inclination may have been toward esoteric music, yet as a Sony Music A&R executive, he also had a responsibility to sign acts that bolstered the company's profit margin. In Jeff, he saw something he had rarely before imagined: a talent who could tap into a musical heritage Berkowitz appreciated yet who could, with his charisma and looks, potentially sell records, unlike most of Berkowitz's other signings. Berkowitz began attending Sin-é with increasing frequency. Almost immediately, he sensed Jeff's wariness toward the business, so he limited the conversations to music. In the past year, Jeff's tastes had shifted again, toward blues and jazz as well as the likes of Holiday and Garland, and Berkowitz was more than happy to discuss his own love of those styles.

Another regular at the shows was George Stein, the lawyer Jeff had retained to help him sort out Gods and Monsters's contract with Imago. The forty-five-year-old Stein, who had started as an FCC lawyer before going to work for his father's law firm, had had years of experience negotiating record contracts but was itching to make the leap into management. An earlier experience with a band that deserted him for a more powerful manager had left Stein on his guard; he wasn't about to allow another potential star to slip through his fingers. Stein began attending as many Sin-é shows as he could to show his support, even the performances that lasted until the early morning hours, as they often did. "Even *I* wanted to go home," Stein says, "but I wanted to show him I wasn't leaving." Like Berkowitz, Stein sensed Jeff had a disdain for anyone connected to the business. Still, he told Jeff he could make a few calls on his behalf to record executives, and Jeff agreed, without signing any binding paperwork.

As it turned out, Stein didn't have to do as much initial legwork as he thought. Positive word on Jeff had first leaked out after the "Greetings from Tim Buckley" concert, and the weekly Sin-é performances only added to the mystique: The son of a semi-famous rock star was performing in a tiny space in the East Village. Soon, Berkowitz wasn't the only major-label scout in the house. On Monday, May 1, Mitchell Cohen, an A&R man at Arista Records, saw the first of many of Jeff's Sin-é shows. During May, two other A&R men who knew Stein—Dave Novik of RCA and Joe McEwen of Sire—dropped by. Imago's Kate Hyman, eager to sign Jeff as a solo, was also in attendance many nights. Each asked Stein for a tape, and Stein told them all the same thing: There *was* no tape of Jeff singing his Sin-é repertoire, so they would have to come see the show.

About a month later, on June 8, Cohen sent a memo to his boss, Arista president and industry veteran Clive Davis, informing him that Tim Buckley's son was "creating a natural buzz" downtown, that at least three other labels were vying for him, and that perhaps Davis should drop by Sin-é as soon as possible. Before long, limos and car services could be seen parked bumper-to-bumper all along St. Mark's Place.

The irony of the situation was not lost on Jeff: After years of avoiding any connection with his late father, he had awakened the interest of the music business as a result of singing *Tim*'s music, and he was being checked out by veteran record executives old enough to remember and admire his father. "I'm convinced part of the reason I got signed is because of who I am," Jeff said in 1993. "And it makes me sad. But I can't do anything else."

Friends told Jeff that wasn't true, but he had a point. During the summer of 1992, the record industry was scouring the landscape for all things grunge and alternative. A Seattle trio called Nirvana, followed by another Northwest band called Pearl Jam, were suddenly selling millions of records, marking the overdue breakthrough of underground, punk-rooted independent rock into the mainstream. The second Lollapalooza tour was one of the summer's big tickets, grossing a surprising $19.1 million. There *was* a feeding frenzy to sign acts, but the demand was for ersatz Kurt Cobains and pseudo Eddie Vedders, not sentimental-sounding kids with crystalline voices, no band, and a repertoire dating back nearly fifty years. The older record executives interested in Jeff may not have connected with grunge, but in him they found a kindred spirit who shared their taste in classic rock, roots music, and standards—"authentic" music in a supposedly unauthentic time.

Everything was happening absurdly, head-spinningly, fast. Before long, even Jeff's friends could no longer squeeze in to Sin-é to watch their friend perform. "It was fucked," says Willner, who once brought along his friend Marianne Faithfull. "There were big fish with limos, and they'd come back with *bigger* fish and more limos. People would be pouring out into the street with their notepads, looking at each other and nodding their heads. I was a little pissed, because it was almost over."

For George Stein, though, it was merely the beginning. Stein sensed he had a hot, albeit reluctant, property on his hands. One of the reasons Jeff began helping Sin-é's employees wash dishes after shows was to avoid having to schmooze with the A&R suits who would dawdle outside the club. Still, Stein—who was still only acting as Jeff's lawyer, since Jeff seemed wary of even the word "manager"—began setting up introductory get-togethers at the labels' offices.

A meeting at Arista, on Wednesday, June 10, was typical. Jeff arrived over an hour late, wearing a ratty T-shirt and carrying a plastic bag filled with cleaning supplies for his apartment. Eventually, he and Stein sat down with Cohen and began talking music and Jeff's preferred career route. "Well," Cohen said, "what are you looking for in a label?"

"Well, if I went to . . . ," Jeff began. He paused and looked over at Stein. *"Where* are we?" he asked.

"We're at Arista, Jeff," Stein replied calmly.

Stein thought the remark was merely another indication of how lovably loopy his client could be, but it may not have been so simple. Jeff later told his friend Penny Arcade that he knew very well where he was during such meetings and that he would deliberately make those comments. "He was very proud of the fact that he was very belligerent with the record companies," Arcade says. "He had a real chip on his shoulder about them." If the goal was to push the powers-that-be away, it didn't work. Instead of being offended by Jeff's blithe attitude, Cohen was only more fascinated; it showed that Jeff was "not pretentious." After the meeting, Cohen was only more determined to pursue Jeff.

A short while later, Cohen took Jeff in to meet Davis, the crinkled, mainstream-minded hitmaker whose career extended from Columbia Records in the '60s (where he signed Janis Joplin and Santana, among others) through his current role as head of Arista, where he made stars out of Barry Manilow and Whitney Houston. After some preliminary chitchat, the meeting began with the airing of a five-minute video presentation about Davis's life and career achievements. Jeff was "bemused," says Stein. Afterward, Davis admitted he had yet to see or hear Jeff play but had *heard* he was terrific. "Jeff appreciated that Clive was trying to be candid with him," recalls Cohen. No firm commitment of any kind was discussed, but Davis said he would try to see Jeff perform soon. Afterward, quiet and shaken, Jeff socked back a bottle of beer in Cohen's office.

As much as Jeff recoiled at the music business, often stiffening up and giving less impressive performances when limos would pull up in front of Sin-é, he was also utterly conflicted. "I didn't want it to happen at the time," he said in 1993. "I was flattered and glad and terrified—not terrified, but I had misgivings. The music business is the most childish business in the world. Nobody knows what they're selling or why, but they sell it if it works." For all his misgivings, Jeff was nonetheless a child of rock culture. A contract with a major label meant a vast opportunity to communicate, to have his records distributed around the world, to get his music across to a huge audience. He knew the power of electricity, of rock and roll cranked loud in arenas, of the surge of the crowd, of the mythic proportions of it all. He wanted it on his terms, on his schedule, but part of him wanted it nonetheless.

Sensing heightened industry interest, Stein—with Jeff's cooperation—set up a package deal any label would have to accept if they wanted Jeff: a guarantee of three albums (as opposed to the one or two most new acts received), a $100,000 signing advance, a higher-than-usual royalty rate of 28 percent (which, again, was slightly higher than that for a new, unproven act), and creative control over his music and recordings. Given the six-figure costs of making a single album in the '90s, it was, in essence, a million-dollar deal.

The plan was cocky and not a little arrogant, and it nearly backfired. Since Jeff had few songs of his own and an eclecticism that bordered on a lack of focus, each of the A&R executives who were eager to sign him envisioned him in his or her own light. Sire's McEwen, a former DJ and rock critic, saw Jeff making a Memphis-style R&B/blues record, Imago's Hyman a more Neil Young–influenced rock disc, RCA's Novik "not necessarily a blues recording in the Robert Johnson sense but in the sense of raw emotion."

As eager as they were to recruit Jeff, obstacles arose when each brought his or her boss, the men who would actually sign the checks, down to Sin-é. Arista's Davis finally came down—amusingly, after his office called first to reserve a table and were snidely informed by the Sin-é staff that there were no such things as reservations. "At one point," Cohen recalls, "Clive leaned over to me and said, 'This is great, but I don't know where the songs are going to come from. I don't know what it's going to be. It's a huge investment. We really have to think about it.'" Davis left before Jeff finished his set.

Novik's bosses had the same response: Was he going to sing covers? Form a band? And they want a *million dollars*? Imago, lacking the funds, dropped out; RCA, Sire, and Arista had the money but thought the package deal too high. Everyone sensed Jeff was talented, but who was he? What would they receive for their money?

Fortunately for Stein, there was still one label left standing.

Launched in 1887 by a cousin of Alexander Graham Bell, Columbia Records had been home to everyone from Billie Holiday and Miles Davis to Bob Dylan and Bruce Springsteen, and no one was more eager to rattle off such names than the label's strapping thirty-nine-year-old president, Don Ienner. A former promotion man at Arista, where he was credited with helping break Whitney Houston, Ienner had started in the mailroom of Capitol Records in 1969, while he was still in high school. When a back injury crippled his planned baseball career, he began making his way up the music business ladder. Big and beefy, with a full head of coiffed hair and enough charisma to run for office, "Donny" was known for his enthusiasm, his booming voice, and the demands he placed on his staff to deliver as many hits as possible, as often as possible.

By the summer of 1992, Columbia was in healthy financial shape. The label's owner, the Japanese-owned Sony Corporation, announced that revenue for the music division (which included both Columbia and its sister label Epic Records) was $3.8 billion for the fiscal year ending March 31, 1992. (The entire Sony Corporation, a vast conglomerate with film and electronics divisions, netted nine times that amount, $28.73 billion.) That year, Columbia releases ate up 12.6 percent of the *Billboard* chart, more than any other label, thanks to multimillion-selling albums by mainstream pop acts like Mariah Carey, Michael Bolton, and Harry Connick Jr., as well as dance-music acts like C+C Music Factory.

Still, only a label publicist would believe that any of those acts were the esteemed career artists—or "heritage artists," as they were known in-house—on which Columbia prided itself. As platinum-sated as Columbia was, it was vital to Ienner and his colleagues to prove (for image, if anything else) they could still foster another Dylan or Bruce. It was also important to show Columbia could compete with Epic in the alternative music market: Epic had powerhouses like Pearl Jam and Rage Against the Machine, while Columbia was saddled with ersatz bohos like Poi Dog Pondering and Toad the Wet Sprocket.

An earlier signing, a gaunt, sulking singer-guitarist named Chris Whitley, was meant to be Columbia's next classy "heritage artist," but when his first album failed to deliver in 1991, executives began glancing around for alternatives. To Berkowitz and others, Jeff fit the bill: He was young, attractive, and steeped in everything from classic rock to blues to gospel. While competing labels hemmed and hawed, Berkowitz began a campaign to woo Jeff to Columbia, starting with Berkowitz's colleagues. On July 7, he sent a note to fellow Columbia executives recommending they see Jeff's shows at Sin-é and another club, Tilt. Two days later, Jeff found himself at "Black Rock," the monolithic office building on West 52nd Street that was home to Columbia Records. With Stein, he took a seat in the office of one executive as other employees came in. As each marketing and promotion executive explained his or her job, Jeff sat quietly in a chair, eating a sandwich and saying little.

The hard sell didn't end there. Sony Music employees continued dropping by his shows, including vice president of artist development Paul Rappaport, who took Jeff out to dinner one summer evening and told Jeff he belonged on Columbia. Looking up at Rappaport from under his thick eyebrows, Jeff exuded a mixture of hurt and enthusiasm. "For his age, you could see he had really been through a lot," Rappaport recalls. "He was cautious. The foremost thing on this mind was he wanted to be protected, he wanted to be able to do what he did, and he didn't want someone to make him go a certain way." Eventually, Ienner took a limo down to Sin-é himself for what became his first of many trips there. "I had *no* idea what we could ever do with Jeff on a commercial level," he says, "but [the performance] showed an amazing treasure." Ienner was sold. In Jeff, he saw a raw talent with the potential to sell records and lend the label integrity—Ienner's own Dylan or Springsteen.

As the muggy summer dragged on, and as Columbia executives continued sitting through Jeff's sets in the unair-conditioned Sin-é, it became clear (especially to competing label executives) that a contract with Columbia was Jeff's for the taking. The label desperately wanted to add Jeff to its roster, and its executives were willing not only to meet Stein's demands but to offer up the company's estimable resources. According to Michael Tighe (pronounced "tie"), a young actor pal of Moore's who became one of Jeff's close friends, "Jeff was attracted to Columbia's legacy, but the ability they have to get their artists heard across the world really appealed to him. He liked the idea of traveling and performing for people all over the place. He was very aware of the contradictions—yes, it can hurt you this way, but it can also give you *this*."

Others had doubts. Jeff's LA pal Chris Dowd, who was signed to Columbia through his membership in Fishbone, argued strongly against his friend signing with the label. At home, Jeff and Moore talked about it at length. He was afraid he would lose his soul and be trampled by the same machinery that undid his father, and she was concerned about the effect touring and the music business would have on their eighteen-month-old relationship. Over pizza in Times Square, after yet another industry powwow, Jeff turned to Stein and said, "Do we have to do this with a major? Should we go with an independent?" Stein made his case: A major had resources; an indie didn't, which meant Jeff would still have to worry about paying his rent. Also, Stein said, an indie wouldn't have the money to send Jeff on worldwide tours. "And maybe," Stein added, "you won't be able to put enough aside if you want to have kids and put them through college." Naturally, the arrangement would also benefit Stein: How better to launch a career as a rock manager than with an affiliation with Sony Music?

Back and forth it went. Finally, in late July, Jeff gave Stein the go-ahead. "To be a Columbia recording artist was, in his mind, the fulfillment of a dream," says John Humphrey, his one-time LA roommate, recalling a talk with Jeff. "In his mind it was an extension of John Hammond discovering Dylan and all the cats. He was going to have a shot at being a 'cat,' and he was thrilled to be attached to the lineage of 'greatness.'"

Even as Jeff grappled with the idea of committing himself to a huge record company—and thereby committing himself to becoming a singular "Jeff Buckley," rather than the freeform, amorphous person he had been up to that point—everyone around him sensed a major-league record deal was inevitable, that Jeff was on a path over which he had little control. If it wasn't Columbia, there would most likely be some other conglomerate calling for the services of a young, talented, and attractive potential pop star. The only question was what Jeff's precise route would be.

The first draft of Jeff's contract with Columbia was drawn up on August 6, 1992, and for the next two months, Stein haggled over it with Sony lawyers. In the meantime, Jeff went about his business, continuing to play at Sin-é and other clubs and appearing numerous times on Nicholas Hill's radio show. One of the most memorable appearances came the night of September 6, while Jeff and Moore were having dinner at a friend's apartment in Hoboken, New Jersey. Live on the air, Hill called Jeff at the house. Jeff took the call and, as musicians accompanied him in the miles-away studio, sang an impassioned version of Bob Dylan's "I Shall Be Released" over the phone. His newfound reverence for Dylan was in full swing, and many say it was the sight of a Dylan poster in the Columbia hallways that made Jeff finally decide to link up with the company.

He was still living off the Sin-é money (when he remembered to dip into the jug after a set, that is), as well as anything else he could do to earn a few dollars. He would baby-sit for friends' cats or make compilation tapes for restaurants where Moore waitressed while she pursued her own acting and theatrical career. One of Moore's friends worked for an advertising agency, and Jeff auditioned—albeit unsuccessfully—for a Kmart television commercial, in which he would play a twentysomething shopper. He still kept in contact with his old friend Michael Clouse, who offered Jeff an unusual session gig: playing guitar on a bubblegum-R&B demo being produced by Mariah Carey's brother Morgan. Jeff dutifully took a train to the Long Island studio, cut the track quickly with Carey and Clouse (who had flown in from Los Angeles for the occasion), and spent the night in the Carey family home. Mariah had moved out years before, although Clouse was able to sleep in her childhood bed.

As fall approached, the Columbia contract approached completion. One day Jeff brought it home to Moore, and the two of them stared at it. Neither had ever seen such an imposing document. It wasn't simply its length—sixty pages—but its page after page of single-spaced legalese and alphabetized subheads. There were sixteen eye-glazing pages alone devoted to royalty (and royalty-accounting) details. If any proof was needed that the music business had truly become a wholesale business, there it was, staring Jeff in the face. The days of three- or four-page contracts, like the one Tim had signed nearly thirty years before, were over.

The basics of Stein's demands were typed out in black and white and in the subheads. Sony (as the label was referred to in the contract) was obligated to release three albums by Jeff, with options for four more. He would indeed receive a $100,000 advance upon signing and an inordinately high royalty rate of 28 percent (of the wholesale price of the album, which amounted to about $1.50 per disc). His mechanical publishing (that is, album-sale-oriented) royalty rate for any track he wrote was .066 cents per song (of less than five minutes), or 66 cents per album if the album contained ten tracks. (Rates for songs over five minutes would be calculated based on a formula.) When a second album was to begin, he would receive an advance of $50,000. There was no written mention of creative control; nonetheless, both A&R and management assured Jeff it was a given. Sony gave Jeff approval over album cover art, and the label would not be allowed to "release 'outtakes' on phonograph records without [his] consent."

Otherwise, it was a boilerplate Sony contract, containing many of the standard terms applied to any act. Sony had the right to approve record producers, had to be notified if a song title was changed, and would own the master recordings of Jeff's music. Jeff could perform on another musician's or band's work but could not "render a solo or 'step-out' performance," nor could the song or style be "substantially similar to the characteristic musical style of Recordings made by the Artist for Sony." No movie studio except Sony could use Jeff's music; if another one did, it couldn't use more than two of his songs. More important—and equally standard both for Sony and the music business in general—Jeff had to pay for nearly everything: his producer, half of the independent radio promotion, and half of the cover art (another victory on Stein's part, since most acts have to pay for all of promotion and art). All of these costs—as well as his $100,000 advance and any money Sony would spend on making videos and tour expenses, such as paying for a band, equipment, and buses—would be added to a fund called the recoupable. Only after his record sales matched the recoupable amount would Jeff begin making royalties on his own work. (This applied particularly to the mechanical royalty for song publishing; Jeff's sales would have to exceed his separate publishing advance of $200,000 before he saw that 66 cents per album.)

Shortly before the signing day, Jeff called Berkowitz and asked to get together. They went for one of their usual meals downtown, and around 2 A.M. found themselves at a nondescript bar in the Village. Jeff had something on his mind, and through sleepy, half-closed eyes, he finally articulated it: "Are you signing me because of who my father was?" Berkowitz said of course he wasn't, and added, "Are you interested in working with me because of who *my* father was?" He told Jeff that his father's name had no bearing on Jeff's own music; besides, Berkowitz added, "Your father's not that famous." The conversation seemed to set Jeff's mind at ease, at least for the time being.

The signing was scheduled for October 29. Record contracts can often be initialed by musicians in their own home and then sent back to labels, but everyone at Sony, Ienner in particular, wanted to make a statement that they had landed a major artist. Wearing a black jacket, Jeff went to the legal office at 5 P.M., leaned over the desk, and scrawled his signature on the last page. Then Ienner, Berkowitz, David Kahne (senior vice president of A&R, and Berkowitz's boss), and Sony business executives gathered in front of the Columbia logo in a reception area, and the official commemorative photo was snapped.

Afterward, Jeff came home, jumped on a couch, and told Moore, with both weariness and happiness, "It's done." She had a gift for him, purchased at the deli across the street: a $100,000 Bar candy bar, in honor of his advance. Not long afterward, he deposited his advance check at an ATM; Moore wondered what the bank employee must have thought upon slitting open *that* envelope.

When the photograph of the signing finally appeared in print, in the January 30, 1993, issue of *Billboard,* it would have been easy to mistake it for a post-wedding-ceremony gathering of the bridegroom's closest buddies. The seven men in the photo, especially Ienner, sported broad, satisfied smiles. Standing next to Ienner, Jeff looked stiff and pale, more like someone who was signing up for a flu shot instead of a million-dollar record contract. He was the only one not flashing even the tiniest of grins.

ELEVEN

When Tim fell in love with Judy and Taylor he filled their lives up
again. Judy had a heart reopened and renewed. And Taylor . . . he
woke up again. He was being raised by a long-haired lover-freak . . .
slight disciplinarian . . . in LOVE with his woman and her son. . . .
Listen to me, it was his love that rescued Judy and Taylor from being
frozen by tragedy. And it was their love that rescued my father from his
guilt.

—JEFF BUCKLEY, JOURNAL ENTRY, AUGUST 9, 1995

Janie Goldstein wasn't alone in her puzzlement. To most of Tim's friends, Judy Sutcliffe seemed to materialize out of nowhere. In fact, by the time she had moved into Tim's Park Place home in the fall of 1969, she had already lived several lives and experienced misfortune beyond her twenty-seven years.

Born in St. Louis in October 1942, Judith Fern Brejot only completed high school and, on the eve of her nineteenth birthday, married Darrell Keith Sutcliffe, a local body mechanic four years her senior, in October 1961. By the time of the birth of their son Taylor Keith Sutcliffe in April 1963, the new family had relocated to Waukesha, Wisconsin, where Sutcliffe was born and where he worked at a company called Saghagain Customs. Sutcliffe was a charismatic jack-of-all-trades who, when he wasn't painting or sculpting, was involved in archaeology, adventure travel, and sundry inventions. He and his wife traveled often when they weren't living in Los Angeles, their next home base. Judy claims her husband opened a Native American museum in Arizona and, with film director Carroll Ballard, helped design and construct "blimps," sound-proofing devices that prevent the noise of a movie camera from being recorded by microphones.

One of their trips took them to Tijuana, Mexico, in February 1969, where, driving in their Jeep, they were involved in a serious traffic accident. Severely injured, Darrell Sutcliffe was brought to a Mexican jail; according to Molly LeMay, a friend of the Sutcliffes, the money authorities demanded for his release kept escalating. Before friends and family had a chance to arrange for the official bribe, Sutcliffe died while behind bars. (According to Taylor, "Dad died from penicillin given to him by the Mexican medical staff at a hospital, after he told them he was *allergic* to penicillin.") The incident was later recounted in song by singer, songwriter, and actor Hoyt Axton, a Sutcliffe friend. In "Darrell and Judy," Axton described a friend "hurt bad in a wreck" and of Judy showing up at his house desperate for the $500 needed to bail out her husband. "They gave her his body," sang Axton, "when she gave 'em the dough."

The accident was especially painful for young, blond Taylor, who suffered a broken collarbone and was so traumatized that he stopped speaking for a period. Judy sent him to live with her parents in St. Louis, and she eventually relocated to Venice, near Tim's house. She had already met Tim earlier, at the Troubadour, where she worked at the ticket window while her late husband helped with lights and sound. Tim, she recalls, was "this hippie kid with moccasins and beads," but that was all she knew about him; she had never even heard him sing.

Although Judy was five years older, Tim was immediately drawn to her—and her suffering—after her husband's fatal accident. With her floor-length dresses, penchant for leather vests and shirts, and long, straight black hair that reminded many of Cher, Judy Sutcliffe projected an air of earthy sensuality and slinky intrigue, which also became part of her allure to Tim. Her dry wit and fashion-conscious wardrobe also made her appear more sophisticated and worldly than either Jane or Mary. "Judy was very different from a lot of the little hippie chicks who were around," recalls LeMay. "She had a tremendous style and an elegance about the way she carried herself. She would always have makeup. Even if the clothing was of a particular hippie thing, the rest of the package was totally together, always." Judy was, according to Carter Collins, "the right person at the right time in his life."

By the time Jane stopped by the Park Place home one last time, Judy had already moved in. Tim owned only a tea kettle, two cups, and a bed, but together he and Judy would huddle in the living room and listen relentlessly to Miles Davis's *In a Silent Way* ("the only album he had," Judy recalls). Tim began calling her "Madame Wu," after Wu's Garden, a Cantonese restaurant on Wilshire Boulevard in Santa Monica that was one of Tim's favorite eateries. In turn, Judy nicknamed him "Captain Eddy" after his twelve-string Rickenbacker guitar. "All of a sudden Tim wasn't around," says Dan Gordon. "He was locked in his apartment. When they came out, he said, 'This is Wu—I love her.' And that was it—they were inseparable." Tim and Judy married on April 19, 1970.

Judy sent for her son, and seven-year-old Taylor arrived late one night at the Los Angeles airport and saw a man with a huge Afro in the front seat of a Volkswagen minibus. Arriving in Venice, Taylor walked into the Park Place living room, which was filled with instruments and amplifiers; a giant gong sat in the fireplace. "Go ahead—hit it," Tim said to him. Taylor took a big swing, and the gong reverberated so loudly Taylor felt as if his teeth were about to dislodge from his head. "That's the last time you'll play with that thing," Tim told him. "That's what I use to make my money." Afterward, Tim and his new son took a walk on the beach, Taylor asking this unusual, bushy-haired man what he did for a living and how long he had been doing it.

Perhaps out of guilt over the son in Orange County he wouldn't or couldn't see, Tim quickly took to Taylor. "I fell in love with Tim because of the love he gave my child," Judy says. "He wanted to give us a family. He made Taylor laugh and smile. He made *me* smile and laugh again." Judy herself became instantly devoted to Tim; reporters who stopped by the house found Tim in his high-backed bamboo chair, Judy at his side.

Most likely, Tim also fell for Judy since she appeared to have no pressing desire for a career of her own, despite her ongoing interest in making leather goods. Jane's determination to forge her own life had undermined her relationship with Tim, and as 1970 dawned, the same kind of determination also led to Tim's break with his New York lover, Hope Ruff. Ruff was not only career-oriented but, to add to the competitive air, a fellow musician. For her part, she was disturbed by Tim's increasing reliance on pills, particularly

Seconal, also known as reds. According to Ruff, Tim would visit her New York apartment and ask her to "take this and that."

"It wasn't that I didn't do drugs or drink," Ruff says. "I just couldn't spend all my time getting stoned. He was like an exposed nerve. It was very attractive and very romantic, and it would have killed me. I knew the day would come when I would get a call that he had died. I told him that, and he couldn't refute it. He thought, 'Well, if it happens, it happens.'" Ruff claims that before Judy entered the picture, Tim asked Ruff to marry him, and that she declined. To punish her, she says, Tim slept with another woman the weekend they spent at his friend John King's bucolic country farm north of New York City.

As a wedding gift to Judy, Tim bought his second wife a home in the oceanside community of Laguna Beach, fifty-five miles south of Los Angeles. The house at 2972 Rounseuel Terrace was a wood-shingled split level on a cul-de-sac next to a convent; it was, Judy recalls, "wonderfully quiet." The floors were black marble, and Taylor had his own wing, complete with a sky-light and telescope. Shortly after the Buckley family moved in, Tim had the exterior painted black. To his friends, it felt strangely symbolic, as if Tim were about to enter a new, and very different, period of his life.

Between the time Judy moved into Park Place and she and Tim wed, Tim released not one but two new albums. Starting with *Happy Sad,* Tim found himself in the middle of a creative rush, his artistic fires raging. He felt as if he were on the verge of launching a new art form, an undiscovered terrain that would combine his vast musical influences and loves, and yet not be limited by any fences.

In that regard, *Blue Afternoon,* the first of his albums to be released in the new decade, was something of a false start. By now, Tim was officially on the roster of Herb Cohen's Straight Records. For Tim's first Straight release, though, Cohen needed something more commercial than the fin-ished but still unreleased *Lorca.* With only slight reluctance, Tim agreed to rifle through his sheet music for old, unfinished songs that adhered to standard verse-chorus folk-pop structures. "We had to take one step back-wards," says Underwood, "to please the powers that be."

As backward lurches go, *Blue Afternoon* hardly feels like a compro-mise. Most of the eight songs Tim unearthed are small gems. "I Must Have Been Blind" is imbued with the aching regret of missed romantic opportunity, while "The River," a somber elegy from as early as 1967, was supposedly inspired by R&B crooner Sam Cooke. Its opening line, "I live by the river/And I hide my house away," was written after Tim was riveted by Cooke's "A Change Is Gonna Come" (which opens with "I was born by the river"). "Happy Time," which describes both his passion for his craft and his increasing ambivalence toward the business ("It's such a shame/The way they use your name"), is a number he had begun performing live two years before and had first recorded during the initial *Happy Sad* sessions. A throwaway called "So Lonely" reveals a rare sense of self-mockery, just as "Blue Melody," with its cocktail-lounge piano by Underwood, addresses, with equal rareness, his troubled childhood ("One summer morning, I was raised . . ./One summer morning, I was left"). Even in a hopeful affirmation to his lover called "Chase the Blues Away" (another leftover from the 1968 *Happy Sad* formation period), Tim's voice has a misty, burnished edge, as if things are about to end or change and there is nothing he or anyone else can do about it.

If Tim was forced to concoct "retrogressive business music," as Underwood calls it, he was nevertheless going to do it his way. Recorded just before the breakup of his jazz ensemble, the sessions, held in New York and Los Angeles during 1969, featured Underwood, Friedman, and Miller, but also two jazz musicians, guitarist Steve Khan (who contributed several uncredited guitar solos, including one on "Happy Time") and drummer Jimmy Madison. The songs were melodic and restrained, but Miller's sinuous acoustic-bass lines, Khan's graceful guitar, Friedman's chiming vibe solos, and Madison's perfectly accented brush drums were a further extension of the folk-jazz fusion Tim had been developing. "It was the first time Tim really found himself playing with jazz crossover players," says Miller of what he recalls as relaxed sessions. "It never got *so* out, but it stretched him." The music only went somewhere "out" on the final track, "The Train," which chugged wildly over nearly eight minutes, Tim emitting wails and groans as if he had repressed them during the seven preceding songs.

When it was released in the middle of January 1970, *Blue Afternoon* appeared to mark a return of the old Tim his fans knew and loved. Trade advertisements referred to Tim as a "frail minstrel, solid heartthrob, and major artist from Orange County," three descriptions that most likely made his skin crawl. Like the two albums that preceded it, it made the *Billboard* charts, peaking at number 192 the week of February 14, the day

Tim turned twenty-three. Dubbing him "one of the most underrated, and one of the most gifted, of today's singer-songwriters," the *New York Times* ironically called *Blue Afternoon* "his best to date." The only one who was slightly irritated was Elektra's Jac Holzman, who had *Lorca* in the can, heard the more listener-friendly *Blue Afternoon,* and wondered how it was he ended up with the more esoteric album.

Four short months later, that very record appeared in record store racks. If the public wasn't confused already by two different LPs unveiled within such a short time span, *Lorca* only served to confound them further. Once again, the reviews were kind. The *New York Times* described it as having "Coltranesque modality" and called the title track "a stunning tour de force that has a sensual involvement with sound for its own sake," while *Fusion* magazine favorably compared Tim to jazz saxophonist Pharoah Sanders. Yet *Lorca* was greeted warily by both fans and many of Tim's old friends. Listening to *Lorca* in New York, his former bass player, John Miller, was thankful he was no longer in Tim's band. "I wouldn't have known what to do," he says. "I didn't know the language. It was self-indulgent—or maybe great, and I just didn't understand the language."

Released with little fanfare from Elektra, *Lorca* not surprisingly failed to appear on the charts and sold only between five and ten thousand copies, a heady drop from the days when *Goodbye and Hello* and *Happy Sad* sold several times that amount. "He wanted to do it," says Herb Cohen of *Lorca*. "I told him exactly what it would sell—which was not much—and that it wouldn't help his performance career, because people wouldn't want to hear it. And that's what happened. It's beautiful and esoteric, and," he adds caustically, "it fulfilled my expectations of what it would do." When *Billboard* published a list of its leading "campus attractions" that year, Tim placed at number 17, in between pop singer Oliver ("Good Morning Starshine") and Vegas lizard Engelbert Humperdinck.

Shortly before *Lorca*'s release, Tim and a newly revamped band, including Balkin, Underwood, and Mothers of Invention trumpet player John "Buzz" Gardner, gave a performance at the University of Pennsylvania (one of many colleges at which they appeared at this point). They opened with a howling, incendiary "Gypsy Woman" that extended for twenty minutes. It was just the beginning of a show that featured gongs, flutes, and numerous displays of Tim's electrified yodel. The audience didn't know what to make of it—not until the second set, at least, when Tim played recognizable favorites like "Pleasant Street" and "Morning Glory." The old Timmy, the curly-haired troubadour, was back, or so they thought. Someone then called out, "How about 'Buzzin' Fly?' "

"How about horseshit?" Tim shot back.

A *Rolling Stone* review of the concert, under the headline "Buckley's Yodeling Baffles Audience," praised Tim's attempt to develop "a new form and format . . . but the audience on that night didn't care much; they were just disappointed and confused."

"He knew his fans hated *Lorca*," says Ruff, "and he hated them for hating it." Just as likely, at this point in his career Tim shrugged off the naysayers and went about his art. He already had a grander, more challenging vision in mind.

By early 1970, Larry Beckett had had an eventful eighteen months, albeit in the worst ways. After being drafted, he had been assigned to a fort near Monterey in Northern California and another in Missouri. Desperate to get out before he was shipped to Vietnam, Beckett went AWOL and, upon being caught, was sentenced to the stockades. Beckett did his best to act strange—which his friends say wasn't terribly difficult for the lost-in-his-thoughts Beckett to do—and after a stay in a state mental hospital, he was eventually discharged as unsuitable for combat. Manda Bradlyn, who had become Beckett's lover during the later Venice days, was now living in Portland, Oregon, and Beckett, still sporting his army crew cut, relocated there to live with her. (In terms of his own military obligation, Tim was more fortunate; according to Cohen, he and other Cohen clients like Captain Beefheart and members of the Mothers of Invention were deemed 4-F. "Would *you* want them in your army?" Cohen cracks.)

Back in Portland, Beckett played the first side of *Lorca* and was so disheartened he couldn't bring himself to flip the LP over. Still, he couldn't resist when Tim called and said he wanted to write a new batch of songs with his old friend. Tim flew up to Portland, and the two bore down on a lyric idea Tim said was inspired by a dream. Out came "I Woke Up," the first song Tim and Beckett had written together in two years. Although Beckett wasn't completely happy with the lyric, Tim was inspired by its unorthodox imagery and rhyme scheme (the line "Oh, I see your woman in the raw/Ride a mare of stone and howl" is a lesbian image, according to Beckett). It seemed a fine match for the music he was writing, although Beckett had no idea what that music was.

The duo collaborated on several more songs. "Monterey" began as a

Beckett poem recalling the time Bradlyn left him while he was locked away. Ever since his days in French club at Loara High, Tim had always wanted to sing a song in that language, so Beckett came up with "Moulin Rouge," a jaunty reverie half in French and half in English. Again, Beckett had no idea what the accompanying melodies would be; all he heard were mentions of atonality and various time signatures.

Those elements were the least of it. As Tim told a reporter several years later, "We decided that, now that we're good at this, we'll present a new way of writing a song." By this time, Underwood's role in the band had been quietly usurped by John Balkin. The bass player had turned Tim on to avant-classical composers like Olivier Messiaen and Krzysztof Penderecki, and as he so often did, Tim sucked up the sonic input like an audio vacuum cleaner. For Tim's new project, Balkin assumed an even larger role than he had on *Lorca*. He recruited Buzz Gardner and his saxophone-playing brother Charles "Bunk" Gardner (all three had a side project, the Ménage a Trio, devoted to experimental music). A new drummer, former Janis Joplin sideman Maury Baker, was also hired; with his background in everything from rock to renaissance music to bebop, the native New Yorker had varied tastes that mirrored Tim's own.

The music this ensemble began recording on Thursday, September 10 (once again at Whitney) made *Lorca* seem like a collection of nursery rhymes. Since he couldn't read music, Tim again guided the band by instinct rather than education. He would start a song or indicate a feel for a particular groove, and the band would launch into it, improvising along the way. "There were no charts," recalls Baker. "You just listened." With a bigger, fuller band, the sonic playground was larger this time. The Gardner brothers brought along their slew of woodwind instruments—Tim would regularly imitate their trumpets and saxes during rehearsals—and Baker lugged in his large, booming timpani. (Another drummer, Roy Harte, was also recruited for a later date.) To recording engineer Stan Agol, the scene was like "a bunch of kids having fun. I liked the music, but I didn't quite understand it. You get to the point where you can't tell if it's bullshit or real good." Recorded over the course of seven sessions through September 21, the album was to be the first of many statements of Tim's anything-goes approach to music.

With memories of the timid Tim of *Goodbye and Hello* in mind, Beckett dropped by the studio and was shocked by Tim's new in-control attitude. (Once again, Herb Cohen was listed as executive producer, but no one recalls seeing him.) To Beckett, the change was especially apparent the night of September 20, when he, Tim, and Balkin constructed a piece called "Starsailor." The foundation of the song—a six-line poem by Beckett— was relatively basic, but nothing else about it was. Deciding to transform it into an *a cappella* showpiece, Tim and Balkin painstakingly overdubbed sixteen of Tim's voices, changing the speed on the tape decks and shifting audio channels throughout the process. The result was a ghostly, discombobulated vocal symphony unlike anything a so-called pop musician had ever devised, the sound of purgatory-suspended spirits finding out if they were heading for either heaven or hell. "He'd put something down and listen to it and say, 'Oh, now I have to do this high-pitched shrieking with vibrato,' " Beckett recalls. "It wasn't even pop music anymore, let's face it. It was classical music." Tim so loved the track that he decided to name the album in its honor.

Tim didn't completely turn his back on established pop songwriting forms during the making of *Starsailor*. When everyone discovered the album was running short, the sweet, ersatz-cabaret song "Moulin Rouge" was quickly cut at the end of the sessions. After several earlier stabs at recording "Song to the Siren," Tim also finally decided to include the neglected song on his new project. According to Beckett, Tim hadn't touched it since 1968 because their friend Judy Henske made fun of one line ("I'm as puzzled as the oyster"), prompting Tim, always one to take criticism deeply to heart, to shelve the song. Henske contradicts the story, saying she actually liked the line. Whatever the reason, "Song to the Siren" was retired for at least two years.

Beckett, who had written the original lyrics, rewrote the supposedly offending line, changing it to "I'm as puzzled as the newborn" (Tim added "child" after "newborn," thinking the line was missing a word). When Tim recorded it during the sessions, gone was the soft madrigal performed on *The Monkees*. Accompanied only by his effect-enhanced electric twelve-string, Tim slowed the song down to an exhausted plea, resulting in one of his most subtly anguished performances. For added chills, he overdubbed his own echoey, distant wails in the background. It was as if he were imitating the mythological sirens who lured sailors to the rocks, only to see their vessels crash "amid the breakers" and sink to the bottom of the water.

Starsailor, Tim's third and most challenging release in less than a year, arrived the week of November 7, the same day as Bob Dylan's markedly less ambitious *New Morning*. One can only imagine how Tim's faithful felt when the needle dropped on side one and they were greeted with a flurry of flailing guitar and bass notes, crashing-waves drums, a ghoulish pipe organ, and Tim, his voice low and deliberate, navigating his way through a completely amelodic tune. The song, "Come Here Woman," then shifts time signatures, introduces riffs that come and go, and alters its mood from art-song cerebral to libidinously sexual—all as Tim makes his voice swoop up and down like a trombone. It is merely the beginning of the journey for both Tim and his listeners. On the second cut, "I Woke Up," the fretted instruments imitate the sound of beached whales, while Baker's timpani drum rumbles and splashes as Tim articulates Beckett's pointedly abstract lyrics ("The harbor bells ring slavery/Where the fortune teller sighs to me").

Starsailor only grows more complex as it progresses. "Monterey" is built around a simple, groove-oriented Underwood guitar lick, but as on the other tracks, the music continually shifts and reinvents itself: Different drum patterns and horn figures enter and depart, and there isn't a trace anywhere of a hummable chorus. When Tim reaches one of Beckett's climactic phrases— "I run with the damned, my darling"—he elongates the sound of each word, morphing his voice from a high, sustained yelp to an old witch's bray, before ending with a barrage of squealing and ululating. "Song to the Siren" and "Moulin Rouge," with its muted, Parisian-café trumpet, afford listeners the briefest of respites.

Tim placed the even more difficult songs on the LP's second side. "Jungle Fire" is an impressionistic poem by Tim that, halfway through, lurches into a free-for-all band jam in 5/4 time, Tim repeating the line "Mama lie" in different timbres and registers. It's followed by the *a cappella* piece "Starsailor" and then by the Harlem-inspired "The Healing Festival," another song with an unusual time signature that defies foot-tapping (10/4) and careening jazz contributions from the Gardner brothers. *Starsailor* wraps up with "Down by the Borderline," which begins with Buzz Gardner's bullfight trumpet before giving way to Tim's extended scat section (as he watches "a little girl pass by") and Underwood's flurry of guitar notes. Then the album ends, leaving listeners exhilarated, confused, or perhaps a bit of both. At the very least, his voice once again leaves an indelible impression; its potency and range, and his fluent ability to bend vocal notes and leap up an octave or two within a single line, is a wonder to the ears. By *Starsailor,* Tim has surpassed any of his peers in singing abilities alone, and a range of possibilities—art songs, free jazz, musical theater, R&B—appeared to lay before him.

His stand against the rules of pop and rock didn't end with the album's release. On November 22, the *New York Times* ran an essay he wrote about Beethoven (headlined "Even If You Can't Play Him on the Guitar . . .") on the anniversary of the composer's two-hundredth birthday. The piece was rambling, but as he tried to articulate his feelings about Beethoven, Tim also revealed the dim view he took of the contemporary music scene. He began by writing that after listening to Beethoven's Ninth Symphony, sonatas, and string quartet pieces, he "started to wonder if music is really relevant to people or if it just supports a fashionable movement." Current music was, to him, "no communication, just part-playing—read the [*Bill-board*] charts and fit in." Tim sounded as if he were scolding both the nation and the audience when he wrote, "I think of our culture like I think of bacteria. Rock 'n' roll keeps the traffic moving to an adolescent pulse. . . . Man's music—his bout with the gods—has nothing to do with the latest crimes. It's too personal to isolate, too intimate to forget, and too spiritual to sell." (In an unpublished interview conducted during the same period, Tim claimed that when compared to anything by Miles Davis, rock "comes out sounding like a complete prefabrication.")

If *Starsailor* wasn't evidence enough, the essay was Tim's declaration of independence from the world of pop music, hit singles, and artistic restraints in general. Feeling he had created the best work of his four-year recording career—what he felt was "his masterpiece," Underwood claims—Tim was happy, confident, and ready to share his new vision with the world.

TWELVE

10. 9.93 Up to Bearsville to record for 5 weeks.
11. Jan. '94 Album released.
12. Real work then begins.

—JEFF BUCKLEY, PORTION OF HANDWRITTEN ITINERARY, SUMMER 1993

Wearing a black suit, white dress shirt, and a wide, '70s-style tie, Jeff walked onto the stage of the Anthology Film Archives on Saturday evening, November 21, 1992. His hair was spiky-short, wisps of sideburns framing his cheeks and remnants of acne dotting his face. Without saying a word, he took out a comb, held it up to the microphone, and slowly ran his finger down its teeth, creating a hollow *plunk-plunk-plunk.* He fol-lowed "Comb Music" with an equally unusual performance—"playing" a ceramic vase as if it were a conga and then turning a plastic shower hose into a makeshift trumpet. The audience at the combination movie theater and performance space in the East Village applauded enthusiastically. They had come expecting something striking—the evening, emceed by Larry Miller, had been billed as presentations "from original founders to offspring of Fluxus"—and Jeff didn't let them down.

Although Jeff's Sony contract didn't specify it, the plan following his signing was that there wasn't a plan—that everyone, especially Columbia, would leave him alone for a while. (George Stein claims it was verbally agreed for about two years, although Steve Berkowitz says there was never a set period in mind.) No one, including Jeff, knew where he was headed musically; he still had no band, few original songs, and seemingly limitless options. As the winter of 1992–93 took hold of New York City, Jeff took full advantage of the hands-off arrangement and submerged himself in the city's energy. With his Orange County background, he knew little about the world of avant-garde performance art and theater, and Moore and her friends became his entrée to that world. "Comb Music" was one of several Fluxus-related performances he gave that winter. That same evening, inspired by Yoko Ono's "No Bed for Beatle John" (a 1968 piece in which Ono "sang" the words to a caustic article about the couple's escapades), Jeff turned an article about the Vietnam War into a melody.

Three days later at Judson Memorial Church in the Village, he participated in the Fluxus piece "Three Star à la Carte," in which audience members sat at mock restaurant tables and "ordered" from a menu of oddball acts. As one of the accommodating "waiters," complete with black tuxedo, Jeff threw himself into the work; "diners" who requested "Smooth Events" saw him press his own shirt, using a plugged-in electric guitar as an ironing board, while "Intimidating a Plant" required he yell insults at a potted plant, such as "You make me want to puke!"

Those performances marked the beginning of a creative and relatively carefree time that extended through the dawn of summer. At St. Ann's in March, he performed "Miles of Death," a spoken-word piece sung to the accompaniment of a harmonium keyboard he had bought with a small portion of his album-advance money. (He also finally procured himself a guitar, both instruments purchased at a Bleecker Street music store for about $2,000.) His exploratory arts period also found him attending shows by performance artist Penny Arcade (who instantly became a friend when she bluntly informed Jeff she hated Tim's music due to its folk and jazz tendencies) and acting in one of Moore's pieces at La Mama, in which Jeff played a janitor sweeping a floor. "I thought, 'Two talented kids doing their thing—isn't that great?'" recalls Miller, who became one of Jeff's mentors and one of several father figures he found in New York. Miller feels Jeff's fascination with this downtown art world was little more than a phase, but it was of a piece with Jeff's incessant creativity, which included his relentless journal entries and the animated, cartoon-strewn letters he would write to friends.

Miller, who gave Jeff some of his old clothes and had Jeff teach him guitar as a way of giving the kid some money, wasn't alone in being disarmed by this wide-eyed newcomer. Jeff's ragamuffin image, his lack of funds, and his gentle manner made people, women in particular, instantly want to comfort him, almost as if he were looking for a Manhattan *mother* as well. At Fez, a basement club on Lafayette Street in the East Village, booking agent Ellen Cavolina instructed the staff of the restaurant upstairs to allow Jeff to eat for free, and he more than took her up on the offer: It wasn't unusual to see him sitting at one of the restaurant's green-striped booths eating an egg dish. Before he gave his first show at Fez (which attracted only eleven people), Jeff stopped by to inspect the club, and Cavolina told him how much she liked Tim's music. Jeff stiffened and said, "That has nothing to do with me."

Cavolina instantly apologized. "I didn't mean to offend you," she told him. "But that's the only connection I have to you." Jeff made it clear to her that any such comparisons were expressly off-limits. Nonetheless, he liked the space, and, along with Sin-é, Fez became one of his favorite venues. Cavolina made sure to pay him a minimum of $100 per show, even if only a handful of people came. "I felt he was alone in this city," Cavolina says, "and I wanted to make him feel he could always come here."

"I am busier than any bee ever born," he wrote to his Los Angeles friend Daniella Sapriel that summer. "I can feel the cocoon burning away like a lighted match to a bad smell." He also told her about his first foray into acting. As a result of his Sin-é gigs, he had landed the lead role in Georg Büchner's 1836 play *Woyzeck,* about a lowly German soldier pushed to the brink of murder by jealousy and medical experiments. The play ran for several weeks at a Village space called the Atrium. "I decided to confront the role, confront the fear, slip into another voice and pretend to be a symbol made of real bones and flesh," he wrote. ". . . I don't want to be an actor, I finally found. And I'm happy. *But,* I've derived a certain focus and an entrance sign into some bitchen [*sic*] new skills. . . . Acting is helping me in that direction. But music, for me, just cuts through all the fucking bullshit right on the 'one.' So, I'm never giving it up." Although M. Doughty recalls "an amazing scene" in which Jeff stalked the stage and pretended to shave a fellow officer, Jeff left others with the impression that it was a lark and, in fact, didn't even tell some friends about the play at all.

His artistic side spilled over into whimsical life at home with Moore. Friends would often call simply to hear Jeff's outgoing answering-machine messages, an ever-changing series of tapes about the adventures of Moore's cat, Spinach. In one, Spinach became a rock star and "launches into some killer riffs!" Jeff contributed not only the guitar but also imitations of the cat and a pompous British music business executive. (The days he had spent in high school listening to George Carlin comedy albums before he went to class had clearly paid off.) Rarely taking the subway and preferring to travel on foot, even if it took him hours to go from one Manhattan address to another, he would do vocal exercises as he walked, holding notes as long as he could under his breath to practice breathing and range. One night, he and Moore went to a neighborhood movie house to see *Dragon: The Bruce Lee Story*, a fictionalized account of the life of the late martial-arts star. Repeatedly during the film, Lee, who died at an early age, is haunted by a demon, and at the end, the monster chases after Lee's son Brandon. In an eerie echo of his father's life, the real Brandon Lee—young and on the verge of major stardom—had died more than a month earlier in an accident on the set of his latest movie. Jeff emerged from the theater looking as if he had seen a ghost, and he and Moore walked home in silence.

Although he appeared content on Stanton Street, Jeff was nonetheless encountering problems practicing his songs and playing guitar in the confines of the apartment. He would stop as soon as he heard Moore's key being inserted into the door and the sound of the lock clicking open.

Everyone who worked at Columbia knew when Jeff was up in the offices; they could hear the *clomp-clomping* of his Doc Marten boots, followed by the jangling of the keychain that hung outside his front pocket. Then there he would be, standing with those curious, inquisitive eyes and plopping down on their couches and either watching MTV on their televisions or rifling through music magazines. Sometimes he wouldn't say much; other times he would engage them in conversations about what they did or grab a bunch of free CDs, many of which would be sold for dinner.

One day, months into the Columbia deal, he walked into the office of product manager Leah Reid, closed the door, and told her his life story. It wasn't in-depth or riddled with details, yet he told her about his different homes, the bands he played in around Los Angeles, the influence of Ron Moorhead, and the guitar his grandmother had given him as a child. He talked until nearly 8 P.M. "It felt sad," recalls Reid. "It made me think he was a really intense person and a lot had happened to him." Still, it was a sign he was slowly warming to the business side, learning whom he could trust and letting down his guard one very gradual step at a time.

At that point, other encounters with the label were either innocent or amusing. Both Jeff and current Columbia artist Terence Trent D'Arby happened to be in the offices the same day copies of a Journey boxed set arrived. Reverting to their days as teenage arena-rock fans, they glanced over the song titles together and broke into spontaneous renditions of their favorite cheeseball Journey hits. Not long after, Jeff even attended an outdoor party at Don Ienner's country estate in Connecticut. When a downpour disrupted the activities, everyone gathered under tents. Seizing the moment, Jeff, in army boots and porkpie hat, leapt up on a picnic table with his guitar and began an impromptu set of songs with the word "rain" in the lyric or title, such as Elton John's "We All Fall in Love Sometimes" and Mahalia Jackson's "Didn't It Rain." He also took a playful poke at his new boss, singing Dylan's "Maggie's Farm" but substituting "Donny" for "Maggie." Seated nearby was Mariah Carey, who glanced up at this audacious new act with something resembling surprise and wariness.

Jeff continued to perform at Sin-é and Fez, generally failing to tell Berkowitz or Stein about the gigs; the sight of industry people in the crowd still had the potential to throw him off. At one show, with the bands Glim and Industrial Tepee, he spontaneously broke into the theme from the *Little Rascals*, whistling its melody line. "I just heard that on TV today," he told the audience. "And I just realized it's one of the saddest pieces of music. It's a funny show, but the melody reminds you these kids are all orphans. The melody wants to rise, but it always goes back down."

Nonetheless, the music business machinery was starting to churn. Columbia was sticking to its promise of not recording an album immediately, but they, Berkowitz in particular, still had to decipher exactly what kind of album Jeff would make. To aid that discovery process, the A&R man decided to put Jeff on tape in order to have a rough idea of a starting point. After his signing, Jeff went into the studio twice. The first was a quick one-day session at a budget Times Square studio on November 8, 1992, where Jeff, wearing gloves and a green Army coat and sipping coffee to ward off the cold, sang for several hours.

Then for two days in early February 1993, he settled into the West 21st Street studio of producer-engineer Steve Addabbo, a friend of Berkowitz's who had worked with Suzanne Vega, Shawn Colvin, and other singer-songwriters. Over the course of two eight-hour sessions, Jeff sat in the concrete-walled recording space, had the lights lowered, sipped water, and, accompanying himself on guitar and harmonium, ambled through his repertoire. There were the handful of original songs—"Mojo Pin," "Unforgiven,"

"Strawberry Street," "Grace"—and a slew of the covers he had been performing at Sin-é.

Even as the tapes rolled, though, he was morphing. Often he would start a song, stop, scold himself for not attaining the right tempo or feel, and then resume—in some cases, with an entirely different key and tempo. As Addabbo rolled the tapes, Jeff sang nearly every song he knew: a heart-melting version of the Smiths' "I Know It's Over," a flawless rendition of Benjamin Britten's "Corpus Christi Carol," and, with his harmonium as wheezy accompaniment, Van Morrison's "Madame George." At one point, he began playing a raga-style guitar part, which slid into a gentle pulse that in turn became Sly and the Family Stone's "Everyday People." ("I feel fucking retarded," he scolded himself after forgetting the words.) "You could tell this was a voice to reckon with," Addabbo says. "It wasn't always spot on and it wasn't always controlled, but there were moments where there would be nothing and then this huge sound would come out."

The session was a demonstration of Jeff's talent and potential—and also of his utter malleability as a musical force and a person. One moment he came across supremely confident, the next self-eviscerating. To Addabbo, Jeff seemed bright-eyed ("like a doe") and pensive: "There was a lot going on behind his eyes." As far as his music, Addabbo sensed Jeff's talent but, like the label presidents who had dropped by Sin-é the year before, was at a loss as to where it should venture.

Although the test-session tape was placed in Columbia's vaults (along with further exploratory recordings, with backup musicians, at the Knitting Factory in May), it confirmed that Jeff needed to bear down and figure out what sound, style, and songs would comprise a Jeff Buckley album. More and more, it became evident he needed his own space to do it. In the late spring, Ellen Cavolina was at the Fez when Jeff burst in one day. "I got a *real* apartment!" he told her. With Stein's help, he had found a $900-a-month apartment at 233 East 12th Street, between Second and Third Avenues in the East Village. Scrunched in a tree-lined block of brownstones and old tenements, a fire escape dangling over its entrance, the narrow building had a brown-brick exterior; its narrow, dingy lobby featured circular fluorescent lighting and faded carpet. The apartment itself was a quirky duplex, its first floor housing a small living room, kitchen, and a spiral staircase that connected to the top floor, Jeff's bedroom. One of his new friends, photographer Merri Cyr, helped Jeff move into the new apartment. Giving her a cardboard box, he said, "Be careful with that. That's all I have left of my father."

Although she didn't dare look inside, Cyr felt as if she were carrying an urn. Most likely it contained old articles and artifacts sent to him by Tim friends and fans, such as a 45-rpm single and a program from Tim's 1969 Carnegie Hall concert. "Whatever was in it," Cyr says, "was very precious to him."

To Jeff, the apartment was nothing short of ambrosial. "The upstairs is my living room, my kitchen, my sex room, my thinking room," he wrote in his journal. "The downstairs is where I do my love, hour upon hour when I celebrate my music, my work—the underworld. . . . Someday soon I'll be someone who is known not only as a guy who sings but also the lost world in poetry, surreal . . . innovator supreme, artist, the hardest of the core. . . ." He began to fill it with stacks of books and compact discs, the latter running the taste gamut from classic rock (the Allman Brothers, the Doors, Cat Stevens) to kitsch (Sammy Davis Jr., *The Mighty Wurlitzer*) to alternative rock (Cocteau Twins, Guided by Voices, Sebadoh) to nearly fifty *qawwali* discs. He could step outside and be a block away from a movie theater or an Italian restaurant; Sin-é and Shane Doyle's new bar Anseo, which was two doors away from Sin-é, were a five-minute walk east. Prostitutes roamed the block, and Jeff's devotion to underdogs led him to chat them up or flirt with them whenever he left his apartment.

Although Moore had encouraged Jeff to find a separate work space of his own, the fact that he moved so completely into 12th Street was a telling sign that his romance with her was beginning to wane. "No one will get to see me much for the next years because I'll be working so so slavishly hard and indestructibly deep," he wrote in his journal after he settled in. Although he still loved Moore, he began to hint to friends that he couldn't handle a relationship *and* a career. Adding to his dilemma was the newfound attention he was receiving from women, both in the industry and at clubs. For someone who had long denigrated himself as "monkey boy," the idea that females found him desirable was a surprising, but not unwelcome, development. Jeff himself developed a flirtatious side; his ability to tell a woman exactly what perfume she was wearing became a virtual trademark. It wasn't long before he had a brief affair with a fellow New York musician, "anti-folk" singer-songwriter Brenda Kahn, that she calls "totally clandestine." Engaging in intense one-on-one conversations with women (and men), Jeff conveyed enormous empathy; as Moore says, "He made you feel as if he understood you completely."

At one of his Fez shows that spring, Jeff debuted an in-progress song, "Lover, You Should've Come Over." Built on a languorous riff that recalled Led Zeppelin at their most pastoral, the song revealed another facet of his developing style. Unfortunately, so did the lyrics: "Sometimes a man gets carried away with having his fun/Much too blind to see the damage he's done," he sang in a very apparent elegy to he and Moore's time together. Moore, who was in the audience with Larry Miller, had never heard the song before and was stunned. (A later, more optimistic section of the song, with the refrain "It's never over," was not yet written.) Listening to the lyric, Miller was disturbed. In his mind, it didn't seem to bode well for Moore, Jeff, or whatever changes Jeff was going through.

Jeff was now one the brightest hopes of a major corporation, and word of mouth was beginning to spread beyond the record industry. That spring, he was approached by the Gap to appear in an ad campaign. He immediately rejected the idea—if only because the Gap was part of the same company that owned Banana Republic, the store that had fired him three years earlier.

While not completely averse to the idea, Sony thought it best to hold off. In an internal memo to Ienner dated April 13, Berkowitz wrote: "After he's a somebody, a Gap ad could be a very cool idea. . . . [But] Bob, Bruce, Neil and Van just didn't start as a face in a fashion ad." Berkowitz was smart to evoke Dylan, Springsteen, Young, and Morrison, thereby connecting Jeff with a tradition of enduring, respected, and iconoclastic musicians. Ienner agreed with the memo: Jeff was a heritage artist in the making, and this type of advertising tie-in wasn't appropriate, at least not yet.

In June, Jeff performed at Sony's annual convention, held in Boca Raton, Florida. It was the first time employees from around the world were able to see and hear the new signing, and Jeff rose to the occasion, playing a short set highlighted by "Hallelujah." "It seems evident to all who've followed his career that this next important chapter in the musical odyssey of Jeff Buckley could very well become an equally important chapter in American popular music," read a Sony newsletter distributed at the convention. The write-up listed Jeff's influences as the Bad Brains, Cocteau Twins, Robert Johnson, and Lou Reed. There was no mention of Yes, Rush, any of the jazz fusion guitarists of his formative years, or Tim Buckley.

No one can pinpoint precisely who thought up the idea and when, but one outcome of the Boca Raton performance was convincing many that Jeff's solo performances should be preserved on tape. Hence came the concept of recording Jeff live at Sin-é and releasing an introductory EP, which would serve multiple purposes: It would preserve that period of his career, which everyone assumed would end as soon as he became a bigger star; it would give Jeff more time to write songs; and it would, in Berkowitz's words, "diffuse the big debut release" and the hype that was quickly building around Jeff. "There were a few careers I thought could be emulated: U2, R.E.M., Bob Marley," Berkowitz says. "They all came through the side door, not the front door. I wanted the same for Jeff—an old-style real development where people were allowed to find him, instead of having him jammed down their throat." Releasing a set of four or five songs would be just such a device. Jeff and Stein agreed it was a good idea, and a date for the session—Monday, July 19—was selected.

His mind ever on history, Berkowitz envisioned a recording scenario reminiscent of the illustration on the cover of Robert Johnson's *King of the Delta Blues Singers Vol. 2,* in which Johnson is depicted singing in a parlor, a wire running into a separate room where recording engineers are seated. Not bothering to apply for an official city permit, Berkowitz simply paid Shane Doyle for use of Sin-é, and a mobile recording sound truck arrived in front of the club early that day. Berkowitz and his crew set up microphones in the back and in front (where Jeff would stand), placed recording equipment in another corner, and then ran the wires out of the club, over the fire escape, into a smoke vent, and into nearby Anseo, where the console was set up. The plan was to record two sets, one each in the afternoon and evening.

Wearing his standard white V-neck T-shirt and baggy army pants, Jeff arrived early in the afternoon for a soundcheck and to warm up. Sin-é was nearly empty, yet photographer Cyr, hired to document the event, began snapping away. As the 3 P.M. start time approached, though, Jeff looked nervous, thanks to the recording equipment and the Sony employees who had arrived. The reality—that he was making his first release for Sony— was hitting home.

It had become easy to tell when Jeff was anxious onstage; he would talk more and make exaggerated faces and vocal shrieks. Such was the case during the afternoon show, which included much of his regular set. Afterward, he went to Anseo next door, curled up on two bar chairs, and fell into a deep, instantaneous sleep. Seated next to him, Cyr thought it odd that he could doze in such a way; it seemed to indicate an unusual upbringing.

Refreshed and ready after his nap, Jeff made his way through his second, evening set, the tapes still rolling. By the end of the night, he had sung all of his best-known Sin-é songs: "Unforgiven," two takes of "Eternal Life," and covers of "Lost Highway," Edith Piaf's "Je N'en Connais Pas la Fin," "Corpus Christi Carol," "Strange Fruit," "The Twelfth of Never," Van Morrison's "The Way Young Lovers Do" (which had expanded into a long, impassioned signature piece, often stretching out over ten or fifteen minutes), and Bob Dylan's "If You See Her, Say Hello" and "Just Like a Woman."

Nonetheless, something felt amiss. Sony's archive notes indicate that a version of "Lover, You Should've Come Over" "loses stride." "He was really nervous," says Berkowitz. "I could hear it in his voice. It was constricted. He was not soaring. The Flying Buckleys were not flying." It became even more apparent in the ensuing days, when Berkowitz and his associates listened back to the tapes, which were adequate but unexciting.

The company was caught in a slight bind; the much-anticipated sessions were more or less unusable, and they had spent what is said to be in range of ten to twenty thousand dollars. Still keen on the idea, Berkowitz convinced the label to set up a second session date, but this time he downplayed it to Jeff, telling him they were going to tape another evening's set "just for the hell of it." Almost a month later, on Tuesday, August 17, the tapes rolled at Sin-é once more. Starting with a hot-blooded "Be My Husband," done *a cappella* Nina Simone style, Jeff sang many of the same songs as a month earlier, as well as Dylan's "I Shall Be Released," his stunning version of "Calling You," and Harold Arlen and Ira Gershwin's "The Man That Got Away," made famous by Judy Garland in *A Star Is Born.* But this time, with less pressure in the air and fewer Sony employees in the house, Jeff nailed it. His voice was looser, the performance less uptight—evident when someone half-jokingly called out for Nusrat Fateh Ali Khan, leading Jeff to launch into a six-minute imitation of the *qawwali* singer. (The performance was initially greeted with chuckles, as if it were a put-on, but the laughter soon stopped when everyone realized it wasn't.) Highlights included an exquisite "Lilac Wine," a tighter, nine-minute "Lover, You Should've Come Over," and a version of Dylan's "If You See Her, Say Hello" that took on additional significance in light of his apparent split with Moore. Everyone, Jeff included, felt happier.

Another song Jeff performed both nights was "Dink's Song," a blues that had become one of his signature covers starting with his days in Gods and Monsters. Folklorist John Lomax had originally heard a washerwoman in Brazos, Texas, sing it in 1908 (her name, he wrote, was Dink), and the song, also known as "Faretheewell," had since been recorded by a number of acts, most prominently Bob Dylan (Lucas claims he introduced Jeff to this track on a bootleg).

> One of these days and it won't be long
> Call my name and I'll be gone
> Fare thee well, oh honey, fare thee well

After he sang it that August night, he approached his friend Nicholas Hill and told him it was the last time he would ever perform that song. "It was weird," recalls Hill. "It was like the end of this period." In Jeff's mind, that was precisely what the entire evening performance was.

Jeff was just barely over the hump of the EP when it was time to begin working on his much-anticipated first album. Starting in the spring, Berkowitz had begun gently nudging his signing in that direction, and arranged meetings with potential producers and even songwriters in case Jeff, who was far from prolific, needed assistance. At some point, Berkowitz announced the plan: They would start recording in September.

The names of any number of possible producers—Tom Werman, of Cheap Trick and Ted Nugent fame, among them—were broached, but the search ended when, at the suggestion of a friend and business associate, Berkowitz contacted Andy Wallace. With his silver hair, trim beard, and grandfatherly countenance, the forty-six-year-old Wallace resembled a patient, seen-it-all high-school guidance counselor more than he did a producer, but that he was—and of hard-rock bands at that. Wallace had made a recording-studio name for himself as a mixer and producer for everyone from the Rollins Band to Ozzy Osbourne, and in his role as sound mixer, he had put the just-polished-enough sheen atop Nirvana's breakthrough, *Nevermind*.

By the '90s, many producers had precise sounds and styles associated with them, mirroring the splintering of the pop audience: If you wanted light R&B, grunge, or dance pop, you went with very specific producers. Wallace epitomized the opposite of that approach: He was known more for his efficiency and light touch than for an ability to make singers and bands sound a particular way. The thought of Wallace magnifying Jeff's voice and guitar in the same way the producer brought out the power in metal bands also appealed to everyone, especially Berkowitz. Wallace and Jeff met in June, Wallace landed the job, and the two began to meet and map out a plan. "From the beginning, we understood the album would have a wide variety on it," says Wallace. "It wouldn't be a one-sound album."

Many around Jeff, including Stein, wanted just that, though: a Sin-é-style experience—only Jeff and his guitar—captured in a studio. "I was so afraid that this delicate jewel we had would be run over by a Mack truck by a band and a producer," says Stein. No one wanted to tamper with the sound that had landed Jeff so much media and industry attention. Jeff, however, had other plans: He wanted a band, and he wanted a diverse album. "There was a discussion between myself and Jeff and George and Steve and everyone at Sony, and they were a little concerned," Wallace recalls. "The band thing was a total unknown. He didn't *have* a band." Jeff, however, talked them into it. "Jeff was given a lot of sway at Sony," Wallace adds. "Sometimes too much, but sometimes people were somewhat in awe of him and his dynamic personality and talent."

In typical Jeff style, the band dilemma was solved at the last possible moment. In July, he performed at a Columbia University café, where he met Mick Grondahl, a towering, dough-faced twenty-five-year-old bass player. Born in Denmark, Grondahl had grown up with his divorced mother (who owned a cosmetics company) on the Upper East Side, gradually giving up school sports for a love of drums and punk rock. After graduating from college in 1990 with a degree in art history, he began playing in a number of New York bands. At Columbia, he was, he recalls, "blown away" by Jeff: "The cover songs he did were like you were hearing them for the first time. He did a version of 'Strange Fruit,' and you could taste the experience while he was singing it. It was quite evident to me that this guy was for real."

After attending another one of Jeff's shows, Grondahl asked Jeff if he needed a bass player, and the two jammed late one night in Jeff's apartment, their instruments turned down low so as not to wake the neighbors. Grondahl was not a standard bassist, not one who played traditional walking-blues bass lines, but a more circuitous musician who tended to play around the melody. Cementing their musical and social bond, they flirted with girls at a local pool hall. After several weeks, Jeff informed a surprised

Grondahl that he had a contract with Sony and would have to begin recording soon.

Less than two weeks later, Matt Johnson, a twenty-two-year-old native of Houston, Texas, who had relocated to New York four years earlier, was introduced to Rebecca Moore by a mutual acquaintance. When their friend informed Moore that Johnson was a drummer, Moore flashed on Jeff, who had been having trouble finding the right percussionist. Although she was still unsure of the nature of her and Jeff's relationship, since they hadn't officially broken up, she gave Jeff Johnson's number, and it wasn't long before the long-haired, lean-faced drummer with the marked frown lines found himself at an audition, seated behind a drum kit as Jeff cranked his guitar to ear-splitting levels. The two, and Grondahl, began playing exploratory instrumentals. "It was very hypnotic," Johnson recalls. "There was a moment when were playing and Jeff came up in front of the drum kit and closed his eyes and threw his head back and almost smiled. It was as if he had made a realization within himself that it felt right, like he was getting the okay from his intuition. After we were done, he said, 'I want to play with you.'" The attraction to Jeff must have been clear: Johnson, who had been supplementing his gigging with roof-repair work, could easily shift from the subtlest of brush-drum strokes to crackling rimshots that made it sound as if he were hitting the kit with trees.

By the time Johnson was recruited, though, the trio had a mere six weeks to rehearse before they were set to begin recording at Bearsville Studios, the historic complex in Woodstock, New York. In what Grondahl calls "a kamikaze mission," intensive rehearsals began in the East Village, with Wallace dropping by periodically. "Here's one of the songs we're working on," Jeff would announce, and the band would promptly "start a riff that would turn into a jam, eventually abandoning the riff, and it would go on for ten minutes," says Wallace. "It was interesting, but my first impression was, 'Wait a minute—I thought you guys were learning *songs*. We've got studio time booked!'"

It seemed like madness, but everyone was beginning to learn Jeff worked best under pressure; without a deadline, he could be a major procrastinator. Slowly, during rehearsals and at a few radio and sparsely attended club performances, the band began to develop what Grondahl calls "its own language." Finally, on Monday, September 20, the time to start preserving that language on tape had arrived.

Before he left for Woodstock in the early afternoon, Jeff left a message on

Moore's answering machine. "It's twelve-thirty, and nobody in the band is ready, of course," he said tiredly (the band had played a blistering show at Sin-é the night before). He joked about wearing the "same socks for five days" and told her how much she meant to him. Finally, he said, "In the grand scheme of things, things will work out."

Soon enough, Johnson and Grondahl arrived, and the trio loaded their own guitars and drums into a rented van, piled in, and drove the two hours and ninety-five miles north to Woodstock. As they pulled into Woodstock, Johnson glanced outside and saw row after row of quaint shops on the town's main street. "For me, it was tremendous excitement," he recalls. "It felt so magical."

Andy Wallace's car snaked up the winding road, kicking up gravel with each turn. At the top of the unnamed street, past the private-property signs and hidden behind trees, lay Bearsville Studios. As rustic as its woodsy surroundings, the two-story, barn-like wooden structure off Route 212 had been a musicians' favorite for two decades, thanks to its relaxed environment and isolation. Attesting to the studio's popularity, one office wall was decorated with covers of many of the albums recorded there, from the Band's *Cahoots* and Bonnie Raitt's *Give It Up* to Patti Smith's *Wave* and Metallica's . . . *And Justice for All.* Beyond its association with the rock festival, Woodstock was in 1993 still very much an artists' community, home to Graham Parker and members of the Band and the B-52's. It seemed ideal for Jeff: removed from the potential distractions in New York, yet close enough for quick visits home.

Wallace walked inside the building and down the corridor into Studio A, whose hardwood plank floors, cement walls, and thirty-eight-foot ceiling made it feel like a combination airplane hangar and high-school gymnasium. Seated behind the organ, Jeff was singing and playing "Hocus Pocus," the '70s novelty single by the Dutch prog band Focus; he even had the song's recognizable yodel perfected. "They were," Wallace remembers, "eager to start." Adds Grondahl, "The leaves were just starting to turn. It was a beautiful time of year."

The art of record making had changed dramatically since the '60s. Tim's first album, for instance, had been recorded in two days, the others in roughly a week or two. Back then, it was not unusual for singers to perform live with the backing musicians; everyone would record a take and be done with it. In the '90s, such notions were quaint for all but the most budget-minded of bands. For his first album, Jeff had been allotted five weeks at Bearsville, with the notion that the band would record the basic tracks of the songs—bass guitar, drums, a guitar track or two, and a "guide" (or rough) vocal. Once that was accomplished, everyone would then relocate to another studio to add more instruments, have Jeff insert his polished vocals, and mix the tracks (balancing the levels of the instruments, among other things). At $2,000 a day (including a nearby "writer's cottage" in which Jeff stayed), Bearsville was by no means cheap, which made it vital to get things done as quickly as possible: The more money spent, the higher Jeff's recoupable debt to Sony. Even in those days of less extravagantly produced alternative rock, it wasn't uncommon for major pop acts to take months, even years, to record an album and spend between $500,000 and $1 million on studio costs.

Not surprisingly, given the newness of the band and Jeff's indecisive nature, the first few weeks were unfocused. Although nearly a year had elapsed since he had signed to Columbia, the exact nature of his all-important first album was still unclear. To Berkowitz, the album would be "Jeff Buckley with accompaniment"—that is, Jeff singing his Sin-é repertoire (both originals and cover versions) with unobtrusive accompaniment from Johnson and Grondahl. To warm Jeff up before each day's recording, Wallace even had him perform solo sets of his Sin-é material to an audience of engineers and studio employees. Among the numbers captured on tape were an exultant rendition of Led Zeppelin's "Night Flight" and, with Johnson and Grondahl, a playfully copycat take on Screamin' Jay Hawkins's bug-eyed, leering "Alligator Wine." (One of the performances, "Lost Highway," would later surface as a B-side.)

For Jeff, though, the process was not so simple. As they set up in Studio A, facing each other in the middle of the room, the trio started with "Last Goodbye," as "Unforgiven" was now being called, taking a cue from its opening line. Although Jeff had been performing the song solo for several years, no one was sure how the bass and drums should sound, and numerous patterns were attempted. It soon became apparent that Jeff didn't just have one solid idea for how to approach each song; he had *several*. "Jeff never finalized anything," says Wallace. "He never said, 'This is the arrangement, this is the way it has to be.' It would always be a little bit different—sometimes vastly different—every time he'd play it."

A few of the songs came easily; "Mojo Pin" was nailed in its third or fourth take, and "Grace" in eight or nine. (Burying a hatchet, Jeff invited

Gary Lucas up to Bearsville for four days to record anew the swirling, darting guitar lines he had played on the original recordings of those songs. Lucas found Jeff "more self-assured" than ever.) Still, the proof of Jeff's experimentation lies in the logs of the sessions, which list multiple takes of most of the songs, including over twenty of "Hallelujah" (one described as "angrier, harder"). Grondahl recalls nailing "Last Goodbye" in nineteen takes, by which time a bass line inspired by dub reggae was conceived. "Lover, You Should've Come Over" was still rough and, by session's end, had been whittled down to three versions, each longer than the next. Johnson was given two drum kits—one for a harder rock sound, the other for a jazz feel—and a local string arranger (and jazz-vibes legend), Karl Berger, was hired to write orchestral parts, which were then played by a local string quartet. At the latter sessions, Jeff surprised everyone by writing out some of the notation for their parts; continuing his enigmatic image, he had failed to tell anyone he had attended a music school.

Adding to complications was the presence of a film crew Berkowitz had hired to document the sessions; as with the Sin-é recordings, it was part of a process of preserving Jeff's history for posterity. With the crew filming one day, Jeff stood at a microphone and sang "Grace." "He probably did four or five takes, and every single time he did it was completely different," recalls Leah Reid, who accompanied the filmmakers. "He did one amazing version, really intense, and at the end he said, 'Oh, that was *okay.*' " Wallace wasn't averse to pounding his hand on the console (hence Jeff's reference to him as "The Fist" in the liner notes), but his mild-mannered way of moving the work along, aiding with the arrangements, and keeping a mental note of each take propelled the sessions. The mood of the sessions, Johnson recalls, "was like stir-fried—very quick and a lot of things being thrown together without a lot of time to stew."

After a month, a number of tracks were done, but the album still seemed somewhat nebulous, and there wasn't yet enough for a full compact disc. (The sessions were also temporarily halted when Moore's father Peter passed away, and Jeff returned to the city to be with her.) Then, several days before work was scheduled to end, something happened. Maybe it was the deadline pressure he thrived on, maybe it was a matter of growing accustomed to the studio environment, but Jeff came in one morning and told Wallace, "I have an idea for a new song." Seated in the wood-paneled control room, Wallace liked what he heard—a sulking, mid-tempo instrumental—and asked the trio to bang out a quick take.

"They're into the first verse and I'm like, 'Andy, are you recording this?'" Berkowitz recalls. "And he says, *'Yes.'* We were both stunned. The song ended and we were like, 'Where did *that* come from? What was that?'"

"Oh, I don't know," Jeff replied. "It was something we messed around with last night."

Thinking it had potential, Wallace asked if there were any lyrics. *"Ahhh,* they're not done," Jeff replied. Yet, as Wallace recalls, "he was agreeable and went out and sang the vocal the first pass. I said, 'Damn, that's killer.'" Jeff called it "Forget Her" after its chorus: "Don't fool yourself, she was heartache from the moment that you met her/My heart is frozen still as I try to find the will to forget her." Part lament and part purge, it was startling in its directness, and the ache and hurt built with each passing line until a key change in the final verse sent the emotions into overdrive. Unlike most of his material up to that point, it hadn't been picked over and thoroughly considered; rather, it was a good old-fashioned fiery spew.

It was, according to Berkowitz, the beginning of "the moment." Over the next few days—literally the end of the session—the ideas for instruments, vocal textures, and overall shaping burst out of Jeff. "All of a sudden," Berkowitz recalls, "we were on this roller-coaster ride." The fully produced opus he and other Columbia executives had thought Jeff would make on his second or third album was suddenly materializing. Berkowitz hurriedly received authorization from his bosses to spend an extra week of studio time. Rather than a mere recreation of Jeff's solo and cabaret side, the music began to incorporate Zeppelinesque furor, tunings associated with Pakistani music, and anthemic, windswept rock guitars.

For his part, Grondahl feels Berkowitz's perception of a last-minute rush of creative juices "is coming out of his anxiety or misunderstanding of what was going on. There were some sparks happening six weeks before that." There was no better example than the evolution of one particular track. On the first day of band rehearsals in New York City, Grondahl had played a two-note bass line that Jeff and Johnson picked up on and began building into a denser, swirling instrumental, with suggestions of Indian modality. The piece of music continued to evolve at Bearsville.

After they started recording rough versions of it, the band and Berkowitz would pile into their economy van and drive for hours along the curving, unlit Woodstock roads, repeatedly listening to the tape of the unfinished song. As the tape rolled in the car and the van plowed on into the night, Jeff listened intently, staring ahead. Although the song was nowhere near finished and had no lyrics—only a title, "Dream Brother"—Jeff knew it was a special and meaningful piece of music.

After six weeks, ending the day before Halloween, 1993, the sessions were done. The album was far from complete, but the basics, the soul, were in hand. Equally if not more important, it appeared that Jeff had discovered something else along the way: himself. Even he had no idea what had been unleashed.

The young troubadour: Tim at
seventeen, performing at the
Loara High School hoot night, 1964.
(Loara Seaxe/Courtesy of Chris Turanitza)

The reluctant teenage groom
and Mary Guibert at their
wedding reception, 1965. Larry
Beckett is in background.
(Courtesy of Mary Guibert)

Soldier or dreamer:
Jeffrey Scott Buckley, age two.
(Courtesy of Mary Guibert)

Eight-year-old Jeff taking a ride
on the wild side,
Fullerton, California.
(Courtesy of Mary Guibert)

Tim placing himself before all others, Greenwich Village, 1967.
(© 1967 by David Gahr)

Tim addresses his generation at the New York Folklore Center, 1967.

(© 1967 by David Gahr)

Clockwise from top left:
Roadie Barry Schultz,
Jennifer Stace, Lee Underwood,
an unknown friend, Tim,
Jane Goldstein, and another
unknown friend, Malibu, 1968.

(Courtesy of Jennifer Stace)

Happy, sad: Tim in 1969. *(Joe Stevens)*

Tim and Judy with friends Wess
and Donna Young, Las Vegas,
1974, eight months before
Tim's death.

(Courtesy of the Estate of Tim Buckley)

Tim with friend Jim Fielder at
Knebworth, 1974.

(Joe Stevens)

Jeff practices his jazz fusion
licks in high school,
early '80s.
(Courtesy of Mary Guibert)

Group Therapy, circa 1989: Jack Cook, Jeff, Kathryn Grimm, Mark Frere.
(Courtesy of Kathryn Grimm)

Tim's mother, Elaine Buckley, Mary Guibert, and Jeff
at Jeff's twenty-fourth birthday party, 1990. *(John Humphrey)*

Jeff onstage at the Tim Buckley tribute concert, 1991, backed by Gary Lucas and
Julia Heyward. *(© 1991 by Jack Vartoogian)*

Warming up for the first Sin-é recording sessions, July 1993. *(Merri Cyr)*

Road warriors: Mick Grondahl (back to camera), Michael Tighe, Jeff, and Matt Johnson, outside of Austin, Texas, 1994. *(Merri Cyr)*

Jeff and mother Mary Guibert in the early '90s.
(Courtesy of Mary Guibert)

Backstage with Joan Wasser at Roseland, New York City, 1995.
(Merri Cyr)

Jeff and tour manager Gene Bowen car shopping in Memphis, hours before Jeff waded into the Wolf River. The Ryder van is in the background.
(Foti)

THIRTEEN

I don't dig the choices my father made stylistically. His life was hell.
There are some people who think they only have six minutes left to live
and see a blank slate when they think of the future, and they say that
those people get on stage and just go wild. And that's what he did. The
greatest thing he ever did, Starsailor, *was also his disaster.*

—JEFF BUCKLEY, INTERVIEW WITH THE AUTHOR, SEPTEMBER 1993

On November 13, 1970, about a week after the release of *Starsailor,* Tim
and his band played the first of two nights at New York's Academy of
Music, headlining over Van Morrison and Tim's Venice friend Linda
Ronstadt. Tim performed songs from his new album, along with material
that appeared to be even further out. One number, "You Can Always Tell
a Town by Its Graffiti," was preceded by the sound of the band making
howling noises like a pack of wild animals. Afterward, one reviewer noted
the evening's "extended trips into free forms," while *Billboard* commented that Tim "seemed oblivious to the audience." Given the hall was
half empty, there wasn't much of an audience to ignore anyway.

The fans at those and other concerts Tim gave during late 1970 and
into 1971 were far from the only people taken aback by his most dramatic
shift in direction. "This LP represents a distinct change from the usual
Buckley fare," noted *Billboard* in an atypically obtuse write-up of *Star-*

sailor. "The lyric content is the same, but Buckley has put a slightly more improvisational background behind them to emphasize a spiritual existence in the universe." The British rock newspaper *Melody Maker* deemed it "an album that is very hard going for the listener," concluding it was "a brave but ill-judged project."

The most enthusiastic review was a five-star (out of five) review in the respected jazz magazine *Down Beat* in March 1971. It was actually a joint review, of *Starsailor* and *Lorca.* Reviewer Mike Bourne admired *Lorca,* but in discussing its successor, he dubbed Tim "a consummate vocal technician. . . . Far too few (if any) pop artists exhibit such expressive control of the resonance and general tone of the voice as does Buckley." Added Bourne, "At a point at which Elton John and Leon Russell and other one-dimensionals are being hailed as the new superstar solo performers, *Starsailor* proves Tim Buckley the far greater. . . ." Although Tim wasn't one to pay attention to critics, he was nevertheless thrilled; it was the validation he had been seeking.

As the *Down Beat* review noted, the new decade had brought with it a distinct breed of pop singer-songwriters. Epitomized by John, James Taylor, Carly Simon, and Joni Mitchell, this wave of literate, middle-class balladeers spoke to the rock generation that found itself on the cusp of its thirties. "The New Rock: Bittersweet and Low," *Time* dubbed it in a March 1971 story, complete with Taylor on its cover. Those who had been weaned on Dylan, the Beatles, Simon and Garfunkel—and, perhaps, *Goodbye and Hello*—had little use for bludgeoning new rock bands like Led Zeppelin, Jethro Tull, and Grand Funk Railroad, who wallowed in (and often made genuine art from) bombast and mega-wattage amplification. That was music for the younger siblings of the original rock and roll generation; it didn't appeal to the baby-boom generation in the way Taylor's *Sweet Baby James* or Carole King's *Tapestry* did.

Tim could have capitalized on the boom in mellow, denim-clad musical tranquilizers, and the laid-back ambience and acoustic melodies of *Blue Afternoon* could have been interpreted as a gesture in that direction. But while he occasionally performed its songs onstage that year, Tim seemed to cast aside that album as soon as he made it. He had no interest in profiting from whatever renown he had as a founding father of the music now growing in popularity and record sales. Instead, he took the first of his *Starsailor* bands—Balkin, the Gardners, Baker, and sometimes Underwood—on tour.

As the New York show demonstrated, their early performances con-

sisted primarily of *Starsailor* songs and a degree of new, entirely improvised material. If Tim began barking and howling, as he did at a club gig
in Escondido, the band followed his lead, until the club was filled with
man-made animal sounds, followed by a free-form *a cappella* piece by the
whole ensemble. Time signatures would continually shift, and the numbers—it was sometimes hard to call them "songs"—would stretch out to
nearly three-quarters of an hour, with lyrics either taken from Tim's
poetry or as free-ranging as the accompanying music ("Just got back into
town/Took a vacation where the elephants go down" was one of many
examples of the latter). With the slightest turn of his head, Tim would gesture to players when he wanted them to solo or pull back, and he often
used his voice not so much to sing lyrics but to imitate instruments,
stretching his vocal cords to sky-high shrieks and well-deep lows in the
process. "Tim wanted an adventure every time he got up to the microphone," says Baker, who replaced one of his drum cymbals with a Chinese
gong for additional sonic boom.

One of their performances—albeit a relatively restrained one—was
captured on public television. In the fall of 1970, the band taped an
appearance on *Boboquivari,* a concert series emanating from KCET in
Los Angeles. Wearing a red pullover sweater, Tim sat stage left, the band
forming a semicircle around him. In an impressive display of instrumental
prowess and stamina, the musicians played a continuous, break-free set of
five *Starsailor* songs, along with "Blue Melody" and a new, untitled number. His head often sloping to a 90-degree angle, Tim leaned hard into the
microphone and sang with his eyes closed. By the end of the half hour, he
was drenched in sweat.

The *Boboquivari* audience sat and listened intently, even boogying in
its seats during the concluding "Down by the Borderline." Elsewhere,
though, reaction was decidedly mixed. Old fans not only *didn't* hear
Tim's best-known songs, but requests for them were greeted less than
receptively. "A couple of times, somebody would say, 'Hey, could you play
one of your old tunes?'" recalls Baker. "And he'd say, 'No, I don't play
that anymore. If you don't like it, get the fuck out of here.' He was vehe-
ment. He didn't want to backtrack at all. The first few months out, it was a
shock for most people. Their mouths dropped."

Critics, too, grappled to understand Tim's new musical language:
"Quintet Generates Warmth," read a headline of a bewildered but generally
favorable Vancouver *Sun* review of a show at the Old Cellar in January 1971.

Other writers were less than charitable, even hostile. After a gig at the Lion's Share in San Francisco, a local music critic approached the band and told them he was going to do them "a favor" and not review the concert. The next day, the musicians slogged in a van out to a club near Oakland. "We were staying in a motel and we were all just alone," Balkin says. "We ate in this one Scottish pub every night and then we'd go play the gig. We'd go onstage as a bunch of outcasts. Psychologically, it was depressing."

Despite such hitches, Tim seemed exhilarated to be playing music he enjoyed. Thanks to Judy, he also looked different, more groomed and better dressed than in the past. His hair was shorter and neater looking—a tamed version of his former bushy Afro—and, with Judy's guidance, he began wearing the occasional pair of satin pants and silk dress shirts. Maury Baker was not only a frequent guest at the Laguna Beach house but also something of a mentor to young Taylor, who connected with the rhythm patterns of Baker's drumming. Still, Baker recalls incurring Tim's wrath once, when he broke into a steady, standard drum beat at a gig. Tim's orders to Baker were simple and direct: "Don't ever repeat yourself."

Tim's Volkswagen bus rumbled to a stop in front of Lee Underwood's home on Park Place, and Underwood and his new girlfriend, a New Yorker named Eileen Marder, jumped in. Tim had with him "a bottle of One A Day vitamins—or what *looked* like One A Day vitamins," Marder recalls. In fact, they were reds, and the drugs kicked in just as the Volkswagen reached the driveway of Tim's home in Laguna Beach. As usual, everyone hung out and discussed music, art, and life; by the end of the weekend, there was nothing left in the bottle.

Ever the movie fan, Tim delighted in sitting in the first row of the local theater and making snide comments at the screen if the film wasn't to his standards. Given Tim's sensual expressions and features, it wasn't surprising when his interest in film began to expand beyond screenings. During the late '60s, the rise of counterculture films like *Easy Rider* convinced Hollywood that rock and roll and its biggest stars could lure younger fans into movie houses. Mick Jagger and John Lennon, among others, had tried their hands at acting, and it wasn't long before producers began calling Herb Cohen to inquire about Tim. Cohen had seen the potential for Tim as a movie star as early as 1968, when Tim was sent to meet with director Otto Preminger. Elektra's David Anderle accompanied Tim to Preminger's office. "There was this Tim movie thing going on," Anderle recalls. "'Maybe Tim should be in film' or 'young Jim Dean,' all that." As Preminger (the renowned director of *Anatomy of a Murder, The Man with the Golden Arm,* and *Exodus*) literally looked down upon his guests from his elevated desk, Anderle could tell Tim was instantly turned off, and the Elektra executive's primary concern became making sure Tim didn't blow up or walk out. Tim didn't do either, but he was stonily nonforthcoming, generally looking down or away from Preminger and expressing not the slightest interest in the proceedings. In his car on the way back, Anderle turned to Tim and said, "There's no shot in hell you're ever getting that."

"Yeah," Tim replied.

Other friends of Tim's, like Underwood's girlfriend Jennifer Stace, recall Tim speaking well of Preminger. Either way, nothing came of the meeting, nor did anything come from the announcement the following spring that Tim would star in a film called *Wild Orange,* in which he would play a Native American character named "Fender Guitar" and write the score. Despite a publicized start date of May 1, 1969, the film—described at the time by its writer-director, Robert Cordier, as "a *42nd Street* kinda thing"—fell apart before shooting began.

That year, though, Tim did score a film, *Changes,* directed by Hall Bartlett and costarring Marcia Strassman (later "Mrs. Kotter" on the sitcom *Welcome Back, Kotter*). Backed by his jazz-rooted band (John Miller, David Friedman, and Carter Collins), Tim recorded a handful of wafting songs, including one of his most autobiographical, "The Father Song":

> *I know I'll never be*
> *The man you want me to be*
> *I feel so hungry*
> *So empty inside. . . .*
> *Oh, tell me, father*
> *Is there shame in your heart for me?*
> *Why do you curse the day that I was born?*

Although dreams of Tim's alternate career as an actor faded as the '70s began, they re-emerged after *Starsailor,* as his music grew increasingly freeform. "That was the next direction," recalls Zachary Glickman, a partner in Herb Cohen Management. "At some point it was like, 'Well, if you're going to sing that shit, let's get you an acting career!'"

By chance, there was a role instantly available. At a party in Hollywood that winter, Tim met Victor Stoloff, a fifty-eight-year-old Russian-born director with a wide-ranging résumé that included producing a season of the television cop show *Hawaii Five-O* and directing propaganda films for the U.S. government's Office of Inter-American Affairs, headed by Nelson Rockefeller. Stoloff had been approached by Technicolor to test out a new method of filmmaking: shooting a movie on videotape and transferring it to 35 millimeter film. Unfortunately, the video cameras were so heavy and bulky that a movie involving any sort of exotic location shooting or action sequences was out of the question. Inspired by the national interest in group therapy, Stoloff had an idea: Why not do a film about one of these sessions, which would only require the actors to be seated in a room? He called the film *Why?*—because, he says, "Everyone seemed to be asking questions, like 'Why this?' and 'Why that?' "

Stoloff had already hired most of his cast, but the role of Glen, a drummer in a suddenly defunct rock band, was still vacant. One of the members of Three Dog Night had supposedly been cast but hadn't shown up at rehearsals. At the party, Stoloff asked Tim, who agreed.

The director was immediately concerned when, during his screen test, Tim stopped and crumpled on the floor in the corner in a fetal position. Someone later told Stoloff Tim had taken heroin, which was known to induce stomach pains and cramps. Nervous about hiring anyone who used drugs, Stoloff was nevertheless struck by Tim's "magnificent face" and his celluloid presence, and decided to cast him.

Filmed on a Hollywood set over the course of several weeks in late spring, all for $150,000, *Why?* took place in a fake therapist's "office"—a chintzy-looking apartment set with a fireplace, puke-yellow shag carpeting, and couches. Stoloff hired an actual therapist, Dr. Herb Goldberg, to lead the discussions. Tim's costars included Jeannie Berlin, daughter of actress Elaine May, and an athlete and unproven actor named O. J. Simpson. Prompted by Goldberg, the cast improvised dialogue during rehearsals. Their comments were then transcribed and turned into a script that, strangely, they had to memorize.

Wearing slacks, black leather shoes, and a pullover sweater, Tim easily slipped into the role of the cynical, aimless "Glen." Whether curling up on a couch, half-listening to the other patients, or slouching as he paced the office, he exuded an effortless malaise. Part of the reason may have been that, with his wise-old-man smile and caustic remarks, it was sometimes hard to differentiate "Glen" from Tim. During one exchange, "Glen" talks about his parents' frequent arguments and how upsetting they were to him: "It scared me. . . . When you're a kid, you always think it's your fault when your parents are quarreling." After Simpson's character spoke of the pressures of being an athlete, "Glen" retorted with a tense speech about selling out, about how "when you speak your mind, the money stops coming."

In his longest monologue, "Glen" was asked about his father. He began by recounting his father's fall off a ladder. Then, he said, one day "my father got up and went out on the front porch. He had his rubber sandals on and his dirty chinos rolled up, safety pins rolled 'em together, with his Hawaiian shirt, and his belly hangin' out and a can of beer, and all his war medals on his Yankees baseball cap." Tim chuckled. "And he breaks into this full sprint down the street after this cat. . . . He was robbing jewelry from the tract homes. Pop tackles this guy and puts him over his shoulder and comes down the street singing, 'By the rising of the moon.'" Tim laughed harder. "It was really bizarre. So he throws the guy down on the lawn and calls to the people, 'Who's gonna call the police?' Nobody did. They all go into their houses. Finally I went in and called the police. He yells, 'Get me a beer—I'm losin' energy.'" The police did appear but failed to arrest the burglar, setting him free due to a lack of evidence. "Glen" then said his father "lost face in the whole community. . . . He split and they found him in Mexico trying to get an army together. They caught him and put him in a VA hospital. Couldn't take the quiet life. Great man, though."

Goldberg asked "Glen" how he was involved with his father. "The presence," Tim responded firmly, in character. "I was involved with the presence of the man. He was great."

"And that made you feel close to him?" Goldberg replied.

"'Course it did," Tim said, looking squarely at Goldberg. "Close as you could be to your father."

Tim later told costar Linda Gillen, who played a pregnant junkie, that he was talking about a neighbor, not his actual father, but the similarities—the ladder, the military medals, the drinking—were all too coincidental. "That moment was wonderful," Gillen recalls. "He wasn't acting. It was very real."

With his motorcycle boots and sweater pulled over his hands, Tim would often curl up next to Gillen between takes. "Tim had a body like a cat," she says. "I'd lean over on O.J. and he was like a *rock*. Other times I'd lean on Tim and it was like being on a pile of down pillows." Between takes, Tim would sing to her seductively, songs like the Frank Sinatra–associated "All the Way." The actors were being paid Screen Actors Guild scale of $420 a week, and Gillen asked Tim why he was doing it. "I need the money for my family," he responded.

Tim and Gillen would talk music as well. Both loved Fred Neil, and Tim told her she had to hear Neil's song "Dolphins." "He said, 'It's about this guy and he had this woman and he's madly in love with her and they have this child. And they live at the beach and have this wonderful life and watch the dolphins in the distance. But he leaves her and the child to follow his destiny. Every time she sees the dolphins on the horizon, he wants her to think about him. It's a beautiful song about lost love and how you can't go back anymore.' I thought, 'Wow, that sounds wonderful.'"

Gillen bought a copy of the recording expecting to hear such a story-song, but only heard Neil's far less specific lyric, with no mentions of children or destiny. Later, Tim told her he had a son but gave Gillen the impression he wasn't allowed to see the child and that he felt bad about it. (By this point, Mary, Jeff, and Ron Moorhead were living in Fullerton.) "Then," Gillen says, "I got the feeling of 'she got pregnant and tricked me into marrying her.' It was like talking to two different people."

Not surprisingly, Tim and Simpson didn't banter much and seemed to have little in common. One day, Stoloff said there was a chance of filming in England, and Tim mentioned he was popular there. With the exception of Dr. Goldberg, none of the actors knew much of Tim's musical career. After Tim's remark, Simpson pointed at Tim and began giggling—"Hee hee hee!"—in disbelief.

Why? wouldn't be released for another year, and even then, just barely; it was primarily shown on college campuses and in a few theaters. In terms of Tim's big-screen debut, the film's premature burial was probably for the best: *Why?* was lugubrious, the videotape-to-film method made it resemble the tackiest of soap operas, and the singer-songwriter theme song ("So many lonely people, forever wondering, 'Why?'"), which wasn't sung by Tim, was dreadful. Tim himself hated the film and was openly dismissive of it, but, Judy says, "it was his way of getting exercise for acting gigs."

Years later, Stoloff sent a copy of *Why?* to a mental-health organization in New York. "So lifelike and convincing were the performances," read the response of a company spokesman, "that, had I not known the group members were actors, I would have thought this a documentary."

His first screen role under his belt, Tim resumed working with the *Star-sailor* band, which had changed personnel once again. By 1971, Tim had again parted ways with his longtime friend and collaborator Lee Underwood. Underwood was once again, in his own words, "out of commission" due to personal excesses (which, in turn, had also led to his breakup with girlfriend Jennifer Stace), but others feel Tim's music may have outgrown Underwood's guitar technique.

Ironically, it was through Underwood that Tim met a musician who would replace him. Emmett Chapman, a young jazz guitarist, had created a new way of playing his instrument: Instead of using the body of the guitar, he would tap the fingers of both hands on the fretboard, which allowed Chapman to play guitar and bass parts and orchestral-style sounds at the same time. By the time he had joined Tim's band, Chapman had dispensed with the body of the guitar altogether and simply played an amplified fretboard, which he called the Electric Stick. Tim loved the sound of it; it was a perfect fit with the direction in which he saw himself heading.

With a new band featuring Chapman, drummer Baker, and occasionally trombone player Glenn Ferris, Tim took the *Starsailor* concept to its outer limits. Complete songs *and* set lists flew out the window, and the concerts became entirely improvised, with even the *Starsailor* songs left behind. The scatting and animal sounds ran wild, and the shows, which changed nightly, took on a wild-eyed experimentation that harked back to Tim's high-school days with the Harlequin Three. Offstage, Baker would often goof off with what he called an impersonation of a pregnant flea: "I got down on the ground and did this weird gesture as if the flea was trying to lift its leg but couldn't because it was pregnant," he recalls. "Tim thought it was funny." At one show, Tim stopped the music and, to Baker's surprise, told the audience his drummer would do his pregnant-flea routine, and Baker obliged. The mad science continued in the studio: According to recording engineer Stan Agol, this edition of the *Starsailor* band laid down some music on tape at Paramount Studios in Los Angeles during this period. The only problem was Tim's voice: One of his high notes was so loud that he literally blew out several microphones. "I've never seen it happen with anybody before or since," says Agol.

Tim was enjoying himself, but as word spread of his new repertoire, the crowds began to thin out. The band continued playing bars, roadhouses, and small clubs up and down the California coast, in Santa Cruz, Escondido, and San Francisco, the musicians making as little as $50 per show. (In contrast, the earlier incarnation of the *Starsailor* band could earn as much as $2,000 a night, according to contracts.) *Starsailor* proved to be a commercial disaster, not even approaching *Billboard*'s Top 200 chart. "I didn't think—and neither did he—about the reception, what the record company would think," says Beckett. "Or whether it would make the charts. It was, 'Was it a great piece of art or not?' And if it was, then okay."

Still, it was not fine with Tim's business associates, both Warner Brothers and Cohen (who, as both manager and record-company head, was seeing two sets of profits shrink). "*Starsailor* and *Lorca* were transitional albums," Cohen says. "He was trying to find a voice. He was trying different forms. He was young." Others recall Cohen being far more blunt. At a show in Napa Valley, he was overheard saying, "This shit isn't going anywhere." Tim would return from meetings with his manager and tell friends that Cohen had referred to the music as "masturbating in public."

"The more he was working, the less people liked it," Cohen maintains. "He was howling, making noises, doing songs people didn't want to hear. People would walk out. Club owners didn't want to book him." Indeed, Tim took to booking shows himself in clubs that often held only a few hundred. The days of headlining Philharmonic Hall felt like another lifetime.

"His later albums I had no use for," says Cohen's brother and business partner Martin, nicknamed Mutt. "All that howling and that crap. He was self-destructive, especially in his career. When you're doing what everybody doesn't *want* you to do, you're self-destructive. If you're not trying to sell records and that's the business you're in, you're self-destructive. I don't want to hear any bullshit about art for art's sake. You wanna play that game? That's beautiful. But you don't get into the mainstream and then act like you're not there. And that's what Tim did." A friend who once drove Tim to the Cohens' office recalls them breaking into an argument within a matter of minutes.

By the end of 1971, Tim and his new family had left the house in Laguna Beach and moved into a $200-a-month apartment at 828 Venezia in Venice. Judy and Taylor maintain the move occurred because Tim wanted to be closer to Los Angeles and his musicians and business handlers; Underwood claims Tim's financial problems led to the loss of the house. Nonetheless, the Buckley family began living in tighter quarters.

Dan Gordon recalls seeing what he called the turning point at a roadhouse in Southern California. The club was nearly empty, but he compares the show to "watching a Stravinsky jam session. It was the most exciting stuff he'd ever done. It wasn't yet *good*. But occasionally he'd get this flash of what it could be, and the flash was so brilliant and so extraordinary that you forgave all the bullshit it took to *get* to that point." Afterward, Tim and Gordon went out drinking, and Gordon saw something new: the sight of Tim crying as he recounted the pressure he was receiving from the business side.

Tim had long had a fondness for alcohol, but in the wake of *Starsailor*'s flop and the downturn in his finances, he began drowning his pain and confusion in heavier doses of drink and narcotics. Gordon recalls one evening when Tim returned to his and Judy's apartment and, finding himself locked out, punched his hand through a glass window, unknowingly slicing up his wrist in the process. "We were so drunk that he didn't know it," Gordon says. "That was the level of drinking." Another friend recalls Tim taking an overdose of numbing Percodan pills and walking through a patio door in the Venezia apartment, showering his body with glass. Gordon says he and others began referring to Tim and Judy as "Scott and Zelda."

With Gordon's assistance, Tim channeled some of his building anxieties into another artistic outlet. Gordon brought his typewriter to the Venezia apartment, and over the course of several weeks, the two junior-high friends cranked out a film script called *Fully Air Conditioned Inside*, so named so that people would be lured into theaters (the unwritten sequel would be called *Immediate Seating*). With the help of a bottle of French Bordeaux, Tim and Gordon had an uproarious time improvising and acting out scenes; Judy would wake up from a nap to the sound of both men's hysterical laughter. "We wanted to write the darkest comedy in the history of the world," says Gordon, "a modern Marx Brothers movie."

"Dark," however, doesn't begin to describe the seventy-seven-page script. It opens with a scene of Tim and "Chief Prancing Cloud" ("an old wise Indian") entering a Hollywood office building. "I sense you have a heaviness in your heart, my son," the chief says to Tim's character, also named Tim. Tim responds: "Tacos always give me gas." In an elevator, they encounter two "hippy kids," "Arny" and "Heather," who spout so much inane counterculture babble that the Chief slays them with his tomahawk. With the heads of the kids dangling from Cloud's belt, Cloud and Tim walk into the office of Tim's manager, who happens to be named "Herby."

"I'll be with ya in a second, schmuck," Herby tells them. After attempting to sell a Navajo rug to the Indian chief, Herby tells Tim: "OK schmuck, let's talk about your fabulous career. To begin with, you're all washed up. From there on, it gets depressing. . . . Look schmuck, your airplane fares, you got hotels, you got musicians, you got car rentals, you got booking agents, you got me, your lawyers, you got tax consultants, you got me, not to mention two nasal toned ex-wives." Herby opens two closet doors revealing "ex-wife no. 1" (who whines, "I want a new car") and "ex-wife no. 2 and kid" ("Your son needs braces"). Accountants—including "Guiseppe the poor Italian"—enter, informing Tim of his dire financial straits and telling him, "It was so much easier when you just played a guitar and wore denim."

Singing "Call Me Irresponsible," Tim walks into the desert with Cloud and prepares to die until he is rescued by a talking, jockstrap-wearing vulture named Buttons. In a hospital, Tim is seduced by "Nurse Wu" (clearly Judy), who wears "a slinky white mini-dress with much cleavage, long white leather boots, and black dancer's stockings" and asks him, "Coco butter or Wesson oil? . . . Whips or coals?" After Herby visits him and suggests a lobotomy ("If Tim'd just sing his old songs, he'd have Elvis Presley on his knees"), Tim vows, "I'm gonna make a comeback, Herby, I got it all figured out." At a concert at the Troubadour, Tim instead explodes detonators, destroying the left and right sections of the club ("huge explosion, screaming, mangled bodies, etc.," reads the script); he then beheads the first row of fans with a guillotine. Arrested, Tim endures an absurdist trial (one of the witnesses is a severed hand, from one of the victims of the explosion) and is sentenced to Death Row. Alone in his cell, Tim tells himself, "All I've succeeded in doing has been to commit an elaborate form of suicide. And I think I always knew it . . ." He is saved at the last minute by the vulture, "to the strains of 'I Did It My Way.' " Flying into the sky, Tim and the vulture crash into the sun and explode.

"Well, I think the worst is over," Buttons the Vulture says.

The neatly typed script was alternately self-pitying, moronic, and shockingly racist: There were repeated insults of blacks ("Carter," who tap-dances and is described in the script as "Steppin Fetchit"), "a faggot waiter" ("CR") who calls Tim "Miss Garland," and a stuttering interviewer who asks Tim his opinions on the Beatles ("fags," Tim says) and Will Rogers ("fairy"). Japanese, Hispanic, and Jewish characters were also mocked. Band member Emmett Chapman, who recalls Tim's enthusiasm about the script, feels the trial scene was a metaphor for the meetings Tim was enduring at the time with Cohen and his record company.

"Needless to say, the script did *not* sell," Gordon says. "But I don't think two people ever had more fun than we did when we wrote it." At the very least, *Fully Air Conditioned Inside* allowed Tim to vent his intensifying bitterness and hostility toward the music business (and, it seemed, the world in general) in a way he never did in music or interviews. "It was therapy for him," Judy says.

Even so, the script made for an often disturbing glimpse into Tim's psyche as his career, music, and bank account hung in the balance in the early months of 1972. Instead of garnering acclaim for the courageousness of his new music, he was being told he was washed up, a has-been in his business. He was a husband with a wife and a child, not to mention a divorcé with an ex-wife and another child to support. He was frustrated and depressed. He was also, on February 14, 1972, twenty-five years old.

FOURTEEN

"I'll probably play live till the day I die. It's cool to have a CD, with a condensed moment that's been worked over for weeks, but to do something that will just fly away is kind of special. Every time somebody tells you they love you, that 'I love you' flies away, and you wait until the next one."

—JEFF BUCKLEY, COLUMBIA PRESS RELEASE FOR LIVE AT SIN-É

Hal Willner had grown accustomed to the sound of his intercom buzzer ringing at two or three in the morning, followed by the sight of Jeff at his door, eager for another late-night hang-out session. Somehow, Jeff had even acquired a key to Willner's apartment, and often Willner would arrive home and find Jeff *there*, poring over his collection of unreleased Tom Waits recordings. If it had been anyone else, Willner would have been less than pleased, but like many others, he found it impossible to be mad at Jeff.

On this evening at Willner's apartment in the fall of 1993, though, Jeff was freaking. He had just heard a mix of the Sin-é tapes and wasn't happy. "They're making me sound like Loverboy!" he shrieked. Willner, who had attended the Sin-é sessions, thought Jeff's concerns were a little odd—Jeff, with *that* voice and *that* guitar and *those* songs, resembling those bloated Canadian corporate-rock clowns?—but then, that was Jeff, endlessly wary of the music industry. During the signing process, Willner would run into Jeff at the Anseo bar, where Jeff would tell him about the latest round of meetings he had taken with executives and all the promises they were making to him. He didn't seem to believe a word they were saying.

There *had* been problems with the Sin-é recording from the start. Something within the building—the heating system, perhaps—had emitted an incessant hum, so all the tapes were undercut by a low buzz. The recording engineers did their best to cover up the sonic disturbance, but it could still be heard in the tapes. Then, at the mixing sessions, Jeff would bridle when engineer Michael Brauer began using technology like a deesser, a machine that removes the *ssss*'s from the edge of a singer's voice. "But that's what I *did*," Jeff would say.

"Jeff didn't like any effects on his voice at *first*," says Steve Berkowitz. "It was a big learning experience and a hard one for him. There was a lot of trepidation, a lot of 'What are you turning me into?'" Eventually, the tapes were finessed to everyone's satisfaction, and Jeff and Berkowitz whittled down the selection to four songs, all taken from the second taping in August. In the third week of November 1993, Jeff made his Columbia debut with the EP, fittingly titled *Live at Sin-é*.

He had originally wanted to call it *Café Days: Live at Sin-é,* implying it would be the first in a series of intimate live recordings to be released throughout his career. (It's thought the umbrella title was inspired by the line "these dark café days" in Joni Mitchell's "The Last Time I Saw Richard.") However, Columbia president Don Ienner is said to have been given a mockup of the cover art and instantly put a slash through *Café Days*. In other ways, though, the label bent to Jeff's demands. The mere fact that the EP was released shortly before Christmas, a period when the public focuses on superstar product, befitted the gingerly way Columbia was handling Jeff (and Jeff wanted to be handled). In the United Kingdom, Columbia leased the EP to the independent label Big Cat in order to lend it instant credibility—"an underground spin," as Ienner says. According to sources, the deal also resulted when Sony's UK division declined to release *Live at Sin-é,* thinking a disc with a lengthy Van Morrison cover would have no chance of competing against the likes of Oasis and other new British pop bands. Either way, the ruse was so successful that later European articles would describe Jeff as an indie act scooped up by Columbia.

Merri Cyr's cover photo, taken during the warm-up for the July 19 afternoon set, depicted Jeff tuning up in front of a few patrons who were pointedly ignoring him. "The fact that he chose that shot shows his sense of humor and how he saw himself," Cyr says. "He thought he was just this goofy kid—he couldn't understand why people were going crazy for him." For extra authenticity, Columbia art designer Nicky Lindeman used her coffee-mug-stained napkin from the taping night for the cover art. The publicity materials cited Bob Dylan, Led Zeppelin, and George Carlin as influences, and as in the Sony convention newsletter, the name of Tim Buckley was nowhere to be found.

As a twenty-six-minute condensation of Jeff's developmental period at the club, down to the sounds of clattering silverware and glasses, *Live at Sin-é* serves its purpose. Even years after its release, Jeff's choir-boy voice and unaccompanied guitar sounds like nothing else released in the aftermath of Nirvana. His version of Edith Piaf's "Je N'en Connais Pas la Fin" ("I Don't Know the End of It") implies the enchantment of attending a carnival as a child, down to Jeff's carousel-style guitar, and "The Way Young Lovers Do" captures him at his most rhapsodic, scatting, ululating, and rolling his tongue for ten rapturous minutes. The EP is nonetheless a little disappointing. The renditions of "Mojo Pin" and "Eternal Life" are solid but pale next to the full-bodied band versions Jeff had just recorded in Woodstock, and some of his most evocative Sin-é–associated songs, like "Calling You" and "Dink's Song," are not included. (Berkowitz says the omission of what he calls "cabaret-ish stuff" was intentional: "To the world outside of New York, this guy didn't exist, and suddenly this EP's going to come out and 'What is he, the new Bobby Short?'") Nonetheless, *Live at Sin-é* is a fitting, and appropriate, hint of things to come.

The original plan was to release the EP, have Jeff hit the road for a solo tour, and then release his first album directly afterward, in late winter. However, by the time Jeff left New York in mid-January for his first national tour, the album was far from finished. The foundations of each song may have been done at Bearsville, but the completion of those songs was turning into an endurance test.

At studios in Manhattan and New Jersey, Jeff began overdubbing layers of guitars and numerous other instruments (his harmonium leading into "Lover, You Should've Come Over," Indian tablas and Johnson's vibes on "Dream Brother," a studio musician's organ on "Lover, You Should've Come Over" and "Forget Her"). He sang his vocals over and over, searching for the right inflections and the perfect take. A mantra that was initially sung over the introductory chords of "Last Goodbye" was cut. The songs were all protracted, and Wallace judiciously trimmed some to manageable lengths.

In particular, Jeff repeatedly recorded "Corpus Christi Carol" and "Hallelujah," unable to decide on a final take. One night in New Jersey, he set up, sighed, and began playing "Hallelujah" for the umpteenth time, but in a minor key, and with a slightly different introductory guitar passage. With Jeff unable to make up his mind, Wallace edited together several different takes of the song, including this latest one, to create a composite "Hallelujah"; the same went with "Corpus Christi Carol." The album release date was bumped from January to March, and finally to August. "I'm sure my bosses thought Jeff and I were nuts by this time," says Berkowitz.

Jeff's inability to commit to a final version of a track—until Wallace gently nudged him into a decision—was an outgrowth of Jeff's overflow of ideas and his instinctive creativity. But it was also a microcosm of his personality. He had spent his life on the move, reinventing himself along the way, afraid or unwilling to commit to one style or even relationship. The concept of finishing a song, a final take over which he would have no further control, his style and music forever cemented, spooked him. It meant a commitment to a singular sound, personality, and image, and few things in life were so foreign to him in the winter of 1993.

There were other hitches, such as a December 1993 critique of *Live at Sin-é* in the New York daily newspaper *Newsday* that, to Jeff's horror, combined it with Michael Bolton's latest album ("both awkwardly reach for a balance of emotion and technique, eventually relying on sheer force of will, oversinging, flaking out"). The review also referred to Jeff as a "cipher" who played "folky blues for wounded bohemians." According to Andy Wallace, Jeff was "almost apoplectic. It stopped him cold. If someone had thought, 'Who can I use to really get his goat?' you couldn't have chosen somebody better than Michael Bolton." For two days, work on the album halted as Jeff, whose ability to handle criticism was never strong, agonized over the review. It was a little funny, Wallace thought, but he still felt bad for the kid.

Still, the tour had been set up, so the album was put on hold while Jeff and a road manager, Reggie Griffith, began a two-month trek around the country and Canada in a van. At Jeff's request, he played cozy, intimate venues—coffeehouses, clubs, even record and book stores. He played the songs from the EP, broke into his comedy routines, and previewed songs from his first album, which by now he had decided to title *Grace*. Sometimes, to his dismay, people talked during his gigs, and the schedule was demanding. Before each show, Sony had him visit record stores for glad-handing and career seed-planting. "It was probably a little forced, but it needed to be," recalls Columbia's Leah Reid, who accompanied him to a few of these performances and recalls seeing Jeff reading a magazine during one record-store visit in Boston. Still, Jeff threw himself into his job, doing what was asked of him. The crowds were small but enthusiastic, demonstrating that his performances could translate beyond St. Mark's Place.

During his stop in Los Angeles in late January, Columbia booked studio time for Jeff to work on the album further. In particular, everyone was anxious for him to finish "Dream Brother," the sweeping, Middle Eastern–influenced track he and the band would listen to during their late-night drives around Woodstock. Although the backing music was almost done, the lyrics were not. Late one night at Sony Studios in Santa Monica, Jeff huddled with Clif Norrell, a local engineer who had the streetwise feel of a West Coast Denis Leary. The choruses were done, but there were still no verses. At midnight, Jeff turned to Norrell and said, softly, "How about if I meet you back here at two A.M.?" Norrell groaned to himself but complied, and Jeff left.

On schedule, he returned with finished lyrics and, in only a few takes, recorded them. The "brother" in the title now referred to friend Chris Dowd, who was considering breaking up with a woman pregnant with his child. It was a scenario that reverberated deeply within Jeff, reminding him of his own childhood and his father's early departure. Although one phrase ("I love you and your dance insane") referred to Dowd's manic presence, the lyrics found Jeff pleading with Dowd not to do what his own father had done to him:

> *Don't be like the one who made me so old*
> *Don't be like the one who left behind his name*
> *Because I waited for you like I waited for him*
> *And nobody ever came*

After the session, Norrell was, like so many before him, floored by Jeff's focus in the studio and his vocal and instrumental command. Still, the engineer was haunted by the experience. Jeff seemed so fragile and vulnerable, and he was about to enter a business not known for tolerating either trait. Norrell couldn't put his finger on it, but joining a growing list of people—

from Jeff's friends in New York to Tim's old manager Herb Cohen—Norrell had an unsettling feeling that someday "something was going to happen" to Jeff, and that that something wouldn't be pleasant.

When Michael Tighe arrived with his guitar at New York's Montana Studios in late winter, he assumed it would be for naught. Raised in Manhattan and Brooklyn, the twenty-one-year-old Tighe was an actor by trade, which wasn't hard to assume given his soft features, puckery face, and wavy brown hair. He had appeared in a few downtown theater productions with Rebecca Moore and, through her, had befriended Jeff two years earlier. The two would play pool on Houston Street or sit around and play guitars together.

During the completion of *Grace*, Tighe was one of many whom Jeff called directly from a studio, excitedly playing them the tapes over the phone. Like many who had seen Jeff do solo gigs at Sin-é, Tighe was taken aback: "I had seen him solo, and I couldn't believe how realized the album was." Tighe knew Jeff was in search of another musician to bolster the sound of the trio, and he was surprised and elated when Jeff asked him to audition. Still, Tighe realized his own limitations—he was, at best, a rudimentary guitar player—and he had no experience beyond jamming with friends in high school. He assumed one of the hotshot axe-men who were trying out for the slot would be hired.

When he stepped into Montana, a midtown studio and rehearsal space, Tighe came upon an inspiring and moving scene: Jeff, Grondahl, and Johnson all listening to a finished copy of *Grace*, Johnson mimicking Jeff's guitar parts and Jeff air-drumming with Johnson's performances. Before long, the foursome got down to the audition, instantly veering into a long, unformed jam. Tighe was so nervous that he sat with his head down—he didn't own a guitar strap anyway—but everyone immediately clicked. "The chemicals in my body had never felt like that before," Tighe recalls. "I was just so elated." After one more similar session, Jeff asked Tighe to join the band, and Tighe accepted.

The choice perplexed everyone in Jeff's camp. It was strange enough that he had hired Johnson and Grondahl, newcomers with little professional stage experience; Tighe didn't have any at all. No one, especially Jeff's old (and miffed) Musicians Institute friends back in Los Angeles, could understand why Jeff hadn't opted for more accomplished players to support him. When Columbia executives would call and ask who the new member was and with whom had he played, everyone had no choice but to bluff and say, *Sure, he's got an extensive résumé, don't worry about it,* all the while hoping Jeff hadn't blown an important hire for the inevitable touring he would have to do.

To Jeff, though, the recruitment of Tighe made all the sense in the known universe. Tighe didn't have musicianly chops, but he had something else: a sweet, unassuming, pensive nature that fit into Jeff's idea of a backup band of buddies, not professional musicians. "Michael felt right from the beginning," says Grondahl. "Jeff didn't want anyone more amazing than him. He wanted people who had their own style, but not a shtick."

Tighe began learning the songs from *Grace*, but just as often, the quartet would gather at Montana and improvise for what seemed like endless hours. One night, they went into a two-hour free-form tune later dubbed the "Morning After" tape, featuring Jeff on organ, Grondahl emitting punky screams, Tighe bashing out crude guitar rhythms, and Johnson playing sundry beats and tempos around his kit. It was the sound of men getting to know each other, personally and musically, and becoming their own posse (and, in the process, "smoking a bit of the ol' reefer," according to Grondahl). "It was apparent that it felt very natural and exciting to play with each other," Tighe says. "Jeff wanted the music to always be changing and have musicians who could have it breathe through them in new ways all the time—a band that could move with each other and just go with a feeling and were not afraid to go as far as he was going." One of these jams, "Tongue," would later crop up on a single.

On the first day of a full band rehearsal, Tighe brought with him a gently descending chord progression he had composed. Jeff heard it, liked it, and, as Tighe played the riff, took a seat behind the drums and began singing and playing along to it. Tighe thought he was singing "sorry"; in fact, the phrase was "so real." Although the lyrics weren't finished, the complete song tumbled out effortlessly.

With Andy Wallace unavailable due to prior commitments, Columbia rehired Clif Norrell to record B-sides for *Grace* singles. Although no one at Columbia or at Jeff's management had yet heard it, "So Real" was one of those songs, and with Norrell, the band put it on tape one spring evening at Sony's midtown studio. As usual, Jeff hadn't finalized the lyrics by the time they were set to wrap up the recording, so he went for a walk and returned to the studio with them in hand.

"So Real" became a composite of various female relationships in his life. It's said the "simple city dress" line referred to Moore, while other parts of the song may have been inspired by a dancer with whom Jeff had a brief fling shortly after his separation from Moore. "I love you, but I'm afraid to love you," Jeff spoke in the middle section, somewhat in the tradition of spoken-word parts dating back to Elvis Presley's "I Can't Help Falling in Love with You." He also brought up his mother Mary, who was still back in Orange County:

> *I never stepped on the cracks 'cause I thought I'd hurt my*
> *mother*
> *And I couldn't awake from the nightmare that sucked me in*
> *And pulled me under, pulled me under*

The track was finished at dawn, and in a cab flying downtown as the sun rose, Jeff and Tighe listened to it in the backseat. To Jeff, who didn't say a word, it was affirmation of his idea of a band based on feeling rather than virtuosity. "It showed us we could be a *sound*," says Grondahl, "but not a type of music."

Although "So Real" was initially slated to be a B-side, Jeff was so taken with it that it became something more important, a solution to a lingering quandary. Ever since Columbia executives had heard "Forget Her," they had begun focusing on it as potential breakout hit; of all the songs on the album, it was the most traditional in its arrangement, and its accessible, verse-chorus structure was the type Jeff didn't seem inclined to bang out. ("Typical idiot thinking," says Grondahl of the label's mindset.) The song was the fifth track on a rough tape of *Grace* being passed around the Sony offices, and Ienner imagined it as the album's third or fourth single. Then one day, Jeff told Berkowitz that not only did he not want it to be a single, he didn't want it on the album at all. Instead, he wanted to replace it with "So Real."

The reasons for Jeff's change of heart on "Forget Her" vary depending on the source. One former Sony executive says Jeff said the song was about Moore and therefore too personal to release. Wallace says that "in his head, Jeff envisioned something totally different." (Indeed, Tighe says that when he encountered the band listening to *Grace* at his audition, both Jeff and Johnson grimaced when the song came on.) Some feel its white-blues, power-ballad structure made it too similar to a Michael Bolton track, while others suspect Jeff *knew* Sony wanted to transform it into a monster hit and was deathly afraid of having his intimate feelings soiled in such a crass way. Or, others say, it was a combination of all those thoughts and fears. As everyone was beginning to learn, Jeff had a habit of telling different things to different people.

"Obviously, I did not share Jeff's feeling," Berkowitz says. "I thought that was the song the largest mass of people would be able to identify with." Ienner agreed: "That song struck me as a magic moment on *Grace*, and I felt there was a void on the record for that song." As the mixing and mastering of *Grace* approached its conclusion, Berkowitz continued to warn his bosses that Jeff was pulling the song, but they refused to believe it until, Berkowitz says, "It came to the day where I said, 'Listen, I'm not kidding. He doesn't want it on there.'"

It was time to talk to Jeff. On March 7, Ienner, Berkowitz, and Michele Anthony, a Columbia vice president who was also an avid Jeff supporter and fan, took their new signing to dinner at an Italian restaurant on Manhattan's West Side. Before the food had even arrived, Ienner made his case about why the song deserved to be on the album and why it would connect with so many people. "*Ohhh,* I don't want to talk about that," Jeff said. "It's not ready. I'll come back to it someday."

Ienner persisted until Jeff, firmly but softly, said, "If I hear the song again, I'm going to throw up." With that, the decision was made: The song would not be on the album. The label wasn't happy ("He was being stubborn," Ienner comments), but no one pushed it—at least, not at this point in his career.

The next day, Jeff left New York for his first series of European concerts. It was not an especially lengthy tour, constituting ten club shows between March 10 and March 20, but endurance was not the point; the goal was to establish his presence overseas and set the stage for the album to come. The trip started with a performance at a Sony convention in Gleneagles, Scotland, at which Jeff tweaked his bosses by singing "Tommy Mottola" (Sony Music's president and CEO) to the tune of the Beatles' "Eleanor Rigby." After preliminary shows in Amsterdam and Dublin, Jeff flew into London's Heathrow Airport on March 15. U2's the Edge was on the same flight and disembarked first, but several young women in the lounge ignored him and instead gravitated toward the unknown young man with the fur coat and boots. It was "like the shape of things to come," recalls Big Cat head Steven Abbott, who was there to pick Jeff up. Before he began singing at the first London show, at the 250-seat Borderline club, bar chatter filled the air. But, recalls Abbott, "Within three minutes of the first song, everyone was silent. People were dumbfounded by him. England is where things come and go every week. But Jeff was on a totally different level."

The British public only grew more welcoming as the tour progressed. On March 17, Jeff gave an on-air performance at GLR, the BBC station serving London, and as a result, his gig that same evening, at the 250-capacity Upstairs at the Garage, was packed—with, among others, Chrissie Hynde and her friend, tennis pro and fledgling guitarist John McEnroe, who was so taken with the performance that he carried Jeff's amp down the club's stairs. The following night came what Abbott calls "a turning point," a show at a fifty-seat coffeehouse called Bunjie's in London's Covent Garden district. With the buzz already building, people began lining up hours before the doors opened, and by the time Jeff was scheduled to perform, around 10 P.M., the living-room-size space was so overstuffed and hot that Jeff dispatched his new management partner, Dave Lory, to buy white roses. As he walked into the space, Jeff passed the flowers out to the audience. While doing so, he made a reference to a British pop legend that further endeared him to them: "You must think I'm Morrissey." Since there was no microphone, he turned his guitar down low and sang without amplification, and the combination of intimacy and his vocal power astounded the crowd, which by then included prominent British music journalists.

With Bunjie's scheduled to close after Jeff's hour-long set, tour booker Emma Banks was given the okay to set up another gig immediately and ran up the street. Returning a few minutes later, Banks informed everyone that Jeff would be performing in a few minutes at Andy's Forge, a club on Charing Cross Road, and seemingly everyone at Bunjie's formed a massive posse that followed Jeff up the street for the five-minute walk to the other club. "It was the Pied Piper, it really was," recalls Abbott. At Andy's Forge, Jeff played a nearly ninety-minute set of originals and covers, including Dylan's "All Along the Watchtower." The following week, *Live at Sin-é* arrived in London record stores and instantly sold five thousand copies. "In the space of six weeks," says Abbott, "he went from being someone Sony turned down [in Britain] to the biggest happening thing in London." To say the tour was a critical and public-relations success was an understatement.

Once Jeff arrived back home, though, the "Forget Her" matter was far from the last debate that would occur before *Grace* was released. As he had done with *Live at Sin-é*, Jeff again hired Merri Cyr to shoot the album cover (another victory for him, since Cyr had little album-art experience), and along with a gaggle of art directors and stylists, he dutifully showed up at a studio in Brooklyn for the photo shoot. He brought along a duffel bag of clothes, all of them unwashed and rumpled, as well as one of his latest acquisitions, a woman's gold-sparkle jacket he had found at a thrift store. Loosening up, Jeff goofed around with a prop microphone, took the glitter jacket on and off, and, for one shot, posed with a half-eaten banana in homage to Leonard Cohen's similar pose on the cover of his *I'm Your Man*.

When it came time to inspect the potential covers, Columbia's Reid visited Jeff in Philadelphia in late February, during the *Live at Sin-é* tour, and showed him various mockups. Jeff instantly gravitated toward one: a moody, sullen shot of himself staring to the side, several strands of hair falling in his face, the sparkle jacket and prop microphone in full view. He told her he wanted that photograph because he was listening to a rough mix of "Dream Brother" when it was taken; to him, the photo embodied his immersion in music.

Within the halls of Columbia, the photo was met with not so much enthusiasm as confusion. Given Jeff's penchant for wearing used clothes and his disdain of showbiz trappings, the choice seemed contradictory. "Jeff was quite vocal about not coming across as a pretty boy," Berkowitz says. "When I saw the cover, I said, 'Oh, come on, you don't mean *this* one? This is exactly what he said he *didn't* want!'" Others at Columbia complained that Jeff looked "too gay" or "too much like Adam Ant." "The sparkly jacket sent a different message than we wanted," admits Ienner. "It was a little flashy, we thought, compared to the earthiness of *Sin-é*. We tried to steer him away from it."

Whether Jeff intended it or not, the photo was an accurate embodiment of his contradictions. He was suspicious of the record business yet had signed with one of its biggest companies; he griped about the star-making machinery yet was drawn to it. And he complained about people focusing on his looks instead of his music, yet selected a photo that made him look as glamorous as a James Dean–style movie star.

Ienner also feels, as others do, that Jeff had an ulterior motive for not budging from the photo. "He probably liked it because he wanted to win that point," Ienner says. "He wanted to start off the relationship saying this is what he wanted, and whether it was right or wrong, he wanted us to back him." If that was the case, and Jeff wanted to draw a line in the sand with the record business, he had won. After several days of heated debate—"It was like pulling teeth," says Stein—Columbia relented to use of the picture.

By 1994, the only aspects of the pop music business that seemed to connect it to its formative days of the '50s and '60s were records and musicians. Vaster and more engulfing than ever, the industry by then generated $8 billion a year in revenue. There seemed to be as many different styles and off-shoots of styles as there were acts. There were no longer simply AM and FM radio stations, but formats for classic rock, alternative rock, Top 40, dance music, and hip-hop; even adult-contemporary had split into formats that played relative newcomers (Celine Dion, Mariah Carey), oldies acts (Barbra Streisand, Barry Manilow), and straight-out Muzak. Hundreds of new albums arrived in stores every week, followed by another few hundred the following week, for annual totals of approximately twenty thousand releases a year, a 400 percent increase from the '60s.

Each of those albums—or the major ones, anyway—was accorded a multitiered marketing strategy not unlike military maneuvers, in which precise radio formats and listeners were targeted, music video storylines were proposed and storyboarded, and extensive, multiyear tours were set in place to earn revenue and extend the life of an album. The chance of commercial success was slim; only one half of one percent of those twenty thousand albums a year went gold (500,000 copies) or platinum (one million) or higher, but those daunting odds didn't stop anyone from signing on the dotted lines. In the eyes of the record companies, one blockbuster album paid for all the flops.

In light of so much competition, debut albums had become increasingly, desperately important; the days when Columbia "heritage artists" like Dylan and Bruce Springsteen—or Elektra acts like Tim Buckley or Judy Collins—could take two or three albums to develop a fan base were over. If a major-label debut album wasn't a hit, or didn't at least make inroads with respectable six-figure sales, there was a strong possibility the company wouldn't be interested in doing another. (*Live at Sin-é* supposedly only sold several thousand copies, but, says Berkowitz, "It felt like the right thing to do.")

Jeff's three-album guarantee with Columbia protected him against being dropped after one less-than-successful release. Still, in such a ferocious, accelerated marketplace, he and his debut album needed a plan. "We spent hundreds of thousands of hours talking about artists he liked and walking him through the fact that Marvin Gaye and Elvis Costello sold a lot of records and didn't suck," recalls Berkowitz. It wasn't long before a strategy arrived. Neatly typed out and dated April 5, 1994, the fourteen-page "Marketing Plan 1994–1995" was conceived to do the trick.

Although sources say the plan was ultimately a collaboration between Jeff's management and Columbia executives, the names initially attached to it were George Stein, Jeff's lawyer, and his new partner, Dave Lory. When it became evident that Stein had little experience with the day-in, day-out handling of a rock band (or with the logistics of equipment and touring schedules), a comanager became the logical solution. Lory, who had been a client of Stein's a decade before, fit the bill. With his bony face and mane of brown hair, Lory resembled nothing so much as a Confederate soldier. In fact, the North Carolina native *was* something of a veteran, but of the music business wars. As he never failed to tell anyone in talking distance, he had been Gregg Allman's tour manager in the late '80s and went on to work with the reunited Allman Brothers Band. Wary of the media (as was Berkowitz) and more than willing to side with musicians over record companies, the thirty-six-year-old Lory shared many of Jeff's own beliefs and paranoias. He was also a good recourse for Stein: Few big-name managers were interested in comanaging a new act like Jeff with a lawyer. In February, Stein and Lory officially became Jeff's first managers, splitting a 15 percent commission.

Written with Jeff's knowledge and consent—and, it is said, many of his ideas—the Jeff Buckley marketing plan crystallized the dreams and fears that had been gestating within Jeff since the time he had told his high-school newspaper that rock bands shouldn't start at the top. (He had also taken notes when he dropped into a few of Stein's music-business law classes at New York University.) The plan set rules for music videos ("Although Jeff is open to discussing the idea, he is initially opposed to have any video shot for this album . . . [this] will allow the public a chance to use their own imagination and not focus on a certain preconceived image of Jeff and his material . . . MTV is to be treated warily") and early stages of publicity ("Only alternative fanzines should be allowed to interview Jeff Buckley"). Incidents such as Jeff receiving a phone call from a *New York Times* reporter in September 1993 and doing an impromptu interview without consulting his advisors would no longer be tolerated or allowed. The marketing plan also called for a slow build from small to large clubs, then to theaters; no matter the venue, Jeff would be a head-liner, never an opening act. "Furthermore," it stated, "all parties involved in servicing publicity should let all know in advance that Jeff does not want to speak about any personal matters unless he brings it up in the interview (i.e., Tim Buckley, his personal life, etc.)."

Jeff's image was a particularly touchy part of the package. "The first priority is to make sure that Jeff's image is not perceived as public relations flak, but as a truthful reflection of what Jeff is about," reads the summation. ". . . We do not want Jeff to appear as being too self-absorbed or personified as a 'tortured artist.' We want to keep the mysterious persona and mysticism of Jeff Buckley to [have it] come out naturally." The plan also argued for breaking Jeff internationally, which fit in with Sony Music president Mottola's new goal of global crossover for his acts.

Much like the *Grace* cover photo, the marketing strategy laid bare many of the contradictions that lay within Jeff. He and his managers stressed a low-key campaign, yet they required "sniping" (industry lingo for posters plastered on the sides of buildings, construction site walls, and so forth) in each major city in which he would perform. But the most striking aspect of the plan was the way it demanded Columbia act like a small, independent label—and, in the words of the plan, "avoid the generic marketing approach utilized by most majors." The plan is filled with references to keeping Jeff's image and presentation close to "the street" and "the street level," and to "create more of an 'indie vibe.'" On the *Grace* tour posters, the Columbia and Sony logos were conspicuously absent, as if Jeff were trying to convince himself he wasn't *really* recording for the same label that had given the world Mariah and Bolton.

Much like Stein's initial demands for Jeff's contract, the plan was self-assured and mildly defiant. But again, to the surprise of many involved, Columbia—and Ienner in particular—approved of this incremental approach, which differed from Columbia's standard guns-blazing style of breaking new acts. "I remember him calling one night and saying, 'I wanna sell a *lotta* records! But I want to do it my way,'" Ienner says. "He always pointed out the direction he wanted to go." Raised in an unstable home environment, Jeff now sought control in the life and business world around him. Some friends believe that same instinct also accounted for Jeff recruiting a band of relative newcomers; that way, it would be easier for him to shape and firmly guide his own music.

The marketing proposal was tweaked by Columbia executives but essentially put into action as it was. In June, two months before the album was set for release, Columbia released a promotional EP, a three-song sampler called *Peyote Radio Theatre*. (The name derived from a band in-joke: Seeing a drug-addled man crawling on a street one day, Jeff, Johnson, and Grondahl started joking about the sight resembling "chemical theater.") A teaser for the upcoming album, it included "Mojo Pin," an instrumental mix of "Dream Brother," and a cover of "Kanga Roo" by underground-rock icons Big Star. The plan was to have college radio, which had fewer constraints than more commercially minded stations, start playing the tricky "Mojo Pin." Once that was accomplished (to some degree), Columbia then sent copies of "Grace" to commercial modern-rock stations, since that song's more straightforward rhythm made it a better bet for airplay. It was dubbed an "emphasis track"—in other words, a song sent only to radio, and not for sale to the public. With "Forget Her" now in limbo, the plan then called for the harder-edged "Eternal Life" to eventually be the actual first single released from the album, with the hope that it would cross over into Top 40 the way singles by Pearl Jam and Nirvana had. "Because the album is loaded with ballads," read the Lory/Stein plan, "this particular track will keep Jeff perceived as hip to the 'alternative scene.'"

The idea of rolling out different songs for different radio formats was not uncommon in the music business of the '90s, but "previewing" two songs for different formats and then releasing an actual single was. The idea was to introduce audiences gradually—via the integrity-associated college radio—to Jeff and his challenging album. It was anti-hype that was also subtle hype. The plan was *not* to have a Top 40 hit right away, since that approach could lead to Jeff being perceived as a one-hit wonder. He was not meant to be a flash in the pan, but an artist who would lead Columbia into its second century.

August 23, 1994, was not unlike any other Tuesday in the U.S. music business. Among the hundreds of releases unveiled that day were new albums by alternative bands (Oasis, Sebadoh, Luscious Jackson, the Jesus and Mary Chain), rappers (Public Enemy, the Goats), singer-songwriters (Shawn Colvin, Jules Shear), headbangers (Danzig), pop acts (Amy Grant), boomer-rock veterans (Emerson, Lake and Palmer, J. J. Cale), nouveau-hippie jam bands (Rusted Root), and a singing comedian (Sandra Bernhard), as well as a Van Morrison tribute album. Sony's Columbia and Epic labels alone released a total of fifty-one albums on August 23, ranging from the Oasis and Colvin projects to compact-disc reissues of the company's back catalog (including artists such as Simon and Garfunkel and Weather Report).

Even amidst that barrage, the forty thousand copies of *Grace* Columbia shipped to stores distinguished themselves, not merely during that week but for the year as well. At a time when the throbbing, anguished groan of alternative music was setting the pace for rock and roll, *Grace* stood apart like a priest in a brothel. From the sirenlike drone of Gary Lucas's guitar loop that opens it to the hypnotic, cathartic crash of "Dream Brother" that brings it to a close nearly an hour later, the album unabashedly sets out on its own course.

Even a cursory listen makes it apparent that all the tweaking, remixing, fiddling, agonizing, and spending had paid off. The rough basic tracks of each song that had been done at Bearsville were transformed into full-throttle sonic epics that nonetheless retain an exceptional intimacy. "Mojo Pin" is more deliberate and dreamier than the original Gods and Monsters rendition, with much more vivid dynamics; the shift from its instantly engrossing circular guitar intro to the thrashing riffs and screams at its climax is the sort of leap few in rock were attempting at the time. "Last Goodbye" has likewise matured from its earlier, 1990 incarnation into an anthemic, sweeping lament, tinged with wistfulness and longing. Berger's Eastern-style strings ride the melody but never overwhelm it, an achievement in itself. "Lover, You Should've Come Over" remains a confused, and confusing, lyric that opens with a reference to attending a funeral and then, abruptly, finds Jeff somewhat rationalizing the breakup of his relationship with Moore. (During the sessions, Berkowitz asked Jeff to change the song's shift from third- to first-person, but Jeff declined.) Nonetheless, as a piece of music it is a languid beauty, a picturesque stretch of musical hills and valleys that truly becomes Jeff's very own Led Zeppelin ballad. "Dream Brother" is a shadowy labyrinth of spidery guitars and eerie, wordless vocal chants, propelled by the controlled fury of Grondahl's bass and Johnson's drums to an emotional zenith.

There are nods to the Sin-é period, and to the desires of management and Columbia to simulate that sound. Jeff's version of James Shelton's "Lilac Wine," popularized by Nina Simone, is tender and sensual, his voice sounding as if it is millimeters away from the microphone. Despite the fact that it was spliced together from different recordings, "Hallelujah" adds to both the Leonard Cohen and John Cale versions. Backed by only the supple, shrouded picking of his electric guitar, Jeff turns Cohen's bittersweet musings on the ties between love, faith, sacrifice, and religion into a devotional hymn. Singers more agile than Cohen had long covered his songs, blanding them out in the process, but the prettiness of Jeff's delivery on "Hallelujah" highlights the song's haunted lyric. (A further, nonmusical reminder of his earlier life lies in the liner notes: "P: Thank you for her," Jeff wrote in tribute to Moore's late father Peter.)

Overall, *Grace* more than fulfills Jeff and Wallace's desire to create an album reveling in the many aspects of Jeff's musical personality. It's often hard to believe that the same person singing an almost supernatural rendition of Benjamin Britten's "Corpus Christi Carol" is the same tormented soul spitting out the embittered words (and tossing off scabrous lead guitar lines) in the rumbling tank that "Eternal Life" has become. The album's only disconcerting moment arrives when Jeff's voice takes on a semblance of Sting's in the chorus of "So Real." That aside, the album doesn't merely have breadth; it breathes.

Its sonic approach is far from the only factor that sets *Grace* apart. The album openly reveals a performer unafraid to lurch over the top emotionally and creatively, which set it in direct contrast to the pop tenor of the times. In the year of its release, rock, grunge in particular, had grown testier, angrier, and terser; while fiery, it also tended to be lyrically obtuse. There was no doubting the power of bands like Soundgarden and Smashing Pumpkins, but also no denying that they seemed to be wailing at an unseen enemy in the clouds. Others, like Beck and Pavement, favored cheekiness and ironic distance over passion, as if sentiment was old-fashioned, a cornball relic of rock past. The few bands who attempted what Jeff did, like Live, only demonstrated how hideously overwrought passion could be in the wrong hands. By comparison, *Grace* appeared to exist on a celestial plane all its own, even while an album of Gregorian chants became popular background-music for new-age boomers and floated into the U.S. Top 10. Although grounded in rock rhythms and sensibility, *Grace* seemed to float above the earth, scouring the landscape for spiritual fulfillment.

The wide-screen expansiveness of *Grace* came as a shock to many of Jeff's friends in New York. They had grown accustomed to bare-boned voice and guitar, and now were confronted with drums, strings, and layers of guitars. His former Musicians Institute friends in California were stunned by the singing voice they had never heard. "I didn't like *Grace* initially when I heard it," admits Willner, a commonplace reaction among Jeff's early supporters. "My reaction was, 'That's it?' It came across small to me. But it grew on me. It was a sneaky little record." Some were stunned by the cover photograph alone—what was with the sparkly jacket?

In one regard, though, Willner was onto something. In an increasingly faster-paced pop environment, *Grace* was a rarity: an album intended to be absorbed over time. (To nurture that process and add to the music's mystique, Jeff demanded the song's lyrics not be included in the packaging; he wanted everyone to *listen*.) Everyone knew *Grace* was not the type of album that would make an instant splash onto pop radio. Its first-week sales of two thousand copies made that issue glaringly clear. There was only one way to ensure Jeff and the album connected with the masses, and that meant taking to the road.

FIFTEEN

Yes, someone told me what "Dream Letter" was about. I figured out
"Mountain" on my own. I never really embraced his tunes, they never
really got inside of me like they did to other people who knew him. But
on the albums he is THE only pure, wild, nonderivative thing
happening. That is one thing I'm sure of, we would definitely agree on
a lot of things, artistically. I can just immediately tell from the
recordings what he thinks is true and what grates on him because it's
such bullshit. I'd bet my life on it. And I SHOULD have played with
him. Joe Falsia wracks my body, so do the other guys on the later
albums—those studio cats make me want to EAT FLESH, they ruin so
much good stuff, sometimes. I don't love the music. I only have a
certain respect for it right now.

—JEFF BUCKLEY, UNSENT LETTER, 1990

The Tim who phoned Emmett Chapman early in 1972 didn't sound like
the same person who had hired Chapman a few months earlier. The calls
came late at night, and Tim usually sounded anguished—in Chapman's
words, "at wit's end about how to fight the system." He would tell Chapman about the opposition to his music he was receiving from management
and record company alike, about the executives at conference tables laying
down the laws. Tim sounded panicky, desperate, and, each time, very
drunk. He would ramble on, seemingly unable to solve, or even cope with,

his problems. For whatever reason—contractual, perhaps, although Cohen maintains there was never a signed contract—Tim never seemed to entertain the thought of leaving Herb Cohen Management.

Finally, the calls stopped coming. The *Starsailor* band gigs had already begun to peter out thanks to reluctant club bookers, but eventually band regulars like Chapman and bass player John Balkin simply stopped hearing from Tim altogether. "That period opened him up, and it's what ruined him," says Balkin. "He could get on stage and do whatever he wanted. He had this immense amount of freedom. And then he had someone clip his wings." Balkin, like others, held out hope that Tim would one day return to his experimental mode, but most of the musicians never heard from him again. The studio recordings made with the *Starsailor* band vanished.

One of the few who received an explanatory phone call was drummer and friend Maury Baker. "He felt terrible and he'd cry," Baker recalls. "It was terrible. He'd say, 'I just want to remember what we did and how we did it.'" When Baker asked why Tim was dismantling the band, Tim replied, "Man, I gotta do this—I gotta feed my family. They're going to do this thing, and you can't do this with me."

The "thing" Tim was referring to soon became apparent. With the bills piling up and *Lorca* and *Starsailor* sales fiascoes, Tim needed to reinforce both his finances and his status within the music business. By 1972, another new stream of earnest, guitar-strumming singer-songwriters—from soloists like Cat Stevens to bands like America and Seals and Crofts—were taking up where Tim and his '60s peers had left off, albeit in blander directions, and Tim was on the verge of being completely swept aside.

By chance, one of Martin Cohen's legal clients was a veteran producer and songwriter named Jerry Goldstein. Goldstein's eclectic résumé included cowriting the Angels' 1963 smash "My Boyfriend's Back," coproducing the McCoys's 1965 hit "Hang on Sloopy," and being a member of the garage-rock band the Strangeloves ("I Want Candy"). But it was Goldstein's rising success as producer of the Latin funk-pop combo War that was making him a hot industry commodity. Under his guidance, the band hit the Top 20 in early 1972 with its first major hit, "Slippin' into Darkness." Approached by the Cohens to make Tim more amenable to record buyers, Goldstein accepted the assignment. "Jerry was going to save the day," says Zachary Glickman of Herb Cohen Management. "Herb was excited about that, because he felt that maybe Tim could get back on track and start selling records again and making some money. Deep down, Herb was always hoping the old Tim would come back and resurrect himself and carry on from his peak."

To oversee the sessions, Goldstein turned to Joe Falsia, a New York–bred guitarist and arranger who had added licks and riffs to records by everyone from Barry White to the Four Seasons. Falsia knew Tim's career was "on the outside from the mainstream" and, at their first meeting, found Tim unapproachable and very reserved. Still, Tim dutifully if reluctantly appeared at a rehearsal at Goldstein's Far Out Studios, a massive soundstage on Sunset Boulevard. Falsia had assembled a band of pros that included well-regarded studio musicians like bassist Chuck Rainey and drummer Ed Greene. Tim brought with him a few chord changes of undeveloped songs, and the band began playing along, working out rock-oriented rhythms and arrangements for the melodies. "When the grooves started to work for him, he didn't need pushing anymore," Falsia says. "After the first get-together, it shed new light on where he wanted to go."

"Tim wasn't defeated by anything," maintains Cohen. "He was *aware* of the choices. I told him. He was a smart kid."

Three days after the first jam, Tim returned with a batch of new songs. "That's how energized he was," says Falsia. Throughout the month of May, work proceeded on the album as producer Goldstein and guitarist-arranger Falsia recorded basic tracks with Tim and the rhythm section. Later, during the overdubbing phase, Goldstein brought in more musicians, string and horn sections, and—a first for Tim—shimmying female backup singers. Tim himself was an utter professional, never failing to nail a vocal in one or two takes and always showing up straight at the studios. One night, in a gym in the same building as the studio, he began playing an improvised blues. Falsia jumped in, a tape recorder was hurriedly set up, and as Goldstein and a girlfriend danced and clapped along, Tim went into a musical trance that lasted nearly an hour. Edited down to seven minutes, it became a mesmerizing blues called "Hong Kong Bar."

Although that song recalls the Tim of the '60s, it is atypical of the rest of the material. As unsettling and foreign as *Starsailor* had been two years before, *Greetings from L.A.*, as the new work was called, is as close to a conventional rock record as Tim had ever made. Starting with "Move with Me," which sports a juke-joint sax solo and honky-tonk piano, most of the songs find him and the band vamping over relatively direct chord changes and rhythms. "Nighthawkin'" started as a lyric excerpt from Larry Beckett, inspired by a night he walked into a convenience store and overheard a cab driver telling a clerk about a deranged passenger. Goldstein, Falsia, and Tim turned it into a boogie, complete with slippery lead guitars. (The reference to "a combat paratrooper daddy" could have been inserted by Tim, possibly referring to his father.) "Sweet Surrender," the album's most aching ballad, has a cascade of strings that undercuts Tim's macho cheating-song lyric ("I had to be a hunter again/This little man had to try to make love feel new again"). "Devil Eyes," fueled by a chugging organ that seems to be humping the melody, feels like an outtake from a War album.

As market-minded as the arrangements were, Tim couldn't resist inserting his own wrench into the mix. Inspired, some say, by his lusty passion for Judy, Tim's lyrics to *Greetings from L.A.* are unabashedly carnal, starting with the album's opening line: "I went down to the meat-rack tavern." The song "Move with Me" found Tim propositioning a married woman in a bar (*"Awww!"* cooed the backup singers in a hokey moment, after Tim lamented the woman's husband coming home and "breaking every bone in my body"). Things barely cool down for the rest of the record. The incendiary "Get on Top" is sexual craving incarnate ("we had those bed springs a-squeaking all night long"), from its galloping rhythm to Tim's orgasmic stretch of moans, gargles, and primal-squeal bellows. The dog-in-heat sizzle of the music brought out the panting voodoo child within Tim's voice; his delivery is laced with lasciviousness, as if he's not merely singing in tongues but *with* one. The most extreme example of Tim's newfound lyric sexuality is a Beckett poem called "Victims" that was incorporated into an entirely new track, "Make It Right," with a newly written chorus by Tim: "Beat me/Whip me/Spank me/Aw, come on, make it right again." With its grubby, tacky rock and roll and its blunt, naughty-boy eroticism, the spirited album, as overproduced as it sometimes was, has the feel of a one-night stand at a back-alley bar in the seediest sector of Hollywood.

Tim liked a postcard of smog-shrouded Los Angeles so much that Straight Records bought the rights to the card and reproduced it on the cover of the album. (Linda Gillen, Tim's costar on *Why?*, believes the idea also sprang from Tim watching her fill out Hollywood postcards during downtime on the set.) The back of the album simulated the back of a post-card, on which Tim wrote to Herb Cohen and Warner Brothers president Mo Ostin: "Dear Herb & Mo: Please send 50 copies—have advance sale guarantee for the Apollo Massage Parlor—sounds real great to rub downs." Inside the jacket, Tim posed holding a gas mask. "The message the sleeve was intended to impart was that even in this horrific atmosphere, there can still be a lot of musical activity going down," Tim told *Melody Maker*. "But of course, nobody picked up on that."

To launch the album, Warner Brothers initiated an ad campaign featuring a quote from Tim: " 'The comeback,' says Tim Buckley, 'is an important part of the creative process. In fact, you're nothing unless you've come back three or four times. I am ready for my first comeback.' "

To trumpet the release of *Greetings from L.A.* on August 15, 1972, Tim did his first series of interviews in some time. Rather than tip readers to his musical adventures of the two previous years, he acted as if they didn't exist. Repeatedly, he told writers he had taken time off to be with his family, only mentioning his stabs at acting and writing. The gigs with the *Starsailor* band went unmentioned, replaced by colorful tall tales about working as a taxi driver and Sly Stone's chauffeur. "I decided after *Starsailor* to cool it for about a year or so and not do anything," Tim told the British rock magazine *Sounds*. "And I decided the way to come back was to be funkier than everybody."

In other articles, Tim's ambivalence crept out in spite of his upbeat attitude. He told British journalist Steve Turner that *Greetings from L.A.* was him "doing the best that I could. . . . Ball and chain on the old brain!" On BBC Radio, he said, "I can't write the same thing over and over again. So that's either my problem or my virtue."

Certainly, many of Tim's friends viewed the album as more problematic than virtuous. Many had been excited by his avant-jazz period and were subsequently jolted by his shift to radio-friendly rock. "I thought, 'What the hell is this?' " Beckett recalls upon hearing the album in Portland. "Well, it was pretty obvious what the hell it was: 'Sell some records or get out.' The balmy days of the sixties, where they had so much money and could float arty projects and hope for the best, were gone. And harsher reality prevailed." Judy loved the album, and Underwood maintains Tim "did not 'knuckle under'; he did not 'sell out.' He explored and developed his *Starsailor* concepts from the end of the *Happy Sad* period to the beginning of this rock period. He had thoroughly investigated the *Starsailor* dimensions to the hilt, and he needed a change, new directions, new inspiration." However, most of Tim's friends and business associates take a dimmer view. As Glickman says, it was Tim's "you-gotta-make-a-living record."

To some degree, the album achieved that goal. *Rolling Stone,* by now the nation's preeminent rock magazine, didn't bother reviewing it, but the record received a dollop of complimentary notices, and Tim and Falsia put together a road band to promote it. Before the band went on tour, Cohen took Tim's new drummer, Southern-bred Russell "Buddy" Helm, into his office and, according to Helm, told the drummer, "Look—if you're out on the road and Tim starts doing that yodeling shit, you call me and tell me."

Cohen needn't have worried, at least not at first. Before the first show, at the Boarding House in San Francisco, Tim was nervous, and his anxiety didn't end when a few fans yelled "sell out!" and "cop out!" when the band began its rhythmic, amplified funk-rock. Tim told the audience about how artists change and mollified them with a few old songs. Singing in a voice as strong and elastic as ever, he won over most of the crowd by the end of the set.

The band hit the road for most of the fall and into the winter, playing colleges and clubs. Despite whatever internal reservations Tim had about the overhauled direction of his music, he committed himself to this phase of his career. Led by Falsia, the four-piece band was exceptionally tight and proficient—ideal for the new material Tim had written, less so when it came to older songs like "Buzzin' Fly," which lost some of their fragile beauty amid the funk-rock grind. Though not averse to engaging in vocal pyrotechnics, Tim kept them to a relative minimum, often waiting for the encore, when he would wander into uncontrolled vocalese to the accompaniment of Helm's drumming. The new Tim was also evident in his stage attire. Although Judy has no memory of it, both Helm and Tim's friend Artie Leichter recall Tim wearing white platform-style shoes onstage, which made him seem taller. More than once, he would lean back while wearing the new shoes and accidentally tip over into Helm's drum set.

Helm calls Tim's strategy of drinking on the road the most disciplined and focused the drummer had ever seen. "The band would be out on the road, imbibing whatever, but Tim never did," Helm recalls. "He said his pipes were his whole life, and if he had to sing the next night, he could not drink. His vocal cords would not be able to stand it. If he had two nights off, maybe he could have a beer. If he had three nights off, then he could have a few beers." Only after three days, Helm says, would Tim "cut loose."

Gradually, word of the revamped Tim began spreading throughout the music business, and it became easier for Cohen to book him. At a show at

Max's Kansas City in New York, which became one of Tim's regular venues, *New York Times* critic John Rockwell praised Tim for "a captivating
intensity and musicality" yet noted that "the end result seemed cold and
distant. . . . He made one wonder whether his diversity reflected adven-
turesomeness or a lack of artistic focus."

Although *Greetings from L.A.* garnered favorable reviews and made Tim a
viable concert attraction for the first time since his 1968–9 heyday, it fell
short of making the *Billboard* album chart and did not ignite the comeback everyone had expected. Thanks to its explicit lyrics, airplay was neg-
ligible for both the album and the single "Move with Me." To hear it on
the radio at all, in fact, listeners would have had to have been in Hartford,
Connecticut, or Sacramento, California, or Ithaca, New York—the homes
of three of the only stations to play it, and smaller markets at that. "In *his*
mind, it was a commercial record," gripes Herb Cohen. "It didn't have a
chance in hell at radio."

The results were evident in more than mere industry terms. For the
calendar year 1972, Tim's gross income was $35,218, of which $27,358 was
derived from personal appearances and live gigs. (He earned only $6,521
from recording income and $1,339 in royalties.) But after deducting band
salaries ($6,101), Cohen's commission ($1,290), hotels and meals
($4,643), and his agency's commission ($2,163), among other expenses,
Tim took home only $11,811. In addition, his business manager deducted
money for special education bills for Taylor, who was still coping with the
effects of the death of his biological father. By the spring of 1973, after
seven years of touring and making albums, Tim had only $1,941 in his and
Judy's checking account at the Crocker National Bank.

By the summer, Cohen and Frank Zappa's Bizarre and Straight Records
had been merged into one new, joint-owned label, DiscReet, which was still
distributed by Warner Brothers. Although Warners gave the new label an
infusion of funds, there was still pressure to score hits; DiscReet's only con-
sistent moneymaker was Zappa. Tim was one of the few acts on the label's
roster who could potentially attract a mass audience, so a decision was made
to continue the pop drift of his previous album. "We were surprised *Greetings from L.A.* didn't do better," says Falsia, "so they said, 'Well, let's get
somebody even *more* pop.'"

Indeed, few were more pop-inclined than Denny Randell, a New York–
born producer and songwriter best known for having cowritten Top 40

hits in the '60s for the Four Seasons ("Working My Way Back to You" and "Let's Hang On") and the Toys ("A Lover's Concerto"). He and Zappa had worked together on one of Zappa's Ruben & the Jets '50s-rock parodies, and Randell was subsequently recruited to re-revamp Tim. "Tim was a name and he was respected, but he hadn't busted through," Randell says. "Frank was aware of that. We wanted to come out with something pertinent to the market, not just an esoteric, FM-rock album for his base. We wanted to make a real, honest Tim album that could be *big*."

The sessions, held in New York and then Los Angeles between May and July 1973, were often uncomfortable affairs, as Randell reined in Tim's band and helped Tim pick out the songs he would sing. "The label wanted a hit, *I* wanted a hit, and we wanted to use those songs of Tim's that were to his benefit in terms of bringing the record home," says Randell. As a result, Tim covered other people's songs for the first time on record, including a tune by one of Cohen's new clients, Tom Waits (thereby once again keeping the publishing money in-house). "Tim was struggling with his muse," recalls drummer Helm. "His initial inspiration had dried up. He was in a creative crisis in terms of where his ideas were coming from."

They even cut one of Randell's own songs, "I Know I'd Recognize Your Face," about a Vietnam War veteran. Falsia and Helm insist Tim didn't want to sing it (Falsia calls it "a loser"), although Randell insists "there isn't a song on that album Tim didn't want to sing." Once again, Tim didn't argue; he showed up every day ready to work, never high nor drunk. "He was afraid of being just another commercial act," says Randell, "but he wasn't negative." Leichter recalls dropping by the studio and witnessing the sad sight of Tim, stripped of his twelve-string guitar and singing alone in an vocal booth—symbolically disconected from his music.

When the album, *Sefronia,* arrived on September 7, 1973, its accompanying press kit trumpeted that "Tim does not compromise his subtle lyrics and sophisticated music, offering instead a well-paced insight to a devoted craftsman." Those words notwithstanding, the project sounds as stiff as Tim's awkward half-smile on the album cover. *Sefronia* is, at best, wildly uneven. Tim's straightforward love song "Because of You" is set to a tepid disco-like beat, and the undeniably melodic "I Know I'd Recognize Your Face" features a middle-of-the-road arrangement more befitting Carly Simon. (In fact, Tim's duet partner on the song, Marcia Waldorf, sounded at times like Simon.) On the other end of the spectrum are

"Honey Man" and "Quicksand," which continue the grittier style of *Greetings from L.A.* and kick up a certain amount of dust. Tim turns into a fine junior Sinatra on Waits's "Martha"; perhaps the lyric about reuniting with a former wife ("Lucky you found someone who makes you feel secure/We were all so young and foolish, now we are mature") spoke to him. Nonetheless, the track's orchestration is mawkish. Throughout the album, the phalanx of female backup singers is far gooier than it was on *Greetings from L.A.,* and Tim is reduced to warbling an inane cocktail-hour novelty called "Peanut Man."

After attempting to record it during the *Greetings* session, Tim was, at least, finally able to cut a version of Fred Neil's "Dolphins," complete with former band member and mentor Lee Underwood on guitar. And Tim's old ambitiousness returned, albeit briefly, in the two-part title song. Inspired by Greek and African mythology, "Sefronia—After Asklepiades, After Kafka" and "Sefronia—The King's Chain" feature wide-screen Beckett lyrics about Africa, and its music aims for a relaxed Caribbean groove. But it feels unfinished and slight, Tim's voice strangely pinched-sounding (the result, Randell says, of a cold that couldn't halt the sessions because of a recording deadline). According to Beckett, the song's original title—"I Have a Cow in the Sky But I Can't Drink Her Milk"—was changed so it would fit onto the label on the vinyl LP.

In *Sefronia*'s press bio, Tim reminisced about his early years on the folk and college circuit: "'I don't think they'll ever happen again,' he recalls, the primary difference then being the comradeship of the musicians. 'The comradeship is just not there anymore, and it affects the music.'" It may have been the most downbeat promotional hype ever issued.

SIXTEEN

I love you too. Especially the ones who channel dead spirits from space and also ones who want to murder me. All my hugs and kisses. In Hell, baby . . . here's my kiss for Christmas. All my love . . .

—JEFF BUCKLEY, LETTER MAILED TO FANS, NOVEMBER 24, 1994

It was almost as if they were departing for summer camp. Shortly after noon on Wednesday, June 1, 1994, a fifteen-passenger Dodge van pulled up to Montana Studios at Eleventh Avenue and 56th Street, a strip of Manhattan's West Side lined with car-dealer showrooms and oil-splattered garages. Under hazy, 80-degree skies, Jeff and his three musicians showed up with their luggage one by one. Their inexperience was instantly, comically, apparent: Each had packed far too many clothes, and the bags, along with all their performing gear, had to be crammed into the back of the van by their two road managers, Reggie Griffith and the newly hired Gene Bowen (a friend of Lory's who had toured with everyone from Papa John Creach to symphony orchestras). A few hours later, the van heaved out of Manhattan with all six men aboard.

Before he left on tour, Jeff called a few friends, including Imago Records executive Kate Hyman. "I just called to say goodbye," he told her. "I won't be talking to you for a year." Hyman asked him what he meant, and Jeff replied, "I won't have time to call any of my friends for the next year." Hyman, who didn't detect a trace of sarcasm in his voice, hung up thinking what a sad conversation it had been.

The van first headed for Asbury Park, New Jersey, where, for two days, the musicians rehearsed in private at the Stone Pony, the legendary shore club whose most prestigious graduate was Bruce Springsteen. Then everyone piled back into the vehicle for the six-hour drive to Rochester, New York, to work up to the official start of the 1994–95 *Grace* international tour later that summer.

Much like the album it was designed to promote, little about the *Grace* tour adhered to conventional music-business wisdom. It wasn't merely that rhythm guitarist Michael Tighe had virtually no music-performance experience; there was also the matter of rehearsals. For days upon days at Montana in the spring, the band bore down, but reports filtering back to Jeff's managers were a bit disconcerting: The musicians were spending their time playing long, freewheeling jams instead of rehearsing the *Grace* songs. "Dave Lory wanted us to rehearse songs in the classic way that bands do, but what we wanted to do was basically play catch in the dark," recalls drummer Matt Johnson. "Improvising taught us a lot about each other and our impulses, which on a long-term level was more important. We were going to be out there playing those songs for months. One thing we wouldn't be doing was improvising." Realizing the band needed to work on its live chops—and wanting a slow, grass-roots build for Jeff—Columbia and management agreed to start the tour a full two months before the general public heard *Grace*.

The stage setup would itself deviate from tradition. Defying the rock and roll norm, Jeff would stand on stage right rather than in the middle. Johnson would be at center stage, with Tighe and bassist Mick Grondahl grouped together at stage left. Tighe says the idea emerged from rehearsals, when Jeff would stop singing and gather the band in a circle to improvise. Yet the arrangement subtly revealed an aspect of the nonconfrontational side of Jeff's personality. He was torn about being both a boss *and* a friend to his fellow musicians, so the stage setup allowed him to be both: one of the boys, yet a star set apart from them.

Even with tickets priced as low as $5, audiences during the initial, two-month phase of the tour were sparse. At clubs like Valentine's in Albany on June 9, as few as two dozen people filtered in. In a way, the sight was almost welcome: The band was a bright shade of green, with Grondahl and Tighe often staring at their feet or playing with their backs to the audiences, and the live versions of complex material like "Mojo Pin" and "Dream Brother" were still coalescing. During the first two weeks, Columbia executives were explicitly not invited to the gigs; no one wanted the label to see how unformed everything still was.

On June 17, the band briefly pulled into New York to play three nights at Fez, one of Jeff's favorite clubs. The shows (billed as the "Kiss Me Goodbye" concerts) were the clearest indication yet that the buzz around Jeff was growing louder by the day. The room was packed with Sony executives as well as celebrities from Winona Ryder to U2's the Edge and Soundgarden's Chris Cornell. Wearing his sparkly jacket and debuting his new band, Jeff seemed happy and pumped. Over the next two months, as they awaited the American and European release of *Grace*, the band schlepped across the United States and Canada in their van, doing forty-eight performances from Saratoga, New York, to Seattle, Washington, to Raleigh, North Carolina. On August 19, Jeff flew to London by himself, where he spent time with one of his musical heroes, the Cocteau Twins' Elizabeth Fraser. In addition to carrying on a brief relationship, the two wrote and recorded an impassioned paean to romantic connection, "All Flowers in Time," at a London studio. The band reconvened in Dublin in late August and began a month-long European tour.

This initial, low-key leg of the tour had results both musical (the band seemed to grow tighter with each gig) and personal. On July 9, Jeff and the band pulled into Iowa City, Iowa, to play Gabe's, a three-hundred-seat club to which only a few dozen tickets had been sold. The opening acts were Memphis indie rockers the Grifters and the Dambuilders, a Boston alternative band with an Elektra Records contract.

Backstage before the show, Jeff was introduced to the Dambuilders' violinist, Joan Wasser, and the two instantly connected. Raised in Norwalk, Connecticut, before relocating to Boston to attend college, the twenty-four-year-old Wasser wore her hair in thick dreadlocks that obscured her dark, exotic features. From her extroverted and intense demeanor (her face could switch from an intimidating stare to a warm grin within moments) to her mutual love of Led Zeppelin and classical music, Wasser projected an aura very different, and far more rock and roll, from that of Rebecca Moore. Wasser had never heard Jeff's music before, but when he performed "Lilac Wine" that night, "it pretty much blew my mind," she recalls. "He was *such* a ham. But it was so beautiful to see someone who had such a love of music and was unafraid to go the distance." Wasser and Jeff danced together during the Grifters' set, and Jeff, who was just beginning to plug into harder-edged indie rock, was smitten with both bands.

That night, Jeff and Wasser retreated to his hotel room at the Holiday Inn in Iowa City. Jeff started playing one of his current favorite CDs: a 1971 recording of James Brown at the Olympia in Paris that captured the soul godfather and his JB's at their sweaty, rhythmic best. As Wasser watched, Jeff lipsynched the entire album—playing instruments, mimicking Brown's patented splits, and playing air guitar and air saxophone. "I was completely blown away," Wasser recalls. "When you get attention from someone like that, you feel like a queen." Even after each band went its separate way, the two new friends began staying in touch.

Before he departed for his world tour, Jeff wanted to bid farewell to his old stomping ground Sin-é, but fearing an overflow of fans, the "farewell to Sin-é" concert was actually held at a larger Manhattan club, Wetlands, on August 16. Afterward, the dressing room was packed with industry shakers and movers congratulating Jeff. Moore, who was still very much in touch with Jeff, was seen sitting on a staircase, her head in her hands. She wasn't alone in feeling Jeff wasn't merely waving good-bye to his one-time creative base but to his previous life, and that he was about to enter a larger, scarier, and potentially more overwhelming world.

In the beginning, the road was a new and enthralling place, and Jeff instantly adapted to its trappings. Given his upbringing, the idea of waking up each morning in a different city felt familiar, even comforting, and encountering a new crowd of attentive fans each night meant adoration and attention without commitments. "He loved to perform and to live in the moment," says Wasser, "so touring was perfection."

As wary as Jeff was of the media, his daily schedule began being filled in with interviews, radio appearances, and "walk-throughs," industry lingo for visits to record stores in which the artist literally strolls through a shop, mingling and shaking hands with employees. "Retail parties," at which store owners and other local industryites were invited backstage to share a drink or conversation with Jeff, often took place before or after shows. As with everything else about his career, Jeff was gradually weaned into the process: "Before or after show—no pressure—hang out at Bourgeois Pig—college radio, college press, and retail," read a notation in the official tour book when the band pulled into Los Angeles in July. To start laying the groundwork for publicity in foreign countries, Sony began flying in journalists from England,

France, Italy, and Japan for interviews along the American tour route.

Well aware that promotion and publicity were part of the job, Jeff went along with the schedule. He tolerated the questions about the media hoopla and Tim. (Both Bowen and Howard Wuelfing, Jeff's Columbia publicist, would warn interviewers beforehand not to ask Jeff about his father, but it didn't always work.) After a store walk-through, Jeff would at least be able to climb back aboard the van with a batch of free CDs given to him by record stores; he never seemed to tire of hearing fresh music.

One begrudging step at a time, he also began to confront—and adjust to—the house rules and regulations of the business. The lessons did not always come easily or smoothly. He had received his first humbling experience a year earlier, in November 1993, when Bob Dylan was appearing at the Supper Club in New York. Knowing Jeff was an admirer, Columbia's Steve Berkowitz took his rising star to the show and backstage afterward. Upon being introduced to Jeff, Dylan looked at the young Buckley and wheezed, in his usual mumbled bray, that Jeff looked like Tim and that Jeff was handsome enough to be in the movies. Not knowing what to make of the remarks, Jeff was silent.

Performing at Sin-é a few days later, Jeff went into one of his standard comic impersonations, this time of Dylan and the incident. What Jeff didn't know was that members of Dylan's entourage were in the audience, inspecting Columbia's hot new property. Although Jeff had intended the remarks good-naturedly, they were interpreted as insults, and Dylan's posse complained to Columbia executives the next day. When word got back to Jeff, he was so devastated he called Rebecca Moore in tears: *How could they have taken his remarks as a dis? He loved Dylan!* Seeking to repair the situation, Jeff wrote an apologetic letter to Dylan. Whether Dylan ever saw it or not (Ienner feels he did), the lesson was bracingly clear: The days when Jeff could goof off at Sin-é, saying and singing whatever he chose to his diehard fans and friends, were drawing to a close. There were now, Berkowitz says of that time, "things at stake."

On the road, a much harder lesson was around the bend. Just before the *Grace* tour began, during the same sessions that yielded "So Real," Jeff and the band had recorded Big Star's "Kanga Roo." In the studio, recording engineer Clif Norrell knew Jeff was about to push an envelope or two when Jeff asked how much time could be fit onto one reel of tape. Norrell, sensing Jeff was about to record "a *really* long song," told him fifteen minutes. "Signal me when we get to twelve," Jeff said, and the band began playing the swooning song, which eventually worked its way into a brutal instrumental vamp, Jeff and Tighe hammering the guitar chords repetitively while Johnson drove the music with incessant, hypnotic drum beats. They finished at fourteen minutes and five seconds.

The band's love of "Kanga Roo" didn't end that day. During the tour, it was frequently employed as an encore, and each time it seemed to expand, blob-like, in length. To the band, the tribal performance was both catharsis and collective experience, the essence of musical transcendence. "It was the release after the show," says Tighe. "We had supported him the whole show, and now it was a giveback."

Not everyone shared the band's enthusiasm. On Thursday, September 1, Jeff played his first London show with the band at the Garage, a midsized club in north London. The performance ended with an even longer than usual "Kanga Roo," and the next day, executives at Columbia's New York headquarters received an E-mail from a Sony UK department head who had attended that show. The executive noted that Jeff clearly fit in with the company's long line of "Crown Jewels, i.e., so special and fundamental to the reputation and culture of the company that they would never be let go, no matter what the cost. . . . I saw Jeff last night and am convinced he has the talent to join that group." But he added a proviso: "My only reservation was the 25-minute, one-chord encore number which had the audience talking among [sic] themselves and looking at their watches. . . . I felt he was not doing justice to himself as an entertainer."

The fallout was immediate. At Columbia's next weekly staff meeting, Ienner is said to have barked, "What the *fuck* is Jeff Buckley doing?" (Ienner doesn't recall the particular incident, although others do.) Ienner and his subordinates had been hearing about the "Kanga Roo" jam, but the memo was their (and management's) first tangible evidence that it was potentially damaging to record sales and public relations.

A week later, on Thursday, September 8, the band was sprawled out in Jeff's room at the Norse-lodge-style Rica Traingel Hotel in Oslo, watching *1001 Arabian Nights,* when the phone rang. From Jeff's tense body language and the tone of his voice, everyone knew the conversation was not agreeable. The Sony vice president calling from New York told Jeff there was a problem: "Kanga Roo" was too long, it was alienating fans and hurting his career, and Jeff had to begin to understand the consequences of his actions. Although there was no explicit order to stop playing the song, it was strongly suggested he at least curtail its length. "This was a foreign language to Jeff," Berkowitz says. " 'Really? My band was badass,' he would say. And if you say maybe they didn't get it, he'd say, 'Get *what?*' So when he thought he was getting off, they thought he was going in the wrong direction."

Tighe says Jeff was "the most visibly upset about anything I can remember concerning the record company. It felt violating to him." The band joked it off, but Jeff was quiet. Afterward, the four men visited an art gallery and saw Edvard Munch's painting "The Scream," the well-known and much-reproduced portrait of a man clutching his head in open-mouthed agony. "We could really relate to it," Grondahl says. "They didn't want us to do that as an encore anymore because it cut into their cocktail time. They thought it was very alienating and negative, and not money-making." On a ferry to Copenhagen the next day, Jeff developed a flu and respiratory problems, and a scheduled Berlin show was cancelled.

On September 13, a group of Sony executives flew to see the band play the Knust club in Hamburg. On stage that night, Jeff announced he was dedicating the next number to someone in the club who "didn't have the time" to stay for "Kanga Roo." With that, the band launched into a revamped version of "Eternal Life." Instead of the lumbering, grunge-inflected version on *Grace*, the new take was a musical jackhammer, more Metallica than Pearl Jam. Although the rearranged song was a vivid demonstration of the rapid-fire evolution of Jeff's music, the Sony employees in attendance instantly knew what had inspired it, and that Jeff was channeling his anger at them into music. After the song was over, Jeff glared at the table where the executives were seated.

Despite the warning, the band would continue to end most of their concerts with "Kanga Roo" (albeit at varying lengths) over the next year and a half.

The employees of St. Ann's could barely believe their eyes when, early in the afternoon of Saturday, October 24, an imposing, dark-blue Eagle tour bus pulled up in front of the church. Those who had witnessed Jeff's debut at the same space three and a half years earlier, during the Tim tribute concert, were taken aback. Even more surprised was Susan Feldman of St. Ann's, a friend of Jeff's who was initially told she couldn't step aboard the bus without a laminated pass.

When Feldman finally entered, she found Jeff sitting alone in the front lounge, flanked by two couches, a table, a stereo system, and a television.

Beyond him was a galley kitchen with refrigerator and microwave, a bathroom, an aisle with two levels of bunk beds, and a back-of-the-bus lounge with two closets and another television and stereo. To Feldman, Jeff seemed isolated but happy, gearing up to make his music and spend time with his band. "I love my job," he told her.

That Jeff was on a luxury tour bus at all at this point in his career was an indication of the high regard in which Columbia held him. Baby touring acts on his level only graduated from vans to this style of bus after many months on the road or after huge financial success. As of October, neither was the case with Jeff, with *Grace* out only two months and not yet having made the *Billboard* album chart. Yet it was clear that Columbia wanted to send a message to the music community that Jeff was an important artist who needed to be taken care of, a true heritage artist on the rise. For this fall tour—the first full band jaunt in the United States since the release of *Grace* in August—Jeff was even able to select his own opening act: his friend and onetime partner Brenda Kahn, herself a Columbia recording artist.

As per the laws of the music business, none of this came cheap. The cost of the tour bus and its driver (and the band's combined $1,500-a-week salary) was added into Jeff's recoupable, as was an infusion of record company cash called "tour support." Tour support was the amount of money it took an act to break even on the road: the difference between the amount the act earned at venues and the amount they would have to shell out for expenses. As the concert schedule progressed, the tour-support cash would eventually dwindle, but for Jeff, that day was still far in the distance.

Although Jeff began tracking album sales and pondering the amount of money in his recoupable, the progress of his music remained his top priority and biggest charge. As he had with the band's stage setup, he again went against orthodox concert rules by often opening the shows with a long, wordless mantra, a way of warming up and working his way into the song he had learned from studying Nusrat Fateh Ali Khan. Jeff would perform this alone, accompanied only by his guitar, and the vocal tour de force, with its swooping ululations, would never fail to grab the attention of nearly everyone in attendance.

Generally, that vocal melisma led into "Mojo Pin," which opened many of the early shows, and then they were off. Much like the album they were promoting, the concerts developed into intense, eclectic, and potent affairs. With Johnson, Grondahl, and Tighe clustered off to one side, keeping watchful eyes on their ever-unpredictable leader, the shows moved from the

warmth and romanticism of "Lilac Wine" through a ceiling-rattling rendition of the MC5's 1969 piledriver "Kick Out the Jams." Jeff's lead guitar playing, often so strenuous-looking it appeared as if he were lifting weights while
strumming, ignited the music, and songs like "Dream Brother" and "Grace"
became engulfed in waves of electricity, a beautiful noise. "A lot of the songs
had that feeling of casting a spell," Tighe says, "where you felt him opening
a very beautiful world that people could escape into for that time and that
song." Jeff's mimicry-laden stage patter revealed his standup-comic side, but
during the music, he generally remained stock-still; only during "Kanga
Roo" would he bounce in place, lost in its hypnotic pull.

Soundgarden singer Chris Cornell had met Jeff in London in March
1994, when Jeff came backstage to meet him at one of the band's shows.
Cornell had already been given *Live at Sin-é* by an industry friend but
hadn't yet played it, and after meeting the shy kid, he finally popped it into
his CD player and was stunned by Jeff's range and voice. The two men
became friendly, and during the *Grace* tour, Cornell caught one of the
concerts in his native Seattle. "Jeff would have a way of almost overdoing
the quiet falsetto to the point where it would almost be irritating and get to
the point of uncomfortability," Cornell recalls of the performance. "That
was the punk-rock stage of 'this is dangerous.' There were these twelve- to
twenty-year-olds in flannel shirts standing there, dead silent. These were
young guys who were into really aggressive music and they didn't know
what to make of him. But after a while, they started looking at each other
like, 'Yeah, I kinda like this.' He definitely had a maverick nature to him,
but he wanted to push and entertain himself. That's what he enjoyed."

Although the *Grace* material took up almost the entire set, they did
manage to squeeze in at least one unrecorded song: "What Will You Say,"
written by Jeff, Chris Dowd, and Carla Azar during Jeff's period in Los
Angeles in 1990. A brooding, midtempo number with Indian-music
inflections, it became a regular part of Jeff's set. "It's been a long time and
I was just a child then/What will you say when you see my face?" went its
opening verse. For years afterward, many assumed Jeff had written those
words about Tim. In fact, the song's lyrics, written (and originally sung)
by Dowd, detailed Dowd's feelings about the father who had abandoned
him.

At this early stage, even the monotony of rock and roll touring felt fresh
and invigorating. During long drives between cities, Jeff and the band
mocked current hits (Counting Crows's "Round Here" was a frequent

target), watched oddball movies (documentaries on the Manson family and the doomed Donner expedition) or *Beavis and Butt-head* (Jeff did perfect imitations of both), and drank beer. Jeff's dirty laundry piled up in a spare bunk until he was forced to wash it. In the back of the bus, he hung up a photo of Kurt Cobain, whose pre-suicide balancing act of integrity and commercial success was a path Jeff himself sought to take.

Unlike Cobain, though, Jeff seemed to attract more women than men to his shows. The girls who clustered upfront, screaming during the inevitable moment when Jeff would pull off his overshirt and reveal his lithe, T-shirted frame, revealed he was becoming a cult sex symbol. In Austin in November, female fans threw underwear at him onstage, to which Jeff bemusedly responded, "You don't even *know* me." His charisma was proving to be stronger than perhaps he himself had ever imagined. "There was something insanely vulnerable about him, which made him really attractive to people," says tour mate Brenda Kahn. "That worked against him at Columbia, because people were always wanting something from him and he was vulnerable to it. He didn't have an easy way to say no." As much as he responded to all the attention, it wasn't long before Jeff began to grow suspicious of it. Did all of these women or company employees like him for his music and talent, or for his looks and power? Were they listening to the *music,* or just responding to his cheekbones? As the months dragged on, it was growing harder to tell, and his worldview became a split screen, purity on one side and abject evil and temptation on the other.

The business, which in his mind increasingly fell into the latter camp, was never far away. On November 8, the tour bus pulled into Chicago for a show at the Green Mill. As was becoming standard, the day was packed with promotional chores: a television taping at 11 A.M., an interview at 2 P.M., a retail party backstage at the club at 6:30 P.M. But as Jeff was preparing to go onstage, he was called to a phone; it was, again, a Sony vice president. In an interview, Jeff had insulted MTV, and the label was not happy; despite Jeff's skepticism toward what he viewed as the superficial world of music videos, MTV was still considered an important tool. After the call, Jeff retreated with Kahn to his bus, a bottle of José Cuervo tequila in hand. As Kahn watched, he downed more than half the bottle. "I said, 'You know, you're getting drunk,'" Kahn recalls. "And he said, 'No, I'm not.'"

But he was, and by the time he hit the stage close to midnight, he was plastered. As a puzzled audience watched, songs and monologues started and stopped as Jeff berated himself as, among other things, "a loser." After one false start, the band again tried to play "Grace" and finally succeeded, and the show slowly veered back on track, albeit not completely. It was, as *Chicago Tribune* critic Greg Kot wrote, "pathetic one minute, galvanizing the next. . . . What started out as seemingly good-natured, self-deprecating humor became more twisted and spiteful as the night wore on."

"He was like a sad drunk," recalls Tighe. "I felt sorry for him. It's not a good place to be. But it was also kind of funny." The next night, for his second Green Mill show, Jeff made up for the debacle with a ferocious performance. But back in New York, Sony executives were confronted with Kot's article and its eye-opening headline: "Buckley's Show Sobering for All but Its Vocalist."

As the show demonstrated for all to see, whether they wanted to or not, the almost virginal, untainted Jeff of a few years before was gradually being altered by the rules of the road. He began smoking cigarettes and developed a love of vodka and tequila, and pot was never far away. "It's very alluring for a teenager to have a cigarette, and it's like he was having that experience for the first time," Tighe says. "When he was young and with his mom, he felt he was very much a guiding force in that relationship. He said, 'I never got the chance to do something like that.' He said it felt good to be able to rebel in a certain way." Jeff also began dying his hair black and parting it in the middle; combined with his flannel shirts, it led one concert reviewer to call him "disheveled."

There was, always, the issue of Tim and his fans. A rider in the tour contract stated that any venue that used phrasing like "Son of Tim Buckley" in its ads could be held accountable on grounds of breach of contract; legally, Jeff could refuse to perform. Almost every club complied, but that didn't stop the curiosity seekers and old fans. It had started early on, with the Tim devotees who would show up and yell out for his late father's songs. After a show in Philadelphia, a middle-aged woman approached Jeff and said his father was residing inside her, and that if the two of them had sex, he would finally be able to commune with Tim. "The only man I ever wanted to be with was your father—except for my husband, of course," she said, as her husband stood by, grinning. Jeff stared at her silently before walking away; out of sight, he burst out laughing.

Other incidents were nowhere as amusing. Later in the tour, at a club in Denver, Colorado, a phalanx of Tim fans gathered at the front of the stage and yelled out Tim song titles throughout the show. Finally, exasperated and angered, Jeff succumbed. "You know what—I'll *do* it," he spat out. As he began strumming the chords to "Once I Was," he continued addressing the crowd: "I'm about to sacrifice myself right now. You all love that kind of stuff, I know. Check this out—to show all the hippies how good I can do this song. So they can all go and masturbate naked to their copy of *Hello Goodbye* [*sic*]. And leave the rest of us normal people *alone*!"

He paused, perhaps realizing the harshness of his words. "I just want you to know one thing. I don't hate my father. Sometimes yes." There were a few giggles from the crowd. "But check this out—my father is sort of like that T-shirt: 'I went through the '60s and all I got was this stinking T-shirt.' I was somebody's son, and I was somebody's stinkin' T-shirt. But let me show you how cool this song is, okay? It's the only time you'll see it, I swear to *fucking* God, all right?" Although he forgot some of the words, he sang the song—and gently, like a lullaby.

After it was over, he looked in the direction of the Tim acolytes: "Are you satisfied now? Are you really? Now shut the *fuck* up for the rest of the night. Love and kisses, from the living one, Jeff Buckley." After the show, a few of the Tim diehards followed Jeff out to the tour bus, wanting to talk to him about his father or perhaps commune with Tim through the son; Jeff was patient but curt. Once they had dispersed, he was found sitting alone on a curb by the bus, his head in his hands. The opening act on that leg of the tour was Soul Coughing, a skewed funk-alternative band fronted by Jeff's New York pal M. Doughty. Doughty watched as someone tried to lead Jeff back onto the tour bus, but instead, Doughty recalls, Jeff "got up and started running up and down the parking lot. He was buggin' out."

Whether it was the Tim fans, his intensive schedule, or both, something in Jeff was changing, and Sony executives soon experienced it firsthand. Every December, the company held an annual meeting in New York—complete with performances by the label's top acts—for employees who worked at Sony branch offices around the country. When confronted with his incessant road schedule, Jeff was developing a habit of being less than cordial, even brusque, with these local workers. In order to smooth things over with those employees who were pitching him to regional radio and record stores, it was decided that Jeff and the band would fly up to New York from Orlando, Florida, where they were performing, to play at the national branch managers conference on Wednesday, December 7.

As they sipped drinks and talked among themselves at Sony Studios, the company employees saw a somewhat startling sight. The fresh-faced, short-haired kid of the *Live at Sin-é* solo tour had been replaced by an unshaven, weary-looking young man in an oversized, untucked flannel shirt, his hair long and uncombed. Jeff wasn't thrilled with the situation from the onset ("You're a wedding band," Tighe says of such industry functions). But in the rush to get to New York, the band left behind its sound system and instruments and was presented with temporary amplifiers and guitars. It proved a disastrous move. "The sound onstage was really awful," Tighe recalls. "It sounded very tinny and thin. If you're going to come all this way and do it, you want it to sound good. And when it didn't sound good, it made him very angry."

It was an understatement. After tense performances of "Last Goodbye" and "So Real," in which he looked visibly unhappy, Jeff kicked his foot through an amplifier and stalked off. It was, says Tighe, "a very frustrating moment that came out in a very frustrated expression." Everyone, including Jeff's managers and label representatives, silently piled into an elevator and retreated to a backstage room. "It was a room," says one company employee, "you didn't want to walk into too quickly." It was unlikely that the branch managers' opinion of Jeff was dramatically improved.

By the beginning of 1995, Jeff had received an inordinate amount of positive press, for both his live shows and for *Grace*. *Rolling Stone* praised him for "pulling off some things no other young singer-songwriter in his right mind would even try"; *Spin* commented, "If Buckley continues to evolve in the direction that *Grace* indicates, only good things can result." Reviewing a show at New York's Supper Club in October, the *New York Times*'s Jon Pareles noted, "With his voice, a world of tumult and obsession becomes almost seductive." His fan base in America was still growing, but in the United Kingdom and France, he was instant royalty, the romantic male chanteuse sprung to full, emotional life. At Passage du Nord Ouest in Paris in late September, female fans literally passed out from the heat inside the club and their own bodies. An overseas tour, which would return him to England, Scotland, France, Italy, Holland, and Germany and mark his first visit to Japan, would start in January.

Still, all the media enthusiasm had not yet translated into sales. In America, *Grace* was selling only one or two thousand copies a week and, by the start of 1995, had still not made the *Billboard* charts. Although Columbia continued its cautious approach to marketing Jeff, the time had finally arrived for an official pop radio single and a video. There had been a clip for "Grace," based around lipsynched performance footage filmed for a video press kit, but since "Grace" had not been a single, the video was rarely shown. (Seeing it broadcast in the lobby of a Sony movie theater in Manhattan, Jeff was horrified but turned it into a joke: For the amusement of a friend, he ran up to the candy counter and mock-yelled, "My face should be on these *napkins*! My face should be on these *hot dogs*!") Everyone knew there would eventually be a genuine video—it was an unavoidable part of the business—and everyone equally realized the song with the most crossover potential was not "Eternal Life" but the much more alluring and accessible "Last Goodbye."

Jeff was deeply ambivalent: He didn't want to be known as an MTV poster boy, but he was nevertheless a born performer intrigued by the creative possibilities of videos. He agreed to make one for "Last Goodbye," as long as he was able to hire two friends, photographer Merri Cyr and director John Jesurin, as collaborators. Once again, Columbia bent to his wishes, and the plans proceeded.

As usual, they proceeded only after a series of meetings—in this case, between Jeff, Jesurin, and Columbia executives, at which Jeff announced he didn't want to appear in a conventional video complete with a formulaic storyline. Instead, as Jesurin scribbled notes beside him, Jeff would list random imagery, like flowers, that he wanted to see in the clip. Finally, he and Jesurin settled on what the director calls "an anti-video": The band would lipsynch the song as a stream of esoteric video images (most supplied by Cyr) would be projected on screens behind them. Since the band would be on the road in Europe, their performance footage would be filmed in a French warehouse on January 23 and 24, a week into the tour.

Everything was in place, but once again, as in the selection of the *Grace* album cover, the dichotomy within Jeff—to be famous, or not to be—played itself out during the creation of the clip. "Videos and what they represent are advertising," says Cyr, "and what they're advertising is product, and he didn't want to be 'the product.' " On the day of the shoot, Jeff showed up on the set with unwashed hair, acted hostile toward at least one nervous Sony executive, announced he was going to sing the song live rather than lipsynch, and appeared more interested in drinking wine than making a video. To Jesurin, even the band seemed spaced out and uptight. "There was a bit of frustration that we had to do it at that time, while we were touring," Tighe says. "We came into a scenario that was already set up, and it seemed like it wasn't going to have the fire or impact we had hoped for." As morning stretched into late evening, Jeff's dissatisfaction with his surroundings hardly dissipated, especially when he was informed that he *had* to lipsynch and *had* to finish filming that day. With his bedraggled mop of hair and unshaven countenance, Jeff looked as if he had just woken up, and his friends realized that the surly, tense air he projected—in both his lipsynching and his tense stares—was far from acting.

Not that it was easy to tell in the beginning: In the video's first edit, Jeff kept shots of himself to a minimum, which, not surprisingly, displeased Columbia. During the weeks ahead, roughly two dozen different edited versions of "Last Goodbye" were assembled, with Jeff or Columbia nitpicking over each one. Costs began to mount, especially when edits were transmitted to Jeff in Europe at a cost of $10,000 each. At the last possible minute, the video was handed over to MTV, by which time the price tag had mushroomed to $275,000, more than double the amount usually spent on a video for an artist at Jeff's level. Even worse, the clip was different but somewhat muddled, particularly Cyr's video images, which amounted to a blur behind the musicians. "It ended up being a little bit more machine gun and formulaic," says Tighe of the final version. "It's not what we really wanted."

Afterward, Jeff told at least one Columbia executive he "loved" the video. Other friends thought he was disappointed but basically satisfied; Cyr feels he was "really upset." Such widely disparate impressions were a sign of the increasing compartmentalization of Jeff's life. He had by now developed many different sets of friends, few of whom knew each other, and although not done maliciously, he would often leave each group with a different impression of himself and his state of mind, as if he were accommodating their idea of who he should be. It wasn't uncommon to find him huddling one-on-one with a friend, making that man or woman feel as if he were revealing his utmost secrets to him or her alone—before doing exactly the same thing with someone else at a later time.

With an actual music video and single to work, Columbia went all out to break "Last Goodbye." To some degree, the strategy worked. "Last Goodbye" made it onto MTV, and with it, sales of *Grace* vaulted to seven thousand copies during the week of May 28, 1995. After nine months, the album finally entered the *Billboard* album chart, at number 174. Grunge had peaked the year before, with the death of Cobain, and the pop audience now seemed to want music that was less aggressive and easier to swallow, whether it was the frat-folk of Hootie and the Blowfish or the Birkenstock singer-songwriter pop of Sheryl Crow. Although Jeff was much more diverse than either of those acts, "Last Goodbye" fit, albeit unwillingly, into that category of nonthreatening roots pop.

The combination of the video, album sales, and a co-headlining two-week spring tour with Juliana Hatfield made the klieg lights of celebrity fame rotate toward him. In May, *People* magazine included him in its annual list of the "50 Most Beautiful People in the World." "He was mortified," says friend Nathan Larson, singer and guitarist with Shudder to Think. "We would leave him phone messages like, 'I'm looking for one of the fifty most beautiful people in the world. I wanna ask him how his ass is.' He took it well, but there was a point where you had to stop." When a friend of the Guibert family asked him to sign the article backstage at a California show, Jeff scribbled epithets all over his photo with a black marker. The article embodied two of his worst fears: having no control over his career (the magazine had used a file photo and didn't interview him for the accompanying text, which called him "dishy") and being regarded more for his physical traits than for his music.

"He acted really mad, but he was also laughing about it," says Joan Wasser, who brought Jeff a copy of the magazine. He told her he had never been considered a "hot guy" in high school. "Well, *look*," Wasser replied. "You're getting *everybody* back." To that, Jeff giggled. "He was disgusted," she says, "but he also knew how flattering and funny it was."

Such first-rung fame reared its head in other ways. At the last show of the Hatfield-Buckley tour, at Roseland in New York on June 2, Jeff took the stage in his glittery jacket. When he pulled it off, screams like those once accorded the Beatles filled the hall, like a miniature *Buckleymania*. Watching in the audience were Paul and Linda McCartney; Linda McCartney was particularly struck by the similarities between Jeff and Tim. Ron Moorhead visited his stepson in New York that spring, and Jeff told him it had been mutually decided by him and his managers to turn down offers to appear on *Saturday Night Live* and with Jeff's old favorite, David Letterman. "That's not my crowd," Jeff told him. Moorhead didn't understand, but didn't question his stepson.

On June 4, after the Hatfield tour ended, Jeff and the band were again back in New York, on a break before returning to Europe on June 19 for another round of European concerts. At Sony Studios, they taped a segment for Columbia's nationally syndicated radio show. (Beforehand, Jeff requested Persian rugs for atmosphere, which the label quickly purchased.) Afterward, the band recorded its new, revamped "road version" of "Eternal Life." But while in the studio, Jeff received a call, and from none other than Courtney Love. The Hole leader had been trading messages with him for some time, and this time she had an offer: She had an extra ticket to see a new Broadway production of *Hamlet,* and would Jeff want to join her?

At this point in her career, a little over a year after the suicide of her husband Kurt Cobain, Love was in a curious place. Rumors of her erratic behavior and offstage habits were even more prevalent than before Cobain's death, and she was reported to be linked with a different actor or musician every week. Despite her fame and infamy, Jeff was intrigued; his natural curiosity took over.

The actual experience turned out to be far less appealing than he had imagined. According to friends and published reports, Jeff met Love at her midtown hotel, and Love suggested they walk to the nearby Broadway theater. On the way, Love decided to ask someone for either directions or the time—someone who, it turned out, happened to be a paparazzi photographer. By the time Love and Jeff left the theater, a swarm of photographers was lying in wait outside. Soon enough, their nonexistent "affair" was an item in numerous newspaper and magazine gossip columns.

The incident left a bitter, unpleasant taste in Jeff's mouth. For days and weeks afterward, he recounted the events angrily to friends, feeling as if he had been used. "He was a little bit shocked and grossed out by her," Tighe says. "It was sort of a repugnant experience. He had a lot of conflict about wanting to be famous or not. It was very symbolic of his struggle with that aspect of his psyche." He even called *Rolling Stone* writer Jason Cohen, then in the midst of writing a cover story for the magazine on Hole, and complained, "I went out for one night, and I'm thrust into this weird, rock-star charade heavy thing."

Ironically, Jeff had a steady partner at this time: the Dambuilders' Joan Wasser, whose meeting with Jeff a year earlier had blossomed into an affair. During their bands' respective downtimes, Jeff would often take a bus or train to Boston and camp out for days in Wasser's South End loft, the two of them reveling in each other's company and playing duets on guitar and violin. "He'd show up with *nothing,* just the clothes he had on," Wasser says. "It was really lovely and exciting."

The only problem was that Jeff would rarely tell anyone when, or where, he was going. (He would also rarely warn Stein and Lory when he made guest appearances on other musicians' records, resulting in a flurry of last-minute legal wrangling.) Back in New York, frantic phone calls between managers and coworkers ensued: *Where's Jeff? Has anyone heard from him? What do you mean, he's missing?*

Eventually, Jeff would call in and say, *Yes, I'm here in Boston,* or *I just went out for a drive.* Everyone would breathe a sigh of relief; they'd found him.

From the start, the plan had been to hit the road for at least a year, and in June 1995, as the band departed for Edinburgh, Scotland, to begin their third jaunt through Europe, it had indeed been twelve months since the launch of the *Grace* road tour. The size of the crowds to whom Jeff was playing indicated his ascending stature abroad. He headlined two nights at the Olympia in Paris (where he gave what many consider one of the best performances of his career) and participated in multi-act festivals in Belgium (before 70,000) and Denmark (the Roskilde Festival, which drew 80,000). At the invitation of Elvis Costello, who was coordinating that year's Meltdown Festival, Jeff flew from Belgium to London on July 1, and he stunned the Meltdown crowd with a gorgeous "Corpus Christi Carol," among other songs. That he made converts of both Generation Xers and older musicians like Costello revealed Jeff's potentially wide fan base, but he was also beginning to look and sound bedraggled: His rendition of "Hallelujah" at the Roskilde Festival was deeper and throatier than it had been several years before.

Back in his home country, Columbia was devising ways in which to take *Grace* to the next level once "Last Goodbye" ran its course, peaking at number 19 on *Billboard*'s Modern Rock chart in May. To Jeff, the next single was obvious: the roaring "road version" of "Eternal Life" that had been rearranged in the wake of the "Kanga Roo" squabble. Columbia, and president Don Ienner, resisted, arguing it would be confusing to fans to promote a single that wasn't on the album. Although the label eventually did release the new "Eternal Life"—in Australia only—Jeff felt insulted by the decision and began badmouthing Ienner to friends. Afterward, he and the label struck a deal. They would be granted *their* wish (to release "Hallelujah" as a single at Christmas) if he was granted his: to make a single and video of "So Real," one of his favorite songs on the album. Columbia agreed.

After his troubled experience with the "Last Goodbye" clip, Jeff decided to be more actively involved this time, starting by collaborating with director Sophie Muller on the storyboards. Intentionally surreal, the video—shot in

August in Brooklyn, New York, and at C&C Castle Hamburgers in Kearny, New Jersey—intermingled footage of Jeff on a bicycle and in a gorilla suit with scenes of the band acting as patrons and cooks in a diner. "It was the vision he wanted," says Wasser. "That combination of beauty and freedom with absurdity—that's Jeff right there." He enjoyed the experience so much that at shoot's end, he only reluctantly took off the gorilla suit. Then it was back to the road: Three weeks later, the band embarked on its first trip to Australia, playing multiple nights in Sydney and Melbourne to crowds as ravenous as in Europe. Even down under, though, the standard queries from the press resumed: *When are you going to start making your next album? How many new songs have you written? How well did you know your father?* He didn't want to answer any of those questions anymore.

Whether because of its idiosyncratic video or the fact that it wasn't the simplest ditty, "So Real" was not the smash Jeff thought it would be. Amongst themselves, the band griped that Columbia did an inadequate job promoting it, and Jeff was bitterly disappointed. He'd visited the radio stations and record stores, he'd toured for over a year, he'd shilled for *Grace*, he'd begrudgingly hosted MTV's alternative rock show *120 Minutes*, he'd even gone to Ienner's farm for a corporate party: What more did they want from him? (Columbia, for their part, felt they had done plenty, down to dispatching a massage therapist to his apartment in April when he threw out his back.) When the Australian leg of the tour ended on September 6, Jeff informed Lory and Stein he had had enough. After 207 concerts and hundreds of interviews, television spots, and in-store appearances, he was exhausted. A fall *Grace* tour of the United States was dropped.

With that, the promotion for the album ground to a halt, and plans to release "Hallelujah" as a single fizzled away. By that point, *Grace* had sold 180,000 copies in the United States, and over 500,000 worldwide (primarily in the United Kingdom, France, and Australia, his three biggest markets outside America). At home, *Grace* spent seven weeks on the *Billboard* chart, peaking at number 149. Although one high-ranking Columbia executive diplomatically recalls "feeling a little bit of pressure" to push *Grace* past the 200,000 mark in the United States, that final tally was respectable; in fact, many at Columbia were thrilled that such a hard-to-pigeonhole album had reached the low six figures. Yet while the overall, integrity-directed strategy had worked, no one realized how resistant media outlets would be: Jeff was considered too soft for alternative radio, his videos too arty for MTV.

The original marketing plan had called for him to release a new album in the fall of 1995. As of September, that was clearly both optimistic and impossible. Still, there were plans to make, songs to write, artistic directions to hammer out; a follow-up was beckoning. As he attempted to decompress and return to something resembling a stable home life in New York, Jeff had barely begun writing new material. But he knew where he wanted to take his music, and he knew exactly which producer would help him take it there.

SEVENTEEN

Look at the Fool. *Oh, God, I just can't get through it. And I am
overcome with the desire to grab him and kiss him and plead for him to
please let me be in your band for awhile, so we can stop this white-funk
wierdness* [sic], *we don't need Herb Cohen anymore,* Starsailor *wasn't
a failure. It was an untouchable beauty and I think you must stop
thinking of dying and start dancing with that luscious beauty you
created. Because she is white hot sex waiting to happen and your studio
cats from L.A. ain't gonna get you there. I'll help you even if I fail. But
then . . . I love him anyway. Let's boogie.*

—JEFF BUCKLEY, JOURNAL ENTRY, AUGUST 9, 1995

Once *Sefronia* was finished, producer Denny Randell played it for
Frank Zappa, co-owner of Tim's label, DiscReet. According to Randell,
Zappa "fell in love with the album," and, over breakfast with the producer,
said he felt it would bust his label wide open in the marketplace. Although
Tim seemed less than exuberant about the work, he was a trouper, taking
to the road for scattered dates with his band. On January 29, 1974, he even
managed to score an appearance on the late-night concert television series
Midnight Special, part of a bill that included the Steve Miller Band and
the rising art-rock band Genesis.

But as with its predecessor, an album expressly designed to salvage
Tim's career failed to turn the tide. Despite its studio polish and its hand
cautiously extended to pop radio, *Sefronia* sold even fewer copies than

Greetings from L.A. and only served to alienate Tim's old fans. Britain's *Sounds* magazine deemed it "a marking-time album" that "shows no great strides." In a record store one day, Zappa was furious to discover the album wasn't even in stock. *Sefronia* wasn't helped by a chintzy ad campaign that equated Tim with a new model of a car ("Fully synchromesh musicianship! All power accessories standard! Great musical mileage! Elegant styling which has stood the test of time!"). Once again, Tim had reined in his art for business considerations, and he once again walked away with little to show for it.

Tim still pumped hot-blooded energy into his rock shows, but offstage, his caustic wit and willfulness were starting to curdle into bitterness. His friend Artie Leichter drove him to the office of a potential new agent in Hollywood, and Tim was his usual jokey, friendly self—until they arrived at their destination. "We get off the elevator, and *bing*—he's a different person," recalls Leichter. "The walls go up. We go in and Tim is his asshole self, tight bad vibes and everything." Nothing came of the meeting.

More and more Tim seemed to stay indoors and read, watching any television sports he could find and playing stickball and basketball near his and Judy's Venice apartment. "For a long time he was quiet and reclusive," recalls Taylor, then entering his teen years. "He did a lot of closing up in the room and writing." Although Tim stayed sober on the road, his intake of alcohol and pills increased at home. One evening Leichter recalls walking with Tim to a local pool hall. "We had too many beers like we always did, and he took *way* too many reds, which he always did," Leichter recalls. In the early hours of the morning, they wandered out and saw a carful of African-Americans drive by. Tim began screaming "nigger" at them. The car stopped, and the two men bolted away and through alleyways, running for their lives. "Neither of us has a prejudiced bone in our bodies," Leichter says. "But he had to be on the edge. These people were going to kill us, and they had every right to. But that was him. Tim was in love with the downside of life." Tim's former band member Emmett Chapman caught one of Tim's outdoor shows. Afterward, he said a quick hello to Tim, and Tim's face was, Chapman says, "white and pasty and thick-skinned, in a very unfamiliar way I had never seen before." It troubled him, but as with so many others, Chapman wasn't sure what to do about it.

Throughout the year, such stories became as much a part of Tim's life as his music. The signs pointed to a common psychological condition known as borderline-personality disorder. According to the *Diagnostic and Statis-*

tical Manual of Mental Disorders, its distinguishing traits included "markedly and persistently unstable self-image or sense of self"; "a pattern of unstable and intense interpersonal relationships"; "impulsivity in at least two areas that are potentially self-damaging (i.e., spending, sex, substance abuse, reckless driving, binge eating)"; "recurrent suicidal behavior, gestures or threats"; "chronic feelings of emptiness"; and "inappropriate, intense anger or difficulty controlling anger." Yet few seemed to acknowledge his problems or attempt to deal with them. Although Larry Beckett regularly communed with his friend by phone from Oregon, he knew little of Tim's personal excesses. "Even if it was pretty dangerous, nobody said anything to anybody at any point," Beckett says. "It just wasn't done."

In early 1974, Tim's longtime high-school pal Dan Gordon returned from a year in Israel. He hadn't seen his friend since just before the making of *Greetings from L.A.* Back in town to work on a script for his screenwriting career, Gordon invited Tim, Judy, and a mutual friend to Gordon's hotel room on Wilshire Boulevard. To Gordon's dismay, Tim showed up drunk and stoned. "By that time," Gordon says, "Tim was doing everything—pills and shooting shit, you name it." Eventually, Tim tried to convince the friend he'd brought along to jump off the balcony and into the hotel pool below. Tim laughed; Gordon, who had served time in the Israeli army and had witnessed actual deaths, was appalled by Tim's cavalier attitude and threw them all out.

Back in Israel, Gordon received an odd package from Tim: twenty mimeographed pages from Thomas Wolfe's *Look Homeward, Angel,* with a brief note attached: "Sorry about that night. I was sick at heart and you paid the price." Gordon wrote Tim back, warning his friend it was only a matter of time before he died "and the only people who are really going to care are me and Wu and maybe your kid and that's about it. But the people you're hanging with don't give a shit, and you'll be a footnote in rock and roll history, and for what?" Gordon volunteered to return to Los Angeles at Tim's request. Otherwise, Gordon wrote, Tim was "a dead man—and the one thing I've learned is not to stand next to dead people. You wind up getting killed."

He never heard back from Tim, and it would be the last time they would communicate.

On March 13, 1974, hope again raised its head as Tim began recording his ninth album. He brought to the studio a new batch of funk-oriented songs, some cowritten by mail with Beckett. To fill the producer's chair, he turned to Joe Falsia, his lead guitarist, arranger, and bandleader of two years; it was a comfortable and comforting choice. With the goal of beefing up Tim's sound—"I felt he sounded a little too thin on record"—Falsia summoned a number of name session players, including drummer Earl Palmer and keyboardist Michael Melvoin. "Tim wanted to go for the big one," says Falsia. "He wanted it just as much as anybody else."

The "big one" Tim was aiming for had only grown bigger by 1974. That year alone, $2.2 billion worth of records was sold in the United States, and sales of concert tickets, stereo equipment, and other related goods amounted to another $4 billion worldwide. The same year, the reunited Crosby, Stills, Nash & Young pioneered the idea of an outdoor stadium tour, and its multimillion-dollar success prompted others to follow. Before long, it became commonplace for bands to appear at monolithic festivals before audiences too stoned or laid-back to notice they were baking in the sun. The industry itself was controlled by a handful of major conglomerates like CBS and Warner-Elektra-Atlantic, with the independent labels of the '50s and '60s increasingly marginalized. The top-selling rock bands included the less-than-subtle likes of Bachman-Turner Overdrive and Grand Funk, while newcomers to the charts included a new wave of pop acts: Billy Joel, Kiss, Daryl Hall and John Oates, ABBA, and Barry Manilow. The competition was fiercer, and more polished, than ever.

Tim's label and management were well aware of rock's new world order. The preliminary album sessions had yielded five songs, but Tim had to wait for approval from the higher-ups at DiscReet before he could proceed with more recording. ("They were hesitant about Timmy," says recording engineer Stan Agol. "They were like, 'Oh, my God, if we let him in there, he's gonna come up with another *Starsailor!*' That album freaked them out for years to come.") Once everyone heard the tapes—and the commercial R&B direction in which they were headed—work resumed in early July. To Agol, who had first worked with Tim on *Starsailor,* the sessions were enjoyable, but Tim was "a little bit jaded. It was like he'd been kicked around and beaten up a little bit professionally. By the time we did that album, he was pretty blasé."

Tim's indignation surfaced at least once, during the recording of "Who Could Deny You." Falsia and Agol voiced their dissatisfaction with Tim's lyrics—"they don't mean anything," they told him—and Tim stormed out. He returned the next morning, seemingly still high on one type of pill or another, and barked, "Turn the mic on and play the track!" He then spit out the new, revised lyrics in one take. "Then he said, 'How was that, guys?'" Agol says. "And it was incredible."

With most of the album in the can, Tim returned to the stage. By now, live performance was his main source of income and, according to Falsia, not a bad one at that: The backup musicians earned between $300 and $500 a week, while Tim took home a few thousand at best. When Tim needed a new bass player for the tour, a familiar face from the past returned. After seven years, Jim Fielder—Tim's old Loara High buddy— had left Blood, Sweat & Tears, which he had co-founded. In need of work, he heard Tim was recruiting a touring band and signed up. "When Jim came back," Helm says, "this old feeling came over Tim. He felt safer."

Tim's full-on, exorcism-drenched rock was a pleasant surprise to Fielder. "He tried so many different things at that point," he says. "He was looking for his roots again. He wanted to lay back and let it fly." To Fielder, the sell-out accusations Tim's fans and friends made were understandable, "but at the same time you had to be there with Tim and realize how much *fun* he was having, and how it was its own kind of musical challenge. It was loud and intense from the minute you counted it off until the tune ended; it just kept driving and driving." Fielder found himself playing harder than he had in years, frequently walking offstage drenched in sweat and with a blister or two on his hand.

With Falsia staying in Los Angeles to mix and finalize the new album, the revamped band, featuring Fielder, Helm, keyboardist Mark Tiernan, and guitarist Art Johnson subbing for Falsia, hit the road, which included Tim's first trip to Europe since 1968. On Saturday, July 20, Tim participated in the "Bucolic Frolic," held on the grounds of Knebworth House in Hertfordshire. Opening a day-long bill featuring the Allman Brothers Band, Van Morrison, the Doobie Brothers, and the Mahavishnu Orchestra, Tim took the stage in bright afternoon sunlight. After addressing the crowd with "How ya doin', campers?" he and the band launched into a set of primarily recent material.

The sound was tough and raucous, Johnson adding jagged, Neil Young–style guitar solos even to midtempo songs like "Dolphins"; the band concluded with a twelve-minute "Honey Man" jam, complete with a feverish speaking-in-tongues vocal improv by Tim. But as most of the concertgoers were still straggling in and finding places to lay out their blankets, few heard or saw Tim. To the Allman and Morrison fans, he was merely an obscure opening act from a bygone era.

"It was a strange dichotomy," Fielder comments on that period. "When Tim tried to do something more mainstream sounding, he's all of a sudden turning off his hardcore fans, who were expecting something totally left-field from each album. But in a way, he continued to do that, because to do that mainstream stuff was for *him* a real abrupt change. In a way, he was still making left turns."

Tim still struck Fielder as the same old mischievous kid he had met at Loara High a decade before. After the Knebworth show, the band returned to London and downed drinks in Tim's hotel room in Kensington. In need of a blast of fresh air, Fielder went for a walk. When he returned, the hotel lobby was abuzz: Someone had pulled a fire alarm. Fielder instantly knew who the culprit was. "It was just Tim being Tim," says Fielder, "deciding it was the right thing to do at the time."

A few days earlier, Tim had spotted his old New York friend Joe Stevens, now a London-based rock photographer and writer, at a press reception at a London restaurant. Although Stevens was shocked at the sight of Tim stooping to autograph albums, Tim brightened up when he saw Stevens and said, "Come on, let's get outta here."

Stevens was taken aback—shouldn't Tim stay? "Fuck it," Tim said.

"He needed to get out of it, like 'What have I got myself into?'" Stevens says. As Warner Brothers executives watched with growing anxiety, Tim sauntered out before the press conference was to begin, and spent the next few days at Stevens's apartment, dodging phone calls and watching television. When Stevens and his girlfriend took Tim out for a meal, he opted for two shots of Jack Daniel's. Eventually, guitarist Johnson came and picked Tim up, and Stevens watched as Tim waved good-bye and stepped into a cab on Fulham Road. He never saw him again.

"In LA, you don't really ever get a straight answer ever," Tim told *Sounds* magazine during that trip. "It's what I call the corporate thought. You can't get an answer from one guy, it has to be from a 'jury,' like five or six. . . . Sometimes you're writing and you're just *not* gonna fit in. But you do it 'cause it's your heart and your soul and you've gotta say it, it's the foremost thing in your mind." His future plans amounted to the now standard litany of exaggerations and pipe dreams: He said he was going to write a screenplay based on Thomas Wolfe's *You Can't Go Home Again* ("possibly the best book I've ever read") and turn the stillborn *Fully Air Conditioned Inside* script into a novel. Or, he said, he might become a country singer.

Before the trip, Tim had also spoken to *New Musical Express*—namely, to an expatriate American freelance writer named Chrissie Hynde who was several years away from the start of her own music career as leader of the Pretenders. Hynde was clearly in awe of Tim (she was, she wrote, "still feeling dizzy at just meeting the guy whose singing sends me into raptures . . . I'm even tempted to ask his stud fee, but don't"), but Tim was less than romantic. As always, he offered a less than upbeat perspective on the current rock scene: "Now a concert consists of 13-year-olds passing coffee cans of pills around and listening to Deep Purple."

Returning to the States, Tim played Central Park's Schaefer Music Festival—right before, coincidentally, Blood, Sweat & Tears. Opening acts were not supposed to play sets lasting an hour and fifteen minutes, but Tim did precisely that, with problematic results. "Sections of the audience used every opportunity granted them to show their disapproval of Buckley's vocal pyrotechnics," noted one reviewer. "He squared off with the audience and fought them to a draw."

In the audience was Lee Underwood's former girlfriend Eileen Marder, who had moved back to New York. Marder thought Tim sang well but felt the band was "*way* below him. And if I knew it, then *he* knew it." Backstage, she received a more troubling jolt. Tim was still handsome as ever, but the free-spirited kid she had known five years earlier had given way to an angry, unhappy man of twenty-seven. When Marder began telling him about her own life difficulties, Tim snapped, "What problems do *you* have? You're a woman." It seemed to Marder that Tim was still searching for something, perhaps peace of mind, and he still appeared to be unable to satisfy himself.

That September, Lee Underwood received a disconcerting letter from his old friend. "You are what you are, you know what you know, and there are no words for loneliness, black, bitter, aching loneliness, that gnaws the roots of silence in the night," wrote Tim, ". . . and we are lying there, blind atoms in our cellar depths, gray voiceless atoms in the manswarm desolation of the earth, and our fame is lost, our names forgotten, our powers are wasting from us like mined earth while we lie here at evening and the river flows. . . . and dark time is feeding like a vulture on our entrails, and we know that we are lost, and cannot stir."

Underwood later claimed he suggested Tim try therapy, to which Tim responded, "Lose the anger, lose the music."

Tim wanted to call the album *Tijuana Moon; An American Souvenir* was also batted around. But when DiscReet released it on September 10, it sported a different, more downcast title: *Look at the Fool.* (According to Judy Buckley, Herb Cohen was behind the switch; Cohen denies the allegation, adding, "I might have objected that *Tijuana Moon* might have been misleading about the music, but I wouldn't have *changed* it.") Falsia had the right idea in terms of making a more unified-sounding album than *Sefronia,* and once again, Tim made an album unlike any of its predecessors. Slipping and sliding from an Al Green–style falsetto to guttural moans, his singing on the vocal-showcase title song and "Tijuana Moon" (inspired by the breakup of Beckett's marriage) marks a potentially positive new direction. "Tim wanted to be Al Green," says drummer Helm, "but he hadn't grown up there, so he had to learn a whole new vocabulary."

Still, the rubbery, vaguely seamy white-boy funk of *Look at the Fool* feels like another wrong turn. Tim's voice often verges on grizzled self-parody, and the quality of the songwriting declines with each succeeding track. If it's depressing to hear Tim sing trivial lyrics like "We oughta have a party" and "You know the talk's around town/You do a funky rhumba," it is doubly jaw-dropping arriving at the last song and encountering a blatant "Louie Louie" knock-off called "Wanda Lu." ("It never crossed my mind," says Falsia, with a laugh, of the similarities.) If *Greetings from L.A.* is massage-parlor rock, then this is bordello soul. Recording engineer Agol says every song was edited to be the length of a single; as a result, he says, many of the best performances—Melvoin's keyboard improvisations or Tim's scatting—can only be heard as each track is fading out.

Adding insult to musical injury, the cover featured a woefully second-rate painting of Tim, looking forlorn and sideburned. Even Tim seemed to hate it: During one of his many days lounging around Tim's apartment, Leichter came upon a box of *Look at the Fool* T-shirts. When he went to put one on, Tim retorted, "Don't wear that—they're fucking ugly."

The reviews were less than sympathetic, as if even the critics had been pushed to the limit. *New Musical Express* dismissed the record as "riffs as opposed to songs, constant displays of vocal overkill, and a kind of overall obnoxiousness of purpose and attitude." After ignoring all eight of Tim's previous albums, *Rolling Stone* finally weighed in. Although critic Bud Scoppa noted the album had "some attractive moments," he opined that "*Look at the Fool* may be slightly easier to take than the last two or three albums, but I still find the combination of hyper-speedy funk and Buckley's octave-spanning howls all but unbearable. It's as if Buckley had borrowed the primal scream of Lennon's Plastic Ono Band in order to mock and punish himself, as the title implies. With music like this, he mocks and punishes the listener as well."

By the time the review appeared, in the magazine's January 30, 1975, issue, the damage had already been done. *Look at the Fool* was another stiff, as was its single, "Wanda Lu." Within a short period of time, it took its place alongside *Sefronia* in the cutout bins. Although Falsia has fond memories of it as a "fun record" to make, few of Tim's associates looked kindly on it, with one notable exception. "*Sefronia* and *Look at the Fool* were a step back to what the first albums had been," says Herb Cohen. "If you take out the four in the middle, and went right from *Happy Sad* to *Sefronia*, it makes sense."

Undaunted, Tim decided to make further changes. During the summer, he had openly complained to his band about his manager of eight years, saying it was time to break free. (In his *Sounds* interview, he said of Cohen, "It's hard for me to be around him; it's hard for him to be around me. . . . Well, he believes in me to a certain extent, my earning prowess. It's degrading—to be thought of in terms of dollars. I feel like a race horse.") With an eye on taking an even larger role in Tim's career, Falsia began encouraging Tim to cut his ties to Cohen. In December 1974, Tim's new lawyer fired off a letter to Cohen, dismissing him. Since Cohen co-owned DiscReet, the break also meant Tim was without a recording contract for the first time since 1966. Tim was, in the words of drummer Helm, "excited, but scared." For all their clashes, Cohen had been something of a father figure to Tim, and some felt the loss, despite the aggravations, was unexpectedly hard on Tim.

In need of cash as ever, Tim returned to the clubs, with Falsia, Helm, and two new players, bassist Jeff Eyrich and former Electric Prunes keyboardist John Herren. In January, they debuted a few new songs, including a pounder called "Freedom," at a series of shows at the Starwood in Los Angeles. Both Tim and the musicians were so encouraged that Falsia booked studio time, and the band recorded rough versions of the new material (including two,

"Jesse James" and "Five O'Clock," without vocals). It was, says Helm, "the end of an era and a beginning of a new one," or so everyone hoped.

The weekend before Easter, Tim was preparing for a late-afternoon soundcheck at another local club, the Golden Bear in Huntington Beach, when he was summoned to the phone.

"Hi," the female voice said, "this is Mary. Do you remember me?"

A brief silence followed before Tim replied, "Yeah, yeah. Sure, I remember you. How are you?"

Mary said she was fine, to which Tim responded, "How's the boy?"

"He's fine too," she replied. "He'd like to meet you. Can he come tonight?"

"Yeah, sure," Tim replied. *"Yeah."* He said he would put their names on the guest list.

EIGHTEEN

Dear everyone,

Thank you for your beautiful letters. Sometimes things get my brain in a twist and reading your words of support really does my heart good. I shouldn't think so much.... The band and I are in writing-mode now, doing well together, they send their love. I'm sure you won't see us until the summer of '96—then we're really gonna freak out, man! Maybe we record in the spring? Don't know yet. Also, may you all find the best of happinesses in the year to come. Don't feel down! '96 must rule! New positive mental attitude slogan: "Dude, future . . . it rocks."

—JEFF BUCKLEY, LETTER MAILED TO FANS, DECEMBER 1995

As soon as he walked into the house in Sag Harbor, a former whaling port on the far eastern tip of Long Island, Eric Eidel knew he had entered what he would later call "an unfamiliar situation." Starting with its location—on a block literally called Main Street—the Victorian home was the epitome of normal, near a strip of white-picket-fenced homes and down the road from an upscale-folksy row of antique stores, galleries, and emporiums. But as he stepped into the attic, the twenty-eight-year-old, Westchester-born drummer and guitarist—whose bushy hair and glasses lent him a distinctly collegiate air—immediately smelled incense. The room was also extremely dark, and when Eidel's eyes adjusted, he saw his friends Jeff, Michael Tighe, and Mick Grondahl.

Eidel had known these men for several years; in fact, it had been at his recommendation that Grondahl had ventured up to Columbia University to see Jeff perform. When Eidel had last seen his friends, they were all smooth-faced; now, in the Sag Harbor attic, he noticed all three sported mustaches. Jeff's in particular was pencil-thin, and he was wearing a white sleeveless T-shirt that, combined with his long, black, greasy hair, made him look like anything but a heart-throb rock star.

Since those heady early days when he had seen Jeff perform at Sin-é, Eidel had kept in touch with Grondahl, his neighbor on Manhattan's Upper East Side. He was proud of his friends' success, and was therefore genuinely surprised when he began receiving messages from Grondahl in the fall of 1995 about auditioning for a slot in Jeff's band.

The position, Eidel learned, was drummer. "I was made for the road," Jeff had told the Salt Lake City *Desert News* at the dawn of the *Grace* tour. "I have sort of mastered the art in nomadic travel." Referring to his musicians, though, he added, "I don't know about the others." His fears proved to be warranted. During the first leg of roadwork, Matt Johnson was very much the Texas kid, buying tourist paraphernalia and beef jerky at truckstops and lapping up the new experience. But the indulgences of the road grew to repel him, and before long, Johnson had become a yoga-practicing vegetarian and was experiencing ringing in his ears due to the band's increasingly loud onstage volume. Grondahl, on the other hand, was more than happy to take advantage of the temptations of the rock road lifestyle, and he and Johnson, who had had personality clashes from the start, became an even more combustible duo.

Jeff himself was not immune to enticements. His friend and tour mate Brenda Kahn noticed that every time he briefly returned home from one leg of the tour, Jeff would be in "a completely different place. He'd lost weight or gained weight. He started smoking or gave up smoking. Every time I saw him, another thing was going on. He was completely metamorphosing." Unfortunately, the on-the-road dabblings were not limited to drinking and lighting up. At his first show in Paris, in September 1994, he had reunited backstage with his former high-school crush Holly Jones, who had since married and relocated to France. The two slipped into a deep conversation backstage, during which Jeff was repeatedly approached by one business associate or another. To Jones, the constant tugging seemed demanding and overwhelming, and at one point, Jeff confided to her he had recently sampled heroin. Jones was shocked: The high-school

Jeff had *never* done anything of the sort. When she reminded him about the drug's dangers and its role in his father's life, he simply said, "I know, I know."

Through nothing but happenstance, the *Grace* tour coincided with heroin's comeback in the rock community. The drug had had a lurid reputation for many years—the sad spectacle of Boy George's smack-fueled decline in the '80s hardly made it seem an appetizing experience—but its mystique appealed to a new generation of rockers, particularly in the alternative set. Heroin, says Tighe, "had this awful taboo to it and now was so acceptable, and it was very exciting for a while. It had the intensity and lore around it, so it felt very renegade." At least once on the *Grace* tour, during a stop in San Francisco, Jeff snorted it backstage with a member of Soul Coughing, his opening act.

For Tighe, who maintains his friend "didn't do that much" of the drug, Jeff's reasons for experimenting were self-evident. "In those moments, I remember him talking about the situation with the band and his relationship with women and friends," says Tighe, "and he felt very positive and objective about certain things. Like all drugs, heroin can be very beneficial or at least bring out certain positive things." The fact that Jeff's father had been linked with heroin didn't deter Jeff's own instinctive curiosity; if anything, it may have been the last step in Jeff's journey to understand the inner workings of his father's mind. "A force in him sometimes wanted to commune with that," concurs Tighe. "If your father or mother was buried under an avalanche, someone might go to the place where they died. That's what it felt like he was doing sometimes."

Simultaneously, heroin's ability to make its user feel relaxed and numb to outside pressure may have also factored into Jeff's interest in it, especially in light of the music-industry expectations placed on him once the *Grace* tour was over. A second album had to be created seemingly from scratch, and the band decided the best way to create new music was to isolate themselves, much as they had done in Woodstock. By chance, the Grondahl family owned a house in Sag Harbor, and for $1,600 a month, the band agreed to rent it as a rehearsal space starting November 1, 1995. During this tranquil off-season, Jeff moved into a room on the second floor, while the attic served as both a practice room and Grondahl's crash pad.

After the band had spent a short time working secretively at the house, Steve Berkowitz, Jeff's Columbia A&R man, decided it was time to check in. Arriving in Sag Harbor the last week of January, he found Jeff in his room, his bed surrounded by effects pedals that made his guitar echo, delay, reverberate, and emit any number of scratchy, grinding noises. Eventually, Jeff played Berkowitz some of the piles of cassettes the band had been making, and what blared from the tape deck were long, formless twenty-minute rambles—a veritable symphony of intriguing sounds, but no actual songs. ("It sounded like a constant loop," the A&R man recalls.) Berkowitz listened in silence.

The following morning, over breakfast, Berkowitz bluntly asked Jeff, "Uh, buddy . . . what's goin' on?" Ultimately, it was clear what was happening: The band was purging itself of the *Grace* songs they had been playing nonstop for eighteen months and was taking steps toward a new, albeit unformed, direction, one Tighe describes as "more of a very raw and electric place."

As Berkowitz and Jeff's managers also learned at that point, the band wanted more than a new sound. Jeff floated the idea that his next album not be credited to "Jeff Buckley" but to the band itself, which would be called the Two Ninas. (The inspiration for the name derived from a photograph of Jeff and Grondahl that made them look so feminine that someone cracked they resembled "a couple of Ninas"; Grondahl also wrote a song for the band with that title.) Clearly, Jeff was not simply weary of his role as band leader and bearer of responsibility; it was as if he were sick of whomever "Jeff Buckley"—*People* magazine beautiful person and adored rock star—had become.

Not surprisingly, both label and management balked at the Two Ninas idea. "It was laughable," says comanager Stein. "It was charming in its naïveté. I just said, 'It doesn't make any sense. You've spent all this time and effort building up recognition with your name.'" Confronted with immediate roadblocks, Jeff dropped the idea.

What no one could alter, though, was the evolution of his music flowering in Sag Harbor. Throughout his life, Jeff had been exposed to a diverse and eclectic range of music, but the jarring, full-throttle roar of punk and indie rock was rarely experienced; in the mid-'80s, he was exploring jazz and fusion while many his age were nodding their heads fiercely along with Hüsker Dü and the Replacements. A decade later, Jeff was catching up. A devout fan of alternative music, Jeff's romantic partner Joan Wasser began playing her Polvo and Jesus Lizard albums for Jeff, and as usual, he absorbed every note on them. In his mind, the scuzzy crunch of indie rock had the roughness and visceral passion his music needed to counter his perceived image as pretty boy and balladeer; he felt it would lend his music additional credibility.

With his usual zeal, he hurled himself into underground rock. Offered the chance to rattle off his favorite music in a September 1995 issue of *Rolling Stone*, he led off the list with the Grifters' lurch-and-grind *Crappin' You Negative;* "They destroy me in a really beautiful way," he wrote. Peggy and Kip Hagberg, Jeff's aunt and uncle, visited New York during this time, and while dropping by their nephew's apartment, Jeff pulled out one of the many used CDs he bought out of curiosity and announced, "You guys are gonna love this." What emerged from the stereo was the gay indie-rock duo the Frogs—which, Hagberg recalls, was "so *filthy!*"

Although Wasser feels Jeff was never less than proud of *Grace,* he began disparaging the album to friends; suddenly, it seemed too slick to him. Frequenting one of his favorite East Village bars one evening, he met Inger Lorre, who had made a splash—literally and figuratively—with the LA hard-punk band the Nymphs. In the early '90s, the band was known for both its wailing punk and for the oft-circulated story of Lorre urinating on the desk of a Geffen Records executive. Although Lorre was barely recognizable—she was battling drug and alcohol problems and had mascara running down her face—Jeff spotted her and told her how much he had loved her former band. When Lorre asked Jeff about his own music, he replied, "Oh, my music's kinda corny. It's like love songs. You wouldn't like it." But, he added, "The Nymphs are *really* cool."

Jeff's interest in the louder, harder, and faster was Matt Johnson's last straw. During the *Grace* tour, Johnson, whose Texas upbringing had not exposed him to as much of the arts and the world as his band mates, had begun to feel increasingly isolated from the others in more than just his new lifestyle. "I just couldn't relate to them," he says. "I was like, 'What's everybody talking about?' I didn't *see* that movie or *know* that band. I was still very insecure." In Johnson's mind, Jeff, who had become something of Johnson's mentor, didn't help the situation: "I remember he used to say, 'Oh, Matty, you're like a dog.' I think he meant that I had instincts and was like a dog in that I was loyal. But that always hurt me. I was ultimately resentful." The tight quarters in Sag Harbor, combined with the smell of pot wafting through the house and the lingering Johnson-Grondahl antagonism, only exacerbated the situation. "I found it almost impossible to be with those people at that time," Johnson says. "It was painful. The feeling of there not being anything definite to do was driving me crazy. We would come up with these interesting musical things, but any ideas I put out were falling down a black hole. I was like, 'What's happening? Are there songs coming out of this?' It felt like we were going nowhere." Finally, Johnson told the other three he was most likely going to quit the band. Everyone, especially Jeff, was shaken but decided to keep the news from Jeff's management for the time being.

Band tumult, musical indecision, and pressure from Columbia: Such was the scenario when Eric Eidel arrived at the Sag Harbor house that fall 1995 day. Over the course of six hours, the four men jammed in the attic, drank beer, and played some of the new songs, including a few Grondahl had written and was singing himself. Eidel wasn't sure he was the right man for the drumming job, but he enjoyed playing with his friends, and afterward Jeff and Grondahl said they would be in touch.

With other scheduled plans looming, the Sag Harbor sessions tumbled to a halt shortly thereafter. "It was a mess," says Columbia president Don Ienner. "He knew he blew that and made a mistake." Although Tighe feels a new sensibility and new songs took root there, he too admits it was "a good idea, but impractical," as evidenced by the numerous noise complaints lodged by neighbors. For their part, Lory and Stein took one look at the bill—$25,000 for renting the house and equipment—and were more than happy to see the experiment end.

During this transitional period, Jeff took a breather from New York with a trip to California to reacquaint himself with his mother, relatives, and friends. Everyone, including his old pal Tamurlaine Adams, was jolted upon seeing their once abstinent friend smoking and drinking. During an Orange County bar get-together with his high-school band mate Jason Hamel, Jeff seemed down and "not real comfortable in his own skin," Hamel recalls. He told Hamel his record company was pushing him to make a new album, but that he wanted to do it on his own time and didn't want to be forced into anything. Over the course of the evening, Jeff pounded down double shots of tequila and seemed perfectly happy to play songs on the jukebox and banter with the bar regulars. None of them recognized the kid with the baggy pants held together by safety pins.

Although the Two Ninas proposal fell by the wayside, Jeff was adhering to at least one of his agenda. Several years before, he had befriended Lenny Kaye, guitarist, author, producer, and longtime friend and colleague of Patti Smith. Jeff and Kaye would often run into each other at an East Village bar and, over beers, play doo-wop records on the jukebox. In August 1995, Kaye and Smith walked into the lobby of Electric Lady Studios on East 8th Street, where they were working on Smith's first album in nearly a decade, and Jeff was just *there,* as if he were waiting for them. Smith had become one of Jeff's old-school-punk heroes—he had cheered her on from the sidelines a few weeks earlier at a Lollapalooza concert in New York—and by chance, they needed someone to sing a high choral part on a newly recorded song called "Southern Cross."

After Jeff had easily laid down the vocal, the band began working on another song, "Fireflies." Jeff mentioned he had an instrument at his apartment—an Egyptian bowed instrument called an essrage—that could work with what Smith calls the song's "exotic, mournful quality." "Go home and get it," Smith told him, and Jeff dashed into a cab and returned shortly with the instrument. Sitting cross-legged in a corner of the studio, he played along with the band, adding a firefly-like buzz to the song. Everyone was pleased, although after the session ended, Smith found Jeff sitting alone in a separate room, crying; he felt he hadn't performed well and had let everyone down.

One of the other musicians playing on "Fireflies" was guitarist Tom Verlaine. At forty-six, Verlaine was a legend in New York and punk rock in general, revered for his band Television and his iconoclastic, pale-loner image. Jeff had become enamored of Television's *Marquee Moon* album, and during the session, he and Verlaine connected by way of a few in-jokes, and Verlaine was struck by Jeff's ability to instantly rattle off the name of an obscure chord. "Tom is not easily impressed," says Smith, "and he was extremely impressed with Jeff's gift." Soon after, Jeff made a decision: Verlaine would helm his next album.

In at least one regard, the choice was curious: Verlaine had heard *of* Jeff, but had never heard *Grace.* In other ways, though, the match made perfect sense. Both men were sonic-architect guitarists, and Verlaine's reputation for not compromising his art was one Jeff admired and wanted to emulate. "Jeff was looking for someone with a history in punk rock," says Wasser. "And he hit it off with Verlaine and decided he just might be the dude. It's not like he was looking at anyone's résumé." Verlaine responded to Jeff in an equally musical way: "Everybody out there is just strumming and sampling. There's nobody writing songs with really good guitar settings and strong vocals, and I thought it was great that in this day someone was doing it."

Verlaine was also known for making albums quickly and relatively inexpensively, and money matters were of pressing concern as 1995 drew to a close. Columbia had spent approximately $2.2 million on *Grace,* including $400,000 on recording fees, $600,000 in tour-support money (the band's salary was raised from $500 to $750 a week during the tour), and over $400,000 for the "Last Goodbye" and "So Real" videos combined. The remainder of the money went toward independent radio promotion, advertising on television and radio, the filming of Jeff's electronic press kit ($85,000), "price and positioning" in record stores (the cost of having compact discs placed in racks in the front of record stores, rather than relegated to bins), and other commonplace industry expenses. Of that total amount, Jeff's recoupable—the amount he, in essence, owed the company before he would be able to earn any royalties—was said to be $1.8 million. Although *Grace* had sold three-quarters of a million copies worldwide, that amount was nowhere near the number of copies that would have to be sold—which Stein estimates would have had to have been at least a million—for Jeff to break even. Not only was Jeff not making money from CD and cassette sales, he was barely making any from the road, either. By the end of his tour, he no longer needed "tour support"—that is, his expenses and earnings had evened out. But during the tour itself, according to Stein, he at times earned as little as $100 per show after expenses.

Although Jeff technically did not owe Columbia $1.8 million—at worst, the company would simply write off the expenses—the *idea* of that figure unsettled him deeply. To exacerbate matters, his contract was cross-collateralized, meaning the debt would be transferred over to his second album. In order to start earning record royalties, he would have to sell several million copies of his follow-up in order to make up the costs of both albums. "Debts got you down?" he scribbled in one of his notebooks, using a television ad campaign to make a pointed joke at himself.

Before any serious discussions about Verlaine got underway, Jeff had one last road obligation to wrap up. A series of fifteen shows had been set up in Australia to capitalize on his popularity down under. Between road fatigue and his problems with Johnson, Jeff was less than enthusiastic about the trip. Over a predeparture meal near his apartment, he told his friend (and Fez booker) Ellen Cavolina as much, adding he could be sued if he didn't play the concerts. "So?" she replied. "Would you rather be run into the ground or be sued? Look at yourself—look at what you look like." However, the thought of canceling was too overwhelming, so he packed his bags and boarded a United Airlines flight from New York to Auckland, New Zealand, on Sunday, February 4, 1996.

What was dubbed the "Hard Luck Tour" had, to say the least, an inauspicious start. On the flight out of New York, a gay steward flirted with Jeff and began pumping him and Tighe with rum. By the time the flight arrived in Los Angeles for the changeover, both men were playfully bombed. As soon as the plane to New Zealand took off, Jeff, who was strapped into his seat, vomited. Jumping to attention, road manager Gene Bowen threw Jeff into the first-class bathroom and doused him with after-shave, but as soon as Jeff returned to his seat, his stomach again revolted. By this time, his fellow first-class passengers were in a state of shock and annoyance, as was Johnson. The drummer always brought along spare clothing, and after Bowen asked to borrow one of his extra shirts for Jeff, Johnson launched into a sermon: "*This* is why I left the band—I can't take this anymore!" It would have been typical rock hijinks if it wasn't so por-tentous.

The anxieties continued through the two-month tour. The early shows felt uninspired compared to the controlled fury of the first Australian dates the previous summer; Tighe himself recalls the first concerts as per-functory. To make matters edgier, Johnson was by now barely communi-cating with Jeff and Grondahl. "It felt like such a brotherhood and an intense musical unit," says Tighe, "and Jeff was not able to deal with [the problems] at that time. He was shocked and very confused. He couldn't believe it was happening. It was difficult. It felt like a death."

In other ways, the tour was a welcome diversion. Jeff was headlining theaters that held as many as two thousand, and he was able to hire both the Dambuilders (featuring Wasser) and the Grifters as his opening acts. "Those were wonderful times, for me and for Jeff," Wasser recalls. "We were semi-rock stars there." During the Grifters' own shows at local clubs, Jeff and Wasser could be seen out front, Jeff resembling a lonesome gau-cho with a sliver of a mustache. Grifters frontman Dave Shouse experi-enced Jeff's fame down under firsthand when, during in-store appear-ances with his band, fans approached him with poetry to give to Jeff. Teenage girls lined up in front of the stage, their arms dangling over the barriers, staring longingly at Jeff. At the Palais Theater in Melbourne, a few passed out.

Toward the end of the tour, the band coalesced, and the music lashed out with a newly serrated edge. Jeff began inserting new material into the sets as well: "I Woke Up in a Strange Place," a rocker built around a taut riff and a mood of dislocation (chaotic images of loud music, spilled beer, and mysterious cabs) that was inspired by his travels; Grondahl's dirge-pretty "Edna Frau" (which Grondahl sang himself); "Moodswing Whiskey," an almost rhapsodic ballad undercut by deeply uneasy, savage imagery ("I think of mankind in quotation marks/Ever since I took a drink from you"); and a vaulting, heavy-jangle instrumental called "Vancouver" that the band had first worked up in a studio in that city in late 1994. The exhaustion that had crept into the music during the last legs of the previous tour fell away, replaced by a bristling, electric-socketed charge. Reaching back to his Sin-é days, Jeff also threw in solo performances of Piaf songs and Dylan's "If You See Her, Say Hello." The shows, Tighe says, felt "like a catharsis and a celebration."

Still, it was a celebration to everyone except Johnson, whose sense of isolation from the band had only increased. Although he and Jeff were roommates on the tour, Jeff still felt "very remote" to the drummer; "I didn't understand his process," Johnson recalls. Unable to relax after shows, Jeff would often watch television in their room for hours on end. Old resentments continued to linger. Onstage, Johnson would feel irritated when Jeff introduced him as "Jesus" (because of Johnson's thin face, long hair, and sometime facial hair), and offstage, matters could be just as testy: Once, Jeff poured lotion down Johnson's underwear while the drummer was in a headstand during meditation. "Transcend *this,*" Jeff cracked. Johnson laughed along, but he also felt judged.

Matters came to a head during a band meeting in Perth a week before the tour's end, at which Johnson explicitly critiqued the band's musical and lifestyle shifts. "I was like, 'There are certain people on tour who are doing drugs, certain people who are vomiting all over the place, and *it is a burden,*'" he recalls. "Jeff was resentful of that. The fact that he didn't even meet me on that level and say, 'I don't give a shit but I understand why you do' just pissed me off. I was very angry and I felt very betrayed." Immediately after the last song of the last show, at Selina's in Sydney on March 1, Johnson not only left the stage but the venue, walking to a nearby beach by himself as the crowd screamed for more. He eventually returned in time for an encore. The four men played "Kanga Roo," their longtime bonding song, and then it was over.

"It felt like we wanted to stay and wander off into the country," Tighe says, "because it was so vague what was going to come up." Tighe hardly felt alone in his apprehension.

Jeff may not have been overly concerned about the contents of Tom Verlaine's résumé, but plenty of others were. Although Verlaine was respected in certain sectors of the music business, nothing he had ever done—from his albums with Television through his subsequent solo work—could be described as a commercial hit, and Columbia was more than aware of that. Meetings and conference calls ensued as Jeff argued his case to the label by way of Lory and Stein. "My theory was, 'I don't get it—explain it to me. Why Tom Verlaine?' " recalls Berkowitz. "I never thought there was anything *wrong* with Verlaine. I just didn't get it." Berkowitz began writing flow-chart-style notes to himself, positing different outcomes: "Songs plus band plus production plus time and space plus producer equals realized goal. Songs plus band plus time and space plus Tom Verlaine: question mark." The A&R executive had already begun jotting down lists of potential producers, including Butch Vig (Nirvana), Brendan O'Brien (Pearl Jam), Steve Lillywhite (U2, Dave Matthews), and, again, Andy Wallace.

According to many of Jeff's friends, based on conversations with him during the early months of 1996, Columbia felt the second album had to deliver the commercial goods, especially after the label had spent so much time and money on *Grace*. It was suggested to Jeff that he hire a hit-proven producer like Lillywhite in order to make a more expansive mainstream-rock album that built on the sonic textures of *Grace*. ("They want me to be Dave Matthews," Jeff griped to a friend that spring.) "That's a natural inclination you look for after you make *Sin-é* and *Grace,* and then the payoff is the third record," Ienner confirms. "Take R.E.M. or Bruce. Makes sense." Berkowitz admits any number of producers—from Lillywhite to Brian Eno—were brought up, but Jeff would simply respond, "I don't know." "Jeff was not interested, for no particular reason," Berkowitz says. "He wanted to do what he wanted to do. Maybe it was being provincial, maybe it was fear."

Much like previous clashes with the label over album covers and "Kanga Roo," the use of Verlaine became a symbolic as well as musical stand. The label had promised Jeff artistic control four years earlier, and he intended to have them live up to their part of the deal; knowing what he did about his father's career, he had learned the unfortunate results of record company interference. Berkowitz argued for Verlaine to contribute as a musician, arranger, or co-songwriter—anything but produce. Jeff wouldn't budge. At a meeting of Columbia's A&R department, one of Berkowitz's coworkers openly questioned the hiring of Verlaine, but was informed it was Jeff's wish and the company would proceed, at least for the time being.

As he had done with Andy Wallace before the making of *Grace*, Stein wanted to meet and talk with the producer of Jeff's next project and make sure his—Stein's—input was heard. True to his ornery image, Verlaine was far less receptive than Wallace had been and asked Stein to just chat *now*, over the phone. "I had no interest in talking to any business people about Jeff's music," he recalls. "I could *totally* give a shit less about what they thought." Stein says he "felt a little dissed. I didn't make a big deal out of it. But I didn't feel good about it."

Begrudgingly, the label agreed to budget enough studio time for Jeff and Verlaine to record a few tracks. Maybe the results would be released, maybe they wouldn't; maybe they would make a four-song EP or simply serve as demos. In fact, the sessions were dubbed "demo masters," a seeming contradiction. By now, the label was simply glad to see Jeff working. "The second record was taking so *long*," says Ienner. "Everyone was just waiting for him to write a song, never mind Lillywhite or making it a more commercial record." It was better than nothing, or better than those diffuse Sag Harbor tapes. With that tentative go-ahead, the band assembled at Sorcerer Sound, a downtown Manhattan studio, on the afternoon of Saturday, June 15.

A longtime favorite of Verlaine's, Sorcerer could not have been further removed from the bucolic serenity of Woodstock. Located just north of the chaotic, vendor-clogged Canal Street, Sorcerer could be found behind an unmarked black metal door on the cobblestoned Mercer Street. The eccentric lobby was decorated with framed bugs, a crocodile head, and sundry animal skulls and skeletons. Located on its top floor, Studio A was more cramped than the main room at Bearsville, and a patio-style sliding glass door separated the main work room from a small space for a drum kit. It had the feel of a one-room Manhattan apartment with an attached recording console. Still, the studio had a sense of history—it had been used by punk bands in the '70s—and at the very least, everyone felt the funky, downscale feel would match the equally gritty music Jeff and the band would record.

Once they settled in, though, things didn't proceed quite as smoothly as everyone had anticipated. Columbia had only budgeted enough funds for Jeff and Verlaine to record four songs; indeed, studio billing records indicate the tab came to all of $10,478.95. With little time and much to do, the pressure valve was turned up high.

Verlaine, six feet of lanky, caustic cynicism, was under the impression Jeff's songs were finished and fully arranged, and that the band would quickly bang out recorded versions of them. Such a method was Verlaine's own preferred way of working, as opposed to wasting time and money rehearsing in an expensive recording studio. What he heard instead were songs that were still in formative stages, both musically and lyrically, and a bandleader unsure where he wanted them to go. "After the first day I realized we could be doing takes forever," Verlaine says. "It was hard to read in many ways what he liked and what he didn't like. Should it sound like the band is playing in a coliseum, in a club, or in a crappy rehearsal space? Should it be a cheesy rock sound or a bombastic Led Zeppelin sound? You had to kind of guess to find the direction zone for the tunes, and he wasn't real forthcoming about it." Verlaine quickly grew exasperated, and he was also impatient with new drummer Eric Eidel's skills and lack of studio experience. "We'd be changing parts while we were working," admits Eidel, "and it was a little frustrating for Verlaine." Working in the separate drum room, Eidel felt physically disconnected from the band, which only added to the difficulties.

Nonetheless, Jeff, Verlaine, and the band managed to nail preliminary versions of four songs. One of them, an anthemic wall-toppler called "The Sky Is a Landfill," was inspired by *The Medium Is the Middleman: For a Revolution Against Media,* an anti-media tract by writer Al Giordano. It was the only one of the four tracks that had an airtight arrangement. Verlaine felt "Vancouver" (which now featured lyrics) was "three songs in one. It needed work, and Jeff thought so too." "You & I" dated back to Jeff's session with producer Steve Addabbo in 1993, where it was a long, winding acoustic ballad recalling a dream about an AIDS rally. In a typical example of the evolution of Jeff's music, it had become a love song, and he recorded it one night at Sorcerer by himself, singing it *a cappella* while sitting cross-legged on the studio floor. For additional eerie effect, he and Verlaine added echo and delay effects to the recording, lending it a spooky, darkened-forest ambience. Jeff also brought with him a buttery ballad, "Morning Theft," which Tighe feels was partly about his recurring feelings for Rebecca Moore and partly about Elizabeth Fraser (particularly its line "your precious daughter in the other room, asleep").

"Morning Theft" became symbolic of these turbulent first sessions. Eidel, still very much a newcomer to the band, couldn't nail a beat everyone liked, prompting Verlaine to suggest Jeff fire the drummer. Verlaine also felt the band had to work as quickly and efficiently as possible given their budget limitations, but to the band, Verlaine came across as "slightly bullying," Tighe says. "Tom made us pretty tense and insecure, pretty early. He seemed frustrated and disappointed from the get-go. It wasn't the relationship with a producer that we needed or that he felt we needed."

After six days of band recording (and another five of overdubbing and mixing, ending June 26), the money ran out. The band came away with the four finished songs. (Eidel also recalls them attempting "Pleasure Seeker," an instrumental.) Upon hearing "The Sky Is a Landfill," Berkowitz was somewhat encouraged—"it was the next chapter of U2," he says—but Jeff wasn't. "It wasn't as explosive and huge as we wanted it to be," Tighe says. "It felt like a stage of the songs. Jeff felt that in himself and the band we could get more, that it could be more dynamic and powerful. It felt like it was a little too soon." Disappointed but not crushed, Jeff and the band agreed to work further on the material and reconvene with Verlaine at a later date.

The summer of 1996 was the best, the worst, and the most vexing of times. On the personal front, Jeff was back home in New York, where Wasser had herself relocated, to Brooklyn. Slowly, he wound down from traveling. He and Wasser would shoot pool or hang out with their mutual friend Nathan Larson. (Jeff and Wasser even participated in a one-week May tour with Larson's offshoot band, Mind Science of the Mind, where Jeff took refuge in being the band's non-singing bass player and tooling around the Northeast corridor in a rented van.) At one of his friend Inger Lorre's club shows, Jeff and Wasser were seen ballroom dancing.

Still, old friends noticed distinct changes in him. He looked haggard and acted peculiar, such as the night he was spotted alone, distracted, and talking to himself at a downtown club. He seemed more insular than before, rarely, if ever, introducing friends to Wasser, as if he was wary of media gossip. "He was very gregarious before that," says Wasser. "Suddenly it was much less. He was a little paranoid, and he wanted to have his private life totally private, to the point where I didn't know many of his friends." He unleashed his frustrations in an acidic new song, "Haven't You Heard": "Make sure you learn to beware your neighbor/Bolt the doors and hire your guards," he sang, both to himself and to his friends.

Musician Tom Shaner, who had befriended Jeff during the Sin-é period, was walking past a bar on St. Mark's Place when he saw a man with long hair and a goatee—was it Ethan Hawke?, he thought—beckoning him inside. "I was like, 'Why is this person asking me in?'" Shaner says. It was Jeff, whom Shaner hadn't seen in months. "He said, 'Hey, Tom,' and put his arm around me and we hugged. But I didn't feel I knew this person at all." Shaner asked Jeff if he'd spoken to their mutual friend Daniel Harnett, and Jeff said, "No, no, I gotta get in touch with him." Shaner asked how Jeff was doing, and he simply replied, "Good." Recalls Shaner, "I didn't know what to say. There was no flow, there was nothing." Unable to bear the awkwardness any longer, Shaner continued on his way.

On the musical front, things were even more vague. Plans to release the first Verlaine session as an EP were quickly scotched; says Stein, "We decided at the end of the day it would be neither here nor there." Although his friends noticed his disillusionment with the recordings, Jeff still held out hope, so he and the band resumed rehearsing in Chelsea. "We weren't down and out," says Eidel. "We felt we just needed more time, and we thought we had it." Early in the summer, Jeff began making plans in one of his spiral-bound notebooks:

> *Each day at 7:30 AM to the park and run the reservoir. Sit and write at 10:30 AM. At 10:30 AM, we come back home and we song-make-song-make-song-make-spirit-make-spirit-gum until either rehearsal with the band at 12:30 Mon.–Thurs., or until lunch at 3 PM. Remember, Fri.–Sun. is your free period. . . . Writing takes a long time simply because there is so much to say and to explore, all the memories, phrases and rhythm rises and rhyme-shades to acquaint yourself with; you will need time to concentrate in candid peace & stillness. . . .*

On August 20, he continued this positive mind-set:

> *Your thought is your right, your art is your right. You are allowed to invent and explore your song. You are allowed to make it real through your concentration and hold onto your gift, man, and let go*

*of anything that holds you back from that aphrodisiac, the cigs, the
pot. . . . Smoking calls, smoking hurts and distracts you and
provides only the voice of the slave. It brings congestion and worry
and deviation from your true voice. It will kill you. . . . Resist death
that is self-inflicted, embrace life. . . . Cigarettes pull you down all
the way. Finish your life without them. Carry yourself with
delight. . . .*

A week later, Jeff made his first journal entry about Memphis, Tennessee.
During his last tour of Australia, his friend Dave Shouse of the Grifters had
inserted a bug in his friend's ear about Easley, a relaxed studio where the
Grifters worked. He told Jeff how comfortable and amenable it was, and the
thought of working outside New York began to appeal to Jeff. He and
Berkowitz decided to take a quick trip south to inspect the studio. "Then to
Memphis on the 4th of September," Jeff wrote. ". . . Most of your demos will
be ready and you can be freer for the recording at Easley. Exercise the voice,
stay strong with the song, write freely from the heart." By then, he had sent a
fax to Berkowitz, on July 22, listing all the songs he was considering for the
album he would call *My Sweetheart the Drunk*. There were sixteen in all,
from "Vancouver" and "The Sky Is a Landfill" through new, semiformed
compositions with titles like "Murder Suicide Meteor Slave," "Skyblue
Skin," "Moodswing Whiskey," and "Ever Since Then (Opened Once)."
After each song title, he placed an exclamation mark.

But for all of Jeff's best intentions, the band was not jelling. Eidel was having problems sticking to preordained arrangements ("I wasn't regimented," he
admits. "I wasn't good at thinking, 'These are my parts and this is the way
we're going to do it every single time'"), and he and Grondahl had started to
clash. In September, the band assembled at Sony Studios—this time without
Verlaine—to run through their material for Berkowitz. They played the songs
they had already recorded and a few more they had premiered in Australia, as
well as new, in-the-works numbers like "Demon John" and "Gunshot Glitter."

To the musicians and Berkowitz, the sessions made it painfully clear
Eidel was not working out. "It was a very difficult thing to come by," Eidel
recalls. "I wanted to be the right person. I did everything I could to practice my timing. But if it's not right, it's not right." Afterward, Jeff told
Eidel, "I think I need to look for new drummers," and Eidel, with both
relief and disappointment, agreed.

Jeff's frustrations—with himself, the band, and his music—began to mount. "There was definitely a time when things weren't coalescing," remembers Tighe, "and I could see Jeff wanting to start anew." On October 1, Jeff admitted as much to himself in his journal:

I'm going to lay off the band. I'm going to keep Michael. Mickey—I can't work with that anymore. I don't have any more time for it or tolerance for it and besides our working situation on his side just fucks up the flow. . . . His songs? I can't sing 'em. His bass playing REALLY GOOD when he's happy—but for him it's about control, not music, not flow. I can't sit alongside that. . . . Nor can I take his . . . fucking house in the Hamptons. Not punk rock at all. . . . I need a heavy man on the bass on the drums in my life. Eric is not right. I am not right. I need to go away. . . .

I prepared my entire life to face the future unprepared to face the future. I hope I explode from the lesson. I hope my brain splits open and that my guts blow out of either side of my body. I hope my eyes are open when I die so they can see you for the final breath. I hope that I never come back alive.

One day in the fall of 1996, Jeff called his friend Susan Feldman from St. Ann's and asked her to stop by his apartment immediately. When he persisted, she gave in and walked over to 12th Street, where she discovered he had painted his apartment mint green. "What do you think of the color?" he asked eagerly. She didn't have the heart to tell him it wasn't quite right, he seemed so proud of his labor.

On their way out to dinner, Jeff grabbed a pile of CDs and sold them at a nearby used record store in order to pay for his meal. Feldman thought it an unusual move for a major-label recording act. Then, as they walked down the street, one female fan after another approached him. He was receptive, but it was clearly getting to be too much. He couldn't visit his favorite bar, 2A, without a gaggle of fans whispering around him and making him want to blend into the wood bar and disappear.

He began talking, and writing, openly about leaving New York: "The Lower East Side can kiss my ass goodbye . . . I don't wanna live here, I don't wanna exist," he wrote in his journal. He was easily given to distractions, and the city—the East Village in particular—had too many of them. During the summer, two of his friends, writer Nihar Oza and producer-songwriter Hod David, opened a midtown coffeehouse, the Daydream Cafe, at 405 West 51st Street. Jeff would often stop by the café or David's apartment around the corner, complaining about the downtown distractions. "In a way it was almost like getting out of New York," says David. Almost, though, was proving to be not enough.

It had now been three years since *Grace* had been recorded. "That's it!" he announced at 2A one night to the bartender, his friend Tom Clark. "I'm a has-been. They forgot about me." On top of it, Columbia was growing testy and less inclined to use Verlaine. A meeting with Ienner was set up, for which Jeff arrived three hours late, exasperating everyone. By year's end, several top Sony executives with whom Jeff had worked had left the label, making company relations thornier.

Jeff continued to work on music, but not necessarily his own. Inger Lorre, newly sober and looking to reclaim her music and life, commenced work on her first post-Nymphs solo album, and when her guitarist quit, Jeff volunteered to fill in. In Lorre's Honda, the two began driving to a studio in New Jersey to record. On the morning of October 23, they were passing through East Amwell, a farming town in western Jersey, when Jeff took a sip from a bottle of beer he had in the backseat. ("He had something in his throat," Lorre says.) By almost comical happenstance, they drove past a police car at that precise moment. A siren wailed, Lorre pulled over, and the officer made Jeff step out and empty his pockets, at which time a plastic bag containing enough pot for a joint plopped out. A "brown wooden container with a brown smoking pipe" was also discovered in the car. After being belittled by the cop, Jeff was arrested, brought to the police station, and fined. "When I said, 'Shall I call your manager, Jeff?' everyone's ears perked up," Lorre recalls, "and they wanted to know who he was. Then they started to treat him real special. That made him even sicker." At a subsequent hearing, he arrived over an hour late (leading the judge to lecture him on promptness) and pleaded guilty, and it was ultimately decided that his record would be expunged if he wasn't arrested again within six months.

Although the incident was harmless enough, the bust and rampant Internet rumors about Jeff's mental state set off alarms with Stein and Lory, his comanagers. Recalls Stein, "We confronted him: 'Is it heroin? Is it alcohol? Is there a problem? Tell us.' He said, no, it was nothing." When Jeff visited Stein's doctor for a stomach ailment, Stein instructed the physician to keep an eye out for telltale signs of drug use. He never heard back from the doctor, and he and Lory never received any definitive answers.

Jeff continued to fill his Mead notebooks with volumes of notes, song fragments, and occasionally overwrought prose. ("Nothing more attractive to the outsider than a human being who exudes the seed of lust and depravity and the mountainous drama of life itself locked in a sticky blowjob with death" was one such phrase.) Another read, "Get out of your music: ego and trepidation. Leave in: Pure soul and Truth and the bringing of the All O-Riginole. . . . This is important work. It could be dangerous. Do not fuck around. When you tap into the feel for real for real!! You better be strong enough to withstand the endless void when you tap into the forearm and administer your juicy comets. Never die never die (never say never)." He and Wasser had planned to celebrate his thirtieth birthday that November 17 by attending a Soundgarden concert, but when the show was canceled on account of a band illness, the two wandered over to the nearby Daydream Cafe and danced by themselves in the empty coffeehouse to CDs on the jukebox.

Each Thanksgiving, Tom Clark threw a party at his two-floor apartment in Brooklyn. He always invited Jeff out of courtesy, never expecting him to show, but that November, Jeff did. His face looked drawn, his hair a little thinner, possibly receding, but Clark didn't ask Jeff about business; he was simply glad to see him. The party grew crowded, and Jeff joined in with the eating and drinking.

After a few hours, the festivities moved downstairs to the white-cement-walled basement where Clark had set up drums and guitars. Amidst the clutter, Jeff grabbed a guitar and sang Led Zeppelin songs, then moved to drums, where he and Clark played '60s oldies like "Tequila" and "Shakin' All Over." Eventually he left alone. Few had recognized him.

For all his frustrations with his band, Jeff was nothing if not loyal; he wanted to believe in them, and the idea of a posse was still appealing. (He had only reluctantly allowed his first sound engineer, Paul Wilke, to be dismissed by management after complaints about the band's concert sound mixes.) Just when matters seemed bleakest, something happened that renewed his faith in them, and it stemmed from Grondahl. Grondahl's clashes with drummers Johnson and Eidel made any further recommendations on his part suspect, but in October, he told Jeff he'd run into a friend looking for a gig. Jeff set up an audition at an East Village rehearsal space, and on Halloween 1996, Parker Kindred walked in. Like Grondahl and Tighe, Kindred had only a modest amount of experience under his belt, mostly with punk bands. But he fit the spiritual bill. With his bony face and small frame, the twenty-four-year-old son of a New Jersey jazz musician exuded a down-to-earth sweetness rather than ruthless careerism.

Kindred showed up at the rehearsal space to find Jeff quiet and dragging on a cigarette, and for several hours, he, Jeff, and Grondahl bashed around on covers, including Black Sabbath's "Paranoid." More rehearsals ensued at a basement rehearsal space next to a mental-health office near Port Authority in midtown Manhattan, and soon Jeff began telling everyone he'd found his drummer. It renewed his faith in his band, Grondahl in particular: *This* is why he hadn't sacked them.

Before he made a final decision about hiring Kindred, Jeff left town on December 6 for a nine-day solo tour—just him and his guitar, playing clubs from Westborough, Massachusetts, to Washington, DC, each of them under a pseudonym. (The Crackrobots, Possessed by Elves, Martha & the Nicotines, and A Puppet Show Named Julio were just a few.) The initial plan had been for Jeff to be joined by his half-brother Corey Moorhead as driver and road manager; it would be a long-overdue bonding period between the two. But it was not to be. The plan collapsed when Moorhead left his license behind in California, and Jack Bookbinder, Lory's assistant, took his place.

At the clubs, and a last-minute show at the Daydream Cafe in New York on January 2, 1997, Jeff played *Grace* songs but also tested the new material. The night of the Daydream show, he showed up at the last possible minute, emerging from a cab with his guitar and amplifier just as Oza and David were worried that the hundreds of people crammed into their space wouldn't see a show. Wearing a rumpled suit and reading lyrics from a notebook, Jeff sang many new songs, including one, "Everybody Here Wants You," that was little more than a mantra-like chorus. Jeff, who told Oza not to "tell anybody from Sony" about the gig, was clearly nervous about the fans' responses to his recent songs. He needn't have worried. "It was one of those times where you could hear a pin drop," David recalls. Afterward, Jeff was thrilled, and sat at the bar divvying up the cash with the other performers.

By then, Kindred had been hired. Plunging themselves into an intense regimen, the band rehearsed eight hours a day, Jeff often teaching the band the parts he wanted them to play. "He would sing the *drum* beat to me," Kindred recalls. If the shock of suddenly being Jeff Buckley's drummer wasn't enough, Kindred was further stunned when Jeff informed him they were about to start making an album. "I was like, 'Whoa—we're gonna *record?*' "

he recalls. "I said, 'Man, I don't know,' and Jeff said, 'No, no, just *play*, just simple with feel.' "

But record they would. A trip to Memphis was on the schedule, with the plan to fly down on February 11 to resume work with Verlaine at Easley. The Easley sessions had been scheduled and postponed numerous times, enough to drive the studio's owner, Doug Easley, slightly crazy. But this time it was on: Hotel rooms were booked, plane tickets were purchased.

Before they left, Verlaine wanted to hear what the new drummer sounded like, so five hours were booked at Sorcerer on Friday, January 24. Kindred's fears about his own lack of studio experience turned out to be well-founded. Staring at the band through glass in the separate drum cubicle, Kindred felt as discombobulated as Eric Eidel had been; to make matters worse, Jeff would start playing songs no one had heard before. "It was so bad," Kindred recalls. "I'm like crying to myself. Headphones falling off my little head. I couldn't even begin to understand the songs to any degree."

Verlaine was even more dissatisfied with Kindred than he had been with Eidel, calling Kindred "a great-spirited guy, but his timing and dynamics were not happening in my ears at all." To compound matters, Verlaine said as much in the studio, and Kindred overheard the remark. The band didn't feel any kinder toward Verlaine, either, but Tighe says they were "feeling better about the songs. There was momentum and excitement about the future."

Based on the first batch of tapes they'd heard, both Columbia and Jeff's management were still underwhelmed by the results of the Verlaine sessions. "Sometimes Jeff would come into rehearsals and not be able to play because he had a bad meeting," says Kindred. "He'd be like, 'Why are they so fucked *up*?' " Still, everyone was sticking to plan; maybe, just maybe, something positive would emerge from Memphis.

Jeff's last week in New York before his departure for Memphis became a blur of activity. On Tuesday, February 4, he played a solo performance as part of the tenth anniversary of the Knitting Factory, the downtown club where he had gigged early in his career. Despite recurring guitar sound problems, his own complaints about his voice (he told the crowd it was "totally shot"), and nerves (Jeff was all too aware of the fact that Lou Reed was watching from the balcony), Jeff sailed through a gripping seven-song set of mostly new material. The set included a breathtaking one-man version of "The Sky Is a Landfill" (with revised lyrics, including the line, "Oh, it's not the way I was raised/I just feel us heading for darker days"), a graceful take on "Morning Theft," and a gently propulsive new love song, "Jewel Box," that he equated onstage with the '60s TV music series *Hullabaloo*. He even called his old bandmate Gary Lucas onstage for a reunion and a reprise of "Grace." Lucas had conversed with Jeff before the show, and when Jeff headed for the dressing room, Lucas says his former bandmate "turned at the top of the stairs and shot me a look of such pathos, like, 'I am in the grip of something, I'm going through so much angst right now.' I thought, 'Am I being manipulated here?' He had the ability to make people hop around him. But my heart went out to him." At the end of the set, Jeff bid adieu to the audience with a Smashing Pumpkins reference: "Despite all my rage, I'm still just a rat in a cage. Go figure."

The next day, the band reassembled for another session—with Verlaine and Jeff's friend Michael Clouse, but without Sony's knowledge—at a Chelsea studio. To Tighe, it felt as if the band were being put through a series of tests. But as the band played huddled around Kindred, sunshine drenching the room and the wood floors, the mood noticeably improved. "It was more spirited," admits Verlaine, "and some of the tunes sounded a lot better." Maybe, some thought, it was Sorcerer's configuration and ambience that had thrown everyone off.

Four days later, on Sunday, February 9, the entire band played a secret show at Arlene Grocery, a new club opened by former Sin-é owner Shane Doyle. Sin-é itself had shut down the previous November, two years after Doyle had sold it to a new owner. Arlene Grocery, a small, rectangular space with a tin ceiling, was on Stanton Street, down the street from Jeff and Rebecca Moore's first apartment. The neighborhood had become a little less daunting in those years; its influx of clubs, restaurants, and low-rent coffeehouses was even attracting tourists.

Thanks to the Internet, which Jeff had grown to loathe because of the way it let fans track his every move, word spread about the gig, and it was packed. The band went on at midnight, Jeff wearing a short black dress that Wasser had left at his apartment. (Though not a cross-dresser, Jeff prided himself on his ability to tap into his inner sensitive female. As Wasser says, "Because he grew up with all women, a lot of times he felt like a woman. He would often say I was the man and he was the woman. He was very sensual in a way a lot of women are. He was a diva.") Many of his old friends were in attendance, and it was their first sight of the new drummer and their first exposure to the new material. Most were impressed on both counts. Although their lyrics, dynamics, and chord changes were still in flux, new songs like "Nightmares by the Sea" and "Vancouver" showed promise, and the versions of "So Real" and "Lover, You Should've Come Over" felt more relaxed.

"The minute it started, it was magical," Tighe says, "and Parker sounded so good. It was wild and exuberant and unhinged." Throughout the show, Jeff yanked at his hair and complained about quitting smoking. Finally, he pulled up his shirt to reveal his smoking patch and tore it off. Someone tossed him a cigarette and, with a sly smile, he lit it up melodramatically and inhaled.

Before he left for Memphis on Tuesday, February 11, there was one last matter to attend to. At Sorcerer Sound, his friend Hal Willner had been working on a tribute album to Edgar Allan Poe, featuring a cast of characters including Marianne Faithfull, Deborah Harry, and Christopher Walken, all singing or reciting Poe stories and poems. Jeff had been procrastinating, but finally agreed to tape his contribution on the evening of Monday, February 10.

The champagne and wine were flowing freely before Jeff arrived. When he did, wearing an old gray coat, Willner thought he looked "tired and stressed out"; Faithfull, who had spent some time with Jeff during his Sin-é days, didn't even recognize her old acquaintance. Most likely Jeff was nervous about his trip into the musical and geographical unknown the following day. Nevertheless, Willner asked Jeff to read "Ulalume," Poe's impressionistic 1847 poem. The effects of smoking were again apparent; Jeff's voice sounded deeper and grainier than it ever had.

By coincidence, Allen Ginsberg was also in the studio, and the Beat poet took Jeff through the reading, instructing him on how to stress certain words and phrases. "It was so beautiful to watch," recalls Willner. Afterward, Ginsberg launched into a hilarious reading of a piece by writer Terry Southern for another of Willner's projects, leaving everyone, Jeff included, in hysterics. To Willner, it seemed to snap Jeff right out of his doldrums; the kid he had met nearly six years before had returned.

In the early morning, Jeff headed home; he had to catch a plane to Memphis in a few hours. Later, Willner listened back to the tape of Jeff's performance. A morbid meditation on lost love and death, "Ulalume" was rife with images of "scoriac rivers" and a tomb. Toward the poem's end, Jeff read, "It was surely October/On this very night of last year/That I journeyed, I journeyed down here/That I brought a dread burden down here." At the time, Willner didn't think much of it, other than feeling Jeff had given a riveting performance.

NINETEEN

*That's why he fucked up at Richard Keeling's place—HE FUCKED
UP! I don't care what anyone says. . . . It was only another mistake he
made, it was no murder, it was no real suicide, it's only that Tim's
momentum had been going all that time on 'I'm-gonna-die-no-matter-
what,' that the* dumbest *message in the world became a subconscious
language from so much practice. . . . The man was on a roll. It's so
simple . . . I don't hate him. I just think he had the whole thing
backwards on purpose so that, somehow, he could make sure he was
protected from the enemy. I don't know what it was. . . .*

—JEFF BUCKLEY, UNSENT LETTER, SUMMER 1990

Mary and Jeff took the hour-long drive from Fullerton to Huntington
Beach, an oceanside town ten miles southwest of Orange County, and
arrived at the Golden Bear just before Tim walked onstage. They took a
seat on a bench in the second row, and Mary ordered eight-year-old Jeff a
plate of spaghetti and a glass of white wine.

What Mary calls "an epiphany" had arrived a few days before, as she
flipped through a local newspaper and saw a listing for Tim's upcoming
show. It had been six years since she and her first husband had seen each
other, and nearly as long since they had spoken. Their last conversation had
taken place shortly before her marriage to Ron Moorhead, at which time
Mary claims Tim asked about a reunion with her, which she declined. "He

took that angry exchange as an excuse to never make an effort to be in our lives," Mary says. "I felt responsible for that and took the blame."

By late March 1975, though, Mary was more contrite. "I had the wind knocked out of me," she says. "I wasn't as arrogant and judgmental of him." She felt Moorhead had not turned out to be "the replacement daddy," in her words, and adds she felt "really guilty about not having done something to keep Jeff in touch with his dad. The whole purpose of that meeting was to reciprocate and approach Tim and say, 'I'm sorry.'" Before she called Tim at the club, she asked her son if he wanted to go see his father. Excitedly, he said yes.

Jeff's enthusiasm only grew as they arrived at the Golden Bear. As they sat near the stage, Jeff seemed enraptured, bouncing in his seat to the rhythms of Tim's twelve-string guitar and rock band. "Scotty was in love," Mary says. "He was immediately entranced. His little eyes were just dancing in his head." To Mary, Tim was still a dynamic performer, bouncing on his heels with his eyes shut, but she also felt he looked careworn for someone still in his twenties.

At the end of the set, no sooner had Mary asked her son if he wanted to meet his father than the kid was out of his seat and scurrying in the direction of the backstage area. As they entered the cramped dressing room, Jeff clutched his mother's long skirt. It seemed a foreign and frightening world to him, until he heard someone shout out, "Jeff!" Although no one had called him that before in his life—he was still "Scotty" to everyone— Jeff ran across the room to a table where Tim was resting after the show.

Tim hoisted his son onto his knees and began rocking him back and forth with a smile as Jeff gave his father a crash course on his life, rattling off his age, the name of his dog, his teachers, his half-brother, and other vital statistics. "I sat on his knees for 15 minutes," Jeff wrote later. "He was hot and sweaty. I kept on feeling his legs. 'Wow, you need an iceberg to cool you off!' I was very embarrassing—doing my George Carlin impression for him for no reason. *Very* embarrassing. He smiled the whole time. Me too."

Tim's drummer, Buddy Helm, was sitting next to Tim when Mary and Jeff entered and recalls the initial mood as "chilly" and somewhat awkward, since Judy was also backstage. But Helm remembers Tim being genuinely happy to see his son. "I felt there was some deep connection as far as Jeff goes," Helm recalls. "It was a very personal moment, and I was sort of embarrassed, so I dissolved into the woodwork. The kid seemed very genuine, totally in love with his dad. It was like wanting to connect. He didn't know anything personally about Tim but was there ready to do it." The same seemed to be true of Tim; after years of distance from his son, he seemed to feel it was time to re-cement whatever bond existed between them.

The proof came shortly thereafter. Before the second set began, Judy asked Mary if it would be acceptable for Jeff to spend a few days at their place: Tim would be leaving soon on tour but had some free time. Coincidentally, that weekend was the beginning of Jeff's Easter break from school, so Mary agreed. The next morning, she packed his clothes in a brown paper bag and drove her son to Santa Monica to spend his most extended period of time ever with his father.

Tim and Judy had since moved from the apartment on Venezia to a small complex called the Ocean Aire Terrace, located a few blocks from the beach. Wedged between two larger apartment buildings, the pink, four-story building at 2811 Third Street had the feel of a rundown beach resort, with its wraparound balconies and small driveway slithering up the side. As Jeff remembered it, the following five days—the first week of April 1975—were largely uneventful. "Easter vacation came around," he wrote in 1990. "I went over for a week or so, we made small talk at dinner, watched cable TV, he bought me a model airplane on one of our 'outings.' . . . Nothing much but it was kind of memorable." Three years later, he recalled it with much more bitterness: "He was working in his room, so I didn't even get to talk to him. And that was it."

Mary recalls Jeff telling her he would dash into Tim's room every morning and bounce on the bed, and Jeff's stepbrother Taylor (whom Tim had officially adopted in August 1974, four years after Tim and Judy's marriage) remembers him and Jeff running around a nearby construction site and terrorizing Taylor's pet rabbit. "Dad tried to spend as much time as he possibly could," Taylor says. "But given the rules everybody was going by, contact wasn't an often thing."

The following Thursday, Tim and Judy put Jeff on a bus out of Santa Monica, and Mary picked him up at the bus station in Fullerton. When Jeff stepped off, she noticed he was clutching a book of matches. On it, Tim had written his phone number.

On the surface, Tim's career was still not in the healthiest of conditions in the spring of 1975. He had no record contract and was living in a place Helm describes as "one of those basic seventies apartments without a lot of flashy decor," albeit many books. (Continuing his fascination with dark colors, Tim painted the bedroom black.) According to Judy, she and Tim were renting a car. Discouragingly, Tim could look around and see his old friends being rewarded with the success everyone had once predicted for him. After years of struggle, his former Venice neighbor Linda Ronstadt had fully established herself with the album *Heart Like a Wheel,* while Tim's onetime Orange County club mate Jackson Browne was in the vanguard of the singer-songwriter movement, thanks to his current album *Late for the Sky.*

Still, Tim forged on, attempting to be as upbeat as possible. The acting career that had never ignited beckoned again. When the idea for a film version of the life of Woody Guthrie made the rounds, Tim was immediately interested. On the road, he was seen carrying around a script for the movie, *Bound for Glory,* to be directed by Hal Ashby. "He was excited about it," recalls friend Wess Young. "He wanted to do it. I don't know if he felt so connected to Woody as he did to the content of the film, of the troubadour riding the rail, hobos, that kind of existence." But the film's producer, Harold Leventhal, never recalls Tim's name being mentioned for the role and says it was always intended as a vehicle for its eventual star, David Carradine. Whether Tim's participation was a misunderstanding or another fabrication remains a mystery.

There was also talk of not one but two new albums. For at least a year, Tim had been mulling over recording a series of concerts at his old haunt, the Troubadour (San Francisco was also mentioned), for a double-LP live album of songs spanning his career. He and Larry Beckett, who was by now a divorced computer programmer (and part-time poet) in Portland, had sketched out a working list of songs to be included. Of their own collaborations, they settled on "Song to the Siren"—according to Beckett, both agreed it was their finest song—as well as Tim's own "The River" and "Sing a Song for You." A few labels, including Arista, Asylum, and United Artists, were rumored to be interested in this newly recorded collection of Tim's best-known songs, his greatest non-hits, as it were. Plans were roughed out to tape the concerts later in the year.

Tim's other project would be a return to the song-cycle concept of *Goodbye and Hello,* but on a grander scale. For several years, he and Beckett had discussed turning Joseph Conrad's 1920 novel *An Outcast of the Islands* into an album. (Tim was especially fond of the 1951 film version starring Ralph Richardson.) Around 1971, John Balkin, Tim's bassist and mentor during the *Starsailor* period, had even recorded a few hours of very rough electronic music for the project. By 1975, though, the idea was back on Tim's front burner. Beckett completed the lyrics: eight songs, each based on a different character from the somewhat sodden novel, which detailed the rise and fall of Peter Willems, a clerk in a trading post on a remote island near the Philippines. "Nobody ever created a larger structure with a narrative movement made up of lyrics and with a very hip structure," Beckett says. "To do it in the rock or pop genre would have been most exciting."

Beckett wasn't entirely right; story-driven concept albums like the Who's *Tommy* and the Pretty Things' *S.F. Sorrow* already existed, but Tim's *Outcast* project—with "The" replacing "An" in the title—had grander literary and musical ambitions. The novel's tropical setting meant Tim could return to the vibes-driven feel of his *Happy Sad* period, and Beckett was planning to read portions of the novel between tracks. "It was going to be difficult to negotiate for the ordinary audience member," Beckett confesses. "It wasn't a bunch of pop songs that would jump off the disc. You couldn't even follow it unless you paid attention to every word." Tim told Beckett he was writing music for the lyrics and had even made preliminary tapes. Coming on the heels of three compromised pop-rock albums, the very thought of the *Outcast* project must have struck Tim as a kind of salvation.

In the spring, Tim phoned Jerry Yester, the producer of *Goodbye and Hello*. Although the two hadn't spoken since their falling-out during the making of *Happy Sad*, Tim thought Yester could be just the man to helm the *Outcast* project, according to Beckett. Yester wasn't home when Tim called, and his wife Marlene—the same Marlene Waters with whom Tim had had a brief fling in New York eight years earlier—answered. Tim remembered her, and they talked briefly. He seemed in good spirits, and she said she would give her husband the message. By the time Yester was able to return the call, it would be too late.

While his next projects awaited financing or conceptual completion, Tim needed money to support his family, and Joe Falsia, who was Tim's de facto manager, booked a series of Midwest concerts in June. The band was still playing its slithery funk-rock and still concentrating on recent material. In Detroit, however, they redeemed *Look at the Fool* songs like "Tijuana Moon" and "Helpless" with fiery performances, and Tim even resurrected "Blue Melody." As he had in the past, Tim maintained his road regimen of avoiding drink and drugs; he was even said to have exercised before leaving home. As much as he continued to struggle with his dark side, he began working harder on repairing his physical condition.

On Saturday, June 28, he played before 1,800 at the Electric Ballroom in Dallas. "Dallas was a great place to play," Falsia recalls. "We had a great musical time. I remember a crystal ball with the lights going on in the middle of the dance floor." Helm recalls Tim as "very positive—suddenly, all the doors had opened." Calling home to Santa Monica that night, Tim spoke to Taylor, who recalls his father sounding charged. "He felt there had been a big turn-around," Taylor says. "It was like a mathematician looking for the right formula for years and finally making one little line of chicken-scratch on a chalk-board and saying, 'Oh my God, that's it.' That's the tone I heard in his voice. He sounded a lot better than he had in a long time."

But Tim had other matters on his mind that may not have been so sanguine. Either before or after the show, he called his old friend and band mate Carter Collins in San Rafael, California. Collins was happy to hear from Tim, but Tim sounded upset. He told Collins he had had a phone conversation with Judy, and that she was not feeling well for mysterious reasons (which Judy denies). Tim told Collins he was concerned and wanted to return to Los Angeles as soon as possible. "Tim was definitely concerned about what he was going to do when he got home," says Collins.

On the flight home to Los Angeles the next morning, Tim—wearing his usual blue shirt and brown corduroy pants—slept a little and had two drinks. Now that the tour was over, he could afford to indulge and not worry as much about his vocal cords. But to Falsia, he also seemed preoccupied. When the flight arrived at 3 P.M., Tim had another drink at the bar, then, according to Falsia, "disappeared. He had something on his mind." Tim's bassist, Jeff Eyrich, and his girlfriend offered Tim a ride home, and he took them up on it. "See ya later, babe," he said to drummer Helm, and left.

Eyrich assumed he would be driving Tim home to Santa Monica, but Tim asked to be taken to nearby Venice instead. On the way, he pointed out a few memorable sights: a house where Charles Manson had once lived and a few of the places he had performed (most likely the Santa Monica Civic Auditorium). It was as if he were traversing his life, to happier and more prosperous days of nearly a decade earlier.

"Pull over here," Tim eventually said. They found themselves on Breeze, a narrow, one-car-wide alley of beach houses that ran perpendicular to Venice beach. The car stopped at 31 Breeze. "If this friend of mine is home," Tim told Eyrich, "we can have a party."

It was about 5:30 P.M. Tim stepped out of the car and looked into a window of the house, but no one was home. Soon, a man in swim trunks and sunglasses emerged from behind the structure; it was Tim's old UCLA friend and ethnomusicologist Richard Keeling, who lived there. To Eyrich's surprise, Tim grabbed his bag and said he was staying, rather than going home, and Eyrich and his girlfriend drove off. The bass player later told police that Tim "was in a happy state and feeling good from the couple drinks he had." Eyrich also testified that he thought Tim had used cocaine a bit, but was mostly "very down on hard narcotics."

According to her police testimony, Jackie McGuire, a female acquaintance of Keeling's, had been at the Venice beach promenade with Keeling when Keeling said he thought he saw someone near his house. Ten or fifteen minutes later, he returned with Tim, each holding a drink. The three of them listened to beach musicians for twenty to thirty minutes before returning to Keeling's house.

Inside, again according to McGuire's statement, the three planned to go out for dinner, and McGuire put clothes on over her bathing suit. As she bent over to adjust her shoes, she saw Keeling enter from the kitchen holding what she called a "small white packet." Keeling supposedly emptied the packet and its brown powder onto a shiny stone on the coffeetable. McGuire noticed a couple of one-dollar bills on the floor, and when she asked Tim if the money was his, he said yes. He then took one of the bills, rolled it up, bent over the coffee table, and snorted up the powder.

Tim stood up to leave, but he was "very unsteady on his feet," according to McGuire's statement; he bumped into the coffeetable and, on the way out, the front door. In the alley outside, McGuire and Keeling helped Tim into the front passenger seat of Keeling's car. McGuire sat between them, and Tim slumped to the side, his head falling on her shoulder. To McGuire, he appeared to be asleep.

At that point, about 6:30 P.M., Keeling and McGuire decided it best to take Tim home, so they took the five-minute drive from 31 Breeze to Tim's apartment on Third Street. When they arrived, Tim stepped out and nearly fell in the driveway. As he mumbled incoherently, Keeling and McGuire propped him up and began carrying him up the slatted stairs leading to the second floor, where he and Judy lived. Tim tried to continue on to the third floor, but wound up falling down and crawling on his hands and knees.

When Judy opened the door, Tim "appeared to be in a very intoxicated or sedated state," as she told the police three days later. Although Judy did not recall hearing Tim say a word, McGuire overheard him jokingly mutter something like "lights out" before he fell to the floor and passed out. According to the initial police investigation, Keeling and McGuire helped carry Tim into the bedroom (at Judy's request) and quickly left. "Judy said she was used to seeing him like that," Collins says. "We all were. In those late days of Seconal and downers, Tim would just pass out." Judy intended to let Tim sleep it off for an hour and a half.

According to McGuire's statement, Judy asked McGuire and Keeling what had happened and was told by McGuire that Tim had "done some stuff." Added Keeling, "Don't worry, it's not enough to hurt him. He'll be all right."

As Tim slept, Judy later told police that she sat in bed next to him, watching television. (She says she was under the impression he was merely drunk.) When she turned him over, about an hour later—approximately 7:40 P.M.—Tim's skin felt clammy, and he had turned blue.

At about 8 P.M. (according to McGuire's statement and alluded to in Judy's), Judy called Keeling, saying, "Please come over"; she thought Tim was dead. Keeling and McGuire raced back to Third Street and found Tim lying unconscious in bed. Opening his shirt, they attempted to revive him, but Tim's breathing did not resume. Luckily, a paramedic from the Santa Monica Fire Department happened to live in the complex. As Judy screamed hysterically in the living room, the paramedic attempted to resuscitate Tim with paddles that deliver DC current to the heart, but he too had no success. (Clearly traumatized by the incident, Judy now insists it was Keeling and Michael Cavanaugh—son of Lee Underwood's former girlfriend Jennifer Stace—who brought Tim over, rather than Jackie McGuire, and that "they said that he was drunk and they put him to bed to take a nap. I did call Richard and he said that Tim had taken pills." Also conflicting with her initial police statement in 1975, she says that "Richard had disappeared right away after dropping Tim off and never came back.")

An ambulance soon arrived to transport Tim to Santa Monica Emergency Hospital, where he was pronounced dead at 9:42 P.M. on Sunday, June 29. His last words were said to be "Bye, bye, baby," delivered in a singsong tone. The line and its delivery could have come from Ray Charles's disconsolate "Drifting Blues," one of Tim's favorite Charles songs. He was twenty-eight.

Taylor, then twelve, had gone to see *Jaws*, a huge hit movie that summer, with Judy's sister Michelle and her boyfriend, Tim's former drummer

Maury Baker. All three returned to 2811 Third Street shortly after the body had been taken away. Taylor, Baker recalls, "went totally bananas." Stunned friends and family—including Tim's mother and sister, Jennifer Stace, Artie Leichter, and Falsia—began solemnly making their way to the apartment. Upon receiving the news in Portland, Beckett cried for nearly an entire day.

The next day, Mary received a phone call from Herb Cohen, who, in his typically to-the-point manner, said, "Tim's dead. You better tell the kid." Jeff had been spending the weekend with his stepfather Ron Moorhead in Carbon Canyon, in the southern part of San Bernardino County, and Mary immediately drove over so Jeff wouldn't hear the news from anyone else. Mary and Moorhead took Jeff into the woodsy backyard terrace and sat him down on a stone wall. Mary told him what had happened to his biological father, and Jeff began crying. Afterward, according to Mary, "He said the most amazing thing. He sort of sat there, sobbing a little bit, and said, 'Well, I guess it'll just go back to being the way it was before.'"

Recalling a later conversation with Jeff, Moorhead says, "He was sad, but he also realized this was an individual who wasn't big in his life. It was like losing a distant uncle, if you will." The different recollections could have been yet another result of Jeff's own deeply conflicted views toward Tim, even at the age of eight. Fifteen years later, Jeff attempted to write to a Tim fan who had sent him an article about his father, but he began crying as he wrote. "I haven't lost it completely, though," he wrote to another friend right after, "not since '75 and someone showed me the obituary. I could take it then because I was a small boy and because he didn't quite mean much to me— just enough."

The obituary he may have seen was the Associated Press newswire report picked up by the *Los Angeles Times* on July 1. The brief article listed Tim's cause of death as "a heart attack" and noted that "Mr. Buckley was noted for his recordings of his own compositions of 'Sweet Surrender,' 'Pleasant Street,' and 'Move with Us.'" It was darkly appropriate that those three songs were hardly three of Tim's most famous, and one of them— "Move with Me"—was given the wrong title. "He rose to popularity as a teen-ager and was signed by Electra [*sic*] Records to write and record his own songs and ballads," read the article. "As he grew older, his work became more experimental and his popularity declined." The article stated Tim was survived by a widow, Judy, and a son, Taylor. In those and subsequent reports, there was no mention of any Jeff.

TWENTY

*What is it that I'm supposed to find? I don't know what to do. I don't
know. All I know is me. All I know is what I had before I ever spent the
night in his living room. I don't know anything. Mother, father,
grandma, auntie, son, wife, nothing but splinters, one and all.
Someone who knew him sent me his death certificate. My grandfather's
as well. Splinters, one and all. Who's next?*

—JEFF BUCKLEY, LETTER TO A FRIEND, JUNE 13, 1990

Northwest Airlines flight 779 touched down on the runway of Memphis
International Airport shortly after 1 P.M. on Tuesday, February 11, 1997.
Dispersing into two rental cars, Jeff, his three musicians, and Tom Verlaine cruised into downtown Memphis, winding up at an unremarkable,
hotel-style building at 109 North Main called the Claridge House Apartments. Except for Verlaine, who had his own room, the four musicians
doubled up in the furnished apartments, each of which had a kitchen and
color television. They were less than inspired by the Claridge, finding
both the corporate-style housing and the surrounding district of office
buildings and parking garages less than stimulating, and Tighe immediately contracted the flu; he hadn't been so sick since childhood.

Still, Jeff felt comfortable in Memphis, attracted not only by the presence
of his friends in the Grifters but also by the city's rich cultural soil. Memphis

was forever etched in rock history as home to Elvis Presley and Sun Records, the independent label that first signed him. But dating back at least to the turn of the century, when local musician and executive W. C. Handy introduced the blues to the masses through hits like "St. Louis Blues," American music had been as much a part of the city's fabric as barbecue and soul-food joints. Labels like Stax (home to, among others, Otis Redding, William Bell, and Sam and Dave) and Hi (Al Green) were responsible for some of the greatest R&B ever made, while Indiana native B. B. King first made a name for himself as a disc jockey at Memphis's WDIA, the country's first all-black radio format. The city was immortalized in song by Chuck Berry ("Memphis"), Bob Dylan ("Stuck Inside of Mobile with the Memphis Blues Again"), Marc Cohn ("Walking in Memphis"), and country songwriter Tom T. Hall ("That's How I Got to Memphis"). Alex Chilton—the former Box Tops and Big Star leader who wrote "Kanga Roo"—was born in Memphis, which was also home base for near-mythical songwriters, producers, and musicians like Chips Moman, Dan Penn, and Jim Dickinson, as well as a developing indie-rock scene. Al Green was now the Reverend Al Green, an impassioned minister who led Sunday services at the Full Gospel Tabernacle church in town.

The city itself was nearly as compartmentalized as Jeff. Memphis was a casual sprawl of a town that stretched out its arms over 295 square miles at the southwest tip of Tennessee. Yet there was a spooky, uneasy undercurrent to its mellow ambience, as if the city didn't want anyone to grow *too* comfortable. After years of hard times, Memphis was reaping the rewards of an economic revival, evidenced by the tourists who streamed into Graceland and inhaled beer up and down Beale Street, the city's bawdy music row. Yet one-fifth of its population was unemployed. In its music alone (the blend of white and black musicians and singers at Stax, for instance), the music community was a paragon of racial tolerance. Still, its 600,000 residents, almost equally divided between black and white, seemed to live in separate, distinct parts of town.

Memphis was also separated from Manhattan by hundreds of miles, but those on Jeff's business side weren't troubled by that fact. Everyone was eager to see him back at work, and a city far removed from the diversions of New York seemed an ideal environment. "It didn't really matter *where*—just some place far from New York and not accessible by him and his friends back and forth," George Stein says. "Just get him out there someplace and give him time to himself." The news that Jeff would continue to record with

Verlaine was received with far more skepticism, especially from Columbia, and the precise nature of their work remained ambiguous. Drummer Parker Kindred was under the impression they were recording an album, but Tighe wasn't; Verlaine entered the sessions thinking they would be just another trial run, but was later told by Jeff that, yes, they actually *were* making a full-fledged album.

Despite the living conditions, the new locale initially energized everyone, especially when the band assembled at Easley Studios in late February. Built in 1967 and once owned by the Stax-Volt R&B combo the Bar-Kays, Easley was nestled in a dead-end street of semi-rundown homes in the southeast district of Memphis. The unmarked building—a two-story structure with vertical wood slats on its second-floor balcony and a wide parking lot out front—looked more like a suburban home than a workplace; there was even a Walgreen's supermarket nearby. The offbeat air extended to its folk-art lobby, which housed an Elvis shrine and a velvet painting of John Kennedy. The main recording room, with its twenty-foot ceilings and pale-green concrete walls, was bigger, cozier—and, at $650 a day, cheaper—than Sorcerer Sound in New York. Owner Doug Easley, a musician himself, was a tall, salt-and-pepper-haired man with an easygoing drawl and a mellow smile.

Working again with a small window of time, two weeks this time, the band and Verlaine had little choice but to leap into the fire. Driving from the Claridge to Easley every day, they logged twelve-hour days bearing down on Jeff's second batch of new songs, the ones that had been practiced and played at Arlene Grocery the month before. Bit by bit, the material began taking shape. With Verlaine's aid, "Nightmares by the Sea," which sounded a bit flat at the Arlene Grocery show, took on added dynamics and an ominous, burbling guitar riff; the shift from verse to chorus was sharper and lent additional power to Jeff's dark imagery ("I've loved so many times and I've drowned them all/From their coral graves, they rise up when darkness falls"). Perhaps it was the Memphis air, but "Everybody Here Wants You" evolved from a barely formed chant to a full-fledged smoky R&B croon (with Jeff transforming himself into a one-man soul-gospel ensemble by way of his own overdubbed harmonies) inspired by Jeff's love of Joan Wasser. For added inspiration, Easley propped a Barry White songbook in front of Kindred's drum kit. Often the musicians played with the studio lights turned off, and Jeff himself often ran out to buy Thai or soul food for everyone.

But even in Easley's casual atmosphere, the problems that bedeviled them in New York once more rose up and announced themselves. Verlaine remained dissatisfied with what he saw as Kindred's inconsistent drumming (leading the producer to snap "Hit it *harder!*" at Kindred, which became a band in-joke). While he felt Grondahl was a talented bass player, Verlaine wondered if his "unbelievably laid-back and not too talkative" manner (as he saw it) was due to drug use. For their part, Tighe, Kindred, and Grondahl felt as if they weren't being given enough time to develop the arrangements, thanks to the abbreviated recording schedule and Verlaine's own work methods. "I was psyched to work," says Kindred, "but with some takes, Tom would say, 'We really don't have enough time for this one,' or, 'That one sounded good—why don't you come in and listen?' And Jeff would be halfhearted about it. The whole thing was like a big aluminum ball getting crushed up."

One evening late in the sessions, head Grifter Dave Shouse and his wife Tammy visited Easley with food for the band. As they walked in, they were greeted with the sound of "Everybody Here Wants You" booming from the studio monitors. They felt as if they had accidentally wandered into a Smokey Robinson and the Miracles session; maybe the Verlaine matchup *was* working after all. But Dave Shouse also detected "a curious vibe" manifested in the sight of Doug Easley pacing, something the easygoing recording engineer only did when he was uncomfortable.

Amidst this uncertainty and tense atmosphere, Jeff didn't help the situation by relentlessly fidgeting with the songs. Never one to mechanically crank out melodies or lyrics, he continued to struggle with the songs' music and structures, and told friends he was particularly concerned about perfecting his lyrics. "Nightmares by the Sea" never settled down; just when Jeff seemed to complete the words, he would change the chord progression, and the band would have to relearn the song. According to Verlaine, Jeff wasn't happy with the final version they recorded; Tighe says Jeff was also less than satisfied with "Everybody Here Wants You," feeling it was too conventional and not yet his own. One of the few songs everyone liked was the *qawwali*-infused mantra "New Year's Prayer," which developed from a simple Kindred drumbeat into an everyone-joining-in repeated vamp. While Jeff was realizing his goal of not merely reproducing *Grace*—these recordings were more stripped down and less opulent—the diffuse sound of each song made it glaringly evident he had yet to find a focused substitute for it.

At the Claridge one evening, the band gathered in Grondahl and Tighe's fourteenth-floor room to listen to the tapes. It was a less-than-exuberant experience. "We were all sitting and bumming," Kindred recalls. "Tom and Doug got good sounds, but the energy was just gray." Before the music ended, Jeff walked out and went to his room one floor up, where he paced back and forth, unable to even talk. In the days after, he grew increasingly withdrawn.

In early March, Steve Berkowitz and Dave Lory, Jeff's comanager, flew down to Memphis to survey the progress. ("I had to justify Verlaine to the company," says Berkowitz.) From their perspective, the recordings were still lacking a certain spark (although the songs were tighter), and it was at times difficult to ascertain exactly *what* songs had even been taped. Jeff was especially concerned that Berkowitz not hear "Very Sexy" (later retitled "Yard of Blonde Girls"), a simple, grunge-inflected grinder written by musician Audrey Clark (of the band the 360s) and her poet sister Lori Kramer. Inger Lorre, who was friendly with Clark, had written a few extra verses and had played an early version of the song to Jeff in 1996, and the two recorded a rough take of it for her own pending solo album. According to Lorre, Jeff particularly liked lines like "gold sharks glittering," which he interpreted as being a reference to the music industry.

In Memphis, Jeff and the band recorded the song fast, in two quick takes. But knowing Berkowitz was on the way, and fearing the label would glom onto the song the way it did "Forget Her," Jeff asked Verlaine to hide the tape. "This was a song everybody was saying they loved because it was so much *fun,* and that he didn't actually write," Verlaine says. "Maybe he was a little offended." On the appointed day, Berkowitz arrived at Easley and, while waiting three hours for Jeff and Verlaine to show up, came upon the tape logs. Later, Jeff and Verlaine ran down the songs that had been recorded without knowing Berkowitz had seen a complete list, and when the A&R man asked about the missing songs (which included "Very Sexy"), there was dead silence in the room. Jeff shot Verlaine a glance, began to tear up, and stormed out of the studio and into the parking lot. Recalls Verlaine, "I went to Steve and said, 'I knew you were gonna do that,' and he said, 'I had to. It's my job. I have to look at everything.' I didn't blame him. I knew it was corporation stuff at that point." Outside, Jeff and Berkowitz took a walk around the block, Jeff crying and saying he needed "more time" to finish the songs but shaking his head when Verlaine's name was mentioned. "He was now realizing how the songs could be, and he realized Tom wasn't the guy," says Berkowitz. "It was crushing to him that it wasn't Verlaine."

Shortly after, Jeff congregated with the band and Wasser at the midtown P&H Café and told them they would finish working with Verlaine in the allotted time, but that this phase of the project was over. He never said whether or not he felt let down by the band or Verlaine; instead, he blamed himself for not being prepared. Berkowitz and Jeff's management were also said to have pulled the plug on the sessions after realizing Jeff had already spent at least $354,000 on the Verlaine and Sag Harbor sessions with little releasable work to show for it. But, friends wondered, was Jeff the problem, or was the limited time allotted for the sessions a guarantee history would repeat itself? Knowing his reputation as a perfectionist in the studio, did Columbia realize he would never be satisfied with the results of such curtailed studio work, thereby subtly sabotaging the Verlaine sessions? Given Jeff's tendency to convey varying messages to people in his life, no one could answer those questions with any degree of certainty.

After the last session, the band prepared to fly home. But they would do so without Jeff, who announced he was going to remain in Memphis to woodshed and would send for them in due time. "I felt strange about leaving him," says Tighe. "I'd say, 'Okay, the plan is that you'll be here for a month and then we'll come down?' And he'd say, 'Yeah, maybe, but I might need more time.'" On the morning of March 10, their departure day, the band piled into an elevator of the Claridge as Jeff stood in the hallway, smiling and waving. "Bye, guys—I love you!" he said. Then the elevator door closed.

As it turned out, Jeff's work was not yet done. For three days after the band departed, he and Verlaine returned to Easley and continued tweaking the recordings. Playing all the instruments himself, Jeff recorded "Opened Once," a lovely sigh of a ballad ("I am a railroad track abandoned/With the sunset forgetting I ever happened"), along with a two-minute screaming, ranting punk tune. "My opinion was that the guy was much better without the band," Verlaine says. "They weren't holding him back. But his desire to get stuff right with them was taking time."

Driving back and forth to the studio in Verlaine's rented Chevy Corsica, the two men finally had time to talk. Jeff told Verlaine about the events of the past year, such as the Courtney Love incident ("He said that's the moment he realized what media-manipulated people were like") and his fleeting experimentation with heroin ("He said he got off it real quick because he saw what could happen"). Discussing the tapes they had just completed, Verlaine asked, "You're not happy with any of this, are you?"

Jeff laughed and, according to Verlaine, replied, "No. It's totally my fault. I've been so lazy and on the road. Don't blame yourself for any of this. You're doing a great job. I see what I have to do." He told Verlaine he was going to stay in town another week to spend time with friends.

The morning Verlaine left, in the middle of March, the two met for breakfast at the Grid Iron, a coffee shop adjacent to the Claridge that had become Jeff's preferred downtown eatery; the black waitresses always greeted him warmly. As he had throughout the sessions, Verlaine warned Jeff about the tapes. "Sooner or later someday somebody might put it out," Verlaine told him over coffee. "Anything in that studio now can be released. If anything should happen, you're gonna have lawyers, managers, everybody, arguing, but they'll put it out and then let you sue them. That's the nature of this business. If you don't want any of that shit out, you'd better go in tomorrow and erase it."

Jeff acknowledged Verlaine's comments with a simple "yeah, yeah."

He was alone now, and he needed to live somewhere homier than the Claridge. Months before, on his first exploratory trip to Memphis and Easley, he had met Robert Gordon, a local author and journalist who lived on North Rembert Street, a quiet, inconspicuous block close to the Memphis Zoo and a golf course. Gordon dropped by Easley during Jeff's final work days with Verlaine, and when Jeff told him he had decided to stay in Memphis, Gordon mentioned a house for rent on his block. When Jeff discovered that the home in question was already rented, the landlady, a spunky blonde named Pat O'Brien, told him there was another available, a white cottage with a black shingle roof at 91, for $450 a month.

Jeff instantly adored the cozy, unpretentious structure. Part of the reason, perhaps, may have been its familiarity: Both the working-class block and the house itself were reminiscent of the street in Fullerton, California, where he had lived with his mother and Ron Moorhead. There, they had briefly been a happy family, and Jeff had first fully discovered his love of music in that house. He asked for a three-month lease for 91 North Rembert, and although O'Brien generally didn't agree to such short rental periods, she had a good feeling about the quiet stranger, who told her he was a musician and needed to be alone to work.

Jeff moved in so fast, on a weekend in late March, that he had no electricity or heat the first night. He didn't seem to mind, nor did he seem initially concerned by the lack of furniture. Fortunately, his new friends in

Memphis—Gordon, O'Brien, the Shouses, and Andrea Lisle, a pert writer, music aficionado, and employee of Shangri-La Records, a nearby record store—realized he needed to have *something* in the house and began dropping by with castoff furniture, cutlery, and dishes. Realizing Jeff didn't have anything to sleep on, Dave Shouse gave him a king-size piece of foam that looked like an oversized egg carton; it could be folded over into something resembling a thin mattress. It became Jeff's one and only bed, and he moved it nightly from room to room. The Shouses also gave him a green, crushed-velvet couch that became the principal piece of furniture in the living room, along with a wood chair and a milk crate holding Jeff's four-track recorder (a tape deck with which one could over-dub multiple voices and instruments). A fan with light bulbs extended down from the living room ceiling, and nails where paintings had once been hung punctured its walls. From his bedroom in the back, he could glance out and see only a bricked-up house next door.

When Jeff's friends heard about his accommodations, particularly the lack of a real mattress, some grew concerned: It seemed further proof that Jeff didn't quite know how to nurture and replenish himself. (One visiting friend found the refrigerator stocked with only milk, cereal, and orange juice.) For Jeff, though, the monk-like existence was precisely the point; it symbolized his focus on music over lifestyle. He told Gordon the results of the Verlaine sessions were too "New York brittle," that he wanted something less angry. The house on Rembert seemed the ideal place to refine that concept.

The relaxed feel of the city, especially the midtown section where he lived, proved a gradual restorative. "His mentality fit in really well down here," says Shouse. "Hanging out, living simple, taking it easy." Since Jeff did not yet have a Tennessee driver's license, he took to walking around town, just as he had done in New York. Lisle says he was like "a kitten, going from house to house. We'd feed him and a couple of hours later he'd show up at Robert's house and Robert would feed him." Memphis's sprawling layout was not expressly designed for strolling, but within a few blocks of his house were Shangri-La Records, an inexpensive Vietnamese restaurant called Saigon Le, and the Memphis Zoo. Long fond of butterflies—it had been his nickname for Rebecca Moore—he became a frequent visitor to the zoo's fenced-in exhibit, where he could sit on a bench and watch sundry species of butterflies flutter around him. He bought a mountain bike and cycled over to Saigon Le for take-out so often that the owners gave him a restaurant T-shirt. One day, a customer remarked great it was that Saigon Le had hired that rock star Jeff Buckley as its de ery boy.

He took to wearing his usual baggy slacks and the sleeveless white T-shirts known gruesomely down South as "wife-beaters." He loved the thrift stores where he could buy shirts for a few dollars. He cut back on smoking and stopped dying his hair, allowing it to return to its natural brown. One morning, Gordon knocked on Jeff's door, and Jeff answered covered head to toe in sawdust; he had offered to sand the floor in the hallway for his landlady. Still covered in dust, he and Gordon walked to Huey's, a nearby hamburger joint, for lunch. Jeff also accompanied O'Brien to a local Wal-Mart, where he bought a frying pan and a new pair of cheap black combat boots. "I was like, 'What do you want them ugly boots for?'" O'Brien says. Jeff bought them anyway; later, O'Brien heard it was commonplace for musicians to wear that type of shoe.

He was anonymous, and liked it that way. Once, he and Lisle went to a midtown bar, where Jeff dropped some change into the jukebox, selected Barbra Streisand's "People," and, sitting atop the bar, began singing along. "Now, honey," said the female barkeep, "you have to be a real *good* singer to do that kind of song." Jeff just laughed. Another time, Lisle introduced him to friends who had never heard of a pop star named Jeff Buckley. He told them he had just moved to Memphis, and the female acquaintance asked, "Where do you work?" When Jeff replied "home," she brightly responded, "Oh—*telemarketing*?" Jeff giggled and didn't answer. Lisle also took him to Ellen's Soul Food Restaurant, where he ordered fried chicken *and* lasagna and everyone from the kitchen emerged to watch this thin little white boy polish off both plates.

He would, from time to time, talk about his career and the business. He said he felt "used" by Sony and was considering hiring new managers. "He was frustrated by the amount of baggage, not being able to do anything without calling four or five people," says Lisle. He would talk to the Shouses about, in Dave Shouse's words, "keeping your sanity, when the label wants you to be *this* thing and you don't, and people want you to be *this* thing and you don't." (Visiting the Grifters in a studio, where the band was having difficulties with a producer who wanted to polish up their next album, Jeff remarked, "They're trying to Sonyize it!") He seemed happier just to visit Lisle's home and play with her dog while singing Metallica songs opera-style, or drop by Gordon's house up the block and imitate the gurgling sounds of the Gordons' months-old baby Lila, or dance to James Brown records at Green's Lounge near the airport.

One warm evening in late April, the Gordons invited him for dinner at their house up the block. Jeff arrived almost an hour early, wearing a new green suit and two-tone shoes. ("I like to dress for dinner," he told them.) After the meal, Gordon and Jeff sat on lawn chairs in the backyard. It was a clear, beautiful spring evening. Jeff settled back, looked up—and leapt out of his chair, pointing to the sky.

"My God—what's *that*?" he said. It was a star, Gordon replied. For a minute, Gordon thought he was pulling his leg, but Jeff was completely serious.

He never asked about the Mississippi River, and no one ever warned him about it; anyone who lived in Memphis knew the brown muck with the strong undertow wasn't safe, and assumed everyone else knew that, too. If Jeff had brought it up, his friends would have, at the very least, told him of far more scenic and safer areas to swim, a half hour away. But it was not yet summer, and the topic never came up.

Gradually, Jeff reimmersed himself in his work, this time with an intensity and focus he only rarely achieved in New York. His living room and attic became a clutter of electric guitars, his tape recorder, piles of notes with fragments of lyrics, and stacks of cassettes. He began honing a new batch of songs, rawer and more intricate than the ones he had laid down with Verlaine; to imitate drums, he stomped his foot on the hardwood floor. For fun, he recorded his own version of "Back in N.Y.C.," the miniature rock opera from Genesis's *The Lamb Lies Down on Broadway,* one of the favorite albums from his adolescence.

In his occasionally distasteful job as Sony Music company representative, Steve Berkowitz returned several times to Memphis to check up on his charge. According to friends, Jeff appeared to be somewhat irritated by his A&R man, who became a living, breathing symbol of a ticking clock. ("I was the coach," counters Berkowitz. "It's easy to hate the coach.") The two men also had newly divergent musical interests. When they had first met and worked together five years earlier, Jeff and Berkowitz had similar tastes, but Berkowitz was not as keen on indie rock as Jeff was now.

Berkowitz himself sensed Jeff's wariness about the visits, but during his last trip to Memphis, the week of April 29, Berkowitz also sensed positive change. The two went for long walks, played pool, and ate ribs together. One evening on Beale Street, a scraggly street vendor asked if they wanted to buy some tapes and held up a box of Columbia cassettes—recent releases from the likes of Michael Bolton and Willie Nelson that looked suspiciously as if they had been lifted off a truck. Berkowitz wanted to move on, but Jeff paused, asked how much, pulled about six dollars from his pants, and bought the tapes. "Do you know how much blank tape is?" Jeff told Berkowitz. "I just got ten tapes to record on!" Soon, his own new songs and guitar noises were recorded over Bolton's voice, which, given the earlier comparison to Bolton that had so upset him, particularly delighted him.

When Jeff played his new tapes for Berkowitz at the house on North Rembert, the A&R man heard a breakthrough. The guitar noises and loops that had emerged during the Sag Harbor jams had begun to make sense, and rough songs Berkowitz had first heard in the summer of 1996—"Gunshot Glitter," "Murder Suicide Meteor Slave," "Demon John"—had, in his mind, coalesced. "He was done," Berkowitz says, "and he was a completely different person that week. The four-tracks were the greatest stuff he ever did. He was on the verge of making a major record, like *Sgt. Pepper*." As he played Berkowitz the four-track tapes, Jeff said he intended to record some of them with his band and others with his friends the Grifters.

The day before Berkowitz returned to New York, he and Jeff took another long hike, eventually winding up downtown near the monorail to Mud Island. Jeff asked if he wanted to go swimming.

"Where?" Berkowitz replied.

"Here," Jeff said, indicating the Wolf River below.

Berkowitz looked down at the garbage-strewn shore and the thick, muddy water and said, "You can't swim here! It's really *funky*!"

Jeff replied that he had done it a few times before and that it was "refreshing." Berkowitz still declined, saying he wasn't about to wade in that water, and neither should Jeff.

In terms of working out his new material, though, the house was not enough; he needed to hone them onstage, to an audience. On their second day in Memphis, Jeff and the band had played two low-key shows at Barrister's, a club in a downtown alley, to warm up for the Verlaine sessions. The venue (so named because of all the law firms in the area) was unadorned and clammy; it had a high ceiling but a small stage a few feet off the ground, and held only a few hundred people. Still, Jeff liked its bare-boned ambience. Almost as if he were consciously attempting to re-create his formative years in New York, he approached the owners to see if he could play every Monday night, just as he had at Sin-é. They agreed, and Jeff's weekly gigs began March 31. To get to the club, he would take a bus or call a friend for a ride, usually at the last minute; no one could say no. At his shows, he occasionally played a *Grace* song—mostly upon request—and covers, like "Hallelujah" and Nina Simone's "Wild Is the Wind." But he wanted to live with the new songs, and with each show his unaccompanied electric guitar—again, a connection to the Sin-é period— sounded fuzzier and rawer. He didn't mind if only a handful of people showed up and paid the $5 cover.

Joan Wasser made monthly, weeklong visits to Memphis throughout the spring. With each trip, she noticed Jeff seemed a little calmer. With the permission of his landlords, he had let the grass in his front yard grow wild, and he and Wasser would lie in it, feeling the sun hit them and tiny green insects crawl over them ("like tiny massages," she says). For days afterward, neighbors would see imprints of bodies in the tall weeds. "In New York, he'd be staring at his feet, stressing about something," Wasser says. "He had to be reminded that there's another world; it's not always down, it's also up. There's the vastness of the sky there *for* you. In Memphis, I really felt that opening up." Her instinct was borne out not only in Jeff's new appreciation of nature but in the way he allowed Wasser to paint his toenails green, his favorite color. He'd always been touchy about his feet—the result of a childhood ingrown toenail—and didn't even like to take off his shoes. For her, the toenail-painting session was one of the most positive signs of all.

During one visit, he wanted to play Wasser some of the tapes he had been making. When she mentioned he could actually buy *speakers* for the tape deck, he said he hadn't thought of it, and the two walked to a nearby audio store and bought a pair of used ones. As they sat on the wood floor of the living room, Jeff blasted his reworked version of "Murder Suicide Meteor Slave." The music filled the house, and Jeff seemed elated as the song—*his* song, *his* work—reverberated through the cottage.

Simultaneously, his thoughts were increasingly turning inward. Left to his own mental devices, he had a tendency to overthink situations and previous mistakes. Now, alone in his house, he delved even deeper into his past. One night at the Gordon house, he mentioned that at thirty, he was now older than his father had been at his death. "He said it was important to him," Gordon says. "It was liberating to him that he had outlived his father." It was also intimidating; by the time Tim died, he had made nine albums, and Jeff had only one under his belt. Still, Jeff seemed at peace with Tim's ghost for perhaps the first time in his life; he told friends he had begun to fathom his father's motives for leaving him and his mother, for the call of music and career, for the mistakes of youth. Starting the previous summer, his friend Penny Arcade noticed Tim coming up in Jeff's conversations more. "His realization was that he was starting to feel sorry toward his father for having been so hard on him," she says. "He'd say, 'Gee, maybe I don't know *anything*—I don't know what to believe anymore. And how can I find out?'"

He recognized the legacy of death, alcoholism, violence, and general weirdness in his lineage, and to understand it further, he began shifting his focus beyond the Buckleys and to his mother's side of the family. He hadn't seen his maternal grandfather in over two decades, and he grew intensely curious about him and the true story of the Guibert family. "He had very mixed feelings about his grandfather," Wasser says. "But he also felt, in a way, very related to him, being a *man* in this family. He had been to Ireland, but he was also curious about Panama. He felt it was one of the missing links. He would say, 'My grandfather's gone, Tim's dead, and I have this ball of fire in me and I don't know what to do with it.'"

"The Guibert family that remained in the States shoveled all the dirt on my father—the dysfunction of the family, the emotional and physical abuse," says Mary. "My father became a whipping boy for that, and Jeff wasn't satisfied with that as a conclusion. He wanted to give his grandfather an opportunity to tell his side of the story."

To satisfy his curiosity, Jeff told Wasser that as soon as he finished the album, the two of them would visit Panama and track down his grandfather, and Jeff hoped any lingering, troubling questions about his heritage would finally be resolved. More than once that spring, Wasser heard him use the same phrase: "My blood is cursed."

Little by little, the songs that had been crystallizing for at least a year were coming together, and it was time to start making plans. Upon his return to New York, Berkowitz sent a status-report memo to Columbia president Don Ienner, informing him Jeff was "well energized," commenting on Jeff's "monastic" lifestyle (one of the CDs in evidence was Pat Boone's album of heavy-metal covers), and indicating that plans to record the second album were underway, with either Andy Wallace or Soul Coughing producer Steve Fisk at the helm. In his written response, Ienner asked if

Steve Lillywhite or Brendan O'Brien were still possibilities. Initially, Jeff wanted to produce the record himself, but Lory, among others, felt it best he had a partner, and Wallace's name shot to the fore. Jeff was concerned that Wallace would treat him like the studio newcomer he had been four years before but nevertheless agreed; there was, in fact, little choice.

In the middle of May, Wallace flew down to Memphis to inspect Easley and talk with Jeff about the project. Wearing a T-shirt and baggy pants, Jeff met the producer in the elegant lobby of the Peabody Hotel in downtown Memphis. Over the course of a three-hour talk, Jeff seemed enthusiastic; discussing the previous sessions, he said he had liked Verlaine as a person but that the chemistry hadn't been what he had hoped. When Wallace asked Jeff what he was looking for in his next record, Jeff told him he felt it should be "a road map for people who were lost in love." ("I was expecting, although I probably shouldn't have, a more finite description of what he wanted to do," Wallace says. "I thought, 'Oh, great.' But it made sense in a way.") To Wallace, it appeared as if Jeff had reached a conclusion: that while he loved his band, he had to be in the artistic driver's seat. Wallace made plans to return to Memphis on June 23 to start work, and stay through August 14.

On Monday, May 19, Jeff took an eight-hour bus ride to Atlanta to see Wasser and her friend Mary Timony of Helium perform. As usual, he told no one in New York of his plans. He and Wasser had only an evening and morning together, but they had grown accustomed to such a lifestyle, and at the very least it felt good to see each other. Jeff told her he wanted her to move to Memphis as well. The next morning, they dropped him off at a bus station in Atlanta for the ride back to Memphis, waiting until he stepped aboard to make sure he didn't flake out and miss it. It would be the last time Wasser would see him.

Back in New York, Tighe, Grondahl, and Kindred felt in limbo. They would talk with Jeff on a regular basis—especially Tighe, who remained the closest to him—and ask when they were returning to Memphis. One month had already stretched to nearly three. Finally, an answer of sorts arrived Thursday, May 22, when a batch of tapes (one per man) arrived at Grondahl's apartment. They congregated at the apartment and played the tape, which was labeled "My Sweetheart the Drunk—Rough Demos for My Boys."

The tapes *were* rough—mostly waves of Jeff's scraping, brittle electric guitars and his own multiple singing parts—but they were also harsher and more wild-eyed than anything he'd ever done, a barrage of musical exorcisms. In "Gunshot Glitter," he lacerated himself as a "paranoia politician diva," and "Murder Suicide Meteor Slave" made references to his thoughts on his family ("You know it's not long for you/Sick of all the vomit childhood/Not a trampoline for the freaks/Not even a slave to your father/You're a slave to it all now"). Although there were gentle moments—the midtempo numbers "Jewel Box" and the in-development "Thousand Fold"—the careening complexity of much of the music and the knotty arrangements seemed to match Jeff's own probing mental state. The images were like buckshot, some violent, some reflective. In the most beautiful song, "I Know We Could Be So Happy Baby (If We Wanted to Be)," the line "hang your ruined letters out to dry" apparently referred to a bundle of mail from Rebecca Moore that had been soaked by a broken pipe in his New York apartment. When the tape ended, recalls Kindred, "we sat there with our mouths open."

"When I heard those, I thought, 'Oh, *that's* the sound—he's realized what I felt was hovering around,'" recalls Tighe. "They had those huge sonic landscapes that were extreme but very raw, not polished." There was also a track labeled "Mystery Treat": his original, 1990 demo of "Last Goodbye" (aka "Unforgiven"). The band laughed along with it, partly out of relief; it seemed to demonstrate that Jeff could still have a sense of humor about himself.

Plans were cemented for the band to fly down the following Thursday, May 29; they would stay at his house and finally start *and* finish the second album, with a planned wrap-up date of July 22. Jeff told them that two days after they arrived, cheese-rock kings and queen Styx and Pat Benatar were scheduled to play at the Mud Island amphitheater, and they should all go.

He had acknowledged the ball of fire within him, but he had not quelled it, and sometimes he had no choice but to give in to it. As he had for most of the last two months, Jeff was scheduled to play Barrister's on Monday, May 26. He called his friend Tammy Shouse at 10:30 P.M. to ask for a ride; he had attempted to bicycle down to the club with his guitar on his back but had given up. Even when they arrived at the club, Jeff, who was dressed in a gray suit, sat in her car another half hour writing in his journal. Later, Shouse noticed red glitter from the notebook sprinkled all over her front seat.

With fifty or sixty people in the club, Jeff started his set over an hour late and, according to Gayle Kelemen, a fervent fan who ran an unofficial

Jeff Buckley Web site and was in the Barrister's audience that night, delivered an "aggressive" performance. "His attitude was real sneering," she recalls. He seemed to be stabbing his guitar strings harder than ever. Although some felt he had lately become more accepting of the *idea* of fame, Jeff remained dubious of the Internet and guarded about his life. The sight of diehard fans who had traveled long-distance to see him (like Kelemen) set off something inside him. As he stood at the club's jukebox after the show, Kelemen remarked that Jeff hadn't played two songs she had requested. In response, Jeff screamed at her for ten minutes, things like "This is my private life!" or "I'm not on TV—I'm a person!" and asking her if she was "happy or sad" that one of her other favorite musicians (a member of the band Brainiac) had just died. Everyone remaining in Barrister's watched silently. Refusing to let Kelemen leave, he grabbed her and began slow-dancing with her. Shaken, she left soon after.

"He jumped down her throat pretty hardcore," remembers Shouse. "Jeff felt this was his sanctuary and she had entered it, and it was off-limits. I felt bad for her, but I felt bad for him too. He wanted to make a point with her, and it was the best way he could do that." At 4 A.M., by which time Jeff had lipsynched to a Pixies album on the jukebox, he and Shouse left and drove to her cozy, wood-floored house located a few blocks from Jeff's own. Wired, Jeff began watching the film version of the Who's *Tommy* on television.

Shouse fell asleep; when she awoke, Jeff was still sitting there, eight empty bottles of ginseng spread before him. "The older you get, the less sleep you need," he said. Then, his guitar slung over his back, he walked home. On the way, he ran into his neighbor Robert Gordon. Jeff told him he had been having a hard time sleeping since he stopped smoking, and that he had been walking all night.

Early in the afternoon of Tuesday, May 27, Tammy Shouse stopped by Jeff's house to join him for lunch. By then, he had showered and put on a suit. Despite the rising late-May warmth, he buttoned the shirt up to the top, and his face was beet-red from the heat of the shower. Together, they sat for several hours at the nearly empty Saigon Le, Jeff talking nonstop in what Shouse could only describe as "symbolic, code-like" language; she couldn't understand a word he was saying. "When the pace slowed down for him, he got more active mentally," she says. "Internally he sped up and he was able to spend more time on mental activity. On the one hand he was *more* erratic, but in another way grounded. It was a strange dichotomy."

After, they drove to the zoo and observed the butterflies and tigers (another favorite exhibit) until they were kicked out at closing time. In the late afternoon, he appeared on his bike in Gordon's driveway, returning a copy of Terry Southern's *Red-Dirt Marijuana and Other Tastes* he had borrowed. He told Gordon he was planning to take his band to Green's Lounge on Saturday night and invited him along; Gordon said he would join them if his baby fell asleep.

At 5 A.M. New York time on Wednesday, May 28, an hour ahead of Memphis, Eric Eidel, Jeff's one-time drummer, was awakened by the phone. "Hey . . . it's Jeff," Eidel heard a quiet voice say. "I've been thinking about you and wanted to see if you were doing well. And to say I love you." Eidel told Jeff all was well. "He wanted to see that everything was good with me," Eidel says. "It was quick, but it seemed like it had a point."

Eidel was just one of many friends from throughout Jeff's life who received out-of-the-blue phone calls that week, many on Tuesday or Wednesday. Most were people Jeff had barely seen or spoken to in years. There was his old Sin-é pal Tom Clark, who recalls Jeff as "very laid-back, very dark." He told Clark about the Verlaine sessions, invited him down to Memphis, withdrew the invitation, and then asked Clark again. He spoke for forty-five minutes with his former Los Angeles roommate John Humphrey; in what Humphrey describes as "very flowing and very wordy" language, Jeff repeatedly used Satan as a metaphor for numerous evils and temptations in life. From Jeff's slurred speech, Humphrey wondered if his friend was "high or drinking," but Jeff called back an hour later, sounding more in control and asking for phone numbers of other friends. Another close Los Angeles friend, Daniella Sapriel, spoke with Jeff for two hours. To her, he seemed "all over the map": excited one minute, despairing the next, pessimistic about his ability to make another album the next, then boasting he would do something better than anyone had ever made. Sapriel told him not to take everything so seriously and to get out a little more. Randall Stoll, Jeff's Musicians Institute drummer pal, received a phone message but never had a chance to call back.

They were all glad to hear from him but also distressed: Was he lonely? Upset? Feeling a desire to reach out? And why now? What was *happening* in Memphis?

About an hour after his call to Eidel, he rang Rebecca Moore, who was asleep in her new downtown Manhattan apartment. They had never been completely out of touch (Jeff had played on a few tracks on her 1995 album *Admiral Charcoal's Song*) and he called her almost weekly from Memphis, but Moore knew little about Jeff's current life. This morning he sounded hopeful about the future, talked about starting a theater company in Memphis, and sang to her for almost an hour. Then he paused. "Somebody's here," he whispered. "I have to go."

It was Gene Bowen and his blue-haired friend Keith Foti. As tour manager, Bowen had been assigned the task of transporting the band's equipment—guitars, amplifiers, and the like—from New York to Memphis. Hiring his friend Foti to help him, he rented a yellow Ryder van, and the two men left New York on Tuesday night and drove nonstop to Memphis. Foti had first met Jeff two months earlier, when he and Bowen had driven down after the Verlaine sessions in order to pack up the band's gear and haul it back to New York. (Foti recalls Jeff's room at the Claridge as messy, its coffee table littered with food, wine bottles, and cigarette ashes; he also says there was "an incredible stench," as if "the window hadn't been opened in three years.") When Bowen first asked for directions to the home on North Rembert, Jeff had said, "You'll know which is my house." Sure enough, the overgrown weeds in the front yard made it easy to determine Jeff's residence.

Bowen's first plan of action was to unload the gear from the van and set it up at a rehearsal space beneath an art gallery on Young Avenue. Early in the afternoon, after Foti and Bowen had checked into a hotel, they drove to the space with Jeff and Andy Vannucci, a Barrister's employee. Jeff himself helped haul the instruments and amps down the three flights of stairs into the basement.

After Bowen and Vannucci left to run errands, Jeff and Foti planned to flail away on the drums—until they found themselves accidentally locked out of the basement. For two hours, they instead wandered around the gallery and hung out on the street, rummaging through garbage bins. At one point, Jeff climbed up a fence by the side of the building and, according to Foti, "started screaming. I couldn't understand what he was saying." (He later heard it may have been one of Jeff's new songs.) After a while, puzzled residents emerged from neighboring houses; one threatened to pummel them if they didn't shut up. Jeff and Foti talked a little about music and life, with Foti admitting to Jeff he had once tried a combination of heroin and cocaine. "Are you *crazy*?" Jeff snapped. A few hours later, Bowen returned to find Jeff and Foti sprawled out on the ground near the gallery.

In the late afternoon, they dropped Jeff off at Rembert Street and told him they'd pick him up later for dinner. When they returned, though, he was nowhere to be found. He was, apparently, a few blocks away; Robert Gordon, driving around a transient midtown area during this time, spotted Jeff talking to a cop by the side of a police car. Gordon pulled over, and Jeff hopped in, saying, "Take me home." He told Gordon the cop said Jeff looked familiar and wanted to know who he was. Jeff seemed agitated and stressed, although Gordon didn't ask why.

Around 9 P.M., Jeff wandered across the street and several houses down to the house of his landlady Pat O'Brien and her husband, Jerry Howell. The Howell-O'Brien household was lively and cheerfully chaotic, complete with live ferrets in cages in the living room. For three hours, Jeff sat in their kitchen playing an old guitar as their dog Princess nibbled at his hands and howled along; even Howell joined in, ad-libbing a song about a butterfly to Jeff's accompaniment. Howell served Jeff a vinegar-and-oil salad, and Jeff told them he had applied for a volunteer position at the Memphis Zoo and that 91 North Rembert was the first home he truly loved. After Howell went to bed after midnight, Jeff played in their backyard before heading home. On his way out the front door, he startled O'Brien by planting a kiss on her mouth.

After eating at Saigon Le, Bowen and Foti returned shortly after midnight to Jeff's house, bearing a take-out order of wheat gluten for him. The house was dark when they entered, but they heard Jeff in the bathroom. Bowen walked in to find Jeff soaking in the white wrought-iron tub, a fang-toothed grin on his face and what appeared to be blood dripping down his chin and into the water. In fact, it wasn't blood at all; Jeff was writing in one of his notebooks and had been chewing on one of the red-ink cartridges so hard it had broken open. Even after he realized Jeff wasn't bleeding, Bowen was rattled. He hadn't had much communication with Jeff since March, and he knew he was under the gun, but what exactly was going on?

Out of the tub, Jeff got dressed—in a black hat and short skirt—and played the tapes of his new songs for Bowen and Foti. Jeff asked them to sleep over, but they had already booked a hotel room; besides, the absence of actual beds in Jeff's house didn't make the offer so appealing. Jeff gave Foti his copy of *The Satanic Verses,* and the two men left.

An hour after her long conversation with Jeff earlier that day, Rebecca Moore noticed a new message on her answering machine. She hit play, and out came Jeff's groggy voice, saying, in part, "Think of me and smile.

. . . I'm gonna work my ass off, baby. . . . I'll see you on the other side."
Checking the time, she discovered he had left the message at 3 A.M.
Wednesday, about three hours before they last spoke.

At 8 A.M. on the morning of Thursday, May 29, Pat O'Brien was awakened
by a knock at her front door. To her half-asleep surprise, it was Jeff. The
landlady wondered why Jeff wasn't tired or at least in bed after staying so
late the night before, but Jeff seemed downright jolly. He said he wanted
her to meet his friends—the band—when they arrived that evening, and
she said she would stop by the next day.

In the late morning, he called Wasser. For months, Jeff had been agonizing to her about his body chemistry, his swing from careening highs to
despairing lows. Suddenly, on the phone, he sounded ecstatic. "He had all
these realizations about himself," Wasser recalls. "He realized he had manic-
depressive tendencies, chemical things that mess with your head. He was so
excited to tell me: 'Joan, guess what I realized!' He didn't feel as burdened. It
was as if he opened the door for good, completely, and could see everything—that everyone has certain tendencies to certain degrees, and your
chemistry has so much to do with your emotions and how you feel toward
life. He was bubbling over with excitement over these realizations." To
Wasser, he seemed unusually settled in that regard, almost peaceful.

Eventually, Bowen and Foti arrived at the house, this time with a rented
car for the band as well as the Ryder van. Bowen was glad to see Jeff in a different, more upbeat, frame of mind than the night before. Still, Bowen called
Tammy Shouse and asked her to recommend a local psychologist. Shouse
was shocked; although she didn't know what he was like back in New York,
Jeff's behavior during the preceding days didn't seem particularly odd to
her.

Around 1:30 P.M., Jeff told Bowen he wanted to purchase a particular car,
but hadn't yet talked to the owners about it. The three men drove over to a
gas station. Jeff pointed out an old, dilapidated vehicle with no wheels, saying he wanted to buy it, put it in his front yard, and have his stepfather Ron
Moorhead, who was an automotive-field journalist, fix it up. They walked
into the gas station office, and Jeff asked the owners, "How much for the
car?" He was told it belonged to a customer and wasn't for sale. Again Jeff
asked, "How much for the car?" Again, the attendant told him it wasn't for
sale. To Bowen's and Foti's consternation and puzzlement, Jeff continued

asking, finally storming out and walking down the block. He eventually drove the rental car back to his house while Bowen and Foti took the van.

Jeff's car-buying spree, even if it involved a car that wasn't available, was one of several errands he felt compelled to run, each revealing how much he wanted to take charge of his life and move full-time to Memphis. Next on the list was the opening of a bank account, at a branch inside the nearby Piggly Wiggly supermarket. Before he left the Rembert house, he emerged from his bedroom wearing a wool sport jacket, a green shirt, and a bright wide orange tie. "When you go to the bank, you have to look respectable," he said. During his last few months in New York and in Memphis, he had begun wearing suits more often; they were, for him, symbolic of his transformation into a man who was now taking on adult responsibilities.

Bowen drove Jeff to the supermarket, and they opened the account. Around 5 P.M., back at the house, Jeff told Bowen he needed cash—$9,000 specifically—to fix up his house, and that he wanted to buy it; Bowen made a mental note to stop by the landlady's house later that night to inquire about cost and availability. Jeff called his accountant, Victor Wlodinguer, who was perplexed by the request: Jeff wanted a substantial chunk of money to fix up a *rented* house? Wlodinguer got back on the phone with Bowen and told him it would cost too much to have the funds wired instantly to Memphis via Western Union and that he would instead send it down in the morning (pending approval from Lory and Stein, who were equally hesitant to send Jeff that amount of cash). Nonetheless, after Bowen hung up, Jeff asked Bowen to take him back to the Piggly Wiggly. After waiting on a huge line of customers who were having their paychecks cashed, Bowen asked Jeff why they were there, and Jeff said he was waiting for his money to be wired. The misunderstanding cleared up, Bowen left Jeff at the food store and returned to the house. He had more errands to run, and asked Foti to pick Jeff up at the supermarket in the van.

When Foti arrived at the Piggly Wiggly shortly before 7 P.M., Jeff was seated at the cappuccino bar near the front of the store. On the counter, he had piled a stack of goods—CDs, dog biscuits, plants, toys. "Foti, can you stay there and watch all this stuff?" he asked. Foti obliged, and Jeff went to make a phone call. Foti then watched as his new friend wandered from aisle to aisle, picking up random food or merchandise and dropping it on the counter. Eventually, a store manager approached them and asked if they were planning to purchase the pile, at which point Jeff asked Foti if he wanted a plant. Foti declined. Jeff returned everything to its respective aisle and, with the little cash he had, bought the box of dog biscuits. On the ride home, he and Foti munched on them.

After they had arrived back at 91 North Rembert, between 7:15 and 7:30 P.M., Andrea Lisle stopped by on her way to a casino in nearby Tunica, Mississippi. Jeff had always wanted to join her on a casino trip, but he told her he couldn't tonight; the band was flying in. He seemed so excited by their pending arrival that he gave Lisle a huge kiss on the mouth. He told her that he and Foti were going to play drums at the rehearsal space; to Lisle, he seemed equally animated by the thought of making a loud racket in a private room. He then asked her to visit later that night, after she returned from the casino.

Not long after, between 7:30 and 8 P.M., Jeff changed into his jeans and T-shirt for the trip to the Young Avenue practice space. Foti recalls Bowen asking Jeff if he knew where he was going, and Jeff saying, "Yeah, I know where it is." Bowen said, "You sure?"

"Yeah," Jeff said. They drove off moments later.

After Jeff and Foti had left, Bowen went back to his business of preparing the house for the band's arrival. The spare mattresses eventually arrived. After 8 P.M. he left for the airport, which was a half hour away. The plane touched down a little later than its scheduled 9:08 P.M. arrival time. To Tighe, Bowen seemed unusually quiet as they drove back to Jeff's house.

When Bowen and the band walked in, there was no sign of Jeff or Foti, which seemed odd; they should have been back by now. For a few minutes, the band looked around the house, which was strewn with Jeff's shoes and clothes and his fork-impaled carton of half-eaten Vietnamese food.

Bowen noticed the answering machine light was blinking. When he hit "play," all he heard was an upset-sounding Foti saying something about the water, followed by a string of unintelligible comments.

Bowen didn't have a chance to play the other messages when the phone rang. It was Foti. "I'm down at the water," he said. "Something's happened—Jeff's missing."

Bowen wasn't alarmed at first; Jeff *always* seemed to be truant. But Foti told him this was different. The next voice Bowen heard on the line was that of a police officer, who told him he had best head down to the river.

*   *   *

After calling out Jeff's name for nearly fifteen minutes, Foti realized something was seriously wrong and scrambled back up the river incline to the Welcome Center, where he banged on its closed doors until an employee let him in. At 9:22 P.M., he called 911, and the first police units arrived at the river shortly thereafter. Sergeant Mary Grace Johnson, a seventeen-year veteran of the Memphis police force, was driving toward her downtown precinct in her unmarked car when the call came through on channel six: Helicopters and police were needed at the Welcome Center. By the time Johnson arrived at 10:38 P.M., the area around the center was swarming with helicopters and reporters. A kid with blue hair and aqua pants who appeared to be in a state of shock was being questioned by another officer about drug or alcohol use, which he denied.

When Bowen, Tighe, Grondahl, and Kindred arrived, they quietly surveyed the ominous scene, hands in their front pockets. "There's helicopters and it's nighttime and there are flashing lights everywhere, and we're like, 'Oh *God*, man,'" says Kindred. "You look out into this bay and it's pitch black. At that moment, he was gone." After being gently informed by police that the search would continue but that the river current was dangerous, they returned to Rembert Street but were unable to sleep; they kept hoping Jeff would walk in, wet and smiling. "That night was a nightmare," Kindred says. "A nightmare."

Shortly after midnight, there was a knock on the door. It was Andrea Lisle, who was taking her dog for a walk and stopping by to tell Jeff about her trip.

"Who is it?" asked someone behind the door. Lisle announced her name and heard angry voices inside, followed by, "Who's with you?" Lisle said she was alone.

"Go away," went a voice inside. "Come back tomorrow." Lisle thought Jeff was having an argument with his band and returned home.

By half past midnight, Jeff's body had not been found, and the calls began going out: to his mother Mary Guibert in California and to business associates, who in turn called friends. Many had a similar reaction, both that night and over the following few days: Jeff always seemed to be missing—what was the big deal this time? Some wondered if he had decided to relieve himself of work pressures by disappearing for a day or two. There was a brief, but easily dismissed, rumor of a hoax.

As soon as Jeff was reported missing, Lory ordered all of Jeff's possessions, especially recordings, scooped up. Foti, among others, was ordered
to grab anything and everything in the house on Rembert; someone was
dispatched to Sorcerer Sound in New York for the tapes of the Verlaine
sessions. Jeff's friend Inger Lorre, who was staying in his apartment in
New York, was relocated to a hotel while Jack Bookbinder, Lory's assistant, confiscated diaries, tapes, and miscellaneous personal belongings. In
the low-ceilinged attic of 91 North Rembert, the band came across a
temple-like scenario complete with skull candles and notebooks in which,
according to Tighe, Jeff wrote about "transition and reincarnation and
becoming molecules and rain."

Although the Memphis police continued their search on Friday, now
with the help of scuba divers, it was becoming horrifyingly clear Jeff would
not be emerging from the depths of the Wolf River. By the afternoon, most of
Jeff's circle in New York—Wasser, Stein, Berkowitz—had flown down;
Guibert and her sister Peggy arrived from California; Lory flew in from Ireland. Stein and Berkowitz asked Foti to take them to the spot at the river. As
they took in the sight and attempted to comprehend what had happened, a
police boat slowly passed by, its officers trolling the water for a body with the
aid of a long pole.

For the next three days, everyone congregated in stunned silence at the
little house on Rembert Street as friends stopped by with food and sympa-
thy. The Memphis police, most of whom had never heard of Jeff before, were
swamped with calls from around the world. Taylor Buckley, Tim's adopted
son, phoned authorities, asking to be notified when the body was found, but
Mary Guibert insisted to the police that "none of the victim's items . . . be
released to Taylor Buckley." On Monday, June 2, four days after his disap-
pearance, Columbia issued a press release: "Jeff Buckley Still Missing As
Search Continues; Family and Friends Believe He Has Drowned." There
was little else to hope for at that point. On sundry stages around the world,
U2, R.E.M., and Bush dedicated songs in his honor. "I remember lying out
in the driveway in the gravel and seeing the clouds move really swiftly in the
sky," Tighe recalls, "and I got the sense he was moving on." Except for
Bowen, who stayed behind to close up the house and attend to other duties,
everyone began flying back to New York.

At 4:40 P.M. on Wednesday, June 4, a passenger on the American
Queen riverboat near the mouth of the Mississippi informed two crew
members that something appeared to be floating in the water between

Mud Island and the riverbank. The boat employees used a lifeboat to move closer and discovered a body caught in an eddy of branches. Called to the scene, members of the fire department pulled the body ashore as Sergeant Johnson, who immediately drove to the riverbank, attempted to block photographers from taking pictures of the body with the swollen face. Just after 7 P.M., Bowen identified the body; he recognized not only Jeff's face and hands but the gold earring in his belly button. Jeff's Venice Quartz watch was still ticking.

Everyone was struck by two details. After six days in the water, Jeff's body had surfaced mere hours after his closest friends had left town. ("It's almost as if he spared them," says Nathan Larson.) Also, he had drifted up not at the precise place he had drowned—which, according to police, was often the case—but at the slope of Beale Street, a symbol of both Memphis's cultural heritage and American music. It felt like the final verse of a long and darkly poetic folk song.

TWENTY-ONE

In the best tradition of the Irish, Tim's casket was open. At 7:30 P.M. on July 2, 1975, two hundred friends, family members, and fellow musicians gathered at the Wilshire Funeral Home Chapel in Santa Monica to bid farewell, Tim dressed in a black silk shirt handmade by Judy. Grief-stricken, his mother Elaine approached the casket, brushed aside a strand of hair from her son's forehead one last time, and sadly said, "My sweet little curly-haired boy." Emmett Chapman, one of the many musicians in attendance, glanced around and saw a roomful of "all these beautiful, sobbing young women." Approaching the podium to begin his eulogy, Lee Underwood looked down at his late friend and noticed that facial hair had begun sprouting up through Tim's makeup. Underwood then read "Fern Hill," Dylan Thomas's lyrical rumination on the idyllic nature of youth and its inevitable finale.

Dressed in black, Judy sat somberly on a hard-backed chair in the front row as twelve-year-old Taylor attempted to comprehend the loss of another father. "What are we gonna do now?" he was overheard to say. "How are we gonna get food to eat?" Eventually, Tim's drummer, Buddy Helm, escorted Taylor outside to distract him. The other son, Jeffrey Scott, and his mother Mary were nowhere to be seen, since they were not invited. ("There was a lot of confusion," Judy says. "It was chaos. It was simply a mistake.")

Up north in Portland, Oregon, Larry Beckett—who didn't believe in funerals and refused to attend Tim's—had a chilling realization. Less than a month earlier, Beckett had mailed Tim lyrics to potential new songs. In particular, Tim had asked his recurring collaborator to write a lyric based around one line, "I'm walking on the clouds"; he told Beckett it expressed the way he felt when he took heroin. In turn, Beckett wrote the cautionary "On the Hook," with one verse that read: "I saw the gypsy woman and drank her rum and coke/'You'll never be a dream,' she said, ''till you go up in smoke.'" When Beckett heard Tim had been cremated after the funeral, he realized his friend had himself literally gone up in smoke.

In the days after, police interviewed nearly everyone who had been in contact with Tim during the last day of his life, but one of them, Richard Keeling, proved to be elusive. After Jackie McGuire told police that Keeling had brought drugs into the living room (and after Judy Buckley told detectives that Keeling had visited her two days after Tim's death, begging her not to authorize an autopsy), police tracked down and arrested Keeling on July 3 in an office at UCLA, where he was employed as a research assistant in the music department. Behind bars, Keeling declined to talk to authorities, only telling them he didn't use drugs "as he is a health addict, works out, and keeps himself physically fit," according to the police report.

By coincidence, the office of the Los Angeles medical examiner issued its findings the same day. The immediate cause of death was determined not to be a heart attack, as was initially reported, but rather "acute heroin-morphine and ethanol intoxication" due to "inhalation and ingestion of overdose"—in essence, a combination of heroin and alcohol. (Heroin turns into morphine upon entering the bloodstream.) A total of 3.31 milligrams of morphine, enough in itself to kill anyone, was discovered in his blood, and another 0.2 milligrams in his bile. The amount of alcohol in his system was 0.13 percent, equal to four glasses of wine or beer. No needle marks were found, nor any indication of ingestion of barbiturates. The death was deemed accidental.

When word spread of the cause of Tim's death, most of his friends and band members were genuinely surprised. Many knew or suspected Tim had dabbled in heroin, but most saw him as more of a drinker than hardcore drug abuser. Some, including Underwood, speculated Tim's system collapsed *because* he hadn't done that many drugs in a while; his body was on the mend but had been weakened by years of excess. The plans Tim was making for future albums would seem to support that claim, yet others felt he was on a downward spiral no one would have been able to halt. "He wanted to die," says friend Artie Leichter. "There's no doubt in my mind that death held a great fascination for him. There's no way he could have grown old." Beckett concurs: "What Tim did was walk on the edge of a cliff until he fell off. It was going to happen sooner or later. In his not-really-taking-responsibility-for-anything way, that was the way out."

On October 2, Keeling, who had no previous criminal record, was charged with one count of murder and a second of furnishing heroin. Making the charges stick, though, wasn't so simple. As his lawyer, James Epstein, recalls, "Simply giving someone drugs is not endangering human life." A report by the district attorney stated that "the prosecution cannot establish that defendant actually gave the victim the heroin by way of an offer, but merely set it out and the victim helped himself. The facts thus lend themselves to an interpretation that defendant intended only he and Jackie McGuire use the heroin, because defendant knew the victim didn't use the stuff." (In her police testimony, McGuire also stated Keeling told her the heroin in the packet "was returned to him by an unknown party that he had previously sold it to. He stated that the unknown party told Keeling that it was wet. . . . Keeling then told McGuire, 'If it was wet, it should have lost some of its potency, that it should not have hurt Buckley.'") The fact that Keeling and Tim had a "friendly relationship" and that there had been "no conversation at all" between the two before Tim took his fatal snort also aided Keeling, as did the fact that Tim's previously consumed alcohol contributed to the overdose. At a hearing at the Superior Court of California in Santa Monica on November 25, Keeling pleaded guilty to a lesser charge of involuntary manslaughter. The following March, he received a five-year probation and ultimately served 120 days in jail.

To some, the events of that day were straightforward enough: "There wasn't any mystery or controversy," says drummer Maury Baker. "It was pretty straight-ahead." To others, though, there were too many holes in the story, too many inconsistencies. Why had Tim gone to Keeling's rather than directly home? Did he think Judy might be there? Did Keeling owe him money? Did Tim simply want to get stoned? Did he want to shower and shave before he returned to Judy (which, according to friend Wess Young, Tim sometimes did after he returned from the road)? Did—as Judy believes—Tim think he was snorting cocaine rather than heroin, thus explaining the massive intake? Why, according to a police report, had "the paramedics treated him for a possible barbiturate overdose rather than heroin"? (Judy says the rescue workers "found some pills in his pocket, so I thought it was a combination of that and alcohol.") According to substance-abuse specialists, the alternate treatment should not have had any impact on Tim's system, yet the scenario nonetheless planted further conspiracy seeds in certain minds. Stories also made the rounds that Tim had arrived at Keeling's home and began banging on his bedroom door while Keeling was having sex with a woman, and that Tim then snorted up whatever drug was in sight as a way to irritate Keeling. (Keeling himself declines comment on the entire incident.) In keeping with the enigma of his family history, it would never be fully determined if Tim's overdose was accidental or a subconscious form of suicide. All that seemed clear was that he had spent his life pushing the limits until the limits pushed back one time too many.

Theories aside, the reality of the situation was that Tim's rental car was immediately confiscated, and Judy and Taylor were not able to collect on Tim's $25,000 life insurance policy because the Buckleys had not had enough money for the monthly payments. Elaine Buckley was so distraught that she destroyed every photo of her son in her possession, including childhood snapshots. Within a few years of his death, nearly all his albums were deleted from the catalogs of his record companies. The few songwriting royalties that trickled in for the albums made after Tim and Judy's wedding went to Judy; royalties for albums recorded before their marriage were divided among Judy, Taylor, and Jeff, Judy receiving 50 percent and Jeff and Taylor splitting the remaining half.

Several days after Tim's funeral, Wess Young and Taylor pulled out of Marina del Rey harbor in a friend's motorboat. Judy had asked Young to give her late husband a burial at sea, and Young agreed, taking along young Taylor.

About a half mile past the break point, Young cut the engine and turned to Taylor. "Okay, Taylor," he said. "It's your deal, pal. Do what you gotta do."

Taylor opened the small cardboard box he had been carrying and pulled out Tim's ashes, which were in a clear plastic bag tied with a wire twist. Stoically, Taylor opened the bag and, as the ashes began pouring out into the water, turned to Young and grinned. "You know," Taylor said, "it's a hell of a way to treat your old man." Young thought the crack was perfect; Tim himself would have appreciated the mordant humor of it all.

On the way back, the boat's motor broke down, and Taylor and Young had to be towed in.

*   *   *

In the concise words of the autopsy conducted at the University of Tennessee in Memphis, "death was [due] to drowning" in the matter of Jeff Buckley, and "no evidence of other injuries is seen." Verifying Keith Foti's (and Gene Bowen's) statements to the police about the events of the preceding two days, Jeff's blood tested negative for drugs, and only a small amount of alcohol—0.04 milligrams, enough for one glass of wine or a beer—was found in the body. Before the body was cremated, Jeff's family requested a DNA sample be extracted "to test against any bogus paternity suits against the victim," according to the police report. "The victim has traveled around the world and is very well known in France and Australia."

Phone calls flew back and forth between Jeff's numbed friends and family as fans gathered outside Sin-é for a vigil; a distraught Inger Lorre arrived with some of Jeff's clothes from his apartment and passed them out. At first, the only uncloudy facts were the most basic. According to Memphis authorities, the wake created by the tugboat that passed Jeff by was most likely overpowering, especially for an irregular swimmer who had been in the river for fifteen minutes wearing water-logged jeans and boots (albeit lightweight ones purchased at Wal-Mart). On tour in Australia, he had been spotted in at least one hotel pool wearing black jeans, so perhaps the idea of wading in clothes in a river didn't strike him as unusual. Before the cremation, police removed several items from the left rear pocket of his pants: a bottle opener and two key rings with a total of forty-three keys (which he collected, as evidenced by the artwork of *Grace*). Although the keys were not especially heavy, they nonetheless increased Jeff's body weight. There was no evidence of foul play, and the case was closed.

With Jeff's ashes propped next to him, Bowen drove the Ryder van back up to New York. At a wake in comanager George Stein's Upper East Side apartment, the box was passed around, and one of the participants, drummer Parker Kindred, noticed something odd. "There was some heat from it," he says. "I couldn't quite figure it out. It was really strange."

To Kindred, Michael Tighe, and Mick Grondahl, even stranger were the tape-listening sessions that began within weeks after the body appeared, as Columbia's Steve Berkowitz, producer Andy Wallace, and comanager Dave Lory began sifting through all the recordings Jeff had left behind. It was emotional and, in some cases, arduous work; once, they found themselves playing an entire Michael Bolton cassette in order to unearth the one or two songs Jeff had recorded atop it. In their eyes, someone had to catalog the music he had made before the fateful swim. "In the beginning, it was all about protecting," maintains Stein. "It was *never* about exploitation."

To the band, though, the scenario was abhorrent. Kindred in particular says Jeff told them he wanted to burn the Verlaine tapes once the actual second album was complete. "Whether it was actually going to happen or not," Kindred says, "the answer was 'yes' in my mind." For Michael Tighe, the listening dates were "way too soon for me, so I was wary of everyone in that camp in dealing with the record. The whole thing seemed nuts."

Although everyone insists there were no concrete plans to release the tapes to the public, Sony gave Wallace a mastering date for August, and an album consisting of the ten Verlaine tracks—and using Jeff's working title of *My Sweetheart the Drunk*—was penciled in on Columbia's release schedule for October, barely five months after Jeff's death (it was subsequently bumped to November). "They were not the final manifestation," Wallace says in defense of the tapes, "but there was nothing wrong or embarrassing or tentative in my mind about those recordings." Lory and Stein claim they were opposed to a release so early; regarding a possible October unveiling, Stein says, "You had to put something down in case it *was* going to happen, just to cover our bases if somebody in marketing said, 'Yes, there are plans.' " He also claims "Columbia or somebody" mentioned music would have to be released in the fall in order to have the album be considered for a Grammy the following year. ("Everybody Here Wants You," the single eventually released, was in fact nominated in the rock-male-vocal category in 1999; Jeff lost to Lenny Kravitz.)

However, the plan abruptly shut down due to the reappearance of Mary Guibert. At the time of Jeff's death, his mother was living in a small apartment in the Orange County community of Tustin, where she worked as a contract specialist for a PPO, a health-care network of physicians and hospitals. She had recently begun taking acting lessons again in an effort to restart her long-stalled thespian career. Flying to Memphis and then New York, the maternal figure whom few of Jeff's business associates and friends knew gradually began taking charge of his affairs. The road was almost instantly bumpy. On June 11, an informal memorial spearheaded by several of Jeff's friends, including Penny Arcade and Nicholas Hill, took place at St. Mark's Church in the East Village. On the way back from planning a memorial of her own, Guibert (and Stein) stopped by the church in a car, but Guibert declined to enter, only offering a printed statement to be read. "I didn't understand," Stein says. "It was a tribute to her son. I don't know why Mary felt so challenged by it." In response, Guibert says, "They demanded my presence at this impromptu thing, and I was not ready to do anything." Either way, the organizers felt bewildered and slighted.

Guibert's own memorial took place over two days—July 31 for a private service, August 1 for the public—at St. Ann's, the Brooklyn church where Jeff had given his first New York performance six years earlier, singing his father's songs. Part funeral, part musical gala, it included performances by Elvis Costello, Marianne Faithfull, Irish balladeer and friend Katell Keineg (who sang one of Jeff's favorite songs, "Calling You"), and Rebecca Moore (who sang the Jayhawks' "The Man Who Loved Life"), as well as an instrumental requiem by Tighe, Kindred, Joan Wasser, and Nathan Larson. Guibert read from her "Golden Promise" (in honor of Jeff, she asked everyone to "look into your soul and find a Promise you can keep that would make this world a better place"); Lou Reed's lawyer gave St. Ann's' Susan Feldman permission to read his Velvet Underground–era ballad "I'll Be Your Mirror." The original cost of the funeral, $20,000, was trimmed when Guibert was led to believe it would be included in Jeff's recoupable fund to Sony. So, despite the summer heat, St. Ann's sliced $7,000 off the budget by canceling the air conditioning and purchasing handheld fans instead. (Jeff's finances at the time of his death amounted to $7,000 in a bank account and two certificates of deposit of $20,000 each.) Yet another memorial was held at the same Anaheim chapel where Tim and Mary had married. High-school and Los Angeles friends paid their respects as an organist played Procol Harum's "A Whiter Shade of Pale."

Problems between Guibert and Jeff's management loomed during the planning of the St. Ann's memorial. Guibert accused them of making it a "business opportunity" by inviting numerous record industry executives; counters Stein, "Dave and I prepared an industry list because they didn't have a clue who should be invited, who had a role—the record companies, the agents, people who really cared about Jeff." Immediately after the service, Guibert's role only grew larger. The service, she says, "was my first inkling I was going to have a problem with Dave [Lory] that was going to interfere with my ability to execute what I wanted. I thought he was manageable at first; as long as he was going to do my bidding, then he would be okay. But he had other things in mind." Initially, Stein says he and Lory were under the impression Guibert *wanted* them to continue running

Jeff's business affairs: "After Jeff's death, she actually said to Dave and me, 'I don't know much about this business, and you guys were always taking care of everything and that's the way it's going to continue.' It was a very clear statement. She was the mother, she was grieving, she knew nothing about the business. And we proceeded exactly that way."

Nonetheless, Guibert felt she was increasingly kept out of the loop regarding a posthumous album: "First they were copying it and then they were sorting it—there was always an excuse." In August, she hired her own lawyer and began communicating with Lory and Stein only through him. The following month, the album was put on hold when Guibert's attorney delivered a letter to Columbia halting its release and asking for more time to decide its contents. Columbia concurred, Berkowitz was off the project, and a new A&R man (Columbia veteran Don DeVito) was assigned to the task. Guibert was now in charge, and Stein and Lory were, in essence, dismissed.

Over the next few months, Guibert and DeVito decided to expand the album to a two-disc package—one of the Verlaine sessions, another of the homemade four-track tapes to let fans hear the material Jeff had in mind for the sessions that never were. Even then, little seemed to run smoothly at first. Wallace and Stein had never felt the four-tracks should be included; the band felt *only* those tapes were worthy of release, since Jeff was so dissatisfied with the Verlaine productions; Wasser initially felt *nothing* should be put out. Lory suggested having an all-star line-up of Jeff admirers—Chris Cornell, Jimmy Page, Robert Plant, and others—record their own versions of the demos as a sort of tribute album. Concerned that their input was being ignored, Tighe, Wasser, and Larson wrote a strongly worded media statement expressing their concerns. "The band had no power," says Wasser. "We all felt very very protective. So we just wrote down everything we remembered him saying in case there was some sort of release, just to make it clear to the press. I felt I owed it to Jeff to preserve his vision." Fearing reprisals from Sony and other industry powers, they opted not to distribute it. Complicating matters for Larson was a letter his band, Shudder to Think, received from Columbia lawyers. It stated that "I Want Someone Badly," an R&B-style track they and Jeff had recorded together in 1996 for an independent film called *First Love, Last Rites,* could be included in the movie but *not* on a soundtrack album, as it was now the label's property. Eventually a deal was struck whereby the song did appear on the album, but everyone felt the long arm of the corporate music world reaching out to them.

During the completion of the album Guibert decided to call *Sketches for My Sweetheart the Drunk,* Tighe felt the four-tracks should be released exactly as they sounded on Jeff's noise-imbued homemade tapes; others felt they should be sonically cleaned up, which Tighe considered a violation. Guibert invited Soundgarden singer Chris Cornell, an acquaintance of Jeff's, to help with the project, and after listening to the tapes, he offered his opinions on which mixes of the tapes sounded best. In early 1998, Cornell flew to New York, walked into a Sony studio, and witnessed some of the dissension. That same day, he received a call in the studio from his wife and manager, Susan Silver: She had been bitten by their dog, and Cornell instantly flew home to Seattle.

Given Jeff was not married, had no children, and did not have a surviving father, Guibert had a legal right to run the estate. Yet the scenario struck some of his friends as peculiar in light of a falling-out that had taken place between mother and son in late 1996. It began when Guibert went on-line and responded to fans' questions about Jeff's personal life, including the Courtney Love incident and his friendship with Elizabeth Fraser. Upset by her actions and what he saw as the Internet's invasion of his privacy in general, Jeff temporarily detached himself from his mother, telling close friends he wanted a "divorce." ("I had no idea what I was doing when I posted that," Guibert admits. "It was a stupid mistake.") During his months in Memphis, he and Guibert had slowly repaired the breach, even speaking by phone for two hours ten days before he died, but the incident left many of Jeff's associates wary of her. Counters Guibert, "If someone tries to tell me they had an intimate relationship with my son, *but* believes I should be the last person in the world who should handle his work, I'll have to doubt they really had an intimate relationship with my son."

Unfortunately, it was only one case of the rancorous finger-pointing and side-taking that ran concurrent with plans for a posthumous album. Many acquaintances from Jeff's early days in New York blamed Jeff's management and label for wreaking havoc with his mental and physical state, while the business end countered that Jeff was always handled with care and that the accusations were the embittered words of those Jeff had left behind in the course of his career. "It was people competing for the zone closest to him or being the most intimate with him," Tighe says of that period. "He had so many different types of friends and personalities revolving around him that it makes sense that there would be a lot of hostility and confusion." For his part, Tighe wept whenever he picked up his guitar, while Grondahl, deeply shaken by the loss, suffered greatly follow-ing Jeff's death and subsequently checked himself into rehab.

Even when the two-disc album was released (on May 19, 1998, in the United States and a week earlier in Europe and Australia), the controversies did not end. Guibert's decision to include reprints of Jeff's journals, as well as his apologetic letter to Bob Dylan, was greeted with some skepticism. "That was really private," Berkowitz says of the Dylan note. "That was not a public event. I question the taste of having that in the album packaging." ("It was a personal message to Bob," Guibert counters.) Guibert did, however, have any mention of Tim stricken from the liner notes.

Some friends and family were still so grief-stricken that it took months, in some cases over a year, before they could listen to the album at all. When they did hear it, most—the band in particular—realized there was little reason to be ashamed. The qualms that both Jeff and the business side had with the Verlaine productions were easy enough to hear and understand: "New Year's Prayer" is more a mood mantra than a com-pleted song; the occasionally overbaked, unfocused lyrics (such as the media evisceration of "The Sky Is a Landfill") reveal Jeff was still in the midst of sharpening his thoughts; and some of the tracks (like "Witches' Rave") feel thin and tentative, especially compared to the relative opu-lence of *Grace*. Yet there is no denying the soaring tumult of "The Sky Is a Landfill," the kicky interplay between guitars and drums that salvages the still-formative "Vancouver," or the honey-smoked soul of "Everybody Here Wants You." The intimacy of "Opened Once" and "Morning Theft" is accentuated by the songs' pared-down, voice-and-guitar settings. Over-all, the disc of the Verlaine recordings, culled from both the Memphis and New York sessions, feels surprisingly accomplished, especially for such exploratory recordings. Hearing them only reinforced the sense that Jeff's loss—to the music community, at the very least—was tragic.

The rawness of the four-track tapes on the second half makes for diffi-cult listening, and no one will ever know how Wallace and Jeff's band would have transformed ravaged mini-epics like "Murder Suicide Meteor Slave" and "Gunshot Glitter" into polished studio productions. (Whether they would have resulted in a more commercial second album than *Grace* is another question entirely.) Yet the tapes provide bewitching glimpses into Jeff's creative process and mental anguish, and even in such primitive settings, the songs' musicality shines through, from the gothic radiance of "I Know We Could Be So Happy Baby (If We Wanted to Be)" to the bad-boy strut of "Your Flesh Is So Nice" to the shining "Jewel Box." *Sketches for My Sweetheart the Drunk* isn't the album Jeff wanted to make or have heard, but it will have to do.

Many years after he had said goodbye, Tim returned to say hello once more. Starting in the mid-'80s, when the British collective This Mortal Coil recorded three of his songs, Tim's stock as both an innovator and tragic, doomed cult figure began to rise. (Ironically, the singer on one of the This Mortal Coil covers, "Song to the Siren," was none other than the Cocteau Twins' Elizabeth Fraser, with whom Jeff would later have a romantic relationship.) He had never had a chance to become a movie star, but his music began appearing in films, including *Coming Home* and *Twenty Four Seven.* In keeping with technology's increasing role in pop, he would even be electronically sampled: bits of "Song to the Siren" and "Dream Letter" were woven into recordings by Everything But the Girl and Dot Allison, respectively. In 1999, his longtime admirer Chrissie Hynde saluted him with a cover of "Morning Glory"; that same year, the Rhino label began an ambitious reissue campaign to dust off his out-of-print albums and unveil archival material. In the fall, the label released *Works in Progress,* an educational set of unreleased recordings from the transitional, folk-to-jazz period between *Goodbye and Hello* and *Happy Sad,* and an assemblage of UK musicians, including Mojave 3 and a former member of the Cocteaus, contributed to a Tim tribute album. In the early '90s, his estate sued Herb Cohen for back payment of royalties and reached an out-of-court settlement. Tim had also left behind a debt of $106,000 to Warner Brothers and Elektra, and into the '90s, funds were deducted from Judy's royalty statements until the bill was paid off.

The clashes between Mary Guibert and Jeff's management did not end with the release of *Sketches for My Sweetheart the Drunk.* In July 1998, Stein sent a bill to Guibert for $2,612.50 for costs involved in organizing affairs after Jeff's death, such as phone calls to Memphis police and the coroner, terminating the lease on Jeff's New York apartment, and obtaining death certificates, dental records, and an autopsy report. He and Lory then filed a breach-of-contract suit against her; they felt they were entitled to 15 percent of all income derived from all of Jeff's work created during the term of the management contract—in other words, all the music Jeff made during his lifetime. ("Manager's post-term commissions," read the contract, "shall be as follows: 15 percent of gross earnings accruing in connection with the release of the first three albums featured Artist released subsequent to the execution of this agreement.") In turn, Guibert felt the pact was void as soon as Jeff's body was found, and sued Lory and Stein for any of Jeff's tapes and journals they supposedly had in their possession. As of mid-2000, Guibert and Jeff's former managers had not spoken in nearly three years, and despite the appointment of an independent arbiter, settlements and hearings were still in the works.

It was both business *and* personal between both parties, a fact born out by the relatively small amount of money generated by *Sketches for My Sweetheart the Drunk.* In its first week in stores in the United States, eighteen thousand copies were snapped up, and the album entered the *Billboard* chart at number 62. The reviews were sympathetic, and sales as of late 1999 were a respectable, if not groundbreaking, 100,000. Abroad, *Sketches* entered the Australian chart at number 1 and eventually went platinum (after selling sixty-five thousand copies), and Sony moved approximately fifty thousand copies each in the United Kingdom and France. (A music video for "Everybody Here Wants You"—ironically, the song Jeff told friends he didn't want Columbia to hear, fearing they would make it a single—was cobbled together, featuring a plot of a woman alone in an airport lounge as Jeff's image flickered on the bar's television.) But given the total *Sketches* sales figures, the 15 percent commission Lory and Stein felt they deserved would have amounted to only in the neighborhood of $30,000.

As the legal costs and friction mounted, Jeff's family and friends were left to comprehend what had happened on that moist, breezy night in Memphis. Exactly what was he doing in the water that night? In light of the tumultuous events of the preceding year, what had been his state of mind? Could someone else—namely, Bowen—have prevented him from entering the river? Did the very awe in which Jeff was held by his handlers make him feel so invincible that jumping into dangerous waters didn't seem life-threatening? In the days before, why had he placed so many calls to so many people from throughout his life? *Sketches for My Sweetheart the Drunk* didn't make the questions any easier to answer. The lyrics were rife with foreboding imagery: "Stay with me under these waves tonight/Be free for once in your life tonight," from "Nightmares by the Sea," curdled the blood the most. Among the other eerie snippets: "I float just like a bubble headed for a spike" ("Witches' Rave"); "leave your office, run past your funeral" ("New Year's Prayer"); "ah, the calm below that poisoned river wild" ("You & I"); "I am the ghost who comes and goes" ("I Know

We Could Be So Happy Baby [If We Wanted to Be]"). Jeff had never been an easy one to decipher in life; understanding him in death was proving to be equally difficult.

The eerie coincidence of father and son passing away at roughly the same age was noted in nearly every obituary, and everyone knew how much the son would have loathed the analogy. He had spent his entire life avoiding comparisons and establishing his own persona, and now they abounded in death. Yet whether out of grief, solace, or an attempt to comprehend the incomprehensible, many closest to him turned to the idea of fate. Supposedly telltale signs from the past were dug up and interpreted, from the numerous references to mortality in songs dating back to "Eternal Life" to the way the tone of his conversations could veer from supremely confident to utterly desolate. ("I know how that feels—to feel pressed down all the time," he commented forlornly four years earlier. "A lot of times I don't feel like I belong here. . . . I'm sick of the world. I'm trying to stay alive.")

"In the last couple of years, there was always a sense of him going to leave," says friend and photographer Merri Cyr. "That isn't to say he was suicidal. It's not that clear. It's the pervasiveness of the myth, and the myth was that he was conditioned to be his father. He was following the same path because that's what he thought was his fate. And I don't think he felt he could fight his fate." Cyr feels part of Jeff willingly gave in to that myth; others, like Wasser, feel larger forces were at work over which he had no control: "I really feel like he was feeling his destiny working at that time. He felt the momentum getting faster and faster."

The fact that Jeff had returned to the Memphis studio with Verlaine after the band went home lent an additional air of mystery to the scenario. "That's the strange thing about all of this," Tighe says. "Why would he polish it if he was not going to use the stuff? In hindsight, it seems there was something directing him. He felt an urgency to get this stuff down. I can't help but think there was something, not on a conscious level, telling him time was short." Tammy Shouse says Jeff told her he had begun dreaming about his own death two weeks before it actually occurred. "When he died, there was this feeling that you knew it was coming, in a way," adds Larson. "There was a part of him that was very present and very physical, lots of hugs. But part of him was always in another place. Before he died there was this little distance. You felt he was preparing you for his departure."

It could only be conjecture; as they often had in Jeff's life, the definitive answers stayed with him. In the meantime, everyone returned to whatever work there was at hand. Fearing a lawsuit from Sony, Lory sent Guibert a box of eighty-seven live recordings in June 1999. A second posthumous album, *Mystery White Boy*—its title taken from one of the playful names of his tours and comprised of live recordings from 1994 to 1996—was released in May 2000. Guibert, who alone constituted Jeff's estate, also became his chief on-line defender and spokesperson. Tighe, Wasser, and Kindred formed a band of their own, Black Beetle. Attesting to the respect with which he was regarded in the music community, Jeff became the subject of songs by Chris Cornell ("Wave Goodbye"), Hole ("Boys on the Radio"), Duncan Sheik ("A Body Goes Down"), Juliana Hatfield ("Trying Not to Think About It"), and Aimee Mann ("Just Like Anyone"); PJ Harvey also paid tribute to him in an unreleased recording. Meanwhile, an admirer and fledgling songwriter and musician who referred to herself only as "Autumn" moved into the little house on North Rembert in Memphis. Like him, she began using the attic as a workplace.

The Tin Angel, the Bleecker Street bar that was Tim's favorite Greenwich Village eatery, eventually shut down.

In August 1998, just over a year after Jeff's death, the Daydream Cafe— the midtown bistro where he had frequently spent time and played one of his final New York shows—also closed its doors. At year's end, another café opened in its place. The new owners settled on a different name: the Tin Angel.

INDEX